PRIESTS, PROPHETS, DIVINERS, SAGES

PRIESTS, PROPHETS, DIVINERS, SAGES

A Socio-Historical Study of Religious Specialists in Ancient Israel

LESTER L. GRABBE

TRINITY PRESS INTERNATIONAL
VALLEY FORGE, PENNSYLVANIA

Trinity Press International, P.O. Box 851, Valley Forge, PA 19482-0851

Library of Congress Cataloging-in-Publication Data

Grabbe, Lester L.
Priests, prophets, diviners, sages : a socio-historical study of religious specialists in ancient Israel / Lester L. Grabbe.
p. cm.
Includes bibliographical references and index.
ISBN 1-56338-132-X (pbk. : alk. paper)
1. Kings and rulers—Biblical teaching. 2. Priests, Jewish—Biblical teaching. 3. Prophets—Biblical teaching. 4. Divination—Biblical teaching. 5. Wisdom—Biblical teaching. 6. Bible. O.T.—Criticism, interpretation, etc. 7. Sociology, Biblical.
I. Title.
BS1199.K5G73 1995
221.9'5—dc20 95-32747
CIP

Printed in the United States of America

95 96 97 98 99 00 10 9 8 7 6 5 4 3 2 1

to
Heather and Bruce

Contents

Preface

Much has been written on the individual subjects of this study, a considerable amount on prophets and sages and perhaps less on kings, priests, and diviners. Nevertheless, there is to the best of my knowledge no complete study of the major religious specialists and their relationships in ancient Israelite society. The idea had its inception in the spring of 1987 when I began working on a sociological study of Jewish apocalypticism (read at the European Association of Jewish Studies in Berlin, August 1987, and published in 1989). This was followed by a paper on religious specialists in ancient Israel, read at the International Society of Biblical Literature meeting (Sheffield, August 1988, but not published until 1993). It was while doing this latter article that I realized a full study of the subject was needed, though this had to be postponed a number of years because of other projects and commitments. This monograph represents the fuller study.

The present work is meant to be a contribution to scholarship and useful to working scholars, but it is also hoped that it will be accessible to students and non-specialists. All technical terms are explained in the context, and quotations from the original texts are translated. Background is given where this is thought to be helpful to the non-specialist, with apologies to scholars who may find it superfluous. English versions of secondary literature are cited where available.

The study is founded on the text, and the text is the primary focus throughout. Relevant secondary literature is also cited, but considering the enormous number of studies in almost all areas, it would be impossible to cite more than a fraction of it. It is also inevitable that important studies have been overlooked, but this is not necessarily important because of the focus on the text. The bibliography listed at the beginning of each section is mainly composed of those items cited in the section; however, other relevant items (especially recent publications) are sometimes included, especially works aimed at orienting the non-specialist. Apart from a few unavoidable exceptions, I have not listed literature which I have not seen. Brian Schmidt's work *Israel's Beneficent Dead* had not been published when this manuscript was finished, and I know of some of its conclusions only from a couple of conference papers and some private discussions with the author. Chapter 5 was already written when F. H. Cryer's commendable *Divination in Ancient Israel and Its Near Eastern Environment* appeared. Rather than rewrite the chapter, I have let it stand as an independent study.

The present book is organized in the following way: Chapter 1 discusses the problems of historical and sociological study, especially the crucial one of whether the text reflects an actual historical society. Following this are chapters on the five main forms of religious specialist, considered as Weberian "ideal types"—that is, as if each existed in pure form in society. Each chapter on an individual religious specialist begins with a section looking at the data of the OT text. This is followed by examples of cross-cultural parallels elsewhere in the ancient Near East and, in some cases, from modern anthropological studies. After an examination of various aspects of the subject in question, the chapter ends with a Gestalt or composite picture of the specialist, drawing on all sources considered in the chapter. Each of these chapters is meant to be self-contained so that a coherent depiction of the particular religious specialist emerges, with the necessary supporting data. Chapter 7 then begins again with the text before going on to look at some cross-cultural comparisons and finally trying to reconstruct the function of the various religious specialisms in the actual historical society. The final chapter is a summary of the major points and conclusions from all the other chapters: many readers will want to begin here!

The transliteration of Hebrew should be clear to those who know the language. I have used *v* and *f* for the non-*dagesh*ed forms of *bet* and *pe*, while *w* is always used for *waw* (even though now pronounced *v* by most modern users of Hebrew). The New Jewish Publication Society version is the basis for most English translations of the OT, though I have not hestitated to deviate from it if circumstances demanded. I use a number of words purely as descriptive terms without any political or sectarian motivation: "Old Testament" (OT) and "Hebrew Bible" are used interchangably to mean the collection of writings found in the present Hebrew canon. I favor "Old Testament" simply because OT is a well-known abbreviation and because it seems a bit odd to refer to the Septuagint version as "Hebrew Bible." "Palestine" is purely a geographical term, used because it has been widely accepted for many years and because it is difficult to find a suitable substitute. Whenever the term "Exile" is mentioned, it is only a convenient chronological benchmark to refer to the watershed between the monarchy/First Temple period and the Second Temple period, without meaning in any way to beg the question of how many—or even whether—Jews were removed from the land by

Nebuchadnezzar. The divine name for the God of Israel is written as "Yhwh"; although often vocalized as "Yahweh," the precise pronunciation is in fact unknown.

Several colleagues have kindly given up some of their own valuable time to read and comment on my manuscript: Professors Robert Carroll and Hans Barstad read the entire manuscript in an intermediate draft and made many valuable suggestions. I also benefited from Professor Philip Davies's written comments on chapters 1, 7, and 8 and further private discussions on other aspects of the study. Professor W. G. Lambert looked over the sections dealing with Mesopotamia and saved me from many errors. Professor Simon Parker commented on the section on prophetic ecstasy (4.5.2) and clarified his own position on the subject. He also brought to my attention an important article which I had overlooked. I sincerely thank these individuals for their time and expertise, which have significantly improved the present work, whatever faults still remain.

This book is dedicated to my daughter and son. Considering the number of years they had to put up with my cooking, it was the least I could do.

Kingston-upon-Hull
31 October 1994

Abbreviations

AB	Anchor Bible
ABD	*Anchor Bible Dictionary*
AfO	*Archiv für Orientforschung*
AnBib	Analecta Biblica
ANET	J. B. Pritchard (ed.) *Ancient Near Eastern Texts*
AOAT	Alter Orient und Altes Testament
AOS	American Oriental Studies
AV	Authorized Version
b.	"son of" (Hebrew *ben*/Aramaic *bar*)
BA	*Biblical Archeologist*
BCE	Before the Common Era (= BC)
BJS	Brown Judaic Studies
BO	*Bibliotheca Orientalis*
BSOAS	*Bulletin of the School of Oriental and African Studies*
BZAW	Beihefte zu *Zeitschrift für die alttestamentliche Wissenschaft*
CBOTS	Conjectanea Biblica, Old Testament Series
CBQ	*Catholic Biblical Quarterly*
CBQMS	Catholic Biblical Quarterly Monograph Series
CE	Common Era (= AD)
CHI	G. I. Davies, ed., *Corpus of Hebrew Inscriptions*
DBS	*Dictionnaire de la Bible, Supplément*
EI	*Eretz-Israel*
ER	*Encyclopaedia of Religion*
FRLANT	Forschungen zur Religion und Literature des Alten und Neuen Testaments
HdO	Handbuch der Orientalistik
HR	*History of Religions*
HSM	Harvard Semitic Monograph

HSS	Harvard Semitic Studies
HTR	*Harvard Theological Review*
HUCA	*Hebrew Union College Annual*
IDB	*Interpreter's Dictionary of the Bible*
IDBSup	*Interpreter's Dictionary of the Bible, Supplement*
IEJ	*Israel Exploration Journal*
JAOS	*Journal of the American Oriental Society*
JBL	*Journal of Biblical Literature*
JCS	*Journal of Cuneiform Studies*
JEA	*Journal of Egyptian Archaeology*
JJS	*Journal of Jewish Studies*
JNES	*Journal of Near Eastern Studies*
JNSL	*Journal of Northwest Semitic Languages*
JSOT	*Journal for the Study of the Old Testament*
JSOTSup	Supplements to *Journal for the Study of the Old Testament*
JSP	*Journal for the Study of the Pseudepigrapha*
JTS	*Journal of Theological Studies*
KAI	H. Donner and W. Röllig, *Kanaanäische und aramäische Inschriften*
KAT	Kommentar zum Alten Testament
KTU	*Keilalphabetischen Texte aus Ugarit*
LdÄ	*Lexikon der Ägyptologie*
LXX	Septuagint
MT	Masoretic text
NCB	New Century Bible
NEB	New English Bible
NJPS	New Jewish Publication Society translation
NovTSup	Supplements to *Novum Testamentum*
NumSup	Supplements to *Numen*
OBO	Orbis Biblicus Orientalis
OT	Old Testament/Hebrew Bible
OTL	Old Testament Library
OTS	*Oudtestamentische Studiën*
RB	*Revue biblique*
RLA	*Reallexikon der Assyriologie*
SANE	Studies in the Ancient Near East
SBLDS	Society of Biblical Literature Dissertation Series
SBLSCS	SBL Septuagint and Cognate Studies
SFSHJ	South Florida Studies in the History of Judaism
SJOT	*Scandanavian Journal of the Old Testament*
TDOT	*Theological Dictionary of the Old Testament*
TSSI	*Textbook of Syrian Semitic Inscriptions*
TT	Texts and Translations

TWAT	G. J. Botterweck and H. Ringgren, eds. *Theologische Wörterbuch zum Alten Testament*
UF	*Ugarit-Forschungen*
v(v)	verse(s)
VT	*Vetus Testamentum*
VTSup	Supplements to *Vetus Testamentum*
WBC	Word Bible Commentary
WMANT	Wissenschaftliche Monographien zum Alten und Neuen Testament
WUNT	Wissenschaftliche Untersuchungen zum Neuen Testament
ZAW	*Zeitschrift für die alttestamentliche Wissenschaft*
*	Reference back to a book listed at the head of the chapter

1.

Introduction

Scholarship has long been enamored of prophecy. Since the generation of Wellhausen, prophecy has "been where it's at" in OT scholarship. If all the literature written on Israelite prophecy and the prophets were gathered up, it would make a small mountain—or at least a sizable hillock. Long neglected, the Israelite wisdom tradition has now attracted scholars whose publications are rapidly amassing their own pile from which to crow. Much less has been written on the priests, for nineteenth-century Protestants did not much like priests, and nineteenth-century Protestant scholarship still exercises great influence. Such professions as diviner, healer, and the like have with some exceptions been beneath the dignity of scholars who would not wish to waste their time and reputations on such non-serious activities. One might say that the prophets have been kosher, but priests deemed profane, while diviners, healers, and their ilk squatted with the mixed multitude outside the camp.

In recent years, of course, all these groups have come under scholarly scrutiny, though some still rather lightly. What I hope to do, however, has not yet been done: this is to examine all the main forms of religious specialist in Israelite society and attempt to describe their own social interaction and relationships. Within the limits of space, it will not be possible to address every issue raised in the study of each individual religious specialist, but in any case, many elements of this study will have been discussed by scholars in existing secondary literature. Although it is hoped that original observations will be found at various points, it is primarily as a work of synthesis that this study will make its contribution to scholarship.

1.1 AIMS OF THE STUDY

Burke, P. "Overture: The New History, Its Past and Its Future," *New Perspectives on Historical Writing* (1991) 1-23.

Turner, V. W. "Religious Specialists: I Anthropological Study," *International Encyclopaedia of the Social Sciences* 13 (1968) 437-42.

This is a socio-historical study. It combines the task and methods of the historian with those of the social and cultural anthropologist. It attempts to see how one aspect of an ancient society and culture functioned. Whether one calls this social history or historical sociology may be debated, but the place of "history from below" and "total history" is now firmly established in the historical agenda (cf. Burke). My aims are modest. I do not intend a major discussion of sociological theory, though some ground rules and basic bibliography are delineated at 1.6. My procedure will be primarily empirical, always checking theory against data. Nevertheless, the objectives tackled and the tools employed are those of social anthropology and social history.

The historical society in question is ancient Israel; the aspect to be studied is that which anthropologists call religious specialists: "A religious specialist is one who devotes himself to a particular branch of religion or, viewed organizationally, of a religious system" (Turner: 437). This would include all cult functionaries—priests of all sorts (including the Levites of the biblical texts), cult prophets, official diviners, temple scribes, temple singers, any others who had an active part in the cult. All intermediaries between the divine realms and humanity would be included. Some of these intermediaries might be cultic figures (e.g., priests), but non-cultic prophets, seers, diviners, healers, magicians, witch-finders, and astrologers would also count as intermediaries. Teachers with a special revelation or insight into the divine realm would be a constituent of religious specialists, whether or not they were considered intermediaries in a formal sense.

Not all the individual offices or functions cited above were likely to have been found in ancient Israel. For example, in many preindustrial societies witchcraft and concerns about it form an important social activity. There is little evidence that witch-finders played a role in ancient Israelite society, however. Similarly, astrology as a form of divination seems to be mainly a development of the Greco-Roman world and little known in Palestine before Alexander the Great. On the other hand, the king in Israel, as in the surrounding cultures in Mesopotamia and Egypt, seems to have had a significant cultic function. The term "sacral kingship" has been used of the Israelite king as well as of kingship in Egypt and Mesopotamia. Therefore, the question of the king as a religious specialist must also be included in the investigation.

1.2 PROBLEMS OF HISTORICAL RECONSTRUCTION

Carroll, R. P. "Prophecy and Society," *The World of Ancient Israel* (1989) 203-25.
Davies, P. R. *In Search of "Ancient Israel"* (1992).
Jenkins, K. *Re-Thinking History* (1991).
Lowenthal, D. *The Past Is a Foreign Country* (1985).
Stanford, M. *The Nature of Historical Knowledge* (1986).

A number of scholars have recently written on the problem of using the OT for trying to reconstruct the history and society of ancient Israel: Niels Peter Lemche, Thomas L. Thompson, Robert Coote, and Keith W. Whitelam, to name only a selection (see the Bibliography for some of their writings). However, I shall single out the works of Philip Davies and Robert Carroll because they are recent, easily accessible, summarize the main issues, and provide references to the work of others. Davies has put his finger on the problem of using the term "ancient Israel." What is often referred to as "ancient Israel" is the light historicizing of the construct in the literary texts. One reads the biblical text, paraphrases it with a sprinkling of archeological data to give it vitamins, throws in a couple of mineral-rich inscriptions, and . . . voila! a history of Israel. The difficulty is that we cannot be sure that the Israel of the texts was historical, or to be less skeptical, we cannot be sure to what extent the historical people of central Palestine corresponded with the entity described in the biblical literature.

Similarly, Carroll has focused on the problem of text versus society. He has highlighted the ways into which the text cannot be translated automatically into social reality. A literary text has its own integrity. A story can be coherent and give the appearance of immediacy while still being complete fiction. Just as the Leopold Bloom of James Joyce's *Ulysses* is set in a real place and time (Dublin, 16 June 1904), with a portrayal of that city's contemporary society, and yet is completely fiction, so can be the stories about Elijah and Jeremiah. Indeed, we can be less certain about Elijah and Jeremiah because we find it much harder to determine the time and setting of the stories about them. At least with Leopold Bloom we can have some confidence that the society portrayed in his story is close to the social reality of the times; we cannot be so sure about Elijah and Jeremiah. Because Carroll has worked specifically on the problem of prophecy in Israel, his work is especially relevant to our task here.

It is not my aim to resolve all the issues that Davies and Carroll have pinpointed. Rather, I shall use Israel to mean the people of central Palestine in the Iron Age without attempting to address the entire historical question of their relationship to the Israel of the Bible. However, some of the questions I shall seek to answer necessarily impinge on the question of the historical Israel. I shall start from the texts, but most historians do. The problem is how to bridge the gap between the preserved texts and the no-longer-directly-accessible historical Israel.

The problem being discussed is hardly new or unique to biblical scholarship. It is one that historians of all persuasions have long been wrestling with, but it has especially been brought to the fore in what is often called the "new history" (see Burke for a clear description). Many of the certainties so often taken for granted, especially among non-historians, are under attack if not discarded as untenable (see Jenkins for a rather polemical statement of the situation). Thus, contrary to the impression sometimes given by critics of the skeptics, the problem is not something artificially created by a few disgruntled biblical scholars. Quite the contrary: the problems perceived for the biblical literature apply, in some form or other, to all historical writing (cf. Lowenthal; Stanford; Jenkins). The situation is more acute with reference to the history of Israel, though, in that our main source is a collection of traditional religious literature of uncertain age and authorship.

Because of the difficulties, some have abandoned the historical question altogether and engage themselves entirely with the text. For those interested only in theology or literature, that is entirely proper—as one alternative, at least. If one wishes to be a historian, however, one has to ask historical questions. The answers may not be possible, or the answers may not provide the detail one would like, but the questions must be asked. And the ultimate goal of historians—however much they may debate questions of method and historiographical theory—is to try to find a route back to a particular historical situation. To be a historian is to get off the fence and make judgments; it is to try to extract historical data from apparently intractable sources. Pointing out the obstacles is necessary, but we cannot stop there and throw up our hands at the hopelessness of the task, assuming we wish to be historians. We should also not assume that problems with Israel's history are essentially different from those faced by historians elsewhere. No one would attempt to write a history of any other ancient Near Eastern or Mediterranean nation by ignoring all literary data. Literary texts are always problematic, especially if they are not historiographic in nature, but they should not be overlooked for potential data, however great the task of grappling with them.

We can begin with the simplest question: Is it valid to talk about a society known as "ancient Israel" when we have in mind the peoples of central Palestine in the Iron Age? The answer is a definite yes. There was a kingdom known as Israel in this region, at least in the ninth and eighth centuries BCE. We know this not only from the OT text but also from contemporary records such as the Moabite stone (*ANET*: 320-21) and the inscriptions of the Assyrian king Shalmaneser III (*ANET*: 278-79). On the other hand, from these records alone we do not know the precise boundaries of this kingdom or the constituent peoples. We do not know, for example, that the name "Israel" was ever applied to the people of the kingdom of Judah (also known from contemporary Mesopotamian records, such as the inscriptions of Tiglathpileser III [*ANET*: 282]). Texts from the Second Temple Judaism apply the name Israel to the Jews, but we do not know for sure that it was done in the earlier period *from external sources*. Nevertheless, for the sake of convenience, when I use the term "ancient Israel," I shall mean for it to include Judah as well (unless otherwise indicated). My term "ancient Israel" thus refers to what P. R. Davies calls "historical Israel" and seems to differ slightly from his usage of the term. The terms "kingdom of Israel" or the "Northern

Kingdom" and "kingdom of Judah" or "Judah" will be used to differentiate the two separate kingdoms.

1.3 THE NATURE OF THE SOURCES

Laslett, P. "The Wrong Way Through the Telescope: A Note on Literary Evidence in Sociology and in Historical Sociology," *British Journal of Sociology* 27 (1976) 317-42.

We need first of all to remind ourselves of the basic historical task. The work of the historian is—at its core—the same for all periods. We have no direct access to the past. It is gone forever, not just Iron Age Palestine, but our own self and activities of yesterday. Our access to the past is only indirect, through the remains of the past which continue into the present—artifacts, traditions, memories. These are our sources. For all historians, it is a matter of investigating sources and trying to draw inferences from them about the past situation, society, and events. The sources vary, but historians do not usually rule anything out which may be of possible use. All sources have their problems of interpretation, and some are more problematic than others, but they are all grist for the mill. Prehistorians have to work with artifacts because that is all they have. The picture reconstructed from artifacts alone is always severely limited, however. It is never more than a skeleton; flesh comes only with written records. It would not be possible to reconstruct Israelite society from archeology alone. Hope of getting at the society in a significant way is possible only if available written records provide usable data. It is no virtue to argue that we should stick to archeology and ignore written sources.

Different types of sources provide different sorts of data and require different methodological approaches. Some sources are intrinsically more likely to be reliable than others. Contemporary witnesses are at a premium because their data are immediate and direct. Eyewitness reports are the first choice of any historian. Nevertheless, as valuable as they are, it cannot be assumed that even they tell the unvarnished truth. The reports of eyewitnesses have all been filtered through the subjective minds of the witnesses. Their memory has been colored and distorted by the limitations on their ability as observers, and even trained observers have their own biases and prejudices which will influence their memories. Nonetheless, of special value is the ability to interview and question living eyewitnesses and participants.

Unfortunately, there are no eyewitnesses from the past who can be interrogated (even if we do have some reports claiming to have been written by eyewitnesses). The closest thing we have to eyewitnesses are artifacts found in situ by archeologists. These have an objective status greatly prized. That is, apart from careless digging or recording of results, or the occasional deliberate planting of evidence (e.g., the Piltdown man), the finds in an archeological context represent material remains as they were deposited by events in the past. The objects and their location possess information uncontaminated by past human caprice or deception. For this reason, archeological data are highly desirable as controls in any sort of historical interpretation. Yet, like eyewitnesses, there will be strong subjective element in their use. The precise meaning to be extracted from the finds will be a matter of interpretation and may occasion debate. The frequent disputes among archeologists should caution anyone who thinks artifacts speak for themselves.

Unlike the modern historian who will usually have a variety of documents and even living witnesses and oral testimony, the ancient historian is often dependent primarily on literary texts. There are exceptions, where abundant archeological information is available or the textual evidence is primarily in the form of economic or legal texts, but much of the time the foundation of ancient history remains literary texts. Literary relics encompass a variety of potential uses and pitfalls. Texts written contemporary with the events recorded are particularly useful, but they are not all of a piece.

We have to distinguish between "high literature" (written as an aesthetic expression), the literature of everyday life (diaries, letters, memoranda, sermons, and the like), and economic and legal documents (Laslett: 319-20). Documents written for a practical function in society are the most reliable, primarily legal and business documents. These have special value in cross-checking literary sources, as well as providing data not usually available in literature. Nevertheless, they are often unhelpful in reconstructing a historical narrative—try writing history from a collection of bank statements! After these come the public and personal communications necessary to carry out daily life. These had immediate value or were designed for the short-term future but were not usually composed for future generations. These types of documents (including legal ones) might be faked to support dubious claims, but the general content had to conform to contemporary norms for the deception to have any chance of success. The general data regarding society and the economy will still often be usable even in documents meant to deceive contemporaries.

Sources like diaries, sermons, and letters may vary in the amount of conscious interpretation and persuasion intended; for example, some diaries are honest private reflections while others were intended to be made public. Other literary texts were written with the specific intent of interpreting events for the reader: royal inscriptions, political propaganda, scribal literature designed for royal consumption, theological literature, various other writings of ideology. These may be contemporary but present a picture at lesser or greater variance from a straightforward description by a disinterested observer. They interpret events to glorify the monarch (or at least save the monarch from embarrassment), to exalt the native country or tradition, to give the real meaning of events from the perspective of the gods (even if this means rearranging or altering the data), or to bring out hidden truths according to the idealism of the writer (ditto).

A further factor helps determine whether a literary source may be useful or not. This relates to literature written or edited long after the events but drawing on early sources or ongoing traditions. Such literature is not to be rejected out of hand; indeed, for many periods of history these are the main or even only sources available to the historian. Classical historians do not throw up their hands when all they have are Polybius, Livy, or Dionysius of Halicarnasus. And historians of what might be called the "later history of Israel" find Josephus indispensable, in spite of his shortcomings.

On the other hand, each of these represents a different quality of writing and must be used critically. Prior sources, purpose in writing, biases of the author, quality of historical judgment all must be investigated. There is consensus that some late writings and compilations are much more reliable than others, but each must be examined in its own right. Each must be looked at critically.

The first problem we face is that our main source for ancient Israel is the Hebrew Bible, a literary source; it is also a religious document which grew over a long period of time under the hands of many different authors and editors. We cannot assume these writers and redactors have given a dispassionate description of ancient society. History cannot be read straightforwardly from the biblical text. No source can be used uncritically, but some are more reliable historical records than others. Because of the nature of the literature—both because of its origin and development and because of the purpose for which it was written—the OT is not a first-class source for history. It may be a splendid piece of religious writing, but by the criteria of trustworthiness for historical use, it does not rank high overall.

There is nothing special about Israelite history. The historian of ancient Israel uses the same basic historical methods as other historians. The general problems and types of sources are no different. A historian who uses the OT to try to reconstruct Israelite society is not doing anything intrinsically different from the classical historian who draws on Diodorus of Sicily (first century BCE) for the wars of the Diodochi (fourth century BCE). Using the OT for the history of Israel is a priori neither illegitimate nor ill conceived. But such use requires critical justification. Material which has been edited and reworked over centuries—or composed from such traditional material as an original work long after the events—cannot be assumed to have usable historical data without some sort of control. Of course, late compositions may have early material and may have preserved useful historical data. The question is how to determine where this is the case and how to sort out the early from the late.

For example, the main narrative sections of the OT—those purporting to tell the history of Israel—are Genesis to 2 Kings and 1 and 2 Chronicles.

As they presently stand, these writings have a definite theological and moralistic function. They are primarily concerned to teach religious truths. Their success in doing so is one reason they have been taken into the canons of both Judaism and Christianity. As religious documents, they are first-rate in the opinion of many theologians. But canonical literature has no special value to the historian. Parables, myths, fables, hymns, homilies, fairy tales, and admonitions are frequently constituents of religious canons. These are clearly not historical sources, however valuable they may be as religious literature. Similarly, the canonical literature of the OT contains such religious writings as psalms, edifying tales, legendary exploits of ancestral peoples and eponymous heroes, conversations of humans with God, reports of miracles, and so on. We can hardly expect these to function very well as useful historical sources.

It was once thought that the traditio-historical methods of source-, redaction-, and form-criticism would be able to trace the development of the tradition and differentiate the early from the late. Scholarship as a whole is becoming more skeptical that this can be done with assurance. Scholars of a century ago, who would with considerable confidence divide a short verse into three or four different sources, now look decidedly arrogant. It is even being argued that much of the Pentateuch and the Deuteronomistic History (Joshua-2 Kings) was composed in the Persian period or even as late as the Greek period. If so, how much history are they likely to contain? The same applies to the prophetic writings which many would date no earlier than the post-exilic period in their present form. We have few, if any, certainly contemporary sources for Israelite society during the monarchy. Archeology, on the other hand, gives us few data about historical events or many aspects of society.

The question remains, then: How do we get from text to society? Can we use the OT writings to try to reconstruct the place and interaction of religious figures of various sorts? Or are we left only with a literary construct with which we have to be satisfied? I believe we can move from text to society, and that the literary construct can be used as a basis for teasing out data about the society. However, this requires a good deal of methodological care.

1.4 CAN WE GET PAST THE PROBLEM OF THE TEXT?

The OT literature purports to describe a society in operation. This is not a unitary society in that it covers several centuries and several geographical regions, but on the surface it appears to describe an actual society in operation. Nevertheless, this could be a persistent attempt at deception by the writer(s). Based on other narratives known from around the world, several possibilities present themselves:

1. A narrative may be pure fantasy, more or less. A fairy tale, for example, may discuss the slaying of giants and dragons. Giants and dragons have never existed; people do sometimes invent things when telling stories.

2. The narrative is a fiction, and the societal institutions in the narrative represent stereotypes, on the order of the *Characters* of Theophrastus (a fourth-century pupil of Plato). Yet fiction may be a true representative of its own age, and stereotypes too may have their uses; however much they may misrepresent the character of a historical individual, they still often show types of persons or institutions. Even when distorted and unbalanced, they may convey certain truths about society in general.

3. The narrative may refer to actual institutions of a real society. Even such a welcome situation does not necessarily solve all problems, though, for reference to a custom or figure may give few data rather than a full description. Thus, even an authentic contemporary document may be only the starting point toward a historical sociology.

Each of these three basic positions, or some variation on them, is possible for the OT. Which is the right one? Is it only a matter of arbitrary choice? Of making a subjective decision about just how credulous one is prepared to be? There are three considerations which may provide a serious way forward, though each is also subject to abuse: (1) hints in the text itself, (2) cross-cultural comparisons, and (3) some authentic texts.

1.4.1 Hints in the Text

If the biblical text contains earlier material in an unmasticated form, we would expect to discover indications here and there within the text itself. We do find these, suggesting that there is some memory of an earlier society and that all is not just a late invention:

1. Recognition that the past is different from the present. A prime example of this is 1 Samuel 9:9. Here it is stated that Samuel is called a *nāvî'*, "prophet," though formerly such a person had been called a *rō'eh*, "seer." The present text asserts two things: first, it notes that the event was some time ago, a memory of a situation in a past age; second, it lets the reader know that there has been a change, that time has led to a new social situation in which the possessor of certain characteristics went under a new name. Not a lot of information is imparted, but the writer evinces knowledge that the institution had developed in society and that things are now different from what they were.

2. Different types of religious specialist are recognized in the texts. For example, all prophets are not described in the same way. Elijah and, especially, Elisha fit the characteristics often associated with a shaman. Samuel is consulted about lost objects. David obtains revelations by consulting the ephod. Amos claims to have been sent from Judah to another country to deliver a set of messages. Isaiah and Jeremiah, on the other hand, preach in and around the temple, delivering messages to the Judean king.

3. On the question of prophets, the contrast of "true" versus "false" prophets is instructive. The writers may be operating with stereotypes, but if so,

the stereotype is not likely to be a completely invented one. False prophets might well be associated with pagan gods (Deut 13; 18; 1 Kings 18:19-40; Jer 23:13), yet this charge is seldom used in descriptions of so-called false prophets. Rather, most of the supposed false prophets are presented as worshipers of Yhwh (e.g., 1 Kings 22:6-28). The Hananiah opposed by Jeremiah (Jer 28) has much in common with Jeremiah himself (4.1.13), as well as with the Isaiah of Isa 36-39 (//2 Kings 18-19).

If these characterizations of individual prophets were invented, the perpetrator had a distinct lack of imagination. One would have expected a clever inventor to have done better than this. Such a writer surely would have made a greater distinction in the depiction of true and false prophets, such as having false prophets worship foreign gods and true prophets only opposing the monarchy and not sometimes supporting it. The clever inventor might have had "false" prophets engage in interesting and innovative sexual practices or perhaps even wander the streets naked. To do so was good enough for Isaiah, who not only walked around naked for three years (apparently without suffering frostbite) but also had love-children by "the prophetess," whoever that Dark Lady was. Why do not the "false prophets" of the Bible have more nasty attributes? Is it because there was no real difference between them and the "true prophets"?

4. The cult and a number of other societal institutions are not likely to have changed rapidly. Thus, a description of the cult in early Second Temple times will probably not show major differences from the practices of First Temple period. Details may well have been different, but the overall operation of the temple probably shared a good deal.

Thus, we are left with the impression that the biblical text has described actual institutions in society. The picture painted may well have the institutions assimilated to stereotypes, but these stereotypes themselves seem based on real life and are not fantastic creatures of the writers. The text has contradictions; it has non sequiturs; it has "lumps" in it. The data from the past have not all been completely homogenized into the smooth pabulum of the writers' present.

1.4.2 Cross-Cultural Comparisons

Cross-cultural comparisons can be abused. It is easy for them to be used as an aid in the interpretation of the biblical data and then for the synthesis created to be compared with the cross-cultural parallels as evidence that the biblical picture is authentic; such circular reasoning is not unknown in OT scholarship. Yet data from other cultures can be useful for purposes of authentication, if used critically.

The procedure which has to be followed is to take the picture arising from a study of the biblical text and compare it with that drawn by social anthropologists from other societies. There is an immediate problem in that no two societies are exactly alike, even when in close proximity. Comparison has to be made on a more fundamental, structural level. The two pictures—the biblical and the anthropological—have to be compared at the level of underlying assumptions, general institutions, and broad functions within society.

We find that there is a variety of religious specialists in most societies around the world. There are figures comparable to priests, diviners, prophets, and healers. What they are called varies; less interesting than the terminology used is how the figure is presented. Yet we find differences in each individual culture. The basic needs are often similar, but the type of specialist in the society may fluctuate. For example, the shaman may take on the function of priest, prophet, diviner, and healer in many Siberian or North American groups. In some societies, especially Africa, the witch-finder is an important specialist, but this sort of witchcraft has little place in the narratives of the OT. The other Near Eastern countries contemporary with ancient Israel have some interesting things to say. Prophetic figures are well-known from Mesopotamia but rather more problematic for Egypt.

An interesting example is found in the Zakkur inscription (4.3.1). Zakkur, the king of Hamath and Luath, writes that he was threatened by an alliance of sixteen kings led by Barhadad b. Hazael of Aram. However, messages of support were delivered to him by "seers" (*ḥzyn*) and "messengers" (*'ddn*). These messages, from Baal Shamayn ("Lord of the Heavens") began, "Fear not" (*'l tzḥl*), precisely as many prophetic messages to the Israelite king in the OT began. Here is clearly a society with some differences from that in the OT, yet there are also some striking similarities, even to the use of a well-known prophetic formula.

In sum, it is not likely that the images and concepts in the biblical text were borrowed from the outside. Why would the biblical writer need to borrow a concept from outside for his theological message? On the contrary, it is intrinsically probable that Israel had its prophetic figures, seers, healers, and shamans just as did the surrounding cultures. Comparisons with other cultures may not confirm the details, but they will help to show whether the biblical picture is plausible or not.

1.4.3 Some Authentic Texts

Barstad, H. M. "Lachish Ostracon III and Ancient Israelite Prophecy," *EI* 24 (1993) 8*-12*.

It should not be assumed that all remains from the ancient world are as suspect as the OT text as a whole. There are a few references that may fall in the category of contemporary documents. Two are worth mentioning here. One is inscriptions which do make some brief mention of religious specialists. The Lachish letters, for example, refer to an individual known as the "prophet" (3.20: *hnb'*). It has recently been argued that his role in the letter was to intercede with Yhwh for the nation (Barstad). Second, there is widespread agreement that the book of Nehemiah contains at its core an actual writing of Nehemiah himself. Although there is no precise agreement on the limits of the "Nehemiah Memorial," it has gone largely unchallenged as an authentic writing of the Persian governor. In it, he mentions being opposed by Shemaiah the prophet, Noadiah the prophetess, and other unnamed prophets (Neh 6:10-14). What is especially interesting is that these individuals evidently have a good reputation in Jerusalem and are regarded by some members of the Jerusalem establishment as true prophets of Yhwh.

1.5 HOW THE METHOD WORKS

Some brief examples illustrating the method can be given here to sketch how it works in relation to the major types of religious specialist. For more detailed application, the chapters in question should be consulted. The main discussion of trying to recreate the society and the specialists within it will be found in Chapter 7.

Although the text more or less accepts the place of the king (ch. 2), it wants his position strictly limited. According to the general picture of the text, the king has no special cultic functions, and in one example the king who tried to offer incense in the inner sanctum was struck with leprosy. This state of affairs seems strange when we consider that a king such as David is a cult founder and Solomon is a temple builder. In this case, the bias of the text can be partially bypassed through hints that the king did take an active part in cultic activities. David and Solomon make sacrifices, and Solomon himself consecrates a section of the temple court. That it is the king himself and not just the priest acting on behalf of the king is indicated by the graphic description of Jeroboam at the altar. At this point, cross-cultural comparisons are helpful. Other Near Eastern kings were important in the cult. Even though the Israelite monarchy may not have been conceived of precisely as in Egypt or Mesopotamia, the differences are not that great (indeed, have been greatly exaggerated). The analogy would not prove the place of the king, but it helps to confirm and even interpret what can be deduced from the text itself.

Priests are cult figures the world over (ch. 3). There is no reason to question the textual construct at this point. Where the text shows bias is in making monotheistic Yahwism the original religious situation in Israel from Moses on. Here a combination of archeology and Israelite inscriptions, Near Eastern texts, and hints within the text itself show a development from a polytheistic society in which other gods were worshiped without criticism, even though the national or main god seems to have been Yahweh and his cult dominant. The overall picture of the text is of a bifurcation in the priesthood, with the "Aaronites" as the presiding priests and the "Levites" as the lower clergy. Yet a number of texts do not fit that picture, with some stressing only the Zadokites as the presiding priests and others making all Levites priests. This suggests struggles within the priesthood, even if the history of the struggle is a matter of speculation. The text also makes priests act as teachers and judges. It is plausible that they were teachers, especially about the law, but were they judges? Here the text could be presenting a bias from the Second Temple period when priests had an administrative position. The question is not easily answered (see 7.3).

The text is in favor of certain prophets (ch. 4). This pro-prophetic bias may lead it to idealize them and give a distorted picture. This bias is indicated by the fact that no cultic prophets are clearly described, yet there are hints that at least some prophets functioned in the cult. Also, two other factors lead us to believe that the descriptions of prophets are not just a literary construct. One is the enormous variety of prophetic figures, with widely differing actions and characteristics, some of potential embarrassment to later writers. This suggests they are not all invented. A second factor is that "false" prophets seem to be very similar to their "true" contemporaries. One would expect a writer concentrating on a purely theological objective to have made figures such as Jeremiah's opponent Hananiah more reprehensible, with more of the "bad" prophetic characteristics (e.g., making him a Baal worshiper).

The text is definitely biased against most forms of divination (ch. 5). It is also against "aberrant" cults, which may have had esoteric knowledge as a goal. Here the priestly forms of divination, accepted without question, take on a particular significance. This shows an authentic memory, especially when later texts suggest that these priestly lots no longer existed (Ezra 2:63; Neh 7:65). A further point is the extent to which the divinatory techniques are used by some of the prophetic figures, including music and dreams. The detailed description of proscribed divinatory techniques suggests that they were around, and archeological evidence for the cult of the dead makes plausible that consulting the dead for divinatory purposes was extant in Israel—a state of affairs apparently confirmed by some textual references.

The text itself is the main source for information about sages as religious specialists (ch. 6), though much has to be inferred rather than being explicit. The variety of wisdom books in the OT suggests not only the importance of wisdom and wisdom figures, but also shows their place within the religious tradition. The text also speaks of scribes, though without making them authors of the literature. Here we must fall back on the analogy of other ancient Near Eastern peoples and hints within the text to show to what extent the creators of the literature also coincided with those called "the wise" in various texts. Terminology is important for studying all the ideal types, but statistical examination of wisdom terminology is probably more important for this ideal type than some of the others.

1.6 THE CONTRIBUTION OF THE SOCIAL SCIENCES

Dearman, J. A. *Property Rights in the Eighth-Century Prophets* (1988).
Fahey, T. "Max Weber's *Ancient Judaism*," *American Journal of Sociology* 88 (1982) 62-87.
Fiensy, D. "Using the Nuer Culture of Africa in Understanding the Old Testament: An Evaluation," *JSOT* 38 (1987) 73-83.
Laslett, P. "The Wrong Way Through the Telescope: A Note on Literary Evidence in Sociology and in Historical Sociology," *British Journal of Sociology* 27 (1976) 317-42.
Mayes, A. D. H. *The Old Testament in Sociological Perspective* (1989).
Miller, J. M., and J. H. Hayes. *A History of Ancient Israel and Judah* (1986).
Rogerson, J. W. *Anthropology and the Old Testament* (1978).
Weber, M. *Ancient Judaism* (1952).
Wilson, R. R. *Sociological Approaches to the Old Testament* (1984).

A number of books and articles have addressed the question of the social sciences in relation to the OT and can be consulted for background information (Mayes; Rogerson; Wilson). No great theoretical discussion will be given here; rather, my own study will proceed on more empirical grounds, though relevant studies by anthropologists and sociologists will be cited at various points.

Central to the disciplines of sociology and anthropology are the study and observation of living societies in action. Sociologists construct questionnaires, conduct interviews, and draw up statistical tables. Anthropologists do field work in native societies, living among those being observed and cultivating native informants. This is impossible in any historical study. Ancient society is no longer accessible as such. There are no native informants from ancient Israel. The society has long since disappeared. All we have is a collection of religious texts, along with some material remains (including a few inscriptions). Granted, the texts claim to tell us something about that society, but these texts in their present form date from long after the events they appear to describe and do not bear the earmarks of first-class historical sources. Even if they were first-class historical sources, however, they would still be deficient in that we have no way of interrogating them as we might living informants.

Also of major import is statistical analysis. This is part of the bedrock of sociological study under normal circumstances. Unfortunately, many of our data are intractable to statistical study. Not only are we dealing with ancient texts, but the use of literary texts for quantitative purposes is highly problematic, as well illustrated by Peter Laslett. Therefore, even though historians can use some of the techniques developed by sociologists and anthropologists, these have to be adapted to take account of the nature of the available data and to recognize the limits imposed by historical work. The contributions of anthropology and sociology are primarily the following:

1. They show new possibilities and approaches to the familiar texts. They allow us to look with new eyes—to pull ourselves out of the accustomed ruts in which we have a tendency to run.

2. They allow us to interrogate the texts and attempt to derive answers from them about questions which were not the primary concerns of the authors and editors. If such and such is known from such and such modern society, could something similar have been the case in ancient Israel?

3. They provide models which can be tested against the biblical data. Does the priest or prophet or diviner known from a living society seem to fit into Israelite society?

4. They may provide cross-cultural comparisons which help to fill gaps in the biblical data. The OT text tells little about many aspects of society. It may be possible to reconstruct a more coherent picture by appeal to analogy from similarly functioning cultures.

There is a negative side as well, however. A real danger exists that theories and models derived from sociological study might be imposed on the data rather than tested against them and then modified or discarded where necessary. A similar danger is to overinterpret—to find a lot more data in a passage than is warranted. And, finally, the texts themselves may be read uncritically, as if they provided immediate access to the ancient society. It is easy to forget that the biblical texts cannot be treated like anthropological reports. A good example of this is the book of Amos. It has frequently been quoted as evidence about the type of society which existed during the reign of Jeroboam II. The standard and rightly praised history of Israel by Miller and Hayes is nevertheless surprisingly uncritical (312):

> While most of the population consisted of poor peasant farmers who had barely survived the long years of Syrian oppression, a wealthy and privileged upper class had emerged in the process of national restoration which lived in stark contrast to the ordinary citizens. Amos uttered stern maledictions against this wealthy upper class which enjoyed its luxury while ignoring the dismal conditions of those around them. . . . Not only did this upper class enjoy great advantage over the poor, Amos accuses them of increasing this advantage by unjust means. . . . In short, Amos' oracles presuppose a social and legal situation in which even the governmental and judicial officials, those allegedly committed to preserving justice, were the very ones contributing to what the prophet considered an ungodly social imbalance.

Even if we assumed that the entire book represented the words of a prophet about 760 BCE (and many would not concede this), we must keep in mind that this would still represent a very particular and one-sided view of society. The street preacher, the television evangelist, the aspiring politician, the single-issue campaigner—these are hardly the most objective observers of society. Their stock in trade is the isolated example, the broad generalization, the hyperbole. They want to support their overall message by whatever means available, and we could hardly expect a full and fair description of society, even if they were trained sociologists.

Instead of a sociological survey, what we find in the book of Amos is a set of vague, even obscure, references which tell us little more than that the prophet disapproved of what was being done. The reference in 4:1 to the "cows of Bashan" who defraud the poor, rob the needy, who say to their husbands, "Bring, and let's carouse," may be graphic, but what is its significance? How many of these "cows" were there? Fifty? A hundred? Twenty? Five? Three? Whom had they defrauded and how many? How had they robbed the needy? Had they cheated their servants out of their wages? Had they engaged in burglary? Had they robbed them at knife point? Why are the women accused but not their husbands? The striking language makes it easy to overlook what is actually the case: this is only a very generalized charge against some rather unspecified persons.

Similarly, we can consider a passage such as 8:4-6:

> Listen to this, you who devour the needy, annihilating the poor of the land, saying, "If only the new moon were over, so that we could sell grain; the sabbath, so that we could offer wheat for sale, using an ephah that is too small, and a shekel that is too big, tilting a dishonest scale, and selling grain refuse as grain! We will buy the poor for silver, the needy for a pair of sandals."

This passage suggests that some people are greedy and cheat their customers, that other people have lost their property and have become impoverished. We have no reason to disbelieve that such things happened. Such happened then; such happens in every age, including our own. Beyond that, though, we cannot go. We do not know how many people lost property or how. We do not know that people were being deprived of property by illegal means, for example; what was being done may have been strictly according to law. We have no information on whether the peasant population as a whole was losing its livelihood in any greater numbers than, say, under Rehoboam, Ahab, or even David. We do not know that great *latifundia* (agricultural estates) were being developed. We do not know that there was more exploitation by the rich or more suffering by the poor, that there was more class conflict than at other times, that more crime was being committed, or that the level of justice had declined. In short, Amos gives us no coherent or definitive information about the overall social and economic conditions under Jeroboam II.

1.7 THE METHOD OF PROCEEDING

Barstad, H. M. "Akkadian 'Loanwords' in Isaiah 40-55—And the Question of Babylonian Origin of Deutero-Isaiah," *Text and Theology* (1994) 36-48.
Davies, P. R. "God of Cyrus, God of Israel: Some Religio-Historical Reflections on Isaiah 40-55," *Words Remembered, Texts Renewed: Essays in Honour of John F.A. Sawyer* (1995) 207-25.
Rendtorff, R. *The Problem of the Process of Transmission in the Pentateuch* (1990).
Whybray, R. N. *The Making of the Pentateuch* (1987).

As noted in the Preface, I shall conduct my investigation in the following way: The first task is to look at each religious specialist individually. Judging from the data in the OT, there are five of these, though the diviner perhaps covers more diversity than the others. Each of these will be treated as an ideal type. What this means is that each is treated in isolation as a distinct function, with the aim of drawing up its major characteristics. In each chapter, the first section is a study of the major texts and examples from the OT itself. This forms the backbone of the study, the basis on which everything else exists. These texts are looked at generally from a synchronic point of view, as they are found in the final form of the OT text.

What does the text as it now stands tell us about the king or priest or diviner? We must start there since this is the one sure source of data available to us. After a summary of the particular ideal type as found in the text, relevant cross-cultural parallels will be surveyed, sometimes from the ancient Near East alone but sometimes from anthropological study as well. After this follow studies of various considerations important for the particular ideal type in question. Finally, each chapter ends with a summary of the Gestalt of the ideal type, based on a study of all relevant data, primarily the OT text, but also archeology, Near Eastern literature, anthropological data.

The ideal type is a scholarly construct for use as a heuristic device. It may not actually exist in society or not in the precise and clear-cut way it may seem to when studied as an ideal type. Things are usually much messier in real life. So the various religious specialists as they functioned in the society of ancient Israel will have to be considered. Chapter 7 attempts to take a holistic view, approaching the question in the same format as Chapters 2-6. It begins by summarizing the ideal types gleaned from the OT text. It then looks at examples of religious specialists in operation in actual societies. Finally, it brings all considerations together into an attempt to see to what extent the religious specialists in ancient Israel can be situated in their society.

This study differs from the way most studies in the past have approached a subject such as this. The normal procedure would have been to do a form-critical and traditio-historical analysis—a diachronic analysis—of the texts before attempting to use them in the study. My procedure has been, rather, to focus on the texts in their final form—a synchronic analysis. There are several reasons for this approach, two of which can be noted here: First, it is interesting to see how remarkably traditio-historical analyses have followed the theological presuppositions of their practitioners. Much as the historical Jesus discovered by nineteenth-century scholars looked like a good respectable *Bürger*, so the prophet had much in common with the occupiers of the *Evangelische* pulpit. This may be an overstatement, but it illustrates a genuine problem. Only by taking the text as it stands can we have a common starting point that all can agree on. What the text actually says has too often been ignored in favor of the message of a hypothetical "original" text.

Second, a crisis of confidence in the traditio-historical methods has been intensifying in recent years. This has become evident in part by the increasing interest in modern literary studies which rely on the final form of the text but, more worryingly, it has penetrated to the heart of the traditional form-critical bastion so that some of those questioning it are well-known practitioners. This means that some of the most cherished theories about the growth of the tradition are now under attack. For example, the documentary hypothesis with regard to the Pentateuch is undergoing a major assault (Rendtorff; Whybray). Even Deutero-Isaiah is now being reinterpreted as far as its setting (Palestine instead of Babylon), date (Persian instead of neo-Babylonia), and unity (cf. Barstad; Davies). This increasing change of approach does not represent a return to a fundamentalist view of the Bible. On the contrary, some of the recent interpretations are more radical (e.g., dating the text quite late) than the standard critical position. In most cases, it is not doubted that the biblical tradition has a long history and that any earlier material has been thoroughly revised and adapted.

What this means, though, is that the historian can no longer use the old traditio-historical analyses with confidence; indeed, the bewildering variety of analysis for many passages has been one of the factors leading to the crisis. It may be that in the coming decades, a new traditio-historical consensus will develop. If so, it could lead to a much greater refinement of the picture developed here. Nevertheless, my approach attempts to bypass the problem of the nature of the OT tradition by a synchronic study, even if it means only a crude product is presently possible.

1.8 PRELIMINARY CONCLUSIONS ABOUT THE TEXT AND SOCIETY

Barstad, H. M. "No Prophets? Recent Developments in Biblical Prophetic Research and Ancient Near Eastern Prophecy," *JSOT* 57 (1993) 39-60.

At this point, I shall anticipate some of the discussion and resulting conclusions to be laid down in subsequent chapters. For the reasons outlined above (especially 1.4), I believe that a move from the literary picture found in the OT text to a legitimate attempt at describing the living society of ancient Israel is possible. The starting point is the text itself. It alone provides sufficient data to give any hope of recreating the religious aspect of ancient society. Archeology may be very helpful for getting at some aspects of the society, but it provides little for the question of religious specialists. To repeat: we have to begin with the text. The OT text itself does not present such a uniform picture that all earlier sources have been completely ironed out. Within the text are a number of hints which suggest that the text contains memories of a functioning society, even if this has been overlaid to a lesser or greater extent by the ideology of the writer. The use of cross-cultural comparisons suggests that the picture derived from the OT is plausible. The various religious specialists, their functions, and their interactions are believable. Whatever stereotyping there may have been does not seem to have created a completely artificial construct. Plausibility is not the ultimate test, of course, since good fiction is often plausible. But a further confirmation of this general conclusion is supported, finally, by a few contemporary texts or remains which are universally accepted as authentic.

I mentioned fairy tales toward the beginning of this discourse. They are a rather interesting case in point. They occur in a number of cultures, and they have features which bear no relation to reality. We know, despite countless B-movies, that there is no evidence for fire-breathing dragons or giant human beings. But other aspects of the fairy tale do reflect the culture in which it was composed. Beautiful maidens do exist—or so we are assured. Even fiction writers tend to describe what they know and thus often give a broadly accurate representation of society even while inventing characters and events.

We should not exaggerate what we are able to do. We are not able to substantiate actual events or persons described in the text, but we do not need to. In this the social historian has an advantage over the political historian. We do not know whether there was an Elijah or a Jeremiah—I shall leave that thorny question for others to debate. All we can say—and all we need to say—is that there were probably figures like them known to the biblical writers or editors who were believed to do certain sorts of deeds (such as find lost objects or foretell people's future). We are also unable to draw much of a historical sequence. That is, my approach does not allow us to trace the development of institutions over several centuries. We have moved from text to society, but the society reconstructed has to be painted in broad strokes with only a minimum amount of color. We are definitely in the school of the Impressionists, not the Realists.

2.

The King

Johnson, A. R. *Sacral Kingship in Ancient Israel* (1967).
Mettinger, T. N. D. *King and Messiah* (1976).
Sacral Kingship, The: Contributions to the Central Theme of the VIIIth International Congress for the History of Religions (1959).
Whitelam, K. W. *The Just King* (1979).

Unlike the situation with some other religious specialists, there is very little direct evidence about the religious function of the king, but there are many hints that the king was very important, and some historical reconstructions make him central. It is not always easy to proceed very far on the basis of direct statements in the text as would be preferable. Much is said about the kings and their activities, but the impression left from clues in the text is that some important data have been suppressed at a time when the monarchy was no longer a reality. A more indirect approach is needed, with more careful attention paid to inconsistencies, out-of-character statements, and other small pointers within the text.

2.1 SELECTED OLD TESTAMENT TEXTS

2.1.1 Deuteronomy 17:14-20

This passage assumes that the Israelites would want a king after they came into the land. Far from the idea being condemned, a human king seems to be explicitly allowed, though with stipulations attached. He is to be chosen by God from among their own people—no foreigners allowed. He is not to collect large quantities of horses, wives, or silver and gold. He is also to have a copy of "this law" (Deuteronomy?) copied out by the "Levitical priests" and is to keep it by him and read it so that he will follow it faithfully all his life.

2.1.2 The Consequences of Not Having a King (Judges)

The story of Judges is the story of disobedience, punishment, repentance, and deliverance for the people of Israel; it is also an account of the depravity that human beings are capable of. A man's concubine is raped to death. He cuts her up, sends the pieces of her body to the other tribes, and they come to wipe out an entire tribe from among the tribes of Israel. They almost succeed, but a few young men manage to carry on the tribal name by seizing maidens dancing at a festival. The narrator's characteristic refrain after relating such an episode is, "In those days there was no king in Israel; every man did what was right in his own eyes" (AV 17:6; 18:1; 19:1; 21:25).

The judges in many cases acted as miniature kings, so perhaps the distinction between judge and king was a small one. Indeed, Abimelech was proclaimed king by the citizens of Shechem (8:29-9:57), though his reign was rather short-lived. Nevertheless, it is the appearance of the judge at crucial points which brings Israel back to adherence of the law: "Now if only it were to be a permanent institution. . . . " One of the messages of Judges is that a proper Israelite king would have done an immense amount of good for God's people.

2.1.3 The Anti-Monarchy View (1 Sam 8)

This classic statement is often quoted as *the* OT view on the monarchy. It embodies the perspective—frequently advanced in some modern writings—which sees the kingship as an alien institution, a rejection of Israelite social traditions, and a deviation from Yahwistic religious principles: "For they have rejected me [Yhwh] from being king over them" (v 7). The burden to be borne by the people and the arbitrary and high-handed way in which the monarch will act are all spelled out in disturbing detail. He will take their grain and wine to feed his courtiers and pay their wages. He will conscript the young men for the army and the young women as domestic servants. He will take away property to reward his followers and will even impose *corvée* (forced) labor. One day the people would cry out under their yoke and regret their demand.

Despite these warnings, the people persist, and Samuel seeks out Yhwh's choice to be king. However, it should be recognized that the context of this demand for a king arose out of the failure of Samuel's sons to dispense justice in their office as judges (vv 1-2). Lying even further behind that was the abuse of office by Eli's sons when Samuel was still only a lad serving him (1 Sam 2:22-36). The text therefore allows that the people had some understandable reasons to want a new system of government.

2.1.4 Saul (1 Sam 9-31)

As the first king of Israel, Saul provides a useful example. He was chosen by God and anointed by Samuel (10:1; 15:1), being referred to often as Yhwh's anointed (12:3, 5; 24:7; 26:9, etc.). While under threat from the Philistines, he was told to wait for Samuel at Gilgal (ch. 13). When Samuel was delayed, Saul finally offered sacrifice in desperation (vv 8-9). For this Samuel condemned him, but the exact reason is unclear (vv 11-14). The general accusation seems to be one of disobedience, but one might wonder whether the fault was in offering sacrifice, which only Samuel was supposed to do.

In chapter 15 Saul fought and defeated the Amalekites at the command of Yhwh through Samuel. However, he was to pronounce a *ḥerem* (proscription) on them so that all the people and animals were to be killed and the spoils destroyed (v 3). But after defeating the Amalekites, Saul spared the king and the best of the animals and the spoil (vv 8-9), the animals being spared allegedly for purposes of sacrifice (v 15). Saul was condemned for this (vv 16-26). Again, his fault seems to be one of disobedience, and nothing is said about Saul's sacrificing. Even though both these passages could be read as a condemnation of the king for an activity (i.e., sacrifice) reserved for the priests, this seems unlikely in the light of what later kings did (see below).

2.1.5 David

Amerding, C. E. "Were David's Sons Really Priests?" *Current Issues in Biblical and Patristic Interpretation* (1975) 75-86.

Stoebe, H. J. *Das zweite Buch Samuelis* (1994).

Wenham, G. J. "Were David's Sons Priests?" *ZAW* 87 (1975) 79-82.

Texts: 1 Samuel 16—1 Kings 2; 1 Chronicles 10-29.

In Samuel-Kings David is the ideal king, the founder of a new dynasty, and the first king over greater Israel. God and the cult play a much greater role in the account of his life than in that of Saul. A special point is made of his being a divine choice and receiving the rite of anointment (1 Sam 16). In an act which may have symbolic significance, David and those with him were allowed to eat the Bread of Presence, which was normally reserved for the priests (21:2-7). One of his first acts after taking Jerusalem was to make it the home of the main Israelite cult object, the Ark of the Covenant (2 Sam 6). Part of this ceremony was the offering of sacrifice, which David seems to have done himself (vv 13, 18). His aim was to build a temple to replace the tent which had housed the Ark up to this point, but God vetoed this through a prophecy to Nathan; the task was to be left for Solomon because David had blood on his hands (2 Sam 7). At the time of the plague on Israel, after David had ordered a census, he was told by Gad to set up an altar on the threshing floor of Araunah (because the plague stopped at that point). He purchased the threshing floor from Araunah and offered up offerings (2 Sam 24). It was that threshing floor which became the site of the temple built by Solomon.

The picture in 1 Chronicles is the same, only more so. That is, David is not only the ideal king, but the warts-and-all image of Samuel-Kings is toned down so that David comes across in a sanitized version. Furthermore, even though David does not build the temple himself, he assembles all the materials and draws up the plans so that there seems little left for Solomon to do (22; 28:10-19; 29:1-5). He also organizes the Levites and priests and orders the entire temple organization (23-26).

One of the more interesting statements is 2 Samuel 8:18: "and David's sons were priests (*kōhănîm*)." This goes against the teaching in various passages that only those of the tribe of Levi could be clergy. It is hardly surprising that in 1 Chronicles 18:17 the text reads, "and David's sons were first ministers of the king" (*hāri'šōnîm lĕyad hammelek*). Some scholars have been reluctant to accept the plain sense of the text in Samuel and have argued for a textual corruption, based in part on the reading in 1 Chronicles (Amerding; Wenham). Yet there is nothing about 2 Samuel 8:18 that suggests a textual corruption except the embarrassment it causes to the view that only the descendants of Aaron could be priests, a view already contradicted by a number of passages. Rather than 1 Chronicles 18:17 representing an original reading, it is likely to be a theological correction because of the same theological consternation apparently felt by some moderns. The text-critical principle of the *lectio difficilior*—that the more difficult reading is likely to be original—certainly applies here. It is hard to believe that a copyist changed "first ministers" into "priests," but easy to believe the reverse.

2.1.6 Solomon (1 Kings 1-11//2 Chron 1-9)

At the beginning of his reign, Solomon went to Gibeon to offer sacrifices (1 Kings 3:4). The author of 1 Kings explains that since no house for Yhwh had been built, the people still sacrificed at the cult places (*bāmôt*: vv 2-3). It was while sleeping at the old cult site of Gibeon that Yhwh appeared to Solomon and asked what he could give him (vv 5-14). Because Solomon asked for wisdom in order to govern properly, God granted him wealth and riches as well. It has been suggested that Solomon himself slept at the cult site for incubation purposes—to evoke a divine dream—though this is not explicitly stated. Solomon's main religious accomplishment was the building of the temple. Although the presence of Yhwh filled the temple, so that even the priests could not enter, Solomon himself was able to stand and pray before the altar of God (1 Kings 8:10, 22, 54). Because he offered up so many sacrifices, Solomon consecrated the entire center of the temple court for burning the sacrificial parts (v 64). This action was taken by the *king* rather than the priests; Solomon acted as a priest among priests.

2.1.7 Jeroboam (1 Kings 12-14)

Jeroboam I sets the tone for the wicked rule of all the Israelite kings. The constant refrain, summing up the reigns of many of the Israelite kings, is that they walked in the way, or did not depart from the sins, of Jeroboam b. Nebat (1 Kings 15:34; 16:2, 19, 26, 31; 22:53[Eng. 22:52]; 2 Kings 3:3; 10:29, 31; 13:2, 6, 11; 14:24; 15:9, 18, 24, 28; 17:22). His reign is pictured as a falling away from the true religion centered on the temple at Jerusalem. After he took away the northern tribes to form a separate kingdom, Jeroboam is said to have set up national cult places in Bethel and Dan (1 Kings 12:25-33). He was offering an offering when the man of God prophesied against him and the altar (13:1-6). It seems clear that Jeroboam was actually presiding over the altar during the sacrifice (v 1: *'ōmēd 'al-hammizbēaḥ lĕhaqṭîr*), a duty reserved for the priests in the priestly writings (Lev 1-7), yet no comment is made on this in the context. Is this because it was an unexceptional activity on the part of kings during this time?

2.1.8 Asa (1 Kings 15:9-24//2 Chron 14-16)

In 1 Kings Asa is presented as the first cult reformer who cleared the land of certain idolatrous practices, though he did not remove the country cult places (1 Kings 15:9-24). Chronicles expands on this (2 Chron 14-16). Asa also prayed before battle and had his prayers answered by a great victory over a vastly superior force (2 Chron 14:8-14). The spirit of God came upon Azariah b. Oded the prophet who spoke to Asa, promising that Yhwh would be with him as long as he obeyed (15:1-7). Asa took courage and removed the abominations from Judah and restored God's altar (15:8-18). However, when he paid the king of Damascus to force the Israelite king Baasha to withdraw, Asa received a negative message via Hanani the seer, who warned that the king had missed defeating the Arameans by making a treaty with them (16:7-10). Instead of repenting, however, Asa punished the seer.

2.1.9 Joash of Judah (2 Kings 12//2 Chron 24)

Joash (or Jehoash) is said to have done what was pleasing to Yhwh because he followed the teachings of Jehoida the (high) priest, even though the cult places continued to exist. His main achievement was to repair the temple. He ordered that all donations of money were to be used for this purpose; however, when he found that the priests were not carrying out the plan as instructed, he set up a system to ensure that the job was done: he had a large locked chest made with a hole in the top into which the people were to drop their donations. When it was full, the money was to be counted by the royal scribe and the high priest and given directly to the repairmen. In this case, the king took charge of preserving the temple and seems even to have contravened attempts by the priests to avoid his instructions. He sent his own royal scribe to help oversee the task.

2.1.10 Uzziah (2 Kings 15:1-7//2 Chron 26)

Little is said about Uzziah in Kings: he was righteous, even though he did not remove the country cult places, and Yhwh struck him with leprosy which he had until his death. Chronicles, however, claims to know more and describes development of the army and successful military campaigns and great building works. But after such success, Uzziah became arrogant and attempted to enter the temple to offer incense on the incense altar in the Holy Place but was prevented by the priests (2 Chron 26:16-21). The Chronicler puts into the (high) priest's mouth the statement that only the Aaronites were to offer incense in this way; because of this violation Uzziah was struck with leprosy which he had until he died.

2.1.11 Ahaz of Judah (2 Kings 16)

Ahaz, the Judean king just before the fall of the Northern Kingdom, called on Tiglath-Pileser III for help against the attack of Israel and Damascus (vv 5-9). The Assyrian king attacked the kingdom of Damascus and destroyed it, deporting the inhabitants. While Ahaz was paying his respects to him in Damascus, he saw the altar there and was rather taken by it. He sent a sketch of it to the high priest and had a copy made. This was then substituted for the original bronze altar made under Solomon. When Ahaz returned from Damascus, he offered sacrifices and cereal offerings and poured out the drink offerings on the altar and dashed the blood of the well-being offerings against its side (v 13). These actions, reserved for the priests in the priestly literature (Lev 1-7), are here carried out by the king.

2.1.12 Hezekiah (2 Kings 18-20//Isa 36-39//2 Chron 29-32)

Most of the Jewish kings before Hezekiah are said to have been righteous, but he is the first allegedly to have tried to remove the cult places and shrines, even to the point of breaking up a bronze serpent attributed to Moses. In 2 Kings 18:1-8 his religious activities are presented only in summary form; despite their similarity to Josiah's, the text makes no issue of his designating the temple the sole cult place for worship. Matters are quite different in 2 Chronicles 29-31, which goes into great detail about Hezekiah's reform. His reform plainly anticipates Josiah's, even though no law book had been found. He also personally encourages, admonishes, and organizes the temple administration and cult personnel. In both Kings and Chronicles, there is a clear connection between the religious and the political. Hezekiah extends his influence into the territory of the Northern Kingdom, even if the reason is ostensibly to invite the people to worship in Jersualem (2 Chron 30). His rebellion against Assyria and his invasion of Philistia are given no religious justification (2 Kings 18:7-8), though they point up that cult centralization and political expansion fit well together.

Much of the description of Hezekiah's reign is given over to the threat to Jerusalem by the invasion of Sennacherib. The narrative has conventionally been analyzed into three parallel accounts of the siege, each one with a different aim and emphasis, and also mutually irreconcilable (4.1.11). In account B_2 (2 Kings 19:9b-34) Hezekiah seems to take the more active role in going into the temple with Sennacherib's letter and praying directly to God for deliverance.

2.1.13 Josiah (2 Kings 22-23//2 Chron 34-35)

Josiah is the premier cult reformer, even if in the text he is not so much a reformer as a restorer of Israel's original religion and true. In 2 Kings the reform began with the finding of the book of the law, but in 2 Chronicles Josiah had already been underway with his reforms for six years before the book of the law was discovered (2 Chron 34:3, 8). In both accounts he first removed the altars around Judah, but then he advanced north to Bethel and then on into Samaria. This was followed by a Passover such as had not been observed during the entire period of the monarchy. This was successful because the correct priestly organization was restored (2 Chron 35:2-5, 10-16). Thus, Josiah appears in the text as an active figure who takes the lead in seeing that the cult and priesthood are functioning properly.

2.1.14 The Book of Ezekiel

Duguid, I. M. *Ezekiel and the Leaders of Israel* (1994).
Tuell, S. S. *The Law of the Temple in Ezekiel 40-48* (1992).

The significance of the *nāśî'*, "prince," of Ezekiel 40-48 has long been debated. Is he the equivalent of the Israelite *melek*, "king," or does he really hold a different office? Elsewhere in Ezekiel, the term *nāśî'* is used of the Israelite king (12:10, 12; 21:30; 34:24; 37:25), and a case can be made that it was also the intent of Ezekiel 40-48 (Duguid: 11-33). It has been argued that the *nāśî'* is the actual governor in the Persian period, but this is based on an analysis of 40-48 which finds two redactional layers, one from the historical Ezekiel and one by a Persian-period redactor (Tuell).

If we assume that the *nāśî'* is an actual or idealized king (rather than a Persian governor), his relationship to the cult may tell us something about the actual cultic functions of the kings during the monarchy. The *nāśî'* has cultic functions, but his relationship is not that of a priest. The palace is no longer right next to the temple, though it is not far away (45:7-8). Although he cannot eat in the priestly enclosure, he is able to eat in the closed eastern gate (44:1-3). He is also responsible for providing offerings to make expiation for the people (45:17-25), a task elsewhere reserved for the priests (Lev 9:7; 10:17; 16:33). The impression is that the complex of Ezekiel 40-48 wishes to change and restrict the cultic position of the king without reducing him purely to the lay level. If so, this suggests that the position being modified had the king with a more direct and central cultic function.

2.1.15 The Royal Psalms

Since the time of Gunkel, it has been agreed that the royal psalms include at least the following: Psalms 2, 18, 20, 21, 45, 72, 89, 101, 110, 132, 144:1-11. These generally focus on the king's responsibilities as warrior and leader of his people and say little about his role in the cult. Psalm 45 is mainly about a wedding to a foreign princess. Others are about how Yhwh helps the king and saves him from his enemies (Ps 18, 20, 21). The intimate relations between God and the king are a major theme: the king is Yhwh's son (Ps 2:7; 89:27-28); Yhwh comes down from heaven to save him (Ps 18, 21, 144:1-11), and gives the necessary qualities and blessings for him to be a good king (Ps 72).

Although specific references to cultic activities are found only in Ps 20:4, we have other indications of the king's place in the cult. Psalm 110 is an important statement in this regard. First of all, it affirms David's position as a cult and temple founder, agreeing with passages in 2 Samuel and 1 Chronicles (2.1.5). Most important, David is designated a priest (*kōhēn*) forever (v 4) "after the order of Melchizedek" (or perhaps "a rightful king by my decree"—NJPS). Since this seems to be the only place that the king is called a priest, the statement is significant, attesting the king's place not only as a cult founder but even as head of the cult himself. The reference to Melchizedek is itself important since Melchizedek was not only king of Salem (Jerusalem?) but also a priest of El Elyon, the god of the city (Gen 14:18). If this tradition is in some way a commentary on the Jerusalem king, it strongly suggests the combining of kingship and priesthood, with the king as the main priest of Yhwh.

2.2 THE KING IN THE OLD TESTAMENT TEXT

The OT text has an ambivalent view of kingship. On the one hand, there is the strong condemnation in 1 Samuel 8 in which the people's choice of a king was tantamount to rejecting the rule of Yhwh. The forcefulness of this passage has often made writers overlook the other side of the question, which in many ways is even more strongly represented. A passage such as Deuteronomy 17:14-20 specifically allows Israel to choose a king without a hint of condemnation, only ensuring that he rules according to Deuteronomic principles. The unchanging refrain in Judges is that when "there is no king in

Israel, every man does what is right in his own eyes" (2.1.2), producing such horrendous crimes as the raping to death of a concubine and the subsequent destruction of almost an entire tribe in Israel (19-21). Furthermore, the dynasty of David was promised not to fail (2 Sam 7); when it did, despite this unconditional statement, the promise was made that it would be reconstituted in a David *redivivus*—an ideal Davidic king who would institute a paradisal rule (Isa 11:1-10; Jer 33:14-26), an idea which was to lead to the plethora of messianic speculations in Judaism and Christianity through the centuries.

The anti-monarchic tendency in Israel may have placed constraints on the king's power and even influenced how he was viewed, at least some of the time. A tradition was perpetuated that Israel had once been without a king. Thus, the contrast often made between Israelite and kingship elsewhere in the ancient Near East may have some truth to it, but the differentiation goes only so far. The Israelite king was supported by his own theology and mythology. Although not himself divine, he was the "son of God" by adoption (Ps 2) and was considered uniquely responsible for the religious condition of the people. This religious accountability is one of the main themes of the Deuteronomistic History (Joshua–2 Kings). Throughout Kings and Chronicles the success or failure of each king's rule is judged by how he followed God's law (as understood by the Deuteronomist and Chronicler). The political success of the king—how he benefited the people internally or guided the nation in international affairs—is basically ignored. A ruler such as Omri, probably one of the most successful of the Israelite kings, has his reign summarized in six verses (1 Kings 16:22-28) because he was regarded as wicked. His son Ahab has a larger section of the book (1 Kings 16-22), but much of this is taken up with the activities of Elijah.

The people also suffered from the sins of the king or benefited from his piety. David's alleged sin in taking a military census of Israel resulted in a plague on the people (2 Sam 24; 1 Chron 21). During the early part of Solomon's reign, when he was obedient, "every man sat under his own vine and fig tree" (1 Kings 5:5 [Eng. 4:25]). Later on, when he allowed his foreign wives to take him away from pure worship, however, Yhwh raised up adversaries who harassed Israel (1 Kings 11:14-25). It was Hezekiah who interceded with God on behalf of the nation at the time of Sennacherib's invasion, according to one account at least (2 Kings 19:9-34). From these examples, it is apparent that the welfare of the people was very much dependent on the leadership of the king.

Although not a major topic, there are a number of references to the king as a cult official. This is especially noted for individuals like Saul, David, and Solomon. Other examples of kings who officiate at the altar happen to be "wicked" kings, such as Jeroboam I and Ahaz of Judah. Yet they are not criticized for their cultic activities as such, and the only clear criticism of a king for attempting to participate in the cult does not occur until 2 Chronicles

26:16-21 (Uzziah). The impression is that the king's part in the cult was a major one and taken for granted. Later views caused some of this to be suppressed or reinterpreted, but the tradition was too strong to be completely controlled. A variety of examples in the text hint at a different state of affairs underlying the present text.

2.3 KINGSHIP IN THE ANCIENT NEAR EAST

Ahn, G. *Religiöse Herrscherlegitimation im achämenidischen Iran* (1992).
Engnell, I. *Studies in Divine Kingship in the Ancient Near East* (1943).
Frankfort, H. *Kingship and the Gods* (1948).

Israelite kingship has often been contrasted with kingship in other ancient Near Eastern countries. Sometimes the term "divine kingship" has been used of the monarchy in Mesopotamia and Egypt. Perhaps the epitome of such an approach is that of Engnell, who took the "Scandinavian school" to its extreme (though Engnell did not exclude Israel from the idea of divine kingship). More recent study has been critical of that approach, pointing out the differences between Egypt and other Near Eastern monarchies (Frankfort) but also suggesting that even too much emphasis has been placed on the divinity of the Pharaoh (Ahn: 21-23).

2.3.1 Egypt

Baines, J. "Kingship, Definition of Culture, and Legitimation," *Ancient Egyptian Kingship* (1995) 3-47.
Bleeker, C. J. "The Position of the Queen in Ancient Egypt," *The Sacral Kingship* (1959) 261-68.
David, A. R. *The Ancient Egyptians* (1982).
Lanczkowski, G. "Das Königtum im Mittleren Reich," *The Sacral Kingship* (1959) 269-80.
Lichtheim, M. *Ancient Egyptian Literature* (1973-80).
O'Connor, D., and D. P. Silverman, eds. *Ancient Egyptian Kingship* (1995).
Silverman, D. P. "The Nature of Egyptian Kingship," *Ancient Egyptian Kingship* (1995) 49-92.
Trigger, B. G., et al. *Ancient Egypt: A Social History* (1983).

The general view of Egyptian kingship is still dominated by H. Frankfort, who emphasized divinity as an important aspect; however, this was mainly because he focused only on religious inscriptions, whereas a survey of all literature gives a more nuanced view (Silverman: 50). Among Egyptologists, the following summary is widely accepted:

> Kingship is a divine institution, in a way itself a god, or at least an image of the divine and capable of becoming its manifestation; each

> incumbent, each pharaoh, is fundamentally a human being, subject to humankind's limitations. When the king took part in the roles of his office, especially in rituals and ceremonies, his being became suffused with the same divinity manifest in his office and the gods themselves. With this capacity, the king would be empowered to carry out the actual and symbolic acts that contributed to the maintenance and rebirth of cosmos. Indeed, in these contexts, the king acted as a creator deity and *became* the sun-god. On these occasions pharaoh would be recognized by those who saw him as imbued with divinity, characteristically radiant and giving off a fragrant aroma (O'Connor/Silverman: xxv).

Clearly the Egyptian concept of kingship developed and shifted through time and in any case a variety of images might exist in the sources at any period. In addition,

> the variations in both terminology and perception were great. A pharaoh might be: named a god in a monumental historical text, called the son of a deity in an epithet on a statue in a temple, hailed as the living image of a god in a secular inscription, described as a fallible mortal in a historical or literary text . . . or referred to simply by his personal name in a letter. Each source, therefore, will help to provide the elements that together comprise kingship in ancient Egypt, accordng to the written documentation of the Egyptians themselves (Silverman: 50).

The king was the chief religious figure in Egypt (David: 42-43; Trigger: 201). He was the priest to the gods (though in practice he delegated this to the priests in the many temples) and was effective as intermediary between the divine and the human. As a ruler, though, he was required to rule according to *maat* (the principles of order and justice, deified as a goddess), as so persuasively expressed by the *Eloquent Peasant* (Lichtheim: 1.169-84). Official texts tend to emphasize his exalted state, but other texts (especially wisdom and popular texts) recognize that the king is less than a god (Silverman: 52-55). For example, a description of the battle of Kadesh tacitly acknowledges that the king made a poor tactical judgment initially, though he is also pictured as a god-like warrior in the same text. The scribe who pictured queen Hatshepsut in a pornographic caricature was apparently the same one who penned traditional inscriptions honoring her, and these were not seen as incompatible (Silverman: 56-57).

The human origins of the king were not forgotten, but the divine attributes of the office were assumed by the act of coronation and also by means of appropriate rituals (Silverman: 66). He was seen as the visible intermediary with the divine realm and respected for the divine element which raised him above the ordinary human being. The idea that the king was divine probably arose at an early time, but it reached its height in the New Kingdom under Amenhotep III and especially his son Amenhotep IV (Akhenaton). This self-deification was evidently a means of separating the king from the mass of private individuals. As time went on, the people took on more and more of the trappings once unique to the king (e.g., the mortuary cult and the exalted language of biographical inscriptions). For the king to claim divinity while still alive was a way of setting himself apart. The language of divinity alongside the recognition of mortality is well illustrated through Rameses II (Silverman: 87):

> He was a god in the temples and in his capital city; he was a royal living ka; he was "Re of the Rulers," throughout the land. Yet it was this very same individual—who much later would be the inspiration for Percy B. Shelley's *Ozymandias*, "the King of Kings"—he who during his lifetime, could be referred to simply as "the general" by his subjects.

2.3.2 Mesopotamia

Garelli, P., ed. *Le palais et la royauté* (1974).
Jacobsen, T. "Early Political Development in Mesopotamia," ZA 52 (1957) 91-140.
Kuhrt, A. "Usurpation, Conquest and Ceremonial: From Babylon to Persia," *Rituals of Royalty: Power and Ceremonial in Traditional Societies* (1987) 20-55.
Lambert, W. G. "The Seed of Kingship," *Le palais et la royauté* (1974) 427-40.
Larsen, M. T. "The City and its King: On the Old Assyrian Notion of Kingship," *Le palais et la royaut* (1974) 285-300.
Seux, M.-J. *Épithètes Royales akkadiennes et sumériennes* (1967).
____ . "Königtum. B. II. und I. Jahrtausend," *RLA* 6 (1980-83) 140-73.
Wilcke, C. "Zum Königtum in der Ur III-Zeit," *Le palais et la royauté* (1974) 177-232.

As with so much relating to Mesopotamia, one cannot speak of a "Mesopotamian" view of kingship. The matter is difficult because much of our knowledge about kingship ideology comes from titles (Seux 1980-83: 141,143). There was a variety of ideas and views, depending on the particular period and the particular area (Sumer, Assyria, Babylonia). It would be a mistake to extrapolate an item attested in one culture to the region as a whole. For example, in the Sumerian period the city ruler was mostly called *ensi* (a term probably implying supervision of temple estates; in Old Babylonian times it meant a kind of farmer), whereas *lugal*, the term later used for "king" (literally "big man"), was comparatively rare. W. G. Lambert has noted that "the ideal of the Sumerian city ruler as a kind of farm bailiff for the god or goddess of the city prevented the growth of prestige around the person of the ruler" (427).

Before the Old Babylonian period a number of the kings had the divine determinative (DINGIR) prefixed to their names, temples built for them, festivals dedicated on their behalf, and even priests consecrated to them (Wilcke: 179-80). This practice of using the divine determinative became very much attenuated by the reign of Hammurabi. A few examples are found in the Kassite period, and it is also used of Sargon II. By contrast, in the Old Assyrian period the assembly of citizens (*ālum*) held power while the king functioned as its agent. The administrative center was the "city hall" (*bīt ālim*) rather than the palace (Larsen). The title *iššiak Aššur*, "vicar of the god Asshur," is used of the first independent kings of Assyria (Larsen: 287-78; Seux 1980-83: 167-68). The king seems to have a position vis-à-vis the national god similar to that of a governor (or vassal ruler) to the king. He also acted in this capacity as intermediary and chief priest between the god and the people.

Even though the divine determinative might be used with the king's name or he might be referred to as a god, the same may be done to an even minor official out of flattery or admiration. In a hymn to the goddess Inanna, the king prays to her as a protective deity even though the divine determinative is used with his name. Also, the king does not generally become a part of the pantheon after death (Gilgamesh is an exception). Thus, the matter is complicated (cf. Seux 1980-83: 170-72). It has been explained in this way:

> The deification of rulers in Mesopotamia is accordingly to be understood not in terms of the qualitative contrast human: divine, mortal: immortal, etc. but in terms of function of the king, he is the "genius" of the country (Jacobsen: 138, n. 108).

Several kings are explicitly called "god of his city" or "god of his country" or even "of all the lands" (Seux 1967: 107 n. 12; Wilcke: 179). A king might also be the protective deity of the city or country. The title "son of the god/goddess D[ivine]N[ame]," which is found in the early period, becomes practically nonexistent in the royal titles of Assyria and Babylonia (Seux 1980-83: 170); however, as attested in most periods all human beings could profess to have particular divine parents. Separating literal from metaphorical usage is not easy.

The king had an important part to play in the cult. In some periods and areas he was regarded as the chief priest to the gods, while the priests in the various temples were in practice only carrying out these sacerdotal duties under his direction (in theory on behalf of the god). The important place of the Babylonian king in the New Year festival is attested in texts copied out in the Hellenistic period (*ANET*: 331-34). To what extent this festival was celebrated in other cities, and the place of the king in the celebration in earlier centuries, is a matter of speculation. Nevertheless, his place in the cult is well established.

According to convention, it was the duty of the king to oversee and practice justice. A graphic example of this is found in the Prologue to the *Codex Hammurabi*, in which Hammurabi states:

> At that time Anum and Enlil named me to promote the welfare of the people, me, Hammurabi, the devout, god-fearing prince, to cause justice to prevail in the land, to destroy the wicked and the evil, that the strong might not oppress the weak, to rise like the sun over the black-headed (people), and to light up the land (*ANET*: 164).

2.3.3 Ugarit and the Hittites

Gray, J. "Sacral Kingship in Ugarit," *Ugaritica VI* (1969) 289-302.
Gurney, O. R. "Hittite Kingship," *Myth, Ritual, and Kingship* (1958) 105-21.
____ . *The Hittites* (1990).
Langhe, R. de. "Myth, Ritual, and Kingship in the Ras Shamra Tablets," *Myth, Ritual, and Kingship* (1958) 122-48.

The Hittite and Ugaritic kings seem to have been regarded much as their Mesopotamian counterpart. While in this life, the king of the respective nations was not considered divine; however, after death the Hittite king at least was said to have "become a god," and regular offerings were made to him. He was the chief priest and the central figure in the cult as a whole. Much time during the six months of each year when not campaigning was given over to religious duties, especially cultic celebrations. However, the religious could even taken precedent over the military, since the king was known to turn over an important campaign to his staff and return to the capital in order to celebrate a major religious festival. Gurney (1990: 53) summarizes the situation in this way:

> The king was at the same time supreme commander of the army, supreme judicial authority, and chief priest. . . . Only his judicial duties seem normally to have been delegated to subordinates; his military and religious ones he was expected to perform in person, and if the latter were sometimes neglected through preoccupation with distant military operations, this was regarded as a sin which would bring the anger of the gods upon the nation. . . . These [religious duties] involved his personal attendance at each of the main cult-centres of the realm. . . . It is in his capacity as priest that we most often find the Hittite king represented on the monuments.

Less is known about the religious aspects of the Ugaritic kingship; nevertheless, the king of Ugarit seems to have reigned much as the kings of Mesopotamia and the Hittites. The list of Ugarit kings (*KTU* 1.113), each name preceded by the divine determinative *il* ("god"), and the references to the Rephaim suggest that the kings became deified after death (cf. 5.3.4).

2.3.4 Iran

Boyce, M. *A History of Zoroastrianism* (1975-).
Burstein, S. M. *The Babyloniaca of Berossus* (1978).
Cook, J. M. *The Persian Empire* (1983).
Frye, R. N. *History of Ancient Iran* (1984).
Kent, R. G. *Old Persian* (1953).
Widengren, G. "The Sacral Kingship of Iran," *The Sacral Kingship* (1959) 242-57.
Yoyotte, J. "L'inscriptions hiéroglyphiques de la statue de Darius à Suse," *Cahiers de la délégation archéologique française en Iran* 4 (1974) 181-83.

According to the Greek Alexander legend (*Vita Alex. Mag.* 1.39.6; 1.40.5), the Persian Great King had the title "god." This has also been the view of many modern scholars until recently, especially those of the "Myth-and-Ritual School" (cf. Widengren). However, there is no evidence in the actual Persian sources that the Persian king was ever regarded as divine himself or that he was deified after death (Ahn: 180-88; Cook: 132-33). The only possible exceptions are the Egyptian inscriptions which refer to the Persian king as son of Re and a god (Yoyotte: 181-82); however, it has to be admitted that this is traditional Egyptian terminology for the Pharaoh, to whom the Egypt priests writing the inscriptions have assimilated the Persian king. This cannot be used as evidence for the divine nature of the Persian king (Ahn: 185). The king was chosen by Ahura Mazda, regarded as his servant, and dependent on him for his authority and well being. The following passage is only one of many which could be listed (*Behistun Inscription* §9.1.24-26 = Kent: 119):

> Saith Darius the King: Ahuramazda bestowed the kingdom upon me; Ahuramazda bore me aid until I got possession of this kingdom; by the favor of Ahuramazda I hold this kingdom.

Whether the early Achaemenid kings were Zoroastrians (as assumed by Boyce) has been very much debated, though the problem may be more one of definition than anything else (Frye: 120-21; cf. Ahn: 95 n. 1). There has been a tendency among recent scholars to date Zarathushtra (Zoroaster) at least some centuries before Cyrus, which would have made it easy for Zoroastrianism to have spread widely among the Iranian peoples by Achaemenid times. In any case, Ahura Mazda was certainly the chief Iranian god. There is little evidence of direct participation in the cult by the king, yet overall control by the king still seems to be the case.

According to Berossus (bk. 3, fg. 65 = Burstein: 29), an Artaxerxes introduced the use of cult statues and also the worship of Anahita. This king seems to be Artaxerxes II, since we also find in his inscriptions, for the first time, Mithra and Anahita listed alongside Ahura Mazda. This suggests that in addition to the introduction of iconic worship, he promoted the worship of these other deities. (Although Mithra was a traditional Iranian deity, Anahita seems to have been a borrowing from Babylonia.) These examples are parallel to those known from all over the ancient Near East in which the king was an important cultic figure. They point to the importance of the king for religion; on the other hand, they give no more support to the concept of a divine king for ancient Iran than for the Mesopotamian kings.

2.4 THE KING AS A CULT FIGURE

The cultic functions of the Israelite king are nowhere described as such. When we put together the textual data (2.2), we find a variety of views. This information needs to be looked at in the light of the obvious textual bias (that the king's powers should be strictly limited) and the comparative data from the ancient Near East, for there are hints that things were not quite the way the priestly writers would want it. The first question to be discussed concerns the long-held theory that the king was the center of an annual cultic celebration that was later dropped from the tradition.

2.4.1 An Annual Cultic Celebration?

Clines, D. J. A. "The Evidence for an Autumnal New Year in Pre-exilic Israel Reconsidered," *JBL* 93 (1974) 22-40.

____ . "New Year," *IDBSup* (1976) 625-29.

Day, J. *Psalms* (1990).

Eaton, J. H. "The Psalms and Israelite Worship," *Tradition and Interpretation* (1979) 238-73.

Kraus, H.-J. *Worship in Israel* (1966).

____ . *Theology of the Psalms* (1986).

____ . *Psalms 1-59: A Commentary* (1988).

____ . *Psalms 60-150: A Commentary* (1989).

Mayes, A.D.H. *Israel in the Period of the Judges* (1974).

Mowinckel, S. *Psalmenstudien: II. Das Thronbesteigungsfest Jahwäs und der Ursprung der Eschatologie* (1921).

____ . *The Psalms in Israel's Worship* (1962).

Nicholson, E. W. *God and His People* (1986).

Toorn, K. van der. "The Babylonian New Year Festival: New Insights from the Cuneiform Texts and Their Bearing on Old Testament Study," VTSup 43 (1991) 331-44.

Weiser, A. *The Psalms* (1962).

Several theories have developed around the idea that there was once an ancient annual cultic ceremony in Israel. In each case, this festival has to be reconstructed because it is not among the annual festivals listed in several places in the OT (Exod 23:14-17; Lev 23; Deut 16).

2.4.1.1 New Year Festival

Probably the most prominent thesis is S. Mowinckel's theory about an autumnal New Year festival celebrated annually in the temple (1921; 1962). He hypothesized that a series of ceremonies memorialized Yhwh's kingship and also included a ritual re-enthronement of the Israelite king. If the thesis should be correct, it would indicate an ongoing and significant function of the king in the cult. The value of Mowinckel's explanation is that it brings a large number of passages together into a coherent thesis and brings out the prominence of the cult in Israel's worship. This is one of the reasons that the theory was once widely accepted in scholarship and has even been recently defended (cf. Day: 67-87); however, there are some substantial problems with the hypothesis:

1. Israel's New Year may not have begun in the autumn. Clines has given a forceful argument that the normally attested time of New Year in pre-exilic times was the spring. Granted, the beginning of the New Year may not have been consistently observed everywhere throughout the Israel of pre-exilic times. That is, it may have been shifted from spring to autumn or vice versa at different times, and the two kingdoms of Israel and Judah may not have always used the same calendar. Nevertheless, there are good arguments for the belief that the most consistent time for the beginning of the New Year was in the spring, and the idea that reckoning from the spring was only a post-exilic innovation certainly does not stand up.

2. No such festival is described in the surviving texts. There are several celebrations assigned to the seventh month (Day of Trumpets, Day of Atonement, Feast of Tabernacles), but none of these is associated specifically with a New Year celebration. The Day of Trumpets marks the first day of the seventh month, but it is not the primary festival which is used as support. Mowinckel focuses mainly on the Feast of Tabernacles, but this does not occur until the fifteenth of the month in the present festival calendar. Mowinckel has to assume that these present celebrations are mere remnants of the original, which was also divided up and displaced from its original location.

3. No single psalm or other writing contains all the various elements (ritual dethronement and re-enthronement of the king, proclamation of God's kingship, etc.) hypothesized to be a part of the Israelite festival liturgy.

4. The main analogy for the Israelite New Year festival is that of the *akitu* festival in Babylon; however, the evidence for that ceremony is very late, from the Seleucid period. Although it is known to have been celebrated earlier, we do not have details to use in evaluating the OT material. Also,

the Babylonian New Year is not in the autumn but in the spring. But no one, to the best of my knowledge, has attempted to connect the New Year with Passover or Unleavened Bread, which are spring festivals in Israel.

Thus, if there was such a New Year festival as hypothesized, it has been by and large forgotten or almost entirely suppressed in the surviving literature, with somewhat different celebrations substituted for it.

2.4.1.2 Covenant Renewal Festival

A thesis developed to replace Mowinckel's is that of A. Weiser (especially pp. 23-52). He accepted the idea of a New Year celebration but proposed that what was celebrated was the covenant between Yhwh and Israel. This hypothesis depends heavily on another theory, the idea of an amphictyony or tribal league united by a covenant before Yhwh around a central shrine. Weiser in fact gives no concrete evidence that the covenant was renewed on a regular basis. Also in recent years, both the amphictyony and the idea that the covenant was an early concept in Israel's thinking have come under severe attack and are now widely abandoned (Mayes; Nicholson).

2.4.1.3 Royal Zion Festival

This is another alternative to Mowinckel's thesis, developed by H.-J. Kraus (1966: 183-88). Drawing on such passages as 2 Samuel 6 (in which David brought the ark up to Jerusalem), 1 Kings 8 (in which Solomon places the ark in the temple), and the Zion Psalms (46, 48, 76, 87), he argued that the choice of Zion by Yhwh was celebrated each year in a cultic ceremony. Psalm 132 is considered especially important evidence. This theory has not received a great deal of support among scholars. One reason is that Kraus developed it in part because he could not accept that Yahwistic religion might make use of myth as Mowinckel's thesis proposed (1966:15-25, 183). Although the matter is still debated, there is considerable opinion that those who reject any presence of myth in the OT do so partly because of theological presuppositions and perhaps partly over a matter of semantics. Kraus himself admits that the myth of the holy mountain was important for Zion theology (1966: 201-3).

Each of the foregoing scholars has proposed a major annual celebration in ancient Israel. If an early festival has been deliberately edited out of Israel's tradition, it would be difficult to demonstrate that such happened. Each of the theories mentioned is able to draw on some passages which, it is argued, hint at the celebration in question. However, it is difficult to see why such a celebration should have been so thoroughly erased from the tradition and Israel's memory. This is in addition to the other difficulties noted with each one. The one which has had the most widespread currency among scholars is Mowinckel's. There is no doubt that it was developed with a good deal of ingenuity and careful work and made scholarship aware of the importance of the cult in Israelite religion. Nevertheless, in the light of present considerations, Mowinckel's thesis seems too tenuous to be acceptable; the other two have never had the same prominence. Thus, the use of such a support for the place of the king in the cult must be ruled out for now. The place of the king in Israel's cult seems established, but not in the way that Mowinckel and others have argued.

2.4.2 Other Cultic Functions

Even though we have to reject, or at least seriously query, an annual cultic celebration with the king in a pivotal role, the place of the king in the cult is still central. This is plain despite the bias of the text, and the parallels from kingship elsewhere in the ancient Near East add additional weight. As noted above (2.2), the dominant view of the text is rather ambivalent toward the kingship as such. 1 Samuel 8 (2.1.3) stamps the preponderant outlook on the tradition—that Israel should never have asked for a king—and the following chapters of the Deuteronomistic History have much criticism of individual kings, especially those of the Northern Kingdom. Nevertheless, the tradition is also very loyal to David and to those of his successors who are seen as righteous.

The priestly view is certainly that the king's place in the cult is strictly limited to that of patron. In its discussion of the duties of priests and of laity, Leviticus gives no place to the king; he would be simply another layman. Deuteronomy differs from the dominant tradition in taking the kingship for granted (17:14-20). It is not a question of *if* but *when* Israel would have a king. Otherwise, its concern focuses on obedience to the law, with the instruction and guidance of the king under the supervision of the "Levitical priests" (2.1.1). Finally, there is one passage which makes a negative point about the king's participation in the cult. This is 2 Chronicles 26, in which king Uzziah attempts to offer incense on the incense altar in the Holy Place (2.1.10). His punishment is to be stricken with leprosy, a salutary warning to any ruler who might be so bold as to usurp priestly privilege at the altar.

The text is not univocal, though; there are other voices in it. In spite of the prevalent view, there are many passages which suggest that the king had cultic functions. The first Israelite king, Saul, offered sacrifices. Although he was criticized for doing so, this was due to his disobedience to Samuel's instructions, not because of the action of offering sacrifice as such (2.1.4). David is presented as a cult founder who took an active part in bringing up the ark to Jerusalem and in setting up the cult there (2.1.5). He performed a public dance to welcome the ark into Jerusalem. Although this itself does not prove a cultic function, David is also accredited with organizing the cult in preparation for building the temple, even though in the end he himself was not allowed to build it. His son Solomon was the temple builder (2.1.6). Solomon also organized the first cultic celebrations in the temple, making decisions about the celebration which should have been confined to the priests according to Pentateuchal tradition.

Other kings are pictured as presiding at the altar; the two main examples are Jeroboam 1 (2.1.7) and Ahaz (2.1.11). One could argue that both these show unlawful behavior, since Jeroboam is sacrificing at Bethel and Ahaz has installed a new altar modeled on the one seen in Damascus. Yet the action implicitly condemned in each case is not the sacrificial activity of the king but the altar or cult site. The impression one is left with is that the king's part in the sacrifice was normal and not at all new or innovative.

2.5 THE RELIGIOUS GESTALT OF THE KING

From the biblical text, we get more than one opinion about the place of the king in the cult. The dominant view in those parts of the OT usually thought to be priestly or deuteronomistic (Leviticus, Numbers, Deuteronomy, 1-2 Samuel, 1-2 Kings) is that the king had no cultic functions different from those of any lay Israelite. Even kings such as David and Solomon were meant to be subordinate to the priests (or Levitical priests according to Deuteronomy). When one Judean king attempted to offer a sacrifice, he was immediately punished by the plague of leprosy (2.1.10). Other passages suggest a different picture. This is especially true of certain of the psalms, but various passages within 1 Samuel–2 Kings also suggest an important place in the cult for the king. They indicate that he offered sacrifices on behalf of the people and that members of his family might be a part of the cult personnel (2 Sam 8:18). The king was responsible for the well-being of his people, and this was conducted under the eyes of Yhwh, whose "son" was the king (Ps 2, 110).

How to explain these different views is an interesting question. One could argue for historical developments—that the ideal of kingship and the place of the king in the cult changed and developed during the period of the monarchy. This makes a good deal of sense since it is unlikely that the office of kingship remained completely static. There may also have been some differences between kingship in the Northern Kingdom and in Judah. Nonetheless, the Israelite monarchy did not last very long, comparatively, and such an institution is likely to have been fairly stable; historical development can probably account for only a few of the textual discrepancies. A better explanation for most of the inconsistencies is the activity of redactors, especially priestly redactors who would want any future monarch to be subordinate to them in cultic matters, or anti-monarchic redactors who might want to scotch any move to a return to the monarchy.

When we put the OT passages together with parallels from kingship elsewhere in the ancient Near East, the following points seem substantial:

1. The king was responsible to God for the people. He was their shepherd and guardian. He was not just a secular ruler but ultimately the most

important figure in the religious entity of Israel. Among his symbolic titles was that of "son of God" by adoption (Ps 2:7).

2. The king was ultimately responsible for the cult. Some kings such as David and Solomon were cult and temple founders. This was not the lot of most of their successors, but when the cult was changed, reorganized, or cleansed, it was the king who took the initiative in each case, even if advised by priests. Thus, Asa made sure that the temple was repaired despite some opposition or disorganization on the part of the priests (2.1.8). Hezekiah set out to centralize the cult; if the account in Chronicles is followed, he also reorganized the temple administration and personnel (2.1.12). Josiah brought the reform to full fruition (2.1.13).

3. The king exercised his duties in a variety of forms, including cultic acts such as offering sacrifice on behalf of the people. The texts are sometimes ambiguous and could be interpreted to mean only that the king brought the animal(s) for the priests to sacrifice; however, some texts leave us in no doubt that the king himself actually carried out ceremonies at the altar, which only the priest should do according to the priestly tradition (2.1.7; 2.1.11). Some of the royal family seem to have exercised sacerdotal functions (2 Sam 8:18).

4. It has been widely accepted that the king fulfilled a central role in an annual cultic celebration. The nature of that celebration has been variously reconstructed, though the thesis of Mowinckel about an annual autumnal New Year celebration has been most popular. There are too many problems with this thesis, however, and it seems best to abandon it (2.4.1).

5. The Israelite and Judean kings look very much like their counterparts in the other areas of the ancient Near East. The only "divine king" was in Egypt, but even this statement requires qualification; the kings in Mesopotamia and Asia Minor seem to have a tradition of ethical and religious duties not greatly differing from those in the OT tradition. The one exceptional OT tradition is that Israel once had no king and, in the opinion of some, was better off then. This is the one area where Israel seemed to differ from the nations around it.

3.

Priests

Despite their clear centrality to much of the worship in ancient Israel, priests have been the Leah to scholarship's Jacob. There is no doubt a number of (non-scholarly) reasons for this: the (Protestant) antipathy to (Catholic) priests, the nineteeth-century suspicion of formalized religion, the (Christian) view that legalism in worship was a bad thing and the sacrificial cult barbaric. These prejudices have helped to distort the nature of worship in Israel because they have led researchers to concentrate on those elements in worship more amenable to modern sensibilities. Good studies of the OT priesthood have been undertaken, but they have been few and far between compared to some other religious specialists.

3.1 SELECTED OLD TESTAMENT TEXTS

On Ahijah, Saul's priest in 1 Samuel 14, see 5.1.2.

3.1.1 The Priestly Tradition (Leviticus/Numbers)

Grabbe, L. L. *Leviticus* (1993).

The book of Leviticus is the apex of priestly writing in the Old Testament. Its primary focus is the cultic responsibility of the priests, most notably the sacrificial system. They carried out all the activities relating to the altar, whether sprinkling blood or burning the sacrificial parts (see especially chs. 1-7, 21-22). There were other cultic functions, though, such as the ceremonies of the Day of Atonement (Yom Kippur), in which the high priest had a central function (16). The other function mentioned by Leviticus is the task of pronouncing on matters of clean and unclean (11-15), especially in the case of "leprosy" (13-14). Most other priestly texts give the same general picture, despite some differences in detail (cf. Grabbe: 29-38, 66-72).

Although indicated only in passing in Leviticus (25:32-34), priestly texts generally assume a difference between the descendants of Aaron (referred to as "priests") and the other descendants of Levi ("Levites"). This is made especially clear in Numbers. The Levites are lower clergy, with responsibility over the fabric of the temple (or tabernacle, in the wilderness texts); they are also assigned other menial tasks in the cult (Num 1:47-53; 4). The Levites were consecrated to serve Aaron and the priests (3; 8) in place of the first-born, whose role this had traditionally been. Only the priests were allowed to preside at the altar itself and were to receive their support from the sacrificial portions, the first fruits, and the tithe from the Levites (17:5; 18). The Levites received their support mainly from the tithes of the people, though they were to tithe in turn to the priests (18:21-32). The prerogative of the priests over the Levites is graphically illustrated by the story of Korah, who attempted to democratize the priesthood (16). Although chiefs from other tribes (such as Reuben: 16:1-3) were also involved, a special point is made that the Levites were not satisfied with their role and wanted to take over priestly duties as well (16:8-11). When they were slain supernaturally, this was seen as God's considered judgment on such an idea.

Besides the priests' cultic function, Numbers mentions some other duties. Joshua is told to go to Eleazar the (high) priest (son of Aaron) who would seek God's instructions via the Urim, by whose decision they were "to go out and to come in" (Num 27:18-21). A priest was to go on the military campaigns (31:6), taking "holy vessels" (*kĕlê haqqōdeš*: for sacrifice? the Urim and Thummim?) and trumpets (for encouragement? to give orders?). The priests were to help tally the booty and were to receive a portion of it (31:25-30). The existence of a high priest or chief priest (*hakkōhēn haggādōl*) is also indicated in that one fleeing to the city of refuge had to remain there until the high priest died (35:25, 28, 32). Aaron also provides an important model for the office of high priest.

3.1.2 Deuteronomy

Abba, R. "Priests and Levites in Deuteronomy," *VT* 27 (1977) 257-67.
Emerton, J. A. "Priests and Levites in Deuteronomy," *VT* (1962) 129-38.

In contrast to the priestly writings, Deuteronomy makes no distinction between the priests and Levites, instead referring to the "Levitical priests" (17:9: *hakkōhănîm halĕwiyyim*) or "priests, sons of Levi" (21:5; 31:9: *hakkōhănîm bĕnê lēwî*). Although the situation is assumed rather than discussed, one passage suggests that some viewed the matter differently from the position in the priestly writings: 18:1-8 says that the whole tribe of Levi is without inheritance; therefore, any Levite has the right to take his place at the altar and receive its dues. The tribe of Levi has the responsibility of carrying the Ark and attending on Yhwh, having no inheritance (10:8-9). Because of this, the people are told not to forget the Levite within their gates when they rejoice before Yhwh (12:12, 18-19; 26:11). In their use of the festival tithe or the tithe of the third year, the people were to remember the Levite (14:27, 29; 26:12). Thus, despite some objections (e.g., Abba), Deuteronomy seems to regard all Levites as having the right to preside at the altar (cf. Emerton), whether or not they chose to exercise it.

Levitical priests had a number of responsibilities. The cultic duties are taken for granted (10:8-9; 18:6-8; 33:10), including pronouncing on skin diseases (24:8). When Moses wrote down the law, it was given into the charge of the priests, who placed it beside the Ark and read it to the people every seventh year (31:9-13, 24-26). They were teachers of the law in general (33:10). The priests were also judges. If a matter arose too difficult for the local courts, the parties were to go to the place which Yhwh would choose and present it before the magistrates or priests (17:8-13; 19:17). The priests are said to be responsible for all lawsuits and cases of assault (21:5, though it is not certain that *nega'* means "assault"). They were also to address the troops before battle and encourage them by saying that Yhwh was on their side (20:1-4). Finally, they had the Urim and Thummim, the divine lots through which Yhwh often communicated the divine will (33:8).

3.1.3 Micah's Levite (Judges 17-18)

An Ephraimite, Micah, set up a silver image and a house cult, with ephod and teraphim (17:5). He was joined by a young Levite who became priest. Danites seeking territory sent men to spy out the land. When offered hospitality in Micah's house, they inquired of God about their mission through the Levite. Later, when they were migrating to Laish (Dan in the north), they offered the Levite the chance to be their priest, and he accepted. At this point, the Levite is identified as Jonathan, son of Gershom son of Moses (18:30). The name "Moses" (*mšh*) has been altered in the text by the addition of an *-n-* to make it Manasseh (*mnšh*), but the additional letter is written partly above the line. It is generally accepted that the original is Moses. However, not only is the "pagan" priest a descendant of Moses, his ancestor Gershom is said to be a son of Moses, whereas he is normally said to be a son of Aaron (e.g., 1 Chron 6:1). This is clearly a different tradition and an embarrassing one. It seems to be the remnant of a Mosaic priesthood otherwise unrecorded in the OT tradition. No wonder a scribe attempted to change the name "Moses" to "Manasseh"!

3.1.4 Samuel

Texts: 1 Samuel 1-13; 15-16; 19:18-24; 25:1.

Samuel was born of the tribe of Ephraim (1:1). Even though not of priestly descent, he was dedicated by his mother to the shrine at Shiloh and served the high priest Eli there. While still a youth, at a time when there was no vison (*ḥāzôn*) in Israel, Yhwh stood by his bed and spoke to him, revealing to him the future of Eli's house (3:1-14). He was referred to as a "man of God" (9:6), and he functioned as a seer and prophet, as well as a priest. In these capacities, he moved on a circuit around the various (cultic?) sites of Bethel, Gilgal, Mizpah, and Ramah (1 Sam 7:13-14). He not only presided as priest but also exercised a judging responsibility and was available to be consulted about prophetic matters, as he was by Saul who wanted information about his lost asses (9:3-20). Samuel anointed Saul king, at the command of Yhwh (10:1). Samuel continued to advise Saul, sometimes to the latter's consternation (13, 15), as well performing cultic functions. Samuel's diverse tasks provide an interesting example of how a cult figure might make cultic performance only one of many duties.

3.1.5 Zadok and Abiathar

Texts: 1 Samuel 21-23; 30; 2 Samuel 8:17; 15-19; 20:25; 1 Kings 1-2, 4; 1 Chronicles 5:34-38 (Eng. 6:8-12); 12:29(?); 15-16; 18:16; 24; 29:22.

Zadok and Abiathar functioned as a duet of chief priests under David (2 Sam 17:15; 19:12; 20:25). Abiathar was the son of Ahimelech. The latter and many other priests were slaughtered at Nob by Saul because of their aid to David. Abiathar escaped to David, however, and was taken in by him (1 Sam 22:20-23), helping David to avoid Saul by means of the ephod (23:6-12; 30:6-8). Zadok is a curious figure in 1 and 2 Samuel. He first appears in 2 Samuel 8:17 with no introduction as one of two priests. Although he is said to be the son of Ahitub, this verse has long been thought to be corrupt, with Ahitub actually the father of Ahimelech. Surprisingly, therefore, no genealogy is given for him in 1-2 Samuel, and we are left to guess at his origins. The silence here cannot be accidental since a good deal is made of appropriate descent for priests. (According to Num 3:5-10, only the descendants of Aaron could serve as priests in the temple.) This lack is remedied in 1 Chronicles 5:34 (Eng. 6:8) where Zadok is said to be of the line of Eleazar, a son of Aaron. But this looks suspiciously like a later attempt to make Zadok "orthodox" rather than original information. The question of Zadok's origins will be further discussed at 3.6 below. He may also be intended as the "valiant young man" who joined David according to 1 Chronicles 12:29.

Zadok and Abiathar served together under David. The two of them attempted to take the Ark into exile with David during the revolt of Absalom (2 Sam 15:24-37). However, later on, when Abiathar supported Adonijah instead of Solomon, David deposed him, making Zadok sole priest (1 Kings 2:35). Zadok's position seems to have been that of priest in charge of the priesthood and temple in general, though little more specific is heard of him. Although he is never called "high priest," the term "the priest" (*hakkōhēn*) seems to have this force in some contexts (cf. 1 Chron 29:22). His son Azariah was evidently high priest under Solomon (1 Kings 4:2).

3.1.6 Jeroboam I (1 Kings 12-14)

Jeroboam allegedly took the Northern Kingdom away from the dynasty of David. One of his first acts was to keep his people from going to Jerusalem for the annual festivals by establishing cult sites at Bethel and Dan in the north. In actual fact, Dan's place as a cult site existed much earlier, according to the story in Judges 17-18 (3.1.3 above), and Bethel already existed as a cult site in the Jacob story (Gen 28:10-22). Whether the "calf" images represented cult images of Yhwh in the form of a bull or only the mounts on which Yhwh took his stand is debatable. Jeroboam is said to institute a new festival in the eighth month to replace that of Sukkot in the seventh month (1 Kings 12:32-33), but this is possibly due to nothing more than divergent calendars. At the various cult sites he appointed priests, including those allegedly of non-Levitical descent (v 31). Finally, he himself presided over the sacrifice on the altar (13:1-6).

3.1.7 Jehoida the High Priest (2 Kings 11-12//2 Chron 23-24)

Jehoida was the high priest who opposed Athaliah and colluded to depose her in favor of Joash (2 Kings 11). During Athaliah's six-year reign, the child and heir to the throne, Joash, was kept hidden. Jehoida made an agreement with the king's guards (including the Carians, who may have been of foreign descent) and set them to guard the royal palace and the temple, after which he brought out Joash and crowned him. Athaliah knew nothing of this until she heard the people shouting and was thus outwitted and executed. This was followed by a destruction of the temple of Baal and a slaughter of its priest (11:18). According to the text Joash "did righteousness in the eyes of Yhwh" during his forty-year reign, because he was taught by Jehoida (12:3).

Interestingly, despite all his good deeds, Joash allowed the country shrines to Yhwh to remain for the sacrifices and worship of the people (12:4). Yet Joash did not neglect the temple; on the contrary, one of his acts was to set aside some of the temple donations for repair of the fabric of the building.

But when the priests did not carry out the repairs, Joash called Jehoida and a means was arranged for people to place their donations in a sealed chest rather than giving them directly to the priests. The distribution of these funds was overseen jointly by the royal scribe and the high priest (12:11).

The account in Chronicles is similar but with some interesting differences. The woman who hides Joash is said to be Jehoida's wife (2 Chron 22:11). The guard established to protect the king and safeguard the coronation ceremony is composed of priests and Levites rather than the traditional royal guard (23:2-8). This alleviates the problem of having non-priests (and perhaps even non-Israelites) in the temple. Jehoida lives to the ripe old age of 130. Unfortunately, after his death, Joash deviates from the straight and narrow, forsaking the temple and serving idols (24:17-18). Jehoida's son Zechariah (a prophet?: 24:19) stands up and denounces this disobedience and is stoned for his pains (vv 20-22). As a result, Joash is defeated by the Arameans and assassinated by his courtiers (vv 23-25).

3.1.8 Jeremiah

This book often refers to priests together with the king and/or other leaders, prophets, and the people as a way of representing the totality of society (4:9; 8:1-2; 13:13; 29:1; 32:32; 34:19). Priests are also coupled with prophets as spiritual leaders, frequently to condemn both (5:31; 6:13-14; 8:10-11; 14:18). Jeremiah himself is of a priestly family centered in Anathoth (1:1). Although he is not said to have served as a priest at the altar, many of his activities take place in or around the temple. He is able to give a message to the Rechabites in a chamber in the temple (35:2-4), and Baruch the scribe reads Jeremiah's words in the temple chamber of Gemariah son of Shaphan the scribe (36:10). He is once told to perform a sign before the priests and elders (19:1), to preach to worshipers coming to the temple (26:2), and at another time is ordered to be flogged by Pashhur the priest and temple overseer (20:1-2). A letter from Babylon calls on Zephaniah the (high?) priest to control Jeremiah (29:24-27). The message of the text is that the priesthood and temple are very important to Jeremiah, that he carries on many of his activities around the temple, and that some priests oppose him but others are his supporters.

3.1.9 Ezekiel

Duguid, I. M. *Ezekiel and the Leaders of Israel* (1994).

Grabbe, L. L. "Reconstructing History from the Book of Ezra," *Studies in the Second Temple: The Persian Period* (1991) 98-107.

____. "What Was Ezra's Mission?" *Second Temple Studies: 2. Temple and Community in the Persian Period* (1994) 286-99.

Levenson, J. D. *Theology of the Program of Restoration of Ezekiel 40-48* (1976).
Tuell, S. S. *The Law of the Temple in Ezekiel 40-48* (1992).

The sins of the priests are mentioned together with those of the prophets, officials, and the people (22:23-31); however, Ezekiel is himself a priest (1:3). Several important references are found in the temple vision of 40-48. Priests are divided into two categories. Only one group serves at the altar; these are the descendants of Zadok (40:45-46). They are referred to as Levitical priests (*hakkōhănîm halĕwiyyim*) from the seed of Zadok (43:19). The reason for this distinction is that the Levites as a whole followed Israel when it went astray and were punished by being allowed to do only menial duties in the temple (44:10-14). They are to be watchmen and in charge of the gates, to slaughter the sacrifices for the people and serve them (cf. 46:21-24), but they are not to have anything to do with the actual offerings. They are also to have different areas of settlement from the priests (45:3-5).

The Levitical priests descended from Zadok are the only ones to offer the fat and blood on the altar and to go into the temple itself (44:15-31). They are to wear special linen priestly garments, not to shave their heads, not to drink wine when going into the inner court, and to marry only Israelite virgins or widows of priests. In addition to service at the altar, they are to pronounce on sacred and profane and on clean and unclean. They are to act as judges in lawsuits. They are to preserve the teachings (*tôrôt*) and laws relating to holy convocations and to preserve the sanctity of the Sabbath. Because they have no inheritance, they are to receive portions of sacrifices and the first fruits and sacred gifts. They have special chambers in the temple where these offerings are prepared and eaten (42:13; 46:19-20).

Ezekiel is an important indication of how some(one) regarded the organization of the priesthood. Most regard Ezekiel as a theoretical program which was never realized (cf. Levenson; Duguid: 133-42). It is an important source for reflecting the tensions and political maneuverings within the priesthood, but it does not show the actual workings of the temple personnel. S. S. Tuell has argued that Ezekiel 40-48 reflects the real operation of the temple and province of Judah in the early Persian period before the coming of Ezra, though he distinguishes between an earlier layer (going back to Ezekiel himself) and a later redactional layer from Persian times. His thesis depends heavily on taking the book of Ezra at face value, which seems to me to be unjustified by the nature of the book (cf. Grabbe 1991, 1994).

3.1.10 Hosea

Hosea has several references to priests. At least one of these (10:5) seems to have to do with the priests at the shrine of Bethel, a shrine which Hosea apparently opposes (cf. 4:15; 10:5, 15). In no case is the reference clearly positive, but the place of priests in society is recognized (e.g., 5:1-2). A rebuke against priest and prophet is found in 4:4-6. Priests and the royal house are called on to take responsibility for the right conduct of the nation (5:1-2). The priests are like murdering bandits because they have carried out depravity (6:9). Both the people and priests mourn over the "calf" of Beth-aven, which is probably a deliberate twisting of the name Bethel (10:5). The word here for priests is *kĕmārîm*, a term usually applied to the priests of other nations and thus seeming to lump the Bethel priests in with the pagan priests of foreign cults.

3.1.11 Amos

Amos has a specific episode relating to the Bethel cult (7:10-17). The (chief?) priest of Bethel reacts to Amos's preaching by sending a message to King Jeroboam that Amos is preaching conspiracy (vv 10-11). He then confronts Amos directly, telling him to cease prophesying at Bethel and to return to Judah; he further implies that Amos is a professional prophet who earns his living by prophesying, which Amos denies (vv 12-15). Amos then prophesies that Amaziah's wife will be ravaged, his children slain, and he himself exiled to die in a foreign land (vv 16-17). Nothing further is said about Amaziah or whether he in fact suffered this appalling fate. Apart from his opposition to Amos (with whom the text obviously sides), there is nothing unusual about Amaziah. He is a family man, conscientiously carries out his duties at a royal shrine by passing relevant information to his patron the king, and maintains the sanctity and tranquillity of the temple by trying to drive away one whom he regards as a troublemaker and fraud.

3.1.12 Haggai, Zechariah, and Malachi

Glazier-McDonald, B. *Malachi: The Divine Messenger* (1987).
O'Brien, J. M. *Priest and Levite in Malachi* (1990).

All three of these are closely related and are ostensibly associated with the early post-exilic period. A number of references are made to priests. Haggai 2:11-19 seeks a ruling from the priests with regard to a cultic matter. The purpose of this is to introduce a prophecy, but it shows the convention that priests made rulings on such matters.

In Haggai and Zechariah the high priest Joshua is quite important. He and Zerubbabel the governor are the leaders of the restoration and the ones responsible for the rebuilding of the temple. They are the recipients of, or the central actors in, various prophecies and visions. They hear and heed the prophecies of Haggai about rebuilding the temple (Hag 1:12-13; 2:1-4). Several of Zechariah's visions relate to Joshua, often in conjunction with

Zerubbabel or with a messianic figure called the Branch. (It is often thought that the title was intended to apply to Zerubbabel, but the text as it presently stands is somewhat ambiguous.) In Zechariah 3 Joshua is cleansed from impurities of the Exile, clothed in priestly garments, and given charge over God's house. In a subsequent vision, he is one of two olive trees who represent God's anointed, the other being Zerubbabel who would finish building the temple (ch. 4). Finally, 6:9-15 describes how Zechariah is to take members of the community, make crowns, and place a crown on Joshua's head. One called the Branch would rebuild the temple and sit on a throne to rule; alongside him would also sit a priest. Joshua is obviously intended to be the priestly leader of the community, though the identity of the Branch is left indeterminate.

Malachi 1:6-2:9 is a concerted critique of the priesthood, charging the priests with allowing defective animals to be offered on the altar, thus defiling it. Whereas Yhwh's name is honored among the other nations with incense and a pure offering (*minḥāh ṭĕhôrāh*), Yhwh's table in Jerusalem is defiled (1:1-14). God made a covenant with Levi who gave proper instructions (*tôrat 'emet*), because the lips of a priest guard knowledge (*da'at*), and instruction (*tôrāh*) is sought from them; he is the messenger (*mal'ak*) of Yhwh (2:6-7). Unfortunately, the Levites corrupted that covenant and disregarded God's ways (vv 8-9). Malachi's identity is not given in the book; however, there is a good chance that he was himself a priest. Indeed, this is suggested by the name Malachi ("my messenger") which seems to be evoked by the reference to the priest as God's messenger in 2:7. If so, this passage represents an internal critique of the priesthood by one of its own members.

More difficult to answer is Malachi's view of the organization of the priesthood. Is it a two-tier priesthood? Julia O'Brien has argued that Malachi makes no differentiation between priests and Levites (17-18, 111-12). Since no clear distinction is made in the few references to priests, Levites, and "sons of Levi," she may be correct; however, the book is a very short one. Since priests are also "sons of Levi," even in sources which separate the Aaronites from the rest of the Levites, the writer of Malachi may be using "Levites" and "sons of Levi" loosely (cf. Glazier-McDonald). None of the passages seems to be decisive. It would be unusual—and interesting—if a late text like Malachi regarded all Levites as altar priests.

3.1.13 Psalms

Kraus, H.-J. *Psalms 1-59* (1988).

It has been argued since the nineteenth century that psalms were originally connected with the cult, though the question of whether the present-day collection of the book of Psalms owes it origins to the pre-exilic cult is more controversial. Despite the supposed cultic connections, priests are hardly mentioned in the book; nevertheless, the psalms provide important insight into temple worship. They show that the central cultic act of blood sacrifice was enriched by accompanying rites of thanksgiving, singing, praise of God, and instrumental music. The headings of many psalms are thought to refer to musical instruments or musicians (see the summary in Kraus: 21-32). The terms are not always easy to figure out, and many of them are subject to debate, but it is hardly likely that we can dismiss all interpretations to do with music. They supplement those passages which make some of the Levites singers and players (see 3.1.15).

3.1.14 Ezra-Nehemiah

Grabbe, L. L. *Judaism from Cyrus to Hadrian* (1992).
____. "What Was Ezra's Mission?" *Second Temple Studies: 2. Temple and Community in the Persian Period* (1994) 286-99.

With the restoration of Judah under Persian rule, the country became a Persian province. The old monarchial state had been transformed into a much-reduced theocracy with the high priest as the main native spokesman and leader. Even when there was a governor of the province, the high priest was generally an important official and may at times have been appointed governor himself. (See Grabbe 1992: 73-83 for further discussion and references.) The beginnings of this situation can be glimpsed in the books of Ezra and Nehemiah where the priests have an important place in various incidents.

Within the books the division between the priests and Levites is assumed. The genealogies in Ezra 2 and Nehemiah 7 break down the various cultic personnel into Levites, singers, gatekeepers, temple servants, and priests (Ezra 2:36-63; Neh 7:39-60, 72). "Priests and Levites" is a phrase occurring several times (Ezra 1:5; 2:70; 3:12; 6:18, 20; 8:30; Neh 7:72; 8:13; 10:1, 29; 11:3, 20; 12:30, 44). The priestly oracle of the Urim and Thummim had apparently ceased to exist (Ezra 2:63). In the first part of Ezra, the high priest Joshua (or Jeshua) was part of a dyarchy with Zerubbabel the governor in the reestablishment of the cult and temple (Ezra 3-6), but he was assisted by his fellow priests (3:2). When the foundations of the temple were laid, the priests sounded trumpets and the Levites who were sons of Asaph sang songs of praise (3:10).

Ezra the priest and scribe is an important player in the books. His genealogy is quoted as evidence of his pure priestly descent (7:1-5). As well as "scribe," the term "priest" is applied to him a number of times (Ezra 7:11, 12, 21; 10:10, 16; Neh 8:2, 9; 12:26). He is never referred to as the high priest, though some of his activities seem to be those of a high priest; indeed, his activities suggest a variety of offices which the narrative does not actually ascribe to him (cf. Grabbe 1994). His priestly functions are not clearly separated from those as scribe. He is credited with bringing a law—whatever it might be—and teaching it, but this seems to be tied up with his scribal office, at least in part (7:6, 10-11). He eventually reads it to the people (Nehemiah 8). The only other activity of Ezra's actually described (as opposed to being merely a part of instructions to him) relates to marriages with the peoples of the land (Ezra 9-10). This involved priests and Levites as well as ordinary Israelites (9:1). The list of those who renounced their wives includes priests and Levites (10:18-23).

3.1.15 1 and 2 Chronicles

Gunneweg, A. H. J. *Leviten und Priester* (1965) 204-16.
Japhet, S. *I & II Chronicles* (1993).
Williamson, H. G. M. "The Origins of the Twenty-Four Priestly Courses: A Study of 1 Chronicles xxiii-xxvii," VTSup 30 (1979) 251-68.

These books give one of the most complete descriptions of the organization of the priesthood, especially 1 Chronicles 23-26. They picture David as having brought the priesthood into order in preparation for Solomon to build the temple, but other passages such as 2 Chronicles 5 and 7 also refer to celebrations in the temple. Of particular interest are the references to singing and music, which have little place in the Pentateuch or the Deuteronomistic History. These are also associated with prophecy, suggesting a connection between the Levites and cult prophecy (1 Chron 25; 2 Chron 20:14-17 [cf. 4.6]).

The books of Chronicles emphasize the judging and teaching functions of the priests. 2 Chronicles 15:3 states that during the reign of Asa, Israel had gone many days without the true God and without a priest to teach (*môreh*) and without teaching (*tôrāh*). According to 2 Chronicles 19:5-11, Jehoshaphat appointed Levites and priests among the judges in Judah. The high priest Amariah was to be overall in charge of judgments relating to God, with the Levite officers to assist (2 Chron 19:11; cf. 1 Chron 23:4). Levites also filled the office of scribe (2 Chron 34:13; cf. 1 Chron 26:29).

The situation described in Chronicles is difficult to evaluate. On the one hand, the books are late; on the other hand, they often depend on a version of Samuel-Kings perhaps more original than the Samuel-Kings in the MT. It is long been argued that the cultic passages may relate to actual practice during the Second Temple period when the cult may have developed in new ways, and more recent studies tend to confirm this (cf. Williamson), though some mutual contradictions suggest the juxtaposition of material from different sources (cf. Gunneweg; Japhet: 411-66).

3.2 THE PRIESTHOOD IN THE OLD TESTAMENT TEXT

The cult was the center of worship in ancient Israel. Major national cult sites are known, notably the temple in Jerusalem, but also many local ones. The text often inveighs against cult sites outside Jerusalem, but it recognizes their existence. As with priests everywhere, the main function of the priesthood and other temple personnel in Israel was the conduct of the cult. According to the text, the primary form of the cult was blood sacrifice, though cereal and drink offerings also formed a part of the sacrificial system. The cult had the dual function of serving God (with food, praise, and thanksgiving) and removing sin and pollution from the worshipers.

The overall picture of the text is that the priesthood had a bipartite structure, with the priests presiding at the altar and the Levites carrying out many of the more menial duties but responsible also for matters of security and some other administrative posts. There are texts which deviate from this position, though. For example, Samuel, even though of the tribe of Ephraim, nevertheless serves as priest at the altar. Ezekiel gives preference to the Zadokites, and evidently not all the Aaronites are allowed at the altar. On the other hand, Deuteronomy seems to make no distinction between Aaronites and Levites, regarding them all as "Levitical priests" with the right to serve at the altar. And we seem to have one reference to a priest descended from Moses (Judges 18:30). This variation has to be explained in some way or other. It is often explained historically, as evidence for struggles in the priesthood. If so, it was probably very late before the division into priests and Levites became standard.

Judging from various texts (especially the psalms) prayer, singing, and praise of Yhwh seem also to have found their place into the cult from an early time. This had implications for the temple personnel. Singers and similar offices are hardly mentioned in the books of the Former Prophets; however, in 1 and 2 Chronicles the place of singers and those who give praise is outlined in detail. Perhaps the history of the development cannot be traced in the present text, but the text indicates that, in addition to priests at the altar, there were Levites and "temple servants" responsible for security, cleaning, and the temple fabric, and—eventually—singers and players on instruments. We are not told when or where these last carried out their duties, but we are assured that they existed.

According to the text, priests had other responsibilities as well. Some duties were confined to the priests, such as pronouncing on whether a leper was clean or not. They were also the natural ones to interpret the cultic law and determine matters of ritual pollution (Hag 2:10-13). Some texts show that priests were to take their place as judges on various matters (Deut 17; 2 Chron 19:8-11). This does not suggest that the role of lay judges among the people was to be usurped, and their exact place is not spelled out, but the priests "at the place which Yhwh shall choose" are envisaged as deciding cases "too hard" for the local judges.

Cultic prophets are also attested as part of the temple personnel. They are discussed at 4.6.

3.3 CROSS-CULTURAL PARALLELS

3.3.1 Egypt

David, A. R. *The Ancient Egyptians* (1982).
Helck, H. "Priester, Priesterorganisation, Priestertitel," *LdÄ* 4 (1982) 1084-97.
Kees, H. *Das Priestertum im ägyptischen Staat vom Neuen Reich bis zur Spätzeit* (1953-58).
Otto, W. *Priester und Tempel im hellenistischen Ägypten* (1905-8).
Trigger, B. G., et al. *Ancient Egypt: A Social History* (1983).

Egyptian temples had a variety of personnel (Trigger: 301-9; David: 135-37). As the divine king, the Pharaoh was in theory the priest to the gods, while the various priests in the temples were merely his deputies. There were several ranks of priest, though the English translations can be misleading since such terms as "chief prophet" are used for clearly cultic figures: the chief priest or high priest (*ḥmw nṯr*, "servant of the gods") was in charge of a particular temple. He was the First God's Servant (sometimes referred to as First Prophet). In some temples, there were Second, Third, and Fourth God's Servants in addition. A further group (which may have overlapped with the God's Servants) was the Fathers of the Gods (*itw nṯr*). Many of the priests were *web*-priests (*w'bw*), who had to pay particular attention to ritual purity since they were responsible for handling cult objects. The lector-priests (*ẖryw-ḥbt*, "scroll bearers") had responsibility for copying, preserving, and studying the sacred texts.

All priests were appointed by the king and served only at his pleasure; however, the hereditary principle tended to prevail even if it was not absolute. The upper echelons of the priesthood were often held by important officials of the government. The majority of the priests were organized into "watches" (*s3w*), each of which served one month out of four. The rest of the time, they were able to pursue various occupations, many of them apparently involving work in the scribal professions. Women could not preside in cultic functions, but might be among the dancers and singers attached to the temple. These are known in some cases to be high-ranking women.

3.3.2 Mesopotamia and Asia Minor

Gurney, O. R. *Some Aspects of Hittite Religion* (1977).
____. *The Hittites* (1990).

Güterbock, H. G. "The Hittite Temple According to Written Sources," *Le temple et le culte* (1975) 125-32.
Harris, R. "The Nadītu Woman," *Studies Presented to A. Leo Oppenheim* (1964) 106-35.
Jeyes, U. "The Nadītu Women of Sippar," *Images of Women in Antiquity* (1993) 260-72.
Lambert, W. G. "Prostitution," *Xenia: Konstanzer Althistorische Vorträge und Forschungen* 32 (1992) 127-57.
McEwan, Gilbert J. P. *Priest and Temple in Hellenistic Babylonia* (1981).
Renger, J. "Untersuchungen zum Priestertum in der altbabylonischen Zeit," *Zeitschrift der Assyrologie* 58 (1966) 110-88; 59 (1969) 104-230.
Saggs, H. W. F. *The Greatness that Was Babylon* (1962).
____ . *The Greatness that Was Assyria* (1984).
Soden, W. von. *The Ancient Orient* (1994).
Stolper, M. W. "The *šaknu* of Nippur," *JCS* 40 (1988) 127-55.
Wilhelm, G. "Marginalien zu Herodot: Klio 199," *Lingering over Words* (1990) 505-24.

The original cult figures in the small Sumerian city-states were "priest-kings." As time went on, a separation was made between the *en* with the routine priestly function and the *ensi* who ruled (Saggs 1962: 345). The king always remained the main cultic official, and some ceremonies (e.g., the New Year celebration) required his participation in a central role. A variety of temple personnel is known from the texts. Renger has made a central contribution to their study, though he limits himself mainly to the Old Babylonian period (c. 1950-1600 BCE), and the temple personal hardly remained static for the next fifteen hundred years. Despite important scholarly work, the exact function of many temple personnel is still not known. In fact, there is no single Sumerian or Akkadian word corresponding to our word "priest." The most generic term is probably *ērib bīti*, "temple enterer," but this applies to anyone who can go into the shrine (*bītum*) housing the god, including temple workers, craftsmen, and cooks, not just cultic personnel. This makes any description tentative at best.

Renger (1966: 112-14) divides the central temple personnel into three groups: (1) cult priests, (2) incantation priests, and (3) diviners. With regard to cult personnel, the term *sanga* in Sumerian texts often meant "temple administrator." In Akkadian texts, however, the *šangû* is a cultic priest, as well as having administrative functions such as responsibility for financial affairs (Renger 1969: 114). By the Hellenistic period, the term is rare and is often written with the same logogram as "scribe" (McEwan: 8-9). The original *en* (the Sumerian king) left its legacy in the *en*-priests and *en*-priestesses who seem to have been chosen from the royal family (Renger 1966: 126); with one exception, they served the main gods. The *en*-priests are not attested after the Old Babylonian period. The *pašīšum* "anointed," had to maintain cultic purity and had responsibility for non-bloody offerings, among other duties (Renger 1969: 162). He underwent the conventional training for scribes (Renger 1969: 165).

The *kalû*, "lamentation priest," chanted the lamentations (with a drum or harp) and otherwise assisted in various of the temple rituals. He might also be involved in temple purification rites. There were also the *zammeru* and *nâru*, who acted as "singers." Of the incantation priests, the *(w)āšipu* (also called *mašmaššu*) worked in a wide sphere. Although some were included among the temple personnel, they were also found in the palace and the army, and many functioned in society with their services available to ordinary people. Their task was to deal with the threat from malign spirits or bad fortune by the use of incantations and by giving advice on prophylactic measures. As one would expect, their services were especially drawn upon by the king. They might also assist in temple purification rites.

Temples had a number of female personnel, in addition to the *en*-priestesses mentioned above. There were also *nârātu*, the female equivalent of the *nāru*. The question of cultic prostitutes continues to be debated. The *nadītu* women were once thought to be cultic prostitutes. This interpretation has been rejected, with the view that they were unmarried women who lived in a sort of cloister (Harris: 106; Jeyes: 266); however, Lambert has argued that there is evidence that in some periods (though not necessarily all) they did function as prostitutes. The same problem applies to the *qadištu* and their male equivalents. The idea that they were prostitutes has been both rejected (Renger 1967: 179-84) and accepted (von Soden: 195). After a judicious survey, Wilhelm has also argued that some texts show the existence of prostitutes within the temple organization at certain periods; whether they were *cultic* prostitutes is another matter.

The diviners are discussed at 5.3.3.

3.3.3 Ugarit

Soden, W. von. "Zur Stellung des 'Geweihten' (*qdš*) in Ugarit," *UF* 2 (1970) 329-30.
Tarragon, J.-M. de. *Le culte à Ugarit* (1980).

Ugaritic literature lists a number of cultic titles, but many questions remain about the exact place and function of the cultic personnel. This has not prevented some from making some fairly large claims, either based on the OT or, conversely, using the supposed Ugaritic situation to interpret the OT. One of the problems is that the cult personnel are often missing from the ritual texts.

The *khnm* seem to be cognate with the Hebrew word for "priests." The name occurs a number of times in economic texts but not in the ritual texts, making it difficult to be precise about their role. No feminine forms of the term are attested. A *rb khnm* appears to have been at the head of the *khnm*, but it is impossible to say whether he was analogous to the high priest in the OT or not. However, archeology has shown that the residence of one *rb khnm* was quite imposing, suggesting an important post. The colophon of the Baal and Mot text parallels this title with *rb nqdm*, suggesting the same person held both offices (*KTU* 1.6.6.54-55). One would expect the term *nqdm* to mean "pastors," as those in charge of flocks, but this hardly seems appropriate for a city context. Because it is found in the same context as *khnm*, it has usually been thought of as a cultic official.

The *inš ilm* also seem to be cult personnel, partly because they are listed along with *khnm*. The name has yet to be explained, though, and some have thought it was a divine title. Similarly difficult are the *ṯnnm*, also listed with the *khnm*. Some think they may be some sort of administrators in a secular context. The *qdšm* have called for a good deal of comment. A number of writers have proposed—or just assumed—that these were male cultic prostitutes. This idea is now best rejected; there is no evidence for ritual prostitution—male or female—at Ugarit (de Tarragon: 138-41; von Soden).

This brief discussion illustrates how difficult it can be to determine even the basic functions without detailed descriptions. All in all, the Ugaritic material probably presents more problems than solutions.

3.3.4 Republican Rome

Beard, M. "Priesthood in the Roman Republic," *Pagan Priests* (1990) 17-48.
North, J. "Diviners and Divination at Rome," *Pagan Priests* (1990) 51-71.

Rome in the republican period is an interesting example because it presents such a contrast, in many ways, to the situation in the ancient Near East. There was no religious center but rather a variety of priestly groups, most of them only part-time. In contrast to Greece and the Near East, most priests did not function in a specific temple or serve a specific deity. The term *sacerdos* is often translated "priest," but this is problematic. The term was not widely used by Roman writers in the Republic, and in inscriptions of the period it was usually applied to foreign cultic personnel (Beard: 44). Also, Greeks writing about Rome (e.g., Polybius and Dionysius of Halicarnassus) do not usually refer to the various Roman priestly groups by *hiereus*, the Greek word for priest.

Part of the explanation for this particular Roman view is that religion was so closely tied to political life. Cicero noted that the priests and the political leaders were, by and large, the same (*De domo* 1.1). The closest thing to a center of the religion seems to have been the Senate. It was the main mediator between the mundane and the divine in the sense of controlling the modes of worship, officially recognizing prodigies (unusual phenomena seen as divine signs), and resolving the problems of relations between humans and the gods. It seems to have operated in many ways analogously to the king in the ancient Near Eastern states.

Two main groups were the *pontifices* and the *augures*. The *augures* definitely had a mediation function, as we normally think priests to have. They could declare a section of ground sacred for a temple and could rule on omens with regard to the sitting of the assembly. They formed a consultative body responsible for interpreting the auspices, about which they were consulted by the Senate. The *pontifices*, by contrast, had no mediative function between the divine and the earthly. Rather, they had a specialist role in the conduct of ritual and also regulated religious behavior in the community (burial, religious status of individuals, conduct of festivals, etc.). Most *pontifices* were also senators, and the college functioned in many ways like a sub-committee of the Senate (Beard: 38-39).

This well illustrates that even the role of priest, normally straightforward in many societies, is not always easy to describe. In Republican Rome the roles of political leadership, religious leadership, priest, and diviner all overlapped and may have been carried out by many of the same individuals.

3.4 THE JERUSALEM PRIESTHOOD

Albertz, R. *A History of Israelite Religion in the Old Testament Period* (1994).
Cody, A. *A History of Old Testament Priesthood* (1969).
Grabbe, L. L. *Leviticus* (1993).
Gunneweg, A.H.J. *Leviten und Priester* (1965).
Jamieson-Drake, D. W. *Scribes and Schools in Monarchic Judah* (1991).

The overall emphasis in the biblical texts is on the Jerusalem temple and priesthood. This naturally represents the bias of the final editors of the collection, and many indications are found of other views and other realities. The existence of other cults is clearly recognized by the text, but they are declared illegitimate and the result of Israel's disobedience and backsliding from Yhwh. (These cults will be discussed in the next section, 3.5.) According to the text, Jerusalem was made an official cultic center at the very beginning of the monarchy and patronized by the king himself. This view has a long history. Genesis 14 pictures it as having the cult and priest of El Elyon, a deity identified in context with Yhwh (v 22). That it was the sole accepted shrine for Yhwh or that it was the capital of the kingdom at an early time is more debatable. Recent study has suggested that the city was not a major administrative center until the eighth century (Jamieson-Drake).

Nowhere is there a complete description of the temple personnel and cultic operations. Information on both is found in Exodus, Leviticus, Numbers, and Deuteronomy. Although there is broad agreement among these books, there are many differences on things as basic as the *tamid* (daily) offering, the priestly dues, and the offerings to be made for different transgressions (cf. Grabbe). Further differences can be found between these books and the narrative sections of the OT (Joshua-2 Kings, Ezra-Nehemiah, 1-2 Chronicles). A good deal of cultic information is found in 1-2 Chronicles, especially on sections of the temple personnel engaged in singing and activities other than those relating to the altar. Because of the lateness of the books and differences from other sections of the OT, it is often thought that Chronicles is—to a lesser or greater extent—describing the situation in the Second Temple period (3.1.15).

Leviticus and other priestly writings generally assume a twofold division of priests who preside at the altar and Levites who have more menial duties in the temple, whereas Deuteronomy seems to have a single undifferentiated priesthood of "Levitical priests." The differences are often explained as a historical development (Cody; Gunneweg; Albertz: 219-22): With the fall of the Northern Kingdom about 722 BCE, many of the priests migrated to Judah, especially the Jerusalem area. As a product of circles in the Northern Kingdom, Deuteronomy regarded these priests as the equal of those in Jerusalem and expected them to take their place alongside their brethren at the Jerusalem altar. This did not happen, however, and the priests from outside Jerusalem became the inferior clergy, the "Levites." Whether this explanation is anywhere near the truth is difficult to prove because of the problem of the growth of the tradition; however, the basic twofold division between clergy allowed at the altar and inferior clergy is well-documented for the Second Temple period. Other OT texts suggest a complex development in the pre-exilic period, perhaps with rival groups (cf. 3.2; 3.6).

3.5 PRIESTS AT OTHER SITES

Fowler, J. D. *Theophoric Personal Names in Ancient Hebrew* (1988).
Manor, D. W., and G. A. Herion. "Arad," *ABD* (1992) 331-36.
Smith, J. Z. "Native Cults in the Hellenistic Period," *HR* 11 (1971-72) 236-49.
____ . "European Religions, Ancient: Hellenistic Religions," *Encyclopaedia Britannica* (1985), *Macropaedia* 18.925-27.
Smith, M. *Palestinian Parties and Politics* (1971).
Smith, M. S. *The Early History of God* (1990).
Tigay, J. H. *You Shall Have No Other Gods* (1986).
Ussishkin, D. "The Date of the Judaean Shrine at Arad," *IEJ* 38 (1988) 142-57.

Cult places outside Jerusalem and their cult personnel are generally viewed negatively in the OT. Yet it is clear that they existed. Although trying to focus first on the text itself, we have to keep in mind that it has been edited in line with later monotheistic and monocultic ideals. It has long been recognized in some circles, and now is becoming more the consensus, that monotheism and a single cult were late developments in the period of the monarchy (some would say they were post-monarchial developments). From the indications of theophoric names, both in the biblical text and from inscriptional sources, Yhwh was the dominant divine name, though El occurs with great frequency as well (Fowler; Tigay). It is also evident, however, that Baal was well known and not confined to marginal individuals. The books of Chronicles show that figures in 1-2 Samuel, such as Saul's son Ishbosheth and Jonathan's son Mephibosheth, really had Baal names (Ishbaal and Meribaal). The Samarian Ostraca similarly have a number of Baal names (*TSSI* 1.5-15; *KAI* ##183-88; *CHI*: 39-57).

Rather than beginning with a "religion pure and undefiled" from which it continually fell away, despite the best efforts of the "true" prophets, Israel was polytheistic from its earliest origins (cf. Smith 1990). Yhwh was an important national god and originally separate deities such as El, Shaddai, and Elyon became identified with him. Why Baal was not also assimilated to Yhwh is a puzzle, but instead a fierce conflict developed, at least in some circles. (The situation under Ahab should probably not be used as evidence except with considerable caution. Native Baal worship is probably not being criticized in this account; rather Jezebel seems to have introduced a Tyrian cult, and opposition to it probably took the form of a nationalistic movement rather than strict religious objection.) It may well be, as Morton Smith has argued, that there was a "Yhwh alone" movement or tendency from an early time (1971). Such a movement did develop at some point and eventually won out over other views. Members of this movement were also in control of the final formulating of the tradition so that other positions were excluded or interpreted in a negative way. It is only here and there that remnants of a different situation have survived in the text.

If this is correct, the treatment of non-Jerusalem cults in the text is probably quite different from their actual place in the society. The existence of other Yahwistic high places in Judah and of northern Yahwistic centers such as Bethel and Dan, and of non-Yahwistic cults dedicated to Baal and Asherah, is acknowledged but considered examples of apostasy and condemned. "Good" kings supposedly removed such cults, though actually a number of good kings left the Yahwistic shrines in the country (e.g., Asa [2.1.8] and Joash [2.1.9]). The excavations at Arad suggest a non-Jerusalem Judean temple existing into the late monarchy (Manor/Herion; Ussishkin). Only occasionally do we come across any description of what happened in actual practice at these shrines. One example is Amos 7. Another widespread allegation is that such cults involved sexual rites such as ritual prostitution, both heterosexual and homosexual. On this question, see 3.7.

The text gives the impression that the priests of the northern shrines were all illegitimate. For example, 1 Kings 13:33 states that Jeroboam made priests of all who so desired from among the people, suggesting that the priests at Bethel and Dan were not only of non-priestly descent but also self-seeking individuals. 2 Chronicles 11:13-17 further maintains that when Jeroboam broke away and set up a separate kingdom, the priests and Levites all migrated south out of his kingdom to Jerusalem because they were not allowed to serve at his shrines. It naturally ignores the story of Judges 17-18 which implies that the cult at Dan was staffed by Levites (3.1.3).

Thus, the activities at the shrines outside Jerusalem and even at the non-Yahwistic cult places are not likely to have been much different from those at Jerusalem. Images of sexual orgies or secret mystical rites may spice up a dull narrative, but blood sacrifice and vegetable offerings were normal in most cults in the Northwest Semitic area, as far as we can determine. (Mesopotamia was different in that the normal routine was to offer prepared food to the cult statues of the gods, after which it was consumed by the priests.) Mystical rites and secret cults were a development of the Hellenistic world and apparently not known in the ancient Near East until the Greek period (cf. J. Z. Smith 1971-72; 1985).

3.6 THE PLACE OF THE HIGH PRIEST

Bartlett, J. R. "Zadok and His Successors at Jerusalem," *JTS* 19 (1968) 1-18.
Corney, R. W. "Zadok the Priest," *IDB* (1962) 4.928-29.
Cross, F. M. *Canaanite Myth and Hebrew Epic* (1973) 195-215.
Grabbe, L. L. *Judaism from Cyrus to Hadrian* (1992).
Hauer, C. E. "Who Was Zadok?" *JBL* 82 (1963) 89-94.
Johnson, M.D. *The Purpose of the Biblical Genealogies* (1988).
Ramsey, G. W. "Zadok," *ABD* (1992) 6.1034-36.
Stoebe, H. J. *Das zweite Buch Samuelis* (1994).
Wellhausen, J. *Der Text der Bücher Samuelis* (1871).
Wilson, R. R. *Genealogy and History in the Biblical World* (1977).

In the Second Temple period, the high priest was an important figure. There is a straightforward reason for this: There was no longer a king, most of the time, and the nation itself was generally constituted as a theocracy, with the high priest in the main administrative post (see further, Grabbe: 73-83). In the First Temple period, the situation was different since there was a functioning monarchy. The ultimate responsibility for religion lay with the king, who was regularly praised or blamed for his conduct. Nevertheless, a number of passages refer to a high priest and envisage special duties or a special position for him.

A number of references suggest that one of the priests was regularly in charge of the temple. For example, before the building of the Jerusalem temple, there was one who exercised both a priestly and perhaps even a judging function. Eli had this role at Shiloh (1 Sam 1). His successor Samuel did not limit his activities to one site but made a circuit of Bethel, Gilgal, Mizpah, and Ramah (1 Sam 7:16-17). Jehoida evidently exercised a similar responsibility in opposing Athaliah and crowning Joash king (2 Kings 11). Hilkiah is particularly associated with the discovery of the lawbook and the reforms under Josiah (2 Kings 22). All this suggests that texts such as Leviticus were not just theoretical ideas but based on some sort of reality, though the office of high priest may well have had a different significance in the Second Temple period when the high priest was also often head of state.

Apart from Aaron, the prototype of the high priest seems to have been Zadok in the time of David. Zadok has excited a good deal of speculation because, like Melchizedek (Gen 14:17-20), he had "neither father nor mother"; that is, he suddenly appears in the text (2 Sam 8:17) without introduction, and no genealogy or other forms of identification are given to him in 1-2 Samuel. This is rather surprising in light of the fact that appropriate descent was considered the sine qua non of being a priest. The text of 2 Samuel 8:17 does make him the son of Ahitub, but the verse has been widely accepted as corrupt since the time of Wellhausen (176-77). Ahitub was the father of Ahimelech (1 Sam 22:9-12), and the priest contemporary with Zadok was Abiathar, Ahimelech's son (2 Sam 17:15; 19:12; 20:25). The correct reading of 2 Samuel 8:17 is now widely accepted to be "Zadok and Abiathar, son of Ahimelech son of Ahitub." No attempt to make Zadok of the line of Aaron is found until 1 Chronicles 5:34 (Eng. 6:8). The obvious conclusion to be drawn from this is that the Chronicler is attempting to resolve a theological problem. The Chronicler knew that Zadok "must have been" of the line of Aaron, so he made sure that this is indicated in a suitable genealogy. This sort of genealogy creation is well known from anthropological studies (Wilson; Johnson), which shows that genealogies were often created to indicate social relations, support political claims, and reflect class structure. Blood descent and genetic relationships may be of little importance to genealogies. Thus, the question of Zadok's actual parentage is highlighted by the text itself.

A thesis widely accepted since Wellhausen's time argues that Zadok was actually the priest of the Jebusite cult in Jerusalem before its conquest by David (Corney; Hauer). When David acquired the threshing floor from the Jebusite king Arauna, he also took over the existing cult of El Elyon and its priesthood represented by Zadok. Not only are Zadok's origins evidently suppressed, but the root *ṣdq* (meaning "righteousness" but also probably a divine name) is found in a number of names associated with Jerusalem: Melchizedek (Gen 14:17-20), Adonizedek (Josh 10:1, 3), and Zadok himself.

This thesis has not been accepted by everyone (Cross: 209-14; cf. Ramsey). Cross dismisses the significance of *ṣdq* because the element is common in Northwest Semitic names (but such names are not common in Israelite tradition) and because of the different vocalization patterns between Zadok (*qatul* pattern) and the *-ṣedeq-* names (*qitl* pattern). His further argument that David as a "primitive Yahwist of well-documented piety" would not have taken over a Jebusite priest is, however, an example of circular reasoning; it assumes that Yahwism of the time would have excluded the adoption of other worship, that the edited tradition with its later monotheistic bias represents the earlier situation, and—especially—that his own ideal of David would not allow such an act. Cross also attempts to find an Aaronic genealogy for Zadok. This is partly because he assumes that David could not have spurned the Aaronites (how do we know?). He also attempts a different textual critical analysis of 2 Samuel 8:17, but his reconstruction seems to be the result—rather than the cause—of connecting Zadok with Aaron.

In the present state of knowledge, it would be difficult to establish that Zadok had been priest of the old Jebusite cult. The thesis is appealing because it recognizes the bias of the text and the apparent attempt at covering up a theologically embarrassing situation—an approach not unknown among some modern scholars. This is why the thesis is still espoused in the recent commentary by Stoebe. Nevertheless, theories which attempt to establish the true origins of Zadok assume a certain reliability of historical data which are open to analytical extraction. Those who have less confidence in the traditio-historical methods, though, would be agnostic as to whether we can establish anything about Zadok or even whether he existed. What does stand out is the extent to which sometimes one priestly line or family or faction dominates in one text as opposed to another.

This suggests a complicated history for the priesthood, with rival factions which not only maneuvered politically but also literarily by developing traditions which favored their particular group. The actual history cannot be written with any assurance despite the variety of theories which have been developed. From a social history point of view, the more important datum is the existence of such rivalries and what it tells us about the development of the priesthood. There is no reason to assume that the genealogies represent actual blood descent; on the contrary, diverse groups, with diverse origins, seem to have entered the priesthood at different times. A number of these may not have owed their original setting to Jerusalem but to various cults outside Jerusalem and perhaps even to non-Yahwistic cults (cf. the El Elyon of Gen 14:18). The high priest may not always have been chosen from the same group, and the historical reality of Second Temple times often goes against the OT text. Despite Deuteronomy, the Levites functioned only as inferior clergy; despite Ezekiel, non-Zadokite groups presided at the altar and eventually even held the office of high priest (i.e., the Hasmoneans).

3.7 WOMEN IN THE CULT

Barstad, H. *The Religious Polemics of Amos* (1984).
Carroll, R. P. "On Representation in the Bible: An *Ideologiekritik* Approach," *JNSL* 20 (1994) 1-15.
Goodfriend, E. A., and K. van der Toorn. "Prostitution," *ABD* (1992) 5.505-13.
Henshaw, R. A. *Female and Male: The Cultic Personnel* (1994).
Kramer, S. N. *The Sacred Marriage Rite* (1969).
Yamauchi, E. M. "Cultic Prostitution: A Case Study in Cultural Diffusion," *Orient and Occident* (1973) 213-22.

The place of women in the cult is seldom explicitly discussed in the OT texts. The cultic obligations were mandatory for male Israelites (e.g., Exod 23:17; Deut 16:16). Only men were allowed to be priests. On the other hand, women were required to observe the purity regulations, and these included temple sacrifice in some cases, such as after childbirth (e. g., Lev 12; 15:25-30). We also find references to women participating in communal cultic worship. A good example of this is Hannah, the mother of Samuel (1 Sam 1-2).

One issue often taken for granted is the existence of cultic prostitution, primarily female but also male. There have been several reasons for assuming this. Some classical sources reported prostitution in the context of some of the Near Eastern cults in antiquity (e.g., Herodotus 1.199), but this is also a charge often made in religious polemics. Any such allegations need to be treated with care, if for no other reason than that the Greeks did not always understand or correctly interpret what they saw (cf. 3.3.2). It has been widely accepted that "sacred marriage" rites in Mesopotamia may have involved the king in sex with the queen or perhaps a priestess (Kramer), and such has also been proposed for Israel. Nevertheless, there is reason to doubt whether ritualized sex was a normal part of the cult of Baal and Asherah. Some scholars have believed they found evidence for such practices in the Ugaritic texts, such as the cultic figures referred to as *qdšm*; however, no clear evidence has been found for ritual prostitution or the like at Ugarit (3.3.3).

The bias of the biblical and subsequent Jewish and Christian religious traditions was toward the assumption of decadent sexual practices in "pagan" worship, especially among the so-called Canaanites (cf. Carroll). It was therefore easy to believe in "abominations" such as sexual orgies, prostitution, sodomy, and the like as a constituent part of the cults which Israel was to eradicate (cf. Yamauchi). Recent study has called into question many of the assumptions about the "Canaanite" cults and other worship in Israel's environment, as well as the biblical version of the development of Israelite religion (as discussed in 3.5 and 5.6). On the question of cult prostitution in Mesopotamia and elsewhere, the matter is not clear-cut (3.3.2). In the same way, most of the OT references can be interpreted as symbolic language for religious straying, and there is really little support for the oft-repeated assertion that cultic prostitution formed a part of the non-Yahwistic cults (Barstad: 21-33; Goodfriend/van der Toorn).

3.8 THE GESTALT OF THE PRIEST

At first sight, it is easy to characterize priests. They are those who carry out the cult functions at the temple. In most ancient societies, the center of worship was the cult. In Mesopotamia and Egypt, the daily cultic activities focused on feeding and clothing the gods as manifested in the cultic images in the temple. Ancient Israel also had the cult as the main form of worship, but it was centered on the system of blood sacrifice (accompanied by appropriate cereal and wine offerings). Priests were needed to carry out this ritual, as well as personnel to care for the physical needs of the temple. This much is clear, but there is much more. Here are some of the functions, duties, and structure of the priesthood:

1. The first responsibility of the priesthood was maintenance of the cult. This consisted of minimal daily offerings and special offerings on the sabbaths and festivals. There were also private offerings brought by individuals in relation to sins, pollutions, vows, and thanksgiving. Various texts give different messages on who was allowed to preside at the altar, but by the Second Temple period a twofold division of duties and rights seems to have been established. Only the priests allegedly descended from Aaron were allowed to serve at the altar. They had become so numerous by the Persian period that they were divided into twenty-four courses, each serving two weeks of the year (except perhaps for festivals, when all were on duty) and having the rest of the time off. Other duties related to the cult were pronouncing on matters of purity (including whether a leper was clean or not) and otherwise preserving and teaching the priestly law.

2. Other temple personnel—usually called Levites, though some other names are used (allegedly subdivisions of the Levites in our present text but probably historically of a different origin)—saw to it that the cult had the necessary support to function smoothly. They were concerned with supply, storage, cleaning, repair, and security.

3. Some personnel were responsible for singing and playing musical instruments. From the literature, we may infer that singing and praise had an important place in the temple, but the exact place of singing in the ritual is not clear. Such personnel are clearly attested, at least for the Second Temple. It has been suggested that these individuals were descended from the cult prophets. If so, there still seem to have been a few actual cult prophets at the beginning of the Second Temple period (4.6). We know that a number of

the prophets were closely associated with the temple (Isaiah and Jeremiah, just to name two), whether they were strictly cult prophets or not.

4. The priestly forms of divination were also an important contribution to administration. Although we cease to read about the Urim and Thummim and the ephod as the text progresses in its account of Israel's history, they are clearly attested in a number of texts associated with the early monarchy. Where mentioned, they are always treated positively and are considered vital for certain sorts of decisions (e.g., Ezra 2:63//Neh 7:65).

5. Some texts regard the priests as having the duty to act as judges. We would expect this in cultic matters, but they were also responsible for adjudicating in civil and criminal cases, if the texts are to be believed. It is always possible that the texts reflect the situation in the Persian period when the monarchy no longer existed and the state was organized as a theocracy. At that time, the proportion of priests to lay people was quite high, and the high priest as head of the people was likely to have appointed priests as judges in local areas. Unfortunately, we have few details.

6. The priests were the ones with leisure to pursue intellectual activities, especially when they no longer had to serve at the altar more than a few weeks each year. They had the opportunity to learn, teach, study, and preserve traditions. The first focus for these were the cultic and priestly traditions, but we should not expect them to be confined to these. The wisdom pursuits of cosmology, the natural world, and the esoteric arts are likely to have been of interest to some priests. Many of the scribes seem to have been priests or Levites. Having charge of the priestly forms of divination might have provided the occasion to study other forms of knowing the future, just as diviner-priests developed in other cultures. This may well have led to a strong priestly contribution to the mantic wisdom and apocalyptic traditions (6.5).

7. Thus, the priestly duties and skills overlapped those of the diviner and sage. In addition, we know that a number of the prophets were also priests (e.g., Jeremiah and Ezekiel). Although the offices of priest, prophet, and the like can be discussed separately as ideal types, in actual society they were not so clearly distinct and were certainly not mutually exclusive.

4.

Prophets

Blenkinsopp, J. *A History of Prophecy in Israel* (1984).
Culley, R. C., and T. W. Overholt, eds. *Anthropological Perspectives on Old Testament Prophecy* (1982).
Lindblom, J. *Prophecy in Ancient Israel* (1962).
Overholt, T. W. *Channels of Prophecy: The Social Dynamics of Prophetic Activity* (1989).
Wilson, R. R. *Prophecy and Society in Ancient Israel* (1980).

Any study of the prophet in Israelite society immediately runs into a major obstacle: the enormous amount of secondary literature on the subject. It is impossible to have read more than a fraction of it, much less to discuss it here. Even to list some of the more important writings would take up more space than is warranted in this book. Therefore, my discussion will focus on the original texts, with citations of secondary literature only where directly relevant. For a guide to the study of prophecy to about 1982, see Blenkinsopp. As well as his indispensable survey of sociological study, Wilson also summarizes much of recent scholarship on individual prophetic books. The Overholt and Culley/Overholt volumes also address the increasingly important sociological questions. Despite its age, one of the best general studies of prophecy is still the classic work of Lindblom.

4.1 SELECTED OLD TESTAMENT TEXTS

On Balaam (Num 22-24), see 5.1.3.

4.1.1 Deuteronomy

Meeks, W. A. *The Prophet-King* (1967).

Several important references occur in this book. In 13:2-6 criteria are given for knowing whether a message is from God or not when an individual does a "sign" (*'ôt*) or "wonder" (*môfēt*); namely, whether that person suggests going after gods other than Yhwh. The person with the message is referred to as either a prophet or a dreamer of dreams (*ḥōlēm [ha]ḥălôm*). No distinction is made between them except over the matter of whether the person follows Yhwh or other gods.

In 18:9-14 is given a long list of "abominations" (*tô'ăvôt*) supposedly practiced by the other nations but to be avoided by Israel. Then, vv 15-22 go on to discuss the "prophet like Moses." Whether this was to be a special figure or office, as the "prophet like Moses" tradition later became (cf. Meeks), or simply a prophet who might arise in any generation after Moses' death is debatable. In any event, Yhwh's words were to be in this person's mouth (v 18). The prophet was to make God's words known to the people, just as Moses did, because they did not like to hear God speaking directly. At this point, criteria are given for recognizing a false prophet: (a) if he speaks in the names of other gods, and (b) if the word of the prophet does not come to pass. This is similar to 13:2-6 but with a slightly different emphasis: to know whether the prophet comes from God, 18:9-14 places the stress on whether the word comes to pass, whereas in 13:2-6 the emphasis is on whether the person proposes going after other gods.

4.1.2 Samuel and Saul

Texts: 1 Samuel 1-13; 14-16; 19:18-24; 25:1.

Samuel was born of the tribe of Ephraim (1:1). He was dedicated by his mother to the shrine at Shiloh and served the high priest Eli there, even though he was not of priestly descent. While still a youth, at a time when there was little vision (*ḥāzôn*) in Israel, Yhwh stood by his bed and spoke to him, revealing to him the future of Eli's house (3:1-14). This experience is referred to as a "vision" (3:15: *hammar'āh*). As a result, Israel knew that Samuel was a prophet (*nāvî'*) because his predications were fulfilled (3:19-20).

Saul wanted to consult Samuel about lost asses which could not be found (9). Samuel is referred to as a "man of God" (9:6), with all that he says coming to pass. He is also called a "seer" (*rô'eh*), the one called a "prophet" (*nāvî'*) being then called a "seer" (9:9). Yhwh revealed to Samuel's ear that he had chosen Saul (9:15). Saul met with a band of prophets, who were playing musical instruments and prophesying; Yhwh's spirit rushed upon him and he prophesied and became another person (10:5-6, 10).

At Naioth, Samuel presided over an assembly (the meaning of the Hebrew word *lahăqāh* is uncertain) of prophets who were prophesying, and God's spirit even came upon the messengers from Saul so that they prophesied (19:20-21). When Saul himself finally came, he stripped off his clothes, prophesied before Samuel, and lay naked on the ground a day and a night (19:23-24).

4.1.3 Nathan the Prophet and Gad the Seer

Texts: 1 Samuel 22:5; 2 Samuel 7; 12; 24; 1 Kings 1; 1 Chronicles 17; 21; 29:29; 2 Chronicles 9:29; 29:25; Psalms 51:2.

These two were important companions of David, though it is interesting that the two are never mentioned as participating in the same episode. But they do seem almost to alternate at crucial points in David's life, first one playing a significant role (Nathan in the temple and Bathsheba episodes) and then the other (Gad with David in the wilderness and in the census episode). Both of them are credited with having written accounts of David's reign (1 Chron 29:29).

Although Gad is often referred to as "the Seer" (*haḥōzeh*), he is also called Gad "the prophet, the seer of David" (*hannāvî' ḥōzēh Dāwid*: 2 Sam 24:11). He first appears with David when a fugitive from Saul, where he is called Gad the prophet (1 Sam 22:5). It was Gad who brought the message of Yhwh to David after he numbered Israel, offering him a choice of three punishments (2 Sam 24; 1 Chron 21).

When David wished to build a temple to house the Ark, Yhwh sent a message by Nathan about this and about David's dynasty (2 Sam 7; 1 Chron 17); this message is referred to as "these words and this vision (*haḥizzāyôn*)" (2 Sam 7:17). Nathan was also the one to bring the message of condemnation from Yhwh when David had Uriah the Hittite killed and then took Bathsheba (2 Sam 11-12). Nathan later played a crucial role (along with Zadok the priest) in making sure that Solomon succeeded David on the throne (1 Kings 1).

4.1.4 Ahijah the Shilonite

Talshir, Z. *The Alternative Story: 3 Kingdoms 12:24 A-Z* (1993).

Texts: 1 Kings 11:29-39; 12:15; 14:1-18; LXX 3 Kgdms 12:24a-z; 2 Chronicles 9:29; 10:15.

During the reign of Solomon, Ahijah was the prophet who met Jeroboam and prophesied that the latter would rule over ten of the twelve tribes which God would take away from David's line and give to him (1 Kings 11:29-39). Ahijah graphically symbolizes this by tearing his own new robe into twelve parts and giving Jeroboam ten of them. The reason is that "they" (Israel?

David's descendants?) have not kept God's laws but have worshiped the gods of the Phoenicians, Moabites, and Ammonites. This prophecy is also referred to as being among other prophecies about Jeroboam: the words of Nathan the prophet, the prophecy (*nĕvû'āh)* of Ahijah the Shilonite, and the vision (*ḥāzôt*) of Iddo the seer (*haḥōzeh*) (2 Chron 9:29).

Ahijah was also consulted with regard to illness. After Jeroboam became king, his son grew ill (1 Kings 14:1-18). The king sent his wife in disguise to Ahijah in Shiloh. Although Ahijah was blind from old age, Yhwh told (*'mr*) him that Jeroboam's wife was coming to inquire (*drš*) of him about the health of their son (v 5). So as soon as the queen arrived, Ahijah delivered a renunciation of Jeroboam for his sins and predicted that every male of Jeroboam's house would be cut off (vv 6-14). This child would die, but only he of Jeroboam's sons would receive a proper burial. Ahijah then went on to predict that Israel would be struck by Yhwh and exiled across the Euphrates (vv 15-16). The son died as predicted (vv 17-18).

In the MT Ahijah is referred to as a "prophet" (*nāvî'*: 1 Kings 11:29; 14:2, 18). In the "alternative story" in 3 Kgdms 12:24a-z, a parallel but sometimes different account (especially in the arrangement of material and the details) of Jeroboam's rise to power (Talshir), the Greek term *prophētēs* (= Hebrew *nāvî'*) is not used. Rather, the designation is always "man of God" (Greek *ho anthrōpos tou theou* [vv 24l and 24y], presumably a translation of Hebrew *'îš hā'ĕlōhîm*). This indicates that "prophet" and "man of God" could be used interchangeably in certain contexts but also suggests that terminology develops and changes as the story itself evolves and mutates.

4.1.5 The Man of God and the Old Prophet (1 Kings 13)

Carroll, R. P. "Night Without Vision. Micah and the Prophets," VTSup 49 (1992) 74-84.

DeVries, S. J. *1 Kings* (1985) 164-74.

____ . *Prophet Against Prophet* (1978).

Winkle, D. W. van. "1 Kings XIII: True and False Prophecy," *VT* 39 (1989) 31-43.

This is perhaps one of the most curious stories among the many about prophets, and much has been written on it by modern scholars (see the bibliographical survey in Winkle). A man of God from Judah was sent to prophesy against the altar at Bethel. He gave a sign, which was that the altar fell apart. King Jeroboam, who was sacrificing at the time, stretched out his hand against the man of God and could not draw it back. The man of God prayed to Yhwh and his arm was restored. The man of God started his return journey without eating or drinking, for so he had been commanded by God, but an elderly prophet in the town went to him and said, "I am a prophet (*nāvî'*) like you" and went on to claim falsely that an angel spoke a message from Yhwh that the man of God was to come with him and eat (v 18). When the latter did this, the old prophet delivered a message from Yhwh that the man of God had disobeyed and would be punished. Soon after he resumed his journey he was killed by a lion, and the old prophet fetched the body for burial, called him "my brother," and stated that his prophecies would be fulfilled.

A number of questions immediately arise. The man of Judah is generally called "a man of God" (*'îš 'ĕlōhîm*), though the old prophet considers him a prophet (v 18), and he is once referred to in the narrative as a prophet (v 23). He delivers his message, he disobeys but only because of a lie, and he dies without mercy. The old prophet lies to the man of God, but then he seems to deliver an actual message from Yhwh, which comes to pass, and he finally honors the prophet whose death he has caused.

Many of previous discussions have concentrated on a hypothesized development of the tradition. Our concern is with the story as it now stands. The designation of the man of God as a prophet may be the result of editing, but it also suggests that "man of God" could be a generic term, especially when other uses of the term are considered (4.2). Neither of the figures is unambiguously labeled a false prophet; indeed, both receive messages from Yhwh which are fulfilled. On one reading of the story, the old prophet comes across in a more negative light since he seems to put the man of God in an untenable position by a lie. Others have seen this only as a test, though, and thus ultimately from God (cf. DeVries). The old prophet is clearly able to receive messages from Yhwh, even if he lied. The man of God suffers the death penalty even though he gave a correct prophecy and even though he was deceived into disobeying part of his instructions. This story upsets a good deal of stereotypical thinking about prophets and prophecy.

4.1.6 Elijah (1 Kings 17-19, 21; 2 Kings 1-2)

Elijah is called both a "prophet" (*nāvî'*: 1 Kings 18:22, 36; cf. 19:10, 14) and "man of God" (*'îš hā'ĕlōhîm*: 1 Kings 17:18, 24; 2 Kings 1:9, 11), though many of his activities are those traditionally performed by shamans and healers. His public career was inaugurated when he announced an indeterminate drought (1 Kings 17:1). This drought came to an end with the confrontation and contest between Elijah and the prophets of Baal (18). The activity of the prophets of Baal in cutting themselves and calling on Baal is referred to as "prophesying" (nif. *nb'*: 1 Kings 18:29). Later he anointed Elisha as his successor (see 4.1.7).

A number of miracles are associated with Elijah. When he stayed with a widow, her small amount of oil and flour renewed itself sufficiently to feed them all (1 Kings 17:14-16). Then when her son became mortally ill, Elijah healed (resurrected?) him (17:17-24). He called fire down from heaven on two occasions: first, to burn the sacrifice in the contest with the prophets of Baal (1 Kings 18:38) and, second, against the messengers of the king who came to fetch him (2 Kings 1:2-12). He was finally taken up to heaven by a whirlwind preceded by a fiery chariot and horses (2 Kings 2:11).

Elijah's power came from having the "word of Yhwh" in his mouth (1 Kings 17:24). He outran Ahab's chariot when the hand of Yhwh was upon him (18:46). Obadiah was afraid the spirit of Yhwh might take him away (18:12). A voice came to him when in a cave at Sinai (19:13). A messenger or angel (*mal'āk*) of Yhwh told him that soldiers of Ahaziah were coming (2 Kings 1:3, 15).

4.1.7 Elisha (1 Kings 19; 2 Kings 2-9, 13)

Elisha was chosen by Elijah who anointed him as a prophet and placed his mantel on him (1 Kings 19:16-21). Then when Elijah was about to be taken away to heaven, Elisha accompanied him as he visited the "sons of the prophets" at Bethel and Jericho (2 Kings 2:1-5). He asked for and received a double portion of Elijah's spirit (2:9-15). Like Elijah, he is called both a prophet (2 Kings 6:12) and a man of God (2 Kings 6:9).

Also like Elijah, Elisha participated in political events of his own times. When the kings of Israel, Judah, and Edom ran out of water in an expedition against Mesha of Moab, they consulted Elisha (3). After he called for a musician to play, the hand of Yhwh came up on him and he predicted a miraculous filling of the wadis with water (3:11-20). When Ben-Hadad of Damascus inquired of Elisha whether he would recover from an illness, the latter foretold that Hazael (Ben-Hadad's messenger) would rule in place of his master (8:7-15). God made him "see" (hif. *r'h*) that Hazael would be king of Aram, suggesting a vision (v 13). He anointed Jehu to be king in place of Ahab's son Jehoram (9:1-13).

Elisha performed a variety of other miracles, in addition to providing water for the three kings. He healed (*rp'*) the bad land and water of a town (2 Kings 2:19-22). He caused a female bear to savage children who made fun of him (2:23-25). When a widow of one of the sons of the prophets found herself in difficulty over a debt, he caused a miraculous flow of oil until she had enough to sell to pay off the debt (4:1-7). He predicted the birth of a child to a barren couple who had provided hospitality to him (4:8-37). Then, in an action parallel to Elijah's (1 Kings 17:17-24), he healed (resurrected?) the son who had become mortally ill. He detoxified a pot containing soup made from a poisonous gourd (2 Kings 4:38-41). Anticipating Jesus' multiplication of fish and loaves, he caused twenty loaves and some grain to feed a hundred, with some still left over (4:42-44). He healed the Syrian commander Naaman of leprosy and cursed his own servant with the same disease for disobedience and greed (5). He caused a lost axehead to float to the surface of the pool in which it had fallen (6:1-7) and predicted a seven-year famine (8:1-6).

4.1.8 Ahab and Micaiah (1 Kings 22:1-28)

Miller, J. M. *The Old Testament and the Historian* (1976).

When Ahab and Jehoshaphat contemplated fighting as allies against the Arameans, Jehoshaphat requested that they seek (*drš*) the word of Yhwh. Therefore, Ahab consulted his four hundred court prophets. They all predicted victory, prophesying (hitp., nif. *nb'*) before the two kings at the city gate (1 Kings 22:10, 12). Their leader, Zedekiah, made iron horns to show how Ahab would win, quoting a revelation of Yhwh ("thus spoke Yhwh"). Jehoshaphat was not satisfied, however, and asked whether there was another prophet. Micaiah was brought forward and, after some cajoling, predicted defeat. He described a vision of the heavenly court presided over by Yhwh (vv 19-23): Yhwh takes counsel from the other heavenly beings as to what should be done to deceive Ahab. Eventually, a "spirit" (*hārûaḥ*) volunteers to be a lying spirit in the mouths of Ahab's prophets.

Several points stand out from this account. The first is that all the prophets speak in the name of Yhwh; this includes the four hundred court prophets. Therefore, the conflict is between two sets of prophets of Yhwh. When the court prophets predicted victory, Jehoshaphat asked for another prophet. It was quite normal for omens to be tested against each other. What is surprising is that Ahab ignores the bad prediction. Having heard Micaiah's story, Ahab was said to have been displeased and to have thrown him into prison. As will be made clear below (4.3.3), kings wanted to know of bad omens and took them very seriously. For Ahab to be so blind to a contra-indication is unusual; even more surprising is that Jehoshaphat does not react but tamely follows Ahab into battle. What this suggests is that whatever the historical basis of the account, the story has been edited to fit the bias of a certain view about both Ahab and various sorts of prophets. (The story that Ahab fought against the Arameans at Aphek and was killed there is now widely rejected; see Miller: 20-39.)

4.1.9 Huldah (2 Kings 22:11-20; 2 Chron 34:22-28)

When a scroll was found in the temple, King Josiah sent the high priest Hilkiah, the scribe Shaphan, and several other officials to inquire (*drš*) of Yhwh because the contents of the scroll were not being obeyed in Judah (2 Kings 22:13). They went to the prophetess Huldah, the wife of Shallum (v 14). She delivered a message from Yhwh that disaster would be brought on the people because they had disobeyed; however, because Josiah had humbled himself and repented, Yhwh would see that this came about only after Josiah's death so that he would not see it. Two points are to be noted: First, there is no distinction in the story between Huldah and the various prophets in the Israelite tradition. Thus, even though fewer prophetesses are mentioned in the tradition, they otherwise seem to act just like the male prophets. Second, Huldah seems to be married to a temple official, probably a priest or Levite (cf. Jer 35:4). Sadly, there are no other references to Huldah in the text.

4.1.10 Book of Isaiah

Childs, B. S. *Isaiah and the Assyrian Crisis* (1967).
Clements, R. E. *Isaiah 1-39* (1980).
____ . *Isaiah and the Deliverance of Jerusalem* (1980).
Emmerson, G. I. *Isaiah 56-66* (1992).
Whybray, R. N. *The Second Isaiah* (1983).

It has become a scholarly consensus to divide the book of Isaiah roughly into three parts. First Isaiah (1-39) relates to a late eighth-century prophet usually referred to as Isaiah of Jerusalem (Clements 1980a). Second Isaiah (40-55) has usually been placed in the late exilic period in the decade or so before the conquest of Babylon by Cyrus in 539 BCE (Whybray: 2-4, though the place and date are now both being challenged [1.7]). It is often ascribed to one individual, a prophet who was himself among the Jewish exiles in Babylonia. Third Isaiah (56-66) is a collection of oracles, many of which are conventionally dated to the early post-exilic period and are thought to reflect the situation in the Persian province of Yehud in the late sixth century BCE (Emmerson: 53-69).

Isaiah 1-35 (First Isaiah) has little on the prophet himself (chs. 36-39 are treated below). He features only in chapters 6-8 and 20. He first appears as the recipient of a vision in the temple, in which he sees Yhwh and is sent to give a message to the people (ch. 6). The message is rather peculiar: Isaiah is to tell the people to hear and see but not to understand lest they repent and save themselves (vv 8-10). There is a brief reference to his call (8:11-15), though the vision in the temple (ch. 6) could also represent his call by God to be a prophet (some think it was only his commissioning for a specific mission and not his original prophetic call). He next goes with his son to give a message to King Ahaz about the alliance of Israel and Damascus against Judah (ch. 7). This was a message of hope, prophesying that the alliance's plans to replace Ahaz with another king would fail. Isaiah states that, as a sign, a young woman would bear a son who would be named "God (is) with us" (Immanuel). In chapter 8 Isaiah has sexual intercourse with "the prophetess" who bears a son named "Hastens the spoil, speeds the pillaging" (Maher-shalal-hash-baz). This is a further sign that Damascus and Samaria will be taken captive. Who the prophetess was is not elaborated, but the frequent suggestion that it was Isaiah's wife seems unlikely. There is no indication that a prophet's wife was referred to as a prophetess, and the failure to designate the woman as his wife seems strange if she was indeed his wife. Also, she seems to be the "young woman" of 7:14. In chapter 20 Isaiah is told to put off his sackcloth loincloth (his normal attire?) and go around naked and barefoot for three years as a sign of the captivity of the Egyptians and Nubians.

The picture of the man Isaiah in Isaiah 1-35 is a minimal one. To what extent this picture is compatible with the one in Isaiah 36-39//2 Kings 18-20 is a question. Isaiah supports the king (at least, one king on one occasion) rather than opposing him; however, it has been suggested that 22:5-14 shows opposition to Hezekiah's defensive actions against the invasion under Sennacherib rather than approval as chapters 36-39 indicate (Clements 1980b: 32-34).

Most of the book is a collection of various oracles of different lengths (some of them clearly much later than the eighth century BCE, such as chapter 13 against Babylon), many of them prophesying destruction either against Israel and Judah or against other nations. A few have been connected with specific historical situations, such as the invasion of Sennacherib in 701 BCE (e.g., 10:28-34), but most are impossible to set in a specific context (cf. Childs). Interspersed with these are a number of prophecies about an idealized future (e.g., 2:2-4; 9:1-6; 19:16-23; 29:17-24; 35).

There are only a few references to prophets. Isaiah himself is not called a prophet. In the superscription to the book reference is made to the "vision" (*ḥāzôn)* Isaiah saw (*ḥzh*) concerning Judah and Jerusalem (1:1; 2:1). A harsh vision (*ḥāzût*) is announced to him (21:2). Despite this tendency to use other terms for prophet, especially where the reference is positive, the term *nāvî'* occurs several times, usually in a negative sense. Yhwh says that he will remove the props or pillars of society, including the judge, prophet (*nāvî'*), augur (*qōsēm*), elder, and enchanter (*nĕvôn laḥaš*) (3:2-3). He will cut off the head and the tail from Israel: the elder is the head and the prophet who teaches lies is the tail (9:13-14). The priest and prophet are drunk; they are muddled in their vision (*rō'eh*) (28:7). He has spread a spirit of deep sleep over the eyes of the prophets (*nĕvî'îm*) and covered the heads of the seers (*ḥōzîm*); the vision/prophecy (*ḥāzût*) is like a sealed book to them (29:10-11).

Prophecy as such is not discussed in Second Isaiah (40-55) or Third Isaiah (56-66). However, a number of passages in Second Isaiah make the point that Yhwh—and only Yhwh—is able to foretell the future, to declare the end from the beginning (41:21-29; 42:9; 43:9; 44:7-8; 45:20-21; 46:10; 48:3-8, 14-16). Although this is in the context of contrasting Yhwh with other gods and idols, it has implications for prophecy. It makes the ability of Yhwh to see into the future and predict it an important divine characteristic.

Third Isaiah also does not discuss prophecy, though it does seem to refer several times to types of divinatory practice (5.1.9).

4.1.11 Isaiah and Hezekiah (2 Kings 18-20//Isa 36-39//2 Chron 32)

Childs, B. S. *Isaiah and the Assyrian Crisis* (1967).

These chapters cover three episodes in the life of Hezekiah: one on the invasion of Sennacherib in 701 BCE, one on the visit of messengers of the Babylonian king Merodach-Baladan, and a third on Hezekiah's mortal illness. The Isaiah material is usually (if not universally) thought to have been borrowed from 2 Kings; the two accounts agree almost word for word except for some small differences (with the exception of the poem in Isa 38:9-20). Since the nineteenth century, the story of the Assyrian invasion has been commonly analyzed as comprised of three separate versions (Childs: 69-103): Version A (2 Kings 18:13-16) is short and has nothing about Isaiah in it, so our concern is with versions B_1 (2 Kings 18:17-19:9a, 36-37//Isa 36:1-37:9a, 37-38) and B_2 (2 Kings 19:9b-35//Isa 37:9b-36).

If this analysis is correct, it is a useful insight into the text since the image of Isaiah is slightly different in each version. In B_1, Isaiah is the dominant figure. When the Rabshakeh's message of destruction on Jerusalem was brought to Hezekiah, he sent scribes, priests, and officials to Isaiah. The prophet (*nāvî'*) returned the message that Hezekiah was not to be afraid, for the Assyrian king would return to his own land and fall by the sword. Version B_2 has Hezekiah (after receiving a letter from the Assyrian king) go to the temple and pray to Yhwh directly about the matter. Yhwh's answer then comes by Isaiah. The picture is similar to version B_1, but here the king makes direct contact with Yhwh, and Isaiah is the conduit for Yhwh's reply to Hezekiah. The difference is one of emphasis and should not be exaggerated, but in this case Hezekiah is more active and the prophet has a more subordinate role.

2 Kings 20:1-11//Isaiah 38:1-8 concerns a time when Hezekiah contracted a serious illness. Isaiah brought the message that he was going to die. Hezekiah prayed to Yhwh, who sent a second message by Isaiah to say that the king would receive a further fifteen years of life and that God would also protect the city from the hands of the Assyrians. As a sign, Yhwh caused the sun to move back ten steps on the sun dial.

2 Kings 20:12-19//Isaiah 39 has the story of Hezekiah and the messengers from Babylon. If this episode is historical, as it may be, it would probably be dated earlier in Hezekiah's reign, before the invasion of Sennacherib. The historical Merodach-Baladan II was hereditary king of Babylon, but Babylon was a vassal to the Assyrians. Merodach-Baladan spent much of his life rebelling against the Assyrians and attempting to make Babylon independent.

Although Judah was rather remote, it is possible that the Babylonian king was seeking allies even that far afield. In this story, Isaiah first asks what Hezekiah showed to the Babylonian messengers; then, he brings a critical message from Yhwh that one day the Babylonians would carry away Hezekiah's treasures and even make his sons eunuchs to serve in their palace. (Isaiah's message looks suspiciously like something given at a time when Babylon was on the ascendancy, long after the time of Hezekiah.)

4.1.12 Jeremiah

Auld, A. G. "Prophets and Prophecy in Jeremiah and Kings," *ZAW* 96 (1984) 66-82.

This book has much to say about prophets. They are often mentioned together with the king and/or other leaders, priests, and the people as a way of representing the totality of society (2:8; 4:9; 8:1-2; 13:13; 32:27-35; 34:19). Prophets and priests are also referred to together, usually to condemn them (5:31; 6:13-14; 14:18; 29:1), indicating that both had important leadership roles in society. Much of what is said about prophets is negative, including major oracles against them (23:9-40): The prophets of Samaria prophesy by Baal (23:13), but the prophets of Jerusalem practice adultery and other wickedness and lead the people astray (vv 14-15). They speak a vision of their own hearts (*ḥăzôn libbām yĕdabbērû*) rather than having stood in Yhwh's council (vv 16-18, 21-22).

A good deal of biographical information about Jeremiah is intermixed with prophecies in the book. Much of this is in chapters 16-44. Jeremiah was of a priestly family of Anathoth (1:1), and although he is not said to have served as a priest at the altar, many of his activities take place in or around the temple. God called him from birth (1:5) and made him a prophet to the nations (1:5; 25). The word of Yhwh comes to him in visions (1:11-13; 31:26). Although he is called a prophet (*nāvî'*) a number of times (34:6; 37:13; 38:9, 14), this is more frequent in the MT than the LXX (Auld), but he is often told to prophesy (nif. *nb'*: 19:14; 25:30; 26:9, 11-12; cf. 32:3). He is told not to marry or to enter a *marzēaḥ* (funeral drinking house: 16:1-8). Just as he accuses others of being false prophets, he himself is similarly accused (17:14-18; 26:7-8; 28; 29:27-28). At one point, Jeremiah suggests that the prophecies be tested by whether they come to pass (27:16-18), a test which his own prophecies would not necessarily pass (cf. 46 on Egypt and 50-51 on Babylon).

4.1.13 Hananiah (Jer 28) and Uriah (Jer 26:20-24)

One of the most interesting episodes in the book of Jeremiah is the confrontation between Jeremiah and the prophet Hananiah. From the context,

Hananiah is clearly labeled a false prophet. He opposes Jeremiah, and he predicts that the Babylonian threat will soon be removed. In that sense he is the mirror image of Jeremiah. He prophesies by Yhwh (not by Baal, cf. 2:8); he opposes Jeremiah, just as Jeremiah opposed other prophets; and his message is just the opposite of Jeremiah's, in that he predicts salvation from Nebuchadnezzar. On the other hand, in Jeremiah there are prophecies about return of the exiles (16:14-15; 29:10-14; 31), similar to Hananiah's (28:4); further, the prophecies of Hananiah about deliverance from the Babylonians are much like those of Isaiah about deliverance from the Assyrians (4.1.11). Thus, the "false prophet" Hananiah is really little different from the "true prophets" Isaiah of Jerusalem and Jeremiah, except for the specific time and place of his prophecy.

A further comparison can be made with Uriah b. Shemaiah (26:20-24). He prophesied in the name of Yhwh against the city and land, like Jeremiah. When Jehoiakim heard, he sought to put him to death. Uriah fled to Egypt, but Jehoiakim sent men and was able to bring him back. Jeremiah, Uriah, and Hananiah all three prophesy in Yhwh's name but with different messages and different fates. Uriah dies violently for his preaching; Jeremiah, who has a similar message, escapes because of friends at court; and Hananiah dies a natural death, allegedly as a result of Jeremiah's prophecy.

4.1.14 Ezekiel

There is much information in the book about Ezekiel's activities and even thoughts and reactions, as well as visions and prophecies. Ezekiel was a priest (1:3). His reactions to God's inspiration are graphically described by such phrases as "the hand of Yhwh was upon him" (3:14, 22; 8:1), the spirit seizes him and carries him away (3:12), and he prophesies when the spirit falls on him (11:4-5). He is told to prophesy (nif. *nb'*) a number of times (4:7; 6:2; 13:2; 21:2; 25:2; 28:21; 34:2; 36:1, etc.). Two special points of interest can be mentioned. On more than one occasion, the elders of the captivity come to inquire (*drš*) of Yhwh through Ezekiel (14:1-4; 20:1-3). The other point concerns the term "vision," which seems to be used in a way not often noted by commentators. Ezekiel himself experiences a number of visions, including being taken to Jerusalem in a vision (*mar'eh*) after the hand of Yhwh fell on him (8:1-3; 11:24). Of particular interest is the use of the term "vision" (*ḥāzôn*) for revelations which are usually classified as auditions. For example, the "word of Yhwh" comes in a vision (7:13). When the hand of Yhwh comes on him and Yhwh tells him to go out into the valley where he sees God's presence (3:22-23), this is later referred to as a "vision" (8:4). Ezekiel castigates those who say the vision will fail, because it is about to be fulfilled (12:21-28). This last passage applies the criterion of whether something comes to pass, yet in Ezekiel's own corpus are prophecies which did not take place, particularly the prediction that Nebuchadnezzar would conquer Egypt and make it desolate and devoid of humans and animals for forty years (29-32, esp. 29:8-20).

Chapter 13 is a prophecy against the prophets (*hannĕvî'îm*) of Israel. They are said to prophecy out of their own hearts without having seen anything (v 2-3: *lĕviltî rā'û*). They see empty or lying visions (v 7: *maḥăzēh-šāw' ḥăzîtem*; v 8: *ḥăzîtem kāzāv*; v 9: *haḥōzîm šāw'*). They prophecy (nif. *nb'*) to Jerusalem, seeing a vision (*haḥōzîm ḥăzôn*) of well-being when there is none (v 16). This clearly associates prophecy and prophets with visions. Exactly who these prophets are is not said, though one can assume they are regarded as being in a different class from Ezekiel. Why these prophets are condemned is also left vague. They are said to prophesy out of their own hearts or spirits and have not received a message from Yhwh; also they do not provide the support which Israel needs (vv 4-5, 10-16). The only specific charge is that they prophesy well-being when there is none (v 16).

4.1.15 Hosea

Hosea has traditionally been dated one of the earliest of the written prophets, along with Amos. Hosea himself is not designated a prophet, but there are both positive and negative references to prophets in the book. He engages in symbolic action by taking a "wife/woman of whoredom" and producing children with symbolic names (1-3). A rebuke against priest and prophet is found in 4:4-6. God has slain the prophets with the word of his mouth because of the sins of Israel (6:4-5). The prophets and the men of the spirit (*'îš hārûaḥ*) are mad (9:7-9). On the other hand, God spoke through prophets in olden days, apparently during the period in the wilderness, when he gave them visions (*ḥāzôn*) and spoke in parables through them (12:10-11 [Eng. 12:9-10). Verse 14 (Eng. v 13) suggests the reference is to Moses as a prophet.

4.1.16 Amos

Paul, S. M. *Amos* (1991).

Most of the book is a collection of prophecies in the name of Amos. There is some brief information in biographical form in 1:1 and 7:10-17. The claim is made that Amos was originally a "herdsman" (*nōqēd*) and collector of sycamore figs (1:1; 7:14). The significance of the verse has been variously assessed. Although it has often been taken to mean that he was a simple countryman, the discovery of a Ugaritic cultic official referred to as *nqd* has suggested to some that Amos held a similar position (3.3.3; opposed by Paul: 34-35). He has several visions which are interpreted by Yhwh (7:1-2; 8:1-3;

9:1). Several favorable statements are made about prophets. When God raised up prophets and Nazarites, the people made the Nazarites drink wine and told the prophets not to prophesy (2:11-12). Yhwh will do nothing without revealing it to his servants the prophets; God has spoken: who can but prophesy? (3:7-8).

The story in 7:10-17 is quite an important one. The Bethel priest Amaziah first sends a message to King Jeroboam (II) that Amos is conspiring against the king by saying (*'mr*) that he would be slain and Israel exiled. He then addresses Amos as a "seer" (*ḥōzeh*) but tells him to go back and prophesy (nif. *nb'*) in Judah for a living. Amos responds by one of the most enigmatic statements in the prophetic corpus: *lō'-nāvî' 'ānōkî wĕlō' ven nāvî' 'ānōkî* (v 14). Several hundredweight of scholarly discussions have arisen out of this one verse without any clear consensus of what it means (see the discussion in Paul: 244-47). Many have taken the position that Amos is denying that he is a *nāvî'*—that having the term *nāvî'* applied to him is repugnant. Others have seen the context as the key, with Amos explaining that he had not chosen the profession of *nāvî'* but that God had chosen him. According to this explanation, Amos does not deny the title *nāvî'* but denies that he had chosen the office as a profession. In any case, the verbal form *nb'* is used in reference to what he says (vv 12, 13, 15, 16), whether or not he was called a prophet as such. It is also interesting that he does not deny the title *ḥōzeh*. Whether this is because he has no objections to it or whether he equates it with *nāvî'* and is implicitly including it with his statement on *nāvî'* is not clear.

4.1.17 Jonah

Although often ignored, this book brings up a number of issues relating to prophecy. The figure of Jonah is an interesting example of a prophet in action. The basic story is well known, but the significant details are often overlooked. When the message comes to Jonah, he does not embrace it with enthusiasm but attempts to flee. In the end, he travels to Nineveh to deliver his prophecy as commanded. In this case, it is a specific prediction: Nineveh would be destroyed within forty days. The Ninevites heeded, and the king proclaimed a fast and repentance from their evil ways. God relented from the destruction of the city. Jonah himself was incensed at the conditional nature of God's message, which he had been to such trouble to proclaim.

This story provides several interesting points about prophecy: (1) the divine call was resisted by the prophet; (2) the prophet made a very specific prediction; and (3) the prophecy itself was clearly contingent and was, therefore, not fulfilled when the people heeded the message and repented.

4.1.18 Micah

Carroll, R. P. "Night Without Vision: Micah and the Prophets," VTSup 49 (1992) 74-84.

Woude, A. S. van der. "Micah in Dispute with the Pseudo-Prophets," *VT* 19 (1969) 244-60.

Two points of interest arise from this book. One concerns a possible dialogue between Micah and opponents (2). The other is the diatribe against "the prophets" (3:5-8). Although there does seem to be a dialogue in chapter 2, it is not clear that the opponents are meant to be prophets (van der Woude's "pseudoprophets"); they could simply be those who refuse Micah's message (vv 6-7). In 3:5-8 the prophets, along with the seers (*ḥōzîm*) and diviners (*qōsĕmîm*), are condemned for leading the people astray. How they do this is not clear since the passage states that their efforts are ineffectual. However, the prophets are not alone in being criticized; much of the chapter is a denunciation of the rulers and leaders in Israel (vv 1-4, 9-12), including the priests (v 11). This seems to be a general condemnation of the leaders and authorities of society and includes the civil, community, judicial, and religious leaders, among whom the prophets are also numbered (cf. Carroll).

4.1.19 Zechariah

Zechariah is set in the period shortly after the return from exile and the building of the Second Temple in the late sixth century BCE. The book is conventionally divided either into two parts—First Zechariah (1-8) and Second Zechariah (9-14)—or into three parts—First Zechariah (1-8), Second Zechariah (9-11), and Third Zechariah (12-14). Much of Zechariah 1-8 is made up of visions. Indeed, when the "word of Yhwh" comes to Zechariah, it is in a vision (1:8: *rā'îtî*, "I saw"). Several of the visions relate to the leadership of the community, including Joshua the high priest, Zerubbabel the governor, and a sort of messianic figure known as the Branch.

Two passages are of particular interest. In chapter 7 certain men come to ask the priests of God's house and the prophets whether to continue to mourn in the fifth month as was their custom. The word of Yhwh comes to Zechariah to speak to the people and the priests. He says that Yhwh had proclaimed a message to earlier prophets (v 7) to practice justice and not to oppress the widow and orphan (v 9-10), but they refused to hear the instruction (*tôrāh*) and words which Yhwh sent by his spirit (*rûaḥ*) through the earlier prophets (vv 11-12). This suggests not only the existence of cultic prophets alongside the priests, but also that Zechariah was himself numbered among them.

In Second or Third Zechariah in 13:2-6 Yhwh says that he will make the prophets (*hannĕvî'îm*) and the unclean spirit pass away from the land. Then those who prophesy (nif. *nb'*) would be condemned by their own father and mother (v 3). The prophets would be ashamed of their visions (*ḥezyôn*), would cease to wear the hairy mantle characteristic of prophets (cf. 2 Kings 1:8), and would deny being prophets (Zech 13:4-6). This passage takes a rather negative view toward prophets.

4.1.20 Ezra-Nehemiah

Several prophets are mentioned in these books. In Ezra, the prophets Haggai and Zechariah announce the necessity for getting on with the building of the temple (Ezra 5:1-2); this information fits the two books named for these prophets. The other prophets are in the book of Nehemiah, in the context of the heated interchange between Nehemiah and his opponents. According to Nehemiah, Sanballat and his colleagues are claiming that Nehemiah is suborning prophets to proclaim him king (Neh 6:5-7). Nehemiah then goes on to claim that various prophets opposed him. He says that Shemaiah b. Delaiah was uttering a prophecy (*hannĕvûʾāh dibber*) against him, but that this prophecy was not from God, only the result of a bribe from Sanballat (vv 10-13). He also mentions Noadiah the prophetess (*hannĕvîʾāh*) and other unnamed prophets who, he alleges, were trying to intimidate him (v 14). Clearly, true and false prophecy here is in the eye—or ear—of the beholder.

4.1.21 Other Prophets in Kings and Chronicles

Asa is presented as the first cult reformer who cleared the land of certain idolatrous practices, though he did not remove the country cult places (1 Kings 15:9-24). Chronicles expands considerably on the account in 1 Kings (2 Chron 14-16). In an episode not in Kings, the spirit of God came upon Azariah b. Oded the prophet (2 Chron 15:1) and he spoke to Asa, promising that Yhwh would be with him as long as he obeyed (15:1-7). From this prophecy (*nĕvûʾāh*) Asa took courage and removed the abominations from Judah and restored God's altar (15:8-18); however, when he paid the king of Damascus to force the Israelite king Baasha to withdraw, Asa received a negative message. This came through Hanani the seer (*hārōʾeh*), who warned Asa that he had missed defeating the Arameans by making a treaty with them (16:7-10). Instead of repenting, however, Asa punished the seer. According to 1 Kings, Jehu b. Hanani (the son of Hanani the seer just discussed?) then prophesied against Baasha for following in the sins of Jeroboam (1 Kings 16:1-7, 12-13).

The books of Chronicles are important for the question of cult prophecy (4.6). 1 Chronicles 25 describes the Levitical families of Asaph, Heman, and Jeduthun and their organization in the temple service. Their main function is music, both playing instruments and singing. Yet this is referred to as prophesying (vv 1-3, 5-6). Heman himself is mentioned as the seer of the king (v

5: *ḥōzēh hammelek*). 2 Chronicles 20:14-17 relates that the spirit of Yhwh came upon Jahaziel b. Zechariah of the sons of Asaph, who then speaks what looks to be a prophecy to Jehoshaphat, urging him to fight against the Moabites and Ammonites.

Two other passages are of interest. In one episode, Pekah of Israel defeated Ahaz of Judah and took many Jews captive. According to Chronicles (absent from Kings), a prophet of Yhwh named Obed met the soldiers of Samaria and told them they should allow the captives to return home; Judah was defeated only because of sins against Yhwh (2 Chron 28:9-11). 1 Chronicles 24:19-22 relates how Joash refused to heed the words of Zechariah b. Jehoiada but had him murdered—despite Jehoiada's service to the king. In summarizing the fall of the Northern Kingdom, 2 Kings relates that Yhwh warned both Israel and Judah "by the hand of every prophet, every seer" to turn back from their wickedness (17:13).

4.2 THE PROPHET IN THE OLD TESTAMENT TEXT

No other religious specialist has such an abundance of material in the OT as the prophet. Prophets and their alleged pronouncements were clearly important to the OT tradents. Within this body of traditions is a variety of views, however, some of them positive, some negative, and some rather ambivalent. Some prophets are clearly considered "true prophets," while others are "false prophets." Few of the false prophets are treated individually (an exception is Hananiah in Jer 28), and the condemnations of them are usually given in vague and anonymous terms: "they" (whoever they are) lead the people astray (whatever this means), fail to condemn them for their sins, and are only interested in enriching themselves (how?).

Within the text are many figures identified in one way or another as prophets. Many times the terminology does the labeling: *nāvî'*, "prophet," or *ḥōzeh*, "seer," are the most frequent terms. Yet terminology itself is not the only criterion. Many prophetic figures are singled out by their social functions and activities. Prophetic terminology is also usually associated with the person in question, but it only confirms what the text makes clear through other means. One does not have to be called a *nāvî'* to be identified as a prophet. For example, the term "man of God" is used of individuals who act like those elsewhere labeled prophets; in some cases, one version has "prophet" and another "man of God" (e.g., the "alternative story" of Jeroboam [4.1.4]). How can this difference in terminology be explained? There may be a historical explanation, for example, that some terms were favored by some groups or in certain historical periods. Nevertheless, in the text as it now stands, there is clearly an overlap in usage, and the identification of a prophet depends on certain particular characteristics rather than just the terms used in the text.

The individuals recognized as prophets in the text show a wide diversity of activity and characteristics. The one feature common to all the prophets is speaking in the name of a god, usually Yhwh, and claiming to pass on a revelation from that god. Samuel is called a priest and a seer (*rō'eh*), as well as a *nāvî'*. He is consulted about a range of issues, from lost objects to whether Israel should have a king. Samuel is also associated with, and at times leader of, a group of prophets, though the activities of this group are left rather unspecific. Elijah and Elisha denounce, overthrow, and appoint kings. They perform various miracles, including commanding a drought, calling fire from heaven, enlisting the aid of wild animals, multiplying foodstuffs, finding lost objects, healing body and land, and perhaps even raising the dead. These miracles are exceeded by those of Isaiah, however, who causes the death of 180,000 Assyrian soldiers and also performs the sign of moving the sun back ten degrees in the heavens.

For other prophets, we have no stories of miracles, but sometimes their accomplishments in the spirit are just as great. Ezekiel had a vision of the divine throne and journeyed in spirit from Babylonia to Jerusalem. Certain prophets engage in symbolic action, some of a grotesque sort. Jeremiah wears a yoke round his neck to symbolize the yoke of the Babylonians. Isaiah goes around naked for three years and also performs sexual acts with an unknown prophetess. Ezekiel lies on one side for 390 days, then on the other for 40. For many prophets, though, we have nothing but words. About who they were or what they did (besides talk or write, presumably) we are left in ignorance: Micah, Obadiah, Joel, Habakkuk, Malachi, Nahum, Zephaniah.

Divine revelation is a sine qua non of prophecy. How this comes about varies considerably. Many times, we are only informed that "the word of Yhwh came" to so-and-so. Occasionally, though, we get a glimpse into the diverse nature of prophetic revelations. The word most often associated with these revelations is "vision." Reference is often made to the "spirit of Yhwh" or "the hand of Yhwh." Deuteronomy 13 makes no distinction between prophet and "dreamer of dreams," indicating the different ways in which Yhwh might communicate. This is confirmed by 1 Samuel 28:6, in which Yhwh is said to send a message by Urim and Thummim, by prophet, or by dreams. It should also be noted that in many cases the divine message is the consequence of inquiry on the part of the prophet, either on his own behalf or because he has been consulted by others. This common characteristic of biblical prophecy (often ignored or denied by modern scholars) is also an important feature of divination.

"False prophets" are usually presented as an undifferentiated mass or a collection of ciphers. They are simply "the prophets," or they are the mass of four hundred fifty prophets of Baal (1 Kings 18) or the four hundred prophets in Ahab's court. Only for a couple are we given names and some individual characteristics. One of them is Zedekiah b. Chenaanah, who prophesies to

Ahab that he should go up against the Arameans at Rammoth-gilead (1 Kings 22:11-25). Zedekiah engages in symbolic action, using a pair of iron horns to signify how Ahab will "gore" the Arameans. When Micaiah b. Imlah takes the opposite point of view, Zedekiah strikes him on the cheek and asks how Yhwh's spirit could have passed from himself to Micaiah. Similarly, Hananiah breaks the yoke (symbolic of Nebuchadnezzar's yoke) off Jeremiah's neck and predicts that even the captives of the year 597 will soon be returning (Jer 28).

Apart from being wrong (supposedly) in the specific instances, nothing singles out the false prophets from the true. Most of the false prophets are Yahwists. The prophecies of Zedekiah and Hananiah are similar to those of Isaiah at the time of Sennacherib's invasion. There is nothing objectionable about their behavior (contrast Isaiah's). The text itself shows no consistent criteria about how to recognize false prophets. Two main ones are adumbrated in Deuteronomy 13 and 18: Does the prophecy of the prophet come to pass; and does the prophet urge his hearers to go after other gods? Apart from the prophets of Baal, no specified false prophets fit the second category. (Rare are passages, such as Jeremiah 23:13, that refer to prophecy in the name of Baal.) On the other hand, the first criterion is clearly not fulfilled by many OT prophecies; indeed, the book of Jonah and such passages as Jeremiah 18:1-10 and Ezekiel 33:1-20 suggest that prophecy is contingent upon the reaction of the hearers. Jeremiah makes "standing in the council of Yhwh" a significant criterion (Jer 23:16-18, 21-22). This is not very helpful, though, since we do not know who did this. We cannot assume that other prophets did not see themselves as called by God or standing in Yhwh's council.

The ambiguous view of prophecy is well illustrated by two examples. The first is that of Balaam. Overall he is a negative figure, but this is because he is asked to curse Israel and also advises Balak how to lead Israel astray, for which advice he is slain by the Israelites. Yet within the episode of Numbers 22-24, nothing labels Balaam as anything but a true prophet of Yhwh. When first asked to curse Israel, he consults God and refuses to go until allowed by God. When he is taken up to curse Israel, he again does only what God allows, which is to bless them. He is not called a *nāvī'*, but neither is he called anything else within the Pentateuch. The language of divination is used with regard to him, but it also used with regard to some of the prophets. The critical consideration is that the *image* and *activities* of Balaam are those of a prophet. Similarly, the "man of God" and the "old prophet" in 1 Kings 13 are both ambiguous figures. The man of God gives a sign from God and utters a prophecy which is ultimately fulfilled. Yet he disobeys his instructions and is slain as a result. The old prophet lies to the man of God, but he also receives a revelation from Yhwh and buries the man of God with due honors. The clear-cut distinction between true and false prophet implied in some passages has no place in these passages.

4.3 CROSS-CULTURAL PARALLELS

In addition to the examples discussed below, the Hittites provide some interesting parallels. These are discussed at 5.3.5.

4.3.1 West Semitic Prophecy

Cody, A. "The Phoenician Ecstatic in Wenamūn: A Professional Oracular Medium," *JEA* 65 (1979) 99-106.
Ross, J. F. "Prophecy in Hamath, Israel, and Mari," *HTR* 63 (1970) 1-28.

Apart from Israel, prophecy is attested in a couple of texts relating to the Syro-Phoenician area. In the Moabite stone, Mesha mentions that the Moabite god Chemosh "spoke" (*'mr*) to him, but the medium of the divine communication is not otherwise delineated (*TSSI* 1: #16.14; *KAI*: #181.14; *ANET*: 320-21). The two main inscriptions are the tale of Wenamun and the inscription of the north Syrian king Zakkur.

Zakkur was king of Hamath and Luath, according to a stele found near Aleppo (*TSSI* 2: #5; *KAI*: #202; *ANET*: 655). He claims that the god Baalshamayn made him king and then delivered him from the Aramean king Barhadad b. Hazael and his alliance. When besieged by Barhadad, Zakkur prayed to Baalshamayn who answered him through "seers" (A12: *ḥzyn*) and "messengers" (*'ddn*) who said to him, "Fear not (*'l tzḥl*), . . . I shall deliver you" (A13-14). The word *ḥzyn* seems to be cognate with the Hebrew *ḥōzeh*, "seer"; *'dd* is probably a cognate of Ugaritic *'d*, "send" and also "answer, speak" (Ross: 4-8), and may have some relation to the OT prophetic figures with names such as Iddo. Zakkur can say that the god spoke to him even though the actual messages came from prophetic figures.

According to the tale bearing Wenamun's name, he was an Egyptian official on a journey to the Phoenician area. From the date given in the text, the event is usually dated to approximately 1100 BCE. During an offering, an individual was possessed by the god Amon. Amon was an Egyptian god whose image was being carried by Wenamun rather than a West Semitic god; however, the individual possessed may be designated by a Semitic expression. In the Egyptian text, the person possessed by the god is called *'d̲d* '3. The first word is usually translated "youth," which is often its meaning in Egyptian. However, the second word is the word for "great, large" (cf. "Pharaoh" = Egyptian *pr* '3 "great house," originally referring to the palace), which creates problems of understanding. Cody has argued, however, that *'d̲d* is actually a Semitic borrowing, the same word as *'dd* in the Zakkur inscription. Thus, the individual possessed by the Egyptian god was actually a Phoenician prophetic figure, if his interpretation is correct. Unfortunately, nothing is said about any message given by the man whom the god possessed.

4.3.2 Egypt

Frankfurter, D. *Elijah in Upper Egypt* (1993).
Gardiner, A. H. *The Admonitions of an Egyptian Sage* (1909).
Hermann, S. "Prophetie in Israel und Ägypten: Recht und Grenze eines Vergleiches," VTSup 9 (1963) 47-65.
Kákosy, L. "Orakel," *LdÄ* 4 (1982) 600-6.
Lanczkowski, G. "Ägyptischer Prophetismus im Lichte des alttestamentlichen," *ZAW* 70 (1958) 31-38.
____ . *Altägyptischer Prophetismus* (1960).
Lichtheim, M. *Ancient Egyptian Literature* (1973-80).
Schlichting, R. "Prophetie," *LdÄ* 4 (1982) 1122-25.

The question of whether prophecy existed in Egypt is a controversial one, and much depends on how one wants to define prophecy. When we look at the social phenomenon, there are several reasons why prophecy as such seems to have been absent from Egypt:

1. The principle means of determining the future made use of techniques usually classified as divinatory (discussed at 5.3.2, though this evokes the issue of whether prophecy should be classified as a form of divination [5.5]).

2. No evidence of speaking under "inspiration" (in a trance, under the influence of the spirit, or the like) is reported. There is nothing comparable to the Mari prophets or to individuals like Elijah or Amos.

3. The speakers in the skeptical and other literature most similar to the OT prophets do not speak in the name of a deity.

Despite the lack of prophetic oracles as normally defined, what we do find in Egypt are some noteworthy parallels to the *prophetic writings* in the OT. Two works of particular interest are the *Admonitions of Ipuwer* and the *Prophecies of Neferty*. *Admonitions* describes the chaos that may result from the failure of the king to carry out his proper duties. The admonitions very much resemble the destruction of the country because of disobedience and divine abandonment found in the OT Prophets. *Neferty* seems to be a sort of *vaticinia ex eventu* (prophecy after the event) relating to the enthronement of Amenemhet I (c. 1975 BCE). Basic to Egyptian thinking was the concept of order or *maat*. Both of these writings draw on this traditional belief and a strong fear of its opposite, chaos—often associated with foreigners and foreign domination. This belief had early become a literary tradition, sometimes referred to as the *Chaostradition* (Frankfurter: 159-94). Even though there is no appeal to divine inspiration or a direct message from the gods, the actual moral admonitions and social and religious criticism look remarkably similar at times to what we find in the OT prophetic corpus.

Because the context of these writings is not that of a prophet delivering a prophecy, they are often dismissed as of little relevance for prophecy in Israel. This way of looking at the question misses much of the point, for some of the Egyptian writings have much in common with the contents of the OT prophetic books. What they do is to point up quite sharply the possible gap between the prophetic utterances of actual prophets and the long literary "oracles" of the written prophets in the OT. We must remember that a large part of these may have been created by significant editorial work or even composed initially as literary works, much as the oracles of Ipuwer and Neferty seem to have been created.

4.3.3 Old Babylonian Prophecy

Charpin, D. "L'Andurârum à Mari," *MARI* 6 (1990) 253-70.

Durand, J.-M. *Archives épistolaires de Mari I/1* (1988).

Ellis, M. deJong. "The Goddess Kititum Speaks to King Ibalpiel: Oracle Texts from Ishchali," *MARI* 5 (1987) 235-66.

Finkelstein, J. J. "Amiṣaduqa's Edict and the Babylonian 'Law Codes,'" *JCS* 15 (1961) 91-104.

Gordon, R. P. "From Mari to Moses: Prophecy at Mari and in Ancient Israel," *Of Prophets' Visions and the Wisdom of Sages* (1993) 63-79.

Huffmon, H. B. "Prophecy in the Mari Letters," *Biblical Archaeologist Reader* (1970) 3.199-224.

Malamat, A. *Mari and the Early Israelite Experience* (1989).

____ . "A New Prophetic Message from Aleppo and its Biblical Counterparts," *Understanding Poets and Prophets* (1993) 236-41.

Moran, W. L. "New Evidence from Mari on the History of Prophecy," *Biblica* 50 (1969) 15-56.

Noort, E. *Untersuchungen zum Gottesbescheid in Mari* (1977).

Orlinsky, H. M. "The Seer in Ancient Israel," *Oriens Antiquus* 4 (1965) 153-74.

____ . "The Seer-Priest and the Prophet in Ancient Israel," *Essays in Biblical Culture and Bible Translation* (1974) 39-65.

Pardee, D., and J. T. Glass. "Literary Sources for the History of Palestine and Syria: The Mari Archives," *BA* 47 (1984) 88-99.

Parker, S. B. "Official Attitudes toward Prophecy at Mari and in Israel," *VT* 43 (1993) 50-68.

Sasson, J. M. "An Apocalyptic Vision from Mari?: Speculations on *ARM* X:9," *MARI* 1 (1982) 151-67.

Weinfeld, M. "Ancient Near Eastern Patterns in Prophetic Literature," *VT* 27 (1977) 178-95.

Old Babylonian prophecy was, until recently, limited to the Mari texts. The only other prophetic texts from Mesopotamia came from Neo-Assyrian times (4.3.4), after the Assyrians had long been in contact with Syria and the West. This had led to a widespread conclusion in scholarship that prophecy as a mode of divine revelation arose in the West and was only imported into Mesopotamia. Now the prophetic texts from Ishchali, a site in the Diyala valley east of Baghdad, make this conclusion less certain (Ellis). One could argue from this and general anthropological considerations that prophecy was likely to have been a native tradition and not just a foreign import. In any case, the question still seems to be open.

Ever since their discovery in the 1930s, the Mari texts have been of great interest to OT scholars, not least because they preserve one of the few examples of prophecy in the ancient Near East outside Israel. So far, twenty-nine prophetic texts (in the form of letters) have been published (Durand: 421-52 [##195-223]; *ANET*: 623-25), plus another four in the form of letters exchanged with the gods (Durand: 413-19 [##191-94]). Because several of the texts have more than one prophecy, there are close to forty individual prophecies. The oracles were given by a variety of figures, some of them professional (e.g., a priest) but many of them lay people. At least half are women. Two main terms are used in reference to the prophetic figures: *āpilum* (feminine *āpiltum*), "speaker, respondent," and *muḫḫûm* (feminine *muḫḫūtum*), "ecstatic." Apparently, the *muḫḫûm* received messages spontaneously, while the *āpilum* was generally called on to confirm or expand on information received from extispicy, divination from interpreting the inner organs of a sacrificial animal (Durand: 386); however, some of the *āpilum* prophecies seem to have been spontaneous. Several are given by an *assinnum* or a *qammatum*. The *assinnum* was a cultic personage of some sort, though his exact function is still debated. The *qammatum* seems to have been a female cultic figure, though the origin of the term and its significance are still a moot point (cf. Durand: 396, who points out that the older reading *qabbātum* is incorrect). Of particular interest is one text in which the term *nabî* occurs (see below). There is evidence that more than one type of prophet might perform in connection with a particular sanctuary (Malamat 1989: 87).

A number of the characteristics of Mari prophecy are of interest: (1) the messages available to us were not delivered directly to the king but were brought by the prophets to high officials of the court (including the queen, who acted on the king's behalf) for transmission to the king; (2) the king was interested in all omens, bad as well as good; (3) the officials would often forward something from the prophets (usually a lock of hair and a piece of their garment) for testing authenticity (by means of divinatory techniques); this meant that the problem of determining "false prophecy" did not arise in the same way as in the OT texts; (4) many of the prophets received support from the court, suggesting they functioned as "central prophets" (*contra* *Wilson: 100-2); this includes many of the *muḫḫûm*, though there were also lay prophets, the majority of them women; and (5) oracles could arise spontaneously or could be the result of formal inquiry, no distinction being made between them.

The mode of receiving messages varied. Most of the prophets received their messages in the temple where they then stood up and delivered them (characterized by the verb *tebû*, "to arise"). Dreaming was also a recognized and frequent mode of revelation, though only among the lay prophets and not among the temple ones. Two features mark off the *āpilum* from the *muḫḫûm*: First, the *āpilum* often reported his revelation in writing whereas the *muḫḫûm* apparently never did (Durand: 390). A second feature is that the prophecies of the *āpilum* were often (though not always) "instigated," like the diviner's inquiry in which a question was put to the deity, whereas the *muḫḫûm*'s messages always seem to have been spontaneous. Scholars generally interpret the mode of revelation as associated with a trance state and/or the result of ecstatic experiences. The messages themselves are coherent and intelligible. In one case, a woman (*qammatum* of Dagan), who apparently received a message while in a trance, was able to remember it and deliver it later in person to the king's official (A.1047 = Durand #197). The same seems to have been the case with a *muḫḫûm* from Terqa (A.4934 = Durand #221-bis).

The value of the Mari prophecies for understanding OT prophecy has long been debated. There are those who argue against Mari prophecy being prophecy in the OT sense (e.g., Noort: 124ff), but this is simply not borne out when all the published oracle texts are taken into account. As Malamat observes (1989: 83):

> In comparison, had the historiographic books of the Bible (Samuel, Kings and Chronicles) alone survived, we would be faced with a picture closely resembling that at Mari, in which Israelite prophecy, too, was oriented primarily toward the king and his politico-military enterprises.

Naturally, there are differences of emphasis between the Mari prophecies and those in the OT. Although most of the Mari prophetic messages are assurances to the king, there are exceptions. Several prophecies chide the king for failing to support a particular cult as he ought (A.1121 = *ANET*: 625; A.671 = Durand #214; M.8071 = Durand #217; M.14836 = Durand #218). Dagan complains through a *muḫḫûm* that he is not given pure water to drink (A.455 = Durand #215). In one case, a *muḫḫûm* was particularly strident about the building of a gate in Terqa (A.4934 = Durand #221-bis). Some warn the king to uphold his ethical duties: to protect the weak (A. 2925 = Huffmon: 204-5) and to declare a promised *andurārum* (debt amnesty [Finkelstein; Charpin]) when the king conquers a particular country (A.4260 = Durand #194). In one case, several prophetic figures predict the death of the king's daughter (A.3724 = Durand #222). The OT prophets are not alone in criticizing and admonishing the ruler and even bringing bad news.

Of particular interest is the text using the Northwest Semitic word for prophets, *nabûm* (A.2209 = Durand #216). When the writer of the letter arrived in Ašmad, he assembled the Hanean prophets (^{lú}*na-bi-i*^{meš} *ša ha-na-meš*), inquired about the welfare of the king, and was answered by favorable oracles. The word here is clearly a cognate of the common Hebrew word for prophet *nāvî'*. It should be remembered that many people of Mari apparently spoke a Northwest Semitic language (usually referred to as Amorite). Durand has speculated that *nabûm* is actually the original word lying behind *bārû*, "diviner," in some of the Mari texts (378). It should also be noted that in this case the prophecies are instigated rather than spontaneous; that is, the *nabûm* are acting in the same ways as the *āpilūm*.

Just as the Israelite king was told not to make alliances with certain nations (e.g., Isa 30:1-5; 31; Ezek 16-17; 23), so the Mari king was told not to make peace with Ešnunna or the Yaminites (A.1047 = Durand #197; A.925 + A.2050 = Durand #199). He is counselled not to worry about the superior numbers of the enemy or to think that he will prevail by his own strength; rather, it is the gods who will give victory and crush his adversaries (A.996 = Durand #207). In a scene comparable to 1 Kings 22:19-23, the gods themselves discuss a matter and take an oath (in this case, to protect Mari) (A.2233 = Durand #208; cf. Sasson). One strange incident made use of a prophetic symbolic act (A.3893 = Durand #206). A *muḫḫûm* of Dagan called for food. He was given a lamb, which he ate raw. He then assembled the elders of the city at the gate and gave a message in which the devouring of the lamb was evidently a sign of pestilence.

In sum, the Mari prophecies have much in common with prophetic reports and literature in the OT. The statement of Orlinsky that "it is divination, and not prophecy, that finds its parallels in the Mari and other social structures and documents in the Fertile Cresent" (1965: 170; 1974: 58) smacks more of his own predetermined view than a judgment based on evidence. It is certainly not borne out by the corpus of texts now available.

The oracle texts from Ishchali (Ellis 1987) are harder to discuss because there are only two, and much of one is broken off. The legible text (FLP 1674) is in the form of a letter from the goddess Kititum to Ibalpiel, king of Ešnunna, a contemporary of Hammurabi of Babylon and Zimri-Lim of Mari. This format leaves many intriguing questions: Was the prophecy spontaneous or instigated? Who received it? Was it received as an audition, a dream, a vision, or in some other way? The message is that Kititum opens the secrets of the gods to Ibalpiel and will strengthen his throne and reward his rule with peace, increased domains, and prosperity. This is all because the king has honored her by having the utterance of her name in his mouth. The content is thus similar to a number of the Mari prophecies. No demands are made on the king except to continue to listen to the goddess, however, because that is what he has been doing.

Ellis has particularly noted the literary character of this text. Although she accepts that the text is probably based on an actual report of a revelation, she believes that the scribe has clothed it in his own literary form. This has implications for the question of the *ipsissima verba* of the prophets: Even when a prophecy is based on actual speech from a human intermediary, how certain can we be that we have the original words? The same question has come up with regard to the Mari prophecies as well. According to Durand, when the prophecies of the *āpilum* were written down, they were couched in a more sophisticated form of language than would be expected from the original utterances under inspiration (390-92).

4.3.4 Neo-Assyrian Prophecy

Ellis, M. deJong. "Observations on Mesopotamian Oracles and Prophetic Texts: Literary and Historiographic Considerations," *JCS* 41 (1989) 127-86.

Livingstone, A. *Court Poetry and Literary Miscellanea* (1989).

Nissinen, M. "Die Relevanz der neuassyrischen Prophetie für die alttestamentliche Forschung," *Mesopotamica-Ugaritica-Biblica* (1993) 217-58.

Parpola, S., and K. Watanabe. *Neo-Assyrian Treaties and Loyalty Oaths* (1988).

Weippert, M. "Assyrische Prophetien der Zeit Asarhaddons und Assurbanipals," *Assyrian Royal Inscriptions* (1981) 71-115.

The Neo-Assyrian texts have much in common with the Mari texts, even though they are a thousand years later. The Neo-Assyrian and the Mari prophecies together form the main corpus of prophetic texts from Mesopotamia. Although the former have been known longer, they have been difficult of access. Until the forthcoming publication by S. Parpola (from which the NAP [Neo-Assyrian Prophecies] numbers come), one must be content with studies giving some extracts from them (Weippert; Nissinen; Livingstone: 33-35 [#13]). There are twenty-eight oracles, presented as direct divine communications, usually to a named individual. They require no technical interpretation in the way that many divinatory methods would. Despite some objections to designating these prophecies, not to do so seems to apply an artificial definition; on the contrary, the label "prophecy" is quite appropriate (Nissinen: 221-22). Of the dozen prophetic figures named in the tablets, more than half seem to be women. The main deity from whom the messages originate is Ishtar of Arbela (which may partially explain the dominance of prophetesses).

The prophecies are all directed either to Esarhaddon or Ashurbanipal. Like Yhwh in Isaiah 45:5, the deity speaking identifies himself or herself. Most of them are messages of assurance, often making use of the "Fear not!" formula so well known from the OT (e.g., Gen 15:1). In some cases, the god or goddess responds to the king's prayer to deliver him from enemies (cf. NAP 3.3:10-25 [Nissinen: 243] with Psalm 18). Reference is often made to the choice of the king for rulership and promises given about the long continuation of his rule and his descendants after him. This compares well with the oracle to David in 2 Samuel 7:4-17, Psalm 89, and other dynastic promises to Israelite kings. The deity speaks as both a nurturing mother and a warrior fighting on behalf of the king (NAP 7:20-25; NAP 3.3:10-25); similar language is known from Israelite tradition (cf. Isa 66:12-13; Num 11:12; Hos 11:1, 3-4). Some of the Neo-Assyrian prophecies also make use of the language of treaty and covenant, such as *adê*, "treaty," *māmītu*, "oath," *mašû*, "forget," and *haṭû*, "sin" (Nissinen: 236-41), just as OT texts do (cf. Ps 89). The theological themes of divine choice and divine love are known from both sets of texts (cf. NAP 1.6; 1.8 [= *ANET*: 605] with Deut 4:37; 7:6-8; 10:15).

As with the Mari prophecies, the closest parallels are more often found in the Deuteronomistic History rather than the prophetic books; however, Second Isaiah presents a number of interesting similarities (Weippert: 108-11; Nissinen: 249). One of these is the self-proclamation oracle (e.g., *anāku Ištar ša Arbail*, "I am Ishtar of Arbela," compared with Isaiah 45:5: "I am Yhwh") which forms one of four different formal types among the oracles (Weippert: 76-81). As elsewhere, the themes of divine election and love occur in Second Isaiah as well (Isa 41:8-20; 43:1-4; 44:1-5; 45:1-7; 48:12-15). The "royal salvation oracle" or "royal oracle" (similar to the priestly salvation oracle of the OT) is a major type among the Neo-Assyrian prophecies (Weippert: 90-92) and is also found in Second Isaiah (Isa 41:8-13, 14-16; 43:1-4; cf. Weippert: 104-11).

Considering that the Neo-Assyrian prophecies were collected and preserved in the palace archive, it is hardly surprising that they are all favorable to and supportive of the king (cf. Nissinen: 251-52). This is also true of many OT prophecies (e.g., 2 Sam 7; 2 Kings 19//Isa 37); nevertheless, it has been asserted that Israelite prophecy is unique in containing criticism of the king. Such a view does not stand up because it is clear that the prophecies preserved were not the only ones given. Esarhaddon, who was the subject of some of these prophecies, recognized that there were also those who prophesied *against* him in his great succession treaty (Parpola/Watanabe: 33 [#6, lines 108-22]):

> If you hear any evil, improper, ugly word which is not seemly nor good to Assurbanipal, . . . from the mouth of a prophet (LÚ*ra-gi-me*), an ecstatic (LÚ*maḫ-ḫe-e̱*), an inquirer of oracles (DUMU*šá-'i-li a-mat* DINGIR), or from the mouth of any human being at all, you shall not conceal it but come and report it to Assurbanipal, the great crown prince designate, son of Esarhaddon, king of Assyria.

4.3.5 Akkadian Literary Prophecy

Beaulieu, P.-A. "The Historical Background of the Uruk Prophecy," *The Tablet and the Scroll* (1993) 41-52.

Biggs, R. D. "More Babylonian 'Prophecies,'" *Iraq* 29 (1967) 117-32.
____ . "The Babylonian Prophecies and the Astrological Texts," *JCS* (1985) 86-90.
____ . "Babylonian Prophecies, Astrology, and a New Source for 'Prophecy Text B,'" *Language, Literature, and History* (1987) 1-14.
Borger, R. "Gott Marduk und Gott-König Šulgi als Propheten: Zwei prophetische Texte," *BO* 28 (1971) 3-24.
Ellis, M. deJong. "Observations on Mesopotamian Oracles and Prophetic Texts: Literary and Historiographic Considerations," *JCS* 41 (1989) 127-86.
Goldstein, J. A. "The Historical Setting of the Uruk Prophecy," *JNES* 47 (1988) 43-46.
Grayson, A. K. *Babylonian Historical-Literary Texts* (1975).
Grayson, A. K., and W. G. Lambert, "Akkadian Prophecies," *JCS* 18 (1964) 7-30.
Hallo, W. W. "Akkadian Apocalypses," *IEJ* 16 (1966) 231-42.
Hunger, H., and S. A. Kaufman. "A New Akkadian Prophecy Text," *JAOS* 95 (1975) 371-75.
Lambert, W. G. *The Background of Jewish Apocalyptic* (1978).
Ringgren, H. "Akkadian Apocalypses," *Apocalypticism in the Mediterranean World and the Near East* (1983) 279-86.

A number of literary prophecies are known from various periods in Akkadian literature. These include the Šulgi and Marduk prophecies (Borger), the Dynastic Prophecy (Grayson 1975: 24-37), and the Uruk Prophecy (Hunger/Kaufman). The Akkadian prophecies originally labeled A-D (Grayson/Lambert) have been reduced mainly to Prophecy A; Prophecies C and D are now known to be parts of the Šulgi and Marduk prophecies respectively (Borger). Prophecy B is more problematic; it is not a prophecy in the opinion of some, but Biggs—though recognizing its difference from the others—is not yet ready to exclude it (Biggs 1967, 1983). It has been argued that some of the literary prophecies are actually *vaticinia ex eventu*—descriptions of historical events as if they were prophecies in advance. This assumption has allowed scholars to date the various texts to some extent.

The Marduk and Šulgi prophecies seem to relate to the reign of Nebuchadnezzar I in the twelfth century BCE (Borger). The Dynastic Prophecy clearly describes the rise of the neo-Babylonian dynasty, Persian rule, and the coming of the Greeks; it was probably composed in the Seleucid period. The Uruk prophecy has been variously assessed. The reigns of the eleven kings of Babylon described by it may end with Amel-Marduk (Hunger/Kaufman; Beaulieu), Nebuchadnezzar II (Lambert: 10-11), or the son of Merodach-Baladan II (Goldstein), though it may have been composed by a Seleucid scribe who saw parallels between Nebuchadnezzar and Antiochus I (Beaulieu). Hallo has argued that Prophecy A must be related to kings of the Second Isin dynasty (twelfth-eleventh centuries BCE), but this has been rejected by Lambert, who puts it tentatively in the early twelfth century (Lambert: 10).

The Akkadian literary prophecies generally take the format of describing the reigns of a succession of unnamed kings, usually in terms of good or bad—whether good things happen to the country and people or whether they seem to be under a curse. Sometimes, but not always, the length of reign of the king is given. They usually end with the reign of an ideal monarch, who will restore the nation's prestige, right all wrongs, and bring great prosperity. Biggs has demonstrated that these texts have much in common with omen literature, especially the astrological omens (1967; 1985; 1987). They differ in overall structure from most of the OT prophetic literature. On the other hand, they are strikingly parallel with some of the later Jewish apocalypses. The *ex eventu* prophecies remind one very much of such passages as Daniel 11 and the" Animal Apocalypse" (1 Enoch 85-90). Indeed, it has been argued that these Near Eastern prophecies are a forerunner of Jewish apocalypticism (Lambert), and some even prefer the term "Akkadian apocalypses" in place of "Akkadian prophecies" (Hallo; Ringgren). However, this last distinction seems irrelevant if apocalypses are a subdivision of prophetic texts, as argued below (6.5).

Despite differences, these prophecies have characteristics in common with some OT prophetic passages. The description of present troubles to be followed by a promised idyllic future is a well-known motif (cf. the Šulgi prophecy with Isa 34-35; Jer 30-31). Several of the Akkadian prophecies look forward to the reign of an ideal king (Marduk, Šulgi, Uruk; cf. with the prophesied future Davidic king: Isa 9:5-6; Jer 23:5-6; 33:12-18; Ezek 34:23-24; 37:24-25). The listing of good and bad reigns side by side reminds one of the periods of suffering alternating with periods of prosperity in the book of Judges. It is clear that the activities of the Mesopotamian king have a great deal to do with what befalls the nation, a view well known to the Deuteronomist. The *Erra Epic*, which describes a time of divine destruction, ends with a prophecy of future prosperity for Babylon (Tablet V, lines 20-37).

Writers on prophecy, both OT scholars and Assyriologists, often make a distinction between "actual" prophecies, such as the Mari and neo-Assyrian prophecies, and the literary prophecies. Indeed, there is no reason to think the literary prophecies arose from the pronouncements of a seer or ecstatic figure. This has led Ellis to use the term "literary predictive texts" to distinguish these texts from genuine prophecies. The distinction is a useful one if appropriately applied. Unfortunately, the literary prophecies are often dissociated from OT prophecy precisely because they are literary. This ignores the fact that much OT prophetic literature may well be literary in origin rather than merely the recording of oral prophecies. It is here that the Akkadian literary prophecies are very relevant to a study of OT prophecy: they demonstrate that written prophecies can be *scribal* creations.

4.3.6 The Nuer

Beidelman, T. O. "Nuer Priests and Prophets," *The Translation of Culture: Essays to E. E. Evans-Pritchard* (1971) 375-415.
Evans-Pritchard, E. E. "The Nuer: Tribe and Clan," *Sudan Notes and Records* 18 (1935) 37-87.
____ . *Nuer Religion* (1956).
Johnson, D. H. *Nuer Prophets* (1994).

The Nuer are a Sudanese cattle-raising people in the upper Nile region. Beginning in the nineteenth century, a number of prophets have become famous. Evan-Pritchard's pioneering accounts, especially his 1956 study of Nuer religion, have dominated discussion, but more recent studies have brought a needed corrective into the debate. Although Evans-Pritchard downplayed the role of prophets in his later writings, it is now recognized that prophets or something similar have probably always functioned in Nuer society (Beidelman: 395-97). Evans-Pritchard tended to emphasize the political role of the prophets, which led to his minimizing their contribution to Nuer religious life and thought (Johnson: 327). The prophets fulfilled important functions within society, including mediating disputes, serving as peace brokers, healing, stopping epidemics, blessing and cursing, and organizing defense against and attack on enemies. Above all, they gave moral guidance and leadership. Contrary to the way they have often been portrayed (even in anthropological studies), the prophets were not primarily "crisis leaders." Even though they responded to the challenges of change and even crisis, they were created by the internal conditions of their own society and not by the threats of war or other external crises:

> The real test of the prophets' appeal and durability came, not in the momentary hope they may have offered during a "crisis," but in their ability to enunciate a coherent set of ideas which helped the members of contemporary Nuer society comprehend their own time and situation, but which ultimately was not restricted to any one period or condition (Johnson: 123-24, 163, 326-28).

The most famous prophet was Ngundeng (1830s-1906). Prophets have arisen since, even into the present time where one called Wut Nyang has played a prominent role in the Sudanese civil war in the 1990s, but they have all modeled themselves on Ngundeng and his contemporaries and worked within the framework created by them. Ngundeng built a large mound which became a combined shrine and oracle. The remains of this mound were honored in 1989 as a symbol of Nuer independence. In his own time, Ngundeng was often doubted, criticized, and unsuccessful. Paradoxically, his greatest fame has come after his death (as is also true of other Nuer prophets) as his words and sayings continue to be remembered and (re)interpreted in the light of continuing events. He was better known after the end of the first civil war in 1972 than at the time of his death (Johnston: 337-38). His words were passed down as sayings and songs. During the century since his death, it is believed that the truth of his sayings has been demonstrated time and again with the claim that many of the prophecies disbelieved and not understood in his own lifetime became clear as they were later fulfilled. This has happened over and over through the turbulent history of Sudan in the twentieth century. Of course, most of these recollections of his words, and especially their interpretation, have been *post eventum*. Also, as singers have spoken under the inspiration of Ngundeng's prophecies and sayings, younger Nuer have often taken the words of the contemporary singer as those of Ngundeng himself (Johnson: 344). One particular story involved an Ethiopian soldier to whom Ngundeng gave aid in 1898. The current version of the story is that this Ethiopian was Haile Selassie, who helped broker the peace of 1972 (Johnson: 338), even though Haile Selassie was only six years old in 1898.

The words of the prophets are not remembered just as predictions, however. They have been recollected because they seem to speak to the current situation and to interpret it in a meaningful way. On the other hand, Ngundeng's life and teachings have not become submerged by the myth:

> In Ngundeng's lifetime his sayings and songs were applied, quite naturally, to the lives of his contemporaries. After his death his words were recalled whenever a new event brought them to mind. But the historical circumstances of Ngundeng's life have not been forgotten or completely subsumed within later events. The historical circumstances of most of Ngundeng's prophecies are remembered as contributing to what he said, and as elucidating his meaning. They are part of the prophecy itself, part of the remembered truth of Ngundeng's words. Ngundeng may have applied the Aiwel myth [about an archetypal ancestor] to himself, but he has not become a mythological figure in the same sense (Johnson: 351-52).

4.3.7 Handsome Lake, the Seneca Prophet

Grabbe, L. L. "The Social Setting of Early Jewish Apocalypticism," *JSP* 4 (1989) 27-47.

Parker, A. C. *The Code of Handsome Lake, the Seneca Prophet* (1913).

Tooker, E. "On the New Religion of Handsome Lake," *Anthropological Quarterly* 41 (1968) 187-200.

Wallace, A. F. C. "Halliday Jackson's Journal to the Seneca Indians, 1798-1800," *Pennsylvania History* 19 (1952) 117-47, 325-49.

____ . *The Death and Rebirth of the Seneca* (1969).
Wilson, B. R. *Magic and Millennium* (1973) 387-97.

Handsome Lake was the prophet among the Seneca Indians of the American eastern seaboard who founded a new religion (called *Gai'wiio'*, "good word") about 1800. His religion is useful for study because of the quality of the sources for it. We have the witness of Halliday Jackson, a contemporary who knew the community and Handsome Lake's work in it and wrote his observations in a diary (Wallace 1952). The Gai'wiio' "bible" also gives details of Handsome Lake's visions from which many of the teachings of the movement derived. Although the code was added to and systematized and preserved by oral tradition, much of it still goes back to Handsome Lake's own time (Wallace has attempted to reconstruct the original vision from the various reports [1969: 242-48].) His message was revealed to him by means of a series of visions, the first of which came when he was thought to have died from an illness. In the initial vision, he was taken on a heavenly journey by three men who continually explained what he was seeing and experiencing (including a meeting with Jesus); part of his experience was being given the particular message which he was later to teach.

The prophetic persona of Handsome Lake has many parallels with those of the OT prophets. He had a divine call to preach to his people at a time of crisis in the community. His message was not necessarily a popular one but called for repentance and a change of life on the part of hearers. Several of his messages were received in visions, at least one of which seems to fit the characteristics of an apocalypse (Grabbe). His message was a moral one and helped the people adjust to the new social and economic changes in the community, especially the change from a hunter-gatherer society to an agrarian one (Tooker). The values he espoused were those necessary for the restraint and control of a society based on the plow, and those he opposed were the characteristics of independence and individualism important to the old way of life. The strong moral element in no way precluded eschatology and apocalyptic predictions about the end of the world.

4.3.8 The Prophet Smohalla among the Washani Indians

Mooney, J. *The Ghost-Dance Religion and the Sioux Outbreak of 1890* (1896).
Trafzer, C. E., and M. A. Beach, "Smohalla, the Washani, and Religion as a Factor in Northwestern Indian History," *American Indian Quarterly* 9 (1985) 309-24.

Smohalla arose as a prophet among an Indian tribe of the Pacific Northwest in the mid-nineteenth century, a time when there was considerable conflict with the white authorities over the Indian lands. A concerted effort was being made to move the Indian tribes to particular areas away from their ancestral home and to induce them to become farmers and homesteaders. The religion founded by Smohalla may have been to some extent influenced by Christianity, but the fundamentals of it were those of the aboriginal religion in this area.

Although there is no evidence that Smohalla ever advocated violent resistance, he opposed the white plans as contrary to the divine will. According to him the various Indian groups were given particular areas by the creator Nami Piap. A "holy covenant" (!) existed between man and God. One of the conditions which this placed on the Indians was not to divide up the land, farm it, sell it, or otherwise disturb it after the customs of the whites. He preached against those of his fellow countrymen who had abandoned the traditions of the ancestors and had become farmers. Like Jeremiah (Jer 6:16), he called them back to the "old paths," to obedience to God's laws as laid down from the beginning. His message was to denounce law-breaking and violation of the divine covenant as he saw it.

4.4 THE PROBLEMS OF DEFINITION

Auld, A. G. "Prophets Through the Looking Glass: Between Writings and Moses," *JSOT* 27 (1983) 3-23.

____. "Prophets Through the Looking Glass: A Response to Robert Carroll and Hugh Williamson," *JSOT* 27 (1983) 41-44.

____. "Prophets and Prophecy in Jeremiah and Kings," *ZAW* 96 (1984) 66-82.

____. "Prophecy in Books: A Rejoinder," *JSOT* 48 (1990) 31-32.

Barstad, H. M. "No Prophets? Recent Developments in Biblical Prophetic Research and Ancient Near Eastern Prophecy," *JSOT* 57 (1993) 39-60.

Carroll, R. P. "Poets Not Prophets: A Response to 'Prophets Through the Looking-Glass,'" *JSOT* 27 (1983) 25-31.

____. "Prophecy and Society," *The World of Ancient Israel* (1989) 203-25.

____. "Whose Prophet? Whose History? Whose Social Reality? Troubling the Interpretative Community Again: Notes Towards a Response to T. W. Overholt's Critique," *JSOT* 48 (1990) 33-49.

Fohrer, G. *History of Israelite Religion* (1972).

Gray, R. *Prophetic Figures in Late Second Temple Jewish Palestine* (1993).

Hanson, P. D. *The Dawn of Apocalyptic* (1973).

Jepsen, A. *Nabi* (1934).

Knight, D. A., ed. *Julius Wellhausen and His* Prolegomena *to the History of Israel* (1983).

Orlinsky, H. M. "The Seer in Ancient Israel," *Oriens Antiquus* 4 (1965) 153-74.

____. "The Seer-Priest and the Prophet in Ancient Israel," *Essays in Biblical Culture and Bible Translation* (1974) 39-65.

Overholt, T. W. "Prophecy in History: The Social Reality of Intermediation," *JSOT* 48 (1990) 3-29.

____ . "'It Is Difficult to Read,'" *JSOT* 48 (1990) 51-54.
Weber, M. *Ancient Judaism* (1952).
Wellhausen, J. *Prolegomena to the History of Israel* (1885).
Williamson, H.G.M. "A Response to A. G. Auld," *JSOT* 27 (1983) 33-39.

4.4.1 Clearing the Scholarly Thicket

A vexing question arises immediately in any attempt to study prophecy: What is it? We use the term "prophet" in everyday usage primarily to mean someone who is able to predict the future. This image has certainly been influenced by the biblical prophets. The English word "prophet" comes from the Greek *prophētēs*, meaning "interpreter (of the divine will), predictor of the future." Greek *prophētēs* was the usual LXX translation of the Hebrew *nāvî'*, which is generally rendered into English as "prophet." This vision of the prophet as one who foretells the future was the dominant one until the arrival of critical scholarship. Wellhausen is the one most often credited with causing a major rethinking of the OT prophets.

According to Wellhausen, the prophets were the high point of Israelite religion (411-15, 472-74). They were the originators of ethical monotheism. Like his teacher H. Ewald and contemporaries such as B. Duhm, he emphasized the uniqueness of the Israelite prophets, especially the "classical prophets." Rather than being mere predictors of the future, they responded to the historical times with appropriate messages of social criticism (and, occasionally, encouragement). They spoke out in their contemporary situation with the authority of Yhwh. They were not *fore*tellers but *forth*tellers. As has often been pointed out, this description of the prophet was not entirely an empirical one gleaned from the pages of the Bible. It was heavily shaped by the attitudes and prejudices of nineteenth-century Christian Germany, especially by the view that "late Judaism" (Second Temple Judaism) was a degeneration of an earlier, superior form of worship into legalism (cf. *Blenkinsopp: 26-35; Knight).

Despite the later criticisms of Wellhausen, his concept of the prophet has been very influential even to the present day. A recent treatment of prophets in the Second Temple period refers to the OT "classical" prophets as "social, moral, and religious critics and reformers" (Gray: 6). A typical statement in a standard history of Israelite religion is as follows (Fohrer: 237):

> More important than the professional prophets—indeed, second only to Moses in importance for the history of Yahwism—is the small group comprising the great individual prophets, including Amos and Hosea, Isaiah and Micah, Zephaniah and Jeremiah, Ezekiel and in part Deutero-Isaiah. They did not exercise their prophetical ministry as members of a profession but on the basis of a special call that

> snatched them from their original profession. In them Israelite prophecy reached its summit; and although they are lumped with other forms under the common heading of "prophecy," there is more to distinguish them from than to identify them with these forms. They came forward among their people not as members of a guild or of a class, not as representatives of a tribe or of a clan, not as functionaries of a sanctuary or of the king, but as conscious representatives and messengers of their God.

A similar concept is summarized in the articles of Orlinsky on the seer or "seer-priest" in Israel (1965; 1974). Although Orlinsky's study is useful and recognizes the overlap between prophets and diviners, it follows older convention by drawing an ultimate distinction between "classical" prophets and "pre-classical" prophets or seers. He also comes to the rather startling conclusion that classical prophecy did not arise out of pre-classical: "Divination [including the activities of the 'seer-priest'] did not develop into [classical] prophecy, no more than polytheism developed into monotheism" (1965: 170; 1974: 58). His conclusions about prophecy and about monotheism are both very questionable, but only the first concerns us at this point (see 3.5 and 5.6 on polytheism and monotheism). It is worth taking the time to look at his position as an example of the sort of ideas that have been widespread.

Although Orlinsky devotes only a small amount space to classical prophecy, he waxes eloquent on it. His exact points of difference between "prophet" and "seer-priest" are not clearly differentiated but seem to include these (1965: 155-60; 1974: 43-46): first, the seer was often a member of a guild and learned his craft, whereas the prophet was individualistic and did not learn from a mentor. Also, people came to the seer for advice and paid him, whereas one "cannot imagine an Amos, or a Jeremiah, or a Deutero-Isaiah being approached thus and making a living in this manner" (1965: 156). The seer predicted the future and performed miracles, whereas the prophet opposed prediction and miracle working. The seer was a man of action, interpreting dreams, offering sacrifices, predicting events, whereas the prophet was a man of words. The activities of the Israelite seer sometime went beyond Israel (1965: 160):

> But one cannot imagine a canonical prophet in Israel being consulted by a foreign power, or going to another country to address a ruler, or to interfere with his rule, directly; or of a foreign ruler coming to Israel to consult one of the canonical prophets.

Orlinsky's analysis is flawed at a number of points, the main one being an image of the "classical prophet" that is essentially an ideological construct of liberal bias and largely uncontaminated by biblical data. For many of his statements, he provides no supporting evidence, and he ignores or is quick to dismiss any biblical passages which do not match the image. First of all, he does not define precisely what constitutes the classical prophets, though he does seem to include Second Isaiah, Micah, Amos, Hosea, and Jeremiah. Some statements seem to include all the prophetic books of the Hebrew canon, but Ezekiel is surprisingly nowhere mentioned—perhaps not surprisingly, since it confutes many of his supposed distinctions. Jonah is dismissed as unhistorical and subsequent to the canonical prophets (begging the question of what "canonical" means, since Jonah is clearly one of the so-called canonical prophets).

Second, Orlinsky ignores what we do *not* know about some of the prophets he includes in his magical circle of canonical prophets. For example, we have absolutely no data on Micah, apart from his supposed place of origin in Morasheth. Whether he opposed miracle working, was consulted (by a foreign power or otherwise), took pay, performed deeds, belonged to a guild, or studied under another prophet—these are all unknown.

Third, Orlinsky picks and chooses what data to consider. The book of Jonah refutes his statement about the canonical prophets and foreign powers. So, as noted, he dismisses it as unhistorical and "subsequent" to the canonical prophets. This assumes that the undefined canonical prophets are all historical and none of their contents "subsequent." Jonah's preaching in Nineveh is certainly as believable as Jeremiah's going to the Euphrates and burying a garment in the bank, returning, and then going back again after a few weeks (Jer 13:1-11); or of Isaiah causing the sun to go back ten steps on the sun dial.

Orlinsky has included the pre-classical prophets in the category of "seer," even those referred to as *nāvî'*. He questions whether the term *nāvî'* is not a later editorial addition to the text. This represents a rather selective application of skepticism, since the employment of the term for Amos or even Jeremiah could equally be questioned—as it has been (Auld 1984). He is also willing to take the text more or less at face value when considering the development of the seer, except where it contradicts his preconceived image, as with the use of the term *nāvî'* (1965: 171-72). Of course, his so-called canonical prophets are often men of action. Ezekiel lies on his side 430 days. Jeremiah travels to the Euphrates to bury a garment and wears a yoke on his shoulder. Isaiah has sex with an unidentified prophetess and goes about naked for three years. Whether being responsible for the slaughter of 180,000 Assyrian soldiers or causing the sun to go back in the heavens might be considered miracles is not discussed by Orlinsky. This slaughter and the displacement of the sun were both the doing of Yhwh, of course, but they were consequences of prophecies by the "classical prophet" Isaiah (2 Kings 19:32-35//Isa 37:33-36). Surely, it is not going to be suggested that Elisha's miracles were anything but the work of Yhwh and that the prophet had any power beyond prayer and Yhwh's spirit. The difference between his miracles and those of Isaiah is only one of magnitude—Isaiah's look the more spectacular.

The problem with trying to draw a sharp distinction between "classical" and earlier prophecy has been noted by Blenkinsopp at several points. For example, he states (*87):

> The distinction between "primitive" and "classical," for example, generally goes with a negative evaluation of ecstasy and is meant to prepare for the assertion that genuine prophetic authority rests on the word rather than the manifestations of the spirit. This way of emphasizing the "protestant" character of prophecy, however, fails to take adequate account of evidence for ecstatic experiences among prophets of the eighth to the sixth century and the frequency with which verbal communications are described as rooted in extraordinary personal experience; witness the remarkable opening line, "The words of Amos . . . which he saw *in vision*."

(On the question of ecstatic experiences, see 4.5.2 below.)

Thus, when the alleged characteristics of the biblical prophets are examined in detail, there are a good many problematic aspects to the picture described by Fohrer, Orlinsky, and others. If we take each of the supposed characteristics and examine it carefully, we find a poor match in some cases. A good one to consider is social criticism and reform. Nahum, for example, prophesied against Nineveh. His prophecies seem to fit his historical situation, but they do not give much in the way of social criticism or reform of Israelite society. Although no specific dates are given, there is no question that he is making a form of prediction: that Nineveh will fall. Except for the length of his oracles (assuming they are all his), he does not seem to differ from the prophets of Mari, who prophesied that Zimri-Lim's enemies would be destroyed (4.3.3).

Isaiah 1-35 is a good section to illustrate the problematic nature of making the prophets social reformers and critics. In this unit of thirty-five chapters, only a few verses concern what could be called social criticism: 3:14-15, on oppression of the poor (but the rest of chapter 3 talks only vaguely of wickedness); 5:7-9, accumulation of property, and 5:23, perverting justice for a bribe (the rest of chapter 5 talks generally of wickedness and more specifically of drunkenness); 10:1-2, oppressing the poor, widow, and orphan; 11:3-4, justice for the poor; 29:20-21, on perverting lawsuits through false witness; 33:15, on false dealings, bribes, slanders. Apart from a few other passages on such undesirable personal traits as drunkenness and gluttony (5:11-12; 28:1-4), the rest of the references in the book are to rather undefined acts of wickedness, rebellion, and disobedience. If Isaiah was a social critic or reformer, we would not know it from these chapters. Rather, if the contents of the prophecies are anything to go by, he comes across as a political critic. Many of the oracles are detailed descriptions of prophesied destruction to come on Israel and Judah or on a variety of foreign nations. Mixed in are a few prophecies of hope, with visions of an idealized society. The referent and even connotation of many sections are obscure. It is difficult to see how the image of the prophet as social reformer can very well be supported from the contents of Isaiah 1-35.

Some prophets do indeed have social criticism as a part of their message. Amos is often cited as an example of one speaking out against the evils within Israelite society. When looked at closely, though, his criticisms are not all that specific. They talk vaguely about "adding house to house" or about the "fat cows of Bashan" who sit around drinking and being pampered. Comments are made about how the poor are treated, but the exact crime being condemned is not always clear. He could easily be using stereotyped language without any actual examples in mind, much as many modern preachers do. Amos is useful to the modern preacher for the simple reason that he is *not* specific. He talks generally about the evils of society but really tells us little. His comments could be used against any society at any time in history. A good section of the prophecies in his name, such as the prophecies against the foreign nations in chapters 1-3, also have nothing to do with the conventional view of the classical prophet. Prophecies against various nations around Israel are a regular part of the preserved prophetic literature and very much parallel to prophecies known from Mari and the Neo-Assyrian period (4.3.3; 4.3.4). This is why those in Amos and other prophets have often been rejected as unoriginal—rousing the not unreasonable suspicion of unadulterated circular reasoning.

Amos well illustrates the generic quality of much prophetic literature. It abounds in tirades against such things as sin, disobedience, crime, immorality (especially of a sexual nature), and false worship. Most of these prophecies are unspecific and often unsubstantiated. For example, was the land really filled with bloody crimes as Ezekiel asserts (Ezek 7:23)? This sounds like the exaggerations of the tent-meeting revivalist down the ages. You can always make such charges and gain a sympathetic hearing because they are not perceived by most hearers as attacking them directly, and the alleged sins are sufficiently vague as not to require the preacher to provide solid evidence. If necessary, a suitably elaborated anecdote or two would do. No society, no matter how enlightened and paradisal, could be criticized in such a way and fail to find receptive ears.

Interestingly, if we are looking for social criticism and comment, the wisdom writings are filled with it. Proverbs has many sayings with regard to the appropriate behavior in society and before God. The book of Job comments from various points of view—Job's, the three friends', Elihu's, Yhwh's—on life and how to live it and human interaction in the sight of heaven.

Qohelet has much to say about how an individual lives and acts. If we want to find social comment and ideas about social reform, the Prophets are hardly the prime place to look in the OT corpus.

Another feature said to be characteristic of the biblical prophets is speaking to their own historical situation (Hanson 1973: 11-12). It is difficult to fathom how this is peculiar to OT prophets. The writer of Daniel was certainly speaking to his own historical situation—and from the depths of his soul—when he envisaged how God was going to intervene to save the people from their horrendous plight at the time of the Antiochene persecutions. The fact that the kingdom foreseen by Daniel differed in some ways from that of the ideal Davidic rule conceived of by Ezekiel (34:23-30), for example, is irrelevant. His vision was certainly no more fantastic or "other worldly" than that of Isaiah 2:2-4 or Micah 4:1-5, which has the lion lying down with the lamb and even eating straw like a ruminant. It is interesting to see that Wellhausen is unable to recognize the preposterous nature of this last vision, perhaps not surprisingly, since it contradicts his image of the prophet (416).

As for the question of prediction (foretelling), the biblical prophets have much of a predictive nature. Jeremiah is alleged to have predicted a return of the exiles in seventy years (Jer 25:11-12; 29:10), a prophecy reinterpreted to 490 years in Daniel 9:2, 24-27. How is Jeremiah a forthteller in this case, whereas Daniel is a mere foreteller? Jeremiah also predicted that Jerusalem would fall to the Babylonians. His difference from Hananiah, who predicted that the exiles would be returned and the Babylonian threat removed, is only one of degree. Jeremiah may not have given an exact year for the Babylonian conquest in the way that Hananiah spoke of the exiles' return within two years (28:1-4), but he was making a specific prediction. Also in Jeremiah's name are specific predictions about the fall of Babylon (Jer 50-51); in this case, he was as fallible as Hananiah in that Babylon was not sacked and made into a perpetual ruin without inhabitant, as he had predicted. In the same way, the prophecies of the major and minor prophets are filled with statements about the future. They may give "neither the day nor the hour," but they are examples of foretelling, pure and simple.

Of course, the old idea that OT prophets were only predictors of the future is wrong, but the Wellhausen concept does not stand up well, either, despite a long tradition in OT scholarship. The designation "social critics" applies only to some of the prophets and then only in a general way to a few of their prophecies, while "social reformer" seems hardly appropriate to any of them. So far, I have been concentrating on the so-called classical prophets for obvious reasons. When we widen the scope of our discussion to take account of the "pre-classical" prophets such as Samuel, Elijah, and Elisha, the situation becomes much more complicated. Finding a definition of prophet which is not artificial or masking a hidden agenda is quite difficult, and the Wellhausen characterization even less applicable.

In the end, we are thrown back on terminology. Our main information on prophets and prophecy is gained by reference to the terms used. The person is first recognized as a prophet because that is what the text calls the man or woman, or because the person is said to "prophesy." After this, we extrapolate from those labeled "prophet" to those whose activities are analogous to them. In the prophetic legends (mainly about the "pre-classical" prophets) emphasis is on the activities of the prophets, though this can sometimes take verbal form. The main characteristic of the written prophets is the oracle in God's name. Once this statement is made, however, a new problem immediately surfaces: Are the many prophecies in the prophetic books the product of prophets prophesying? Do we have actual prophecies or only literary compositions? This seems to be a central issue of dispute in the debate between Auld (1983; 1990), Carroll (1983; 1990), Overholt, and Williamson (1983). So, now, let us turn to this important question.

4.4.2 Prophets *vs.* Literary Prophecies

Paul, S. M. *Amos* (1991).
Wolff, H. W. *Joel and Amos* (1977).

The often-obscure poetic fulminations of lesser or greater length in the name of God (usually Yhwh) is the main characteristic of the prophetic books. Prophetic oracles make up a large portion of most of the prophetic books. It is not the content so much as the form which makes a prophecy. Prophecies cover a variety of subjects, but they frequently criticize Israel for alleged sins of various sorts, usually failure to follow Yhwh. Sometimes they criticize the king for particular political decisions or actions. Religious and political criticism makes up the bulk of most prophetic books.

The difficulty is to tell how and from whom these poetic units originated. Must they be prophecies spoken by a prophet while in the prophetic mode? Or could they be literary products of the scribe in his study or the priest in his chamber? Are prophets the only ones who could create verse compositions on the subjects of sin, obedience, justice, and appropriate worship? Could "wise men" have imitated genuine prophetic utterances as a vehicle to get across their religious and intellectual concerns? In other words, how can we know that the prophecies in a collection in some individual's name actually originated with that individual?

One could rightly point out that even if the exact words of the prophet are not before us, at least we have some of the theological and ethical themes on which the particular prophet in question discoursed. This may well be the case. Some of the main themes have already been noted above: the disobedience and continual backsliding of Israel, the dangers of going after other gods, the feeble-minded efforts of the king in his dealings with foreign powers, the fecklessness of the national and local leadership (kings, elders, priests, prophets, diviners), and so on. The trouble with suggesting that these themes help us to get at the message of the original prophets is that such topics are by no means confined to prophetic literature. All of these can be found in the Deuteronomic, wisdom, priestly, and other writings. The contents of the prophetic books are certainly not unique in the Bible.

This problem has been long recognized, in one sense, since traditio-historical criticism has attempted to separate "original" sayings from "secondary" accretions. The problem is that beyond some very broad boundaries (e.g., First, Second, and Third Isaiah), there has been little agreement on what is original and what is secondary. And in the prophetic books, the criteria for separating secondary from primary have often created an interpretative circle in which preconceived criteria about the classical prophet have been used to remove those passages which might give a different picture. For example, it has been customary to regard the prophecies against foreign nations as secondary. The main reason normally advanced seems to be that it was customary for cultic prophets to make such prophecies, and since the classical prophets were adamantly opposed to cultic prophecy, they could not have make such prophecies. The number of questions begged in this single sentence is myriad, eloquent testimony to why the traditio-historical methods have not solved the problem before us.

Additional evidence of the continuing crisis is exemplified in the recent commentary on Amos by Shalom Paul in comparison with the classic commentary by Hans Wolff in the same series. Whereas Wolff attempted to sort out the original core from the large secondary overlay in time-honored fashion, Paul has taken most of the book to be a product of the prophet himself. The subjective nature of the whole enterprise could hardly be more strikingly exemplified. Using the contents of the oracles in prophetic books to map the sociological construct of the Israelite prophet is not on. The anecdotes and stories about prophets are precarious sources for detailed historical information, but they are safer guides to uncovering social phenomena than the actual oracles.

If the position of some recent scholars such as Paul is correct and we have a much larger quantity of each prophet's own writings in his particular book, this paradoxically gives little support to those who want to emphasize the uniqueness of the "classical" prophets. In order to maintain this uniqueness, a good many of the prophecies in the final form of the text had to be demoted to clumsy editing or rewriting. If, on the other hand, most of a book is now credited to the prophet in question—Amos, for example—such passages as messages of salvation, oracles against foreign nations, detailed forecasts about the future, predictions of a new age with millennial conditions all become part of the message of the classical prophet. The differences between the pre-classical seer, the classical prophet, the post-exilic prophet, and the apocalyptic visionary dwindle at most to matters of degree rather than kind.

4.4.3 Definition of a Prophet: Summary

Huffmon, H. B. "Prophecy in the Ancient Near East," *IDBSup* (1976) 697-700.
____. "Ancient Near Eastern Prophecy," *ABD* (1992) 5.477-82

Many scholarly discussions of prophecy have, unfortunately, been circumscribed by prejudged concepts held over from the theological concerns and biases of nineteenth-century scholarship. The most important factor is the endeavor to give a privileged place to "classical" prophets and prophecy, fueled to a large extent by the hermeneutical needs of Protestant preaching. In order to do this, however, it has been necessary to ignore much of the data in the texts. The text uses a variety of terms for prophetic activity, and it is also clear that the mode of revelation varies as well (4.5). In many cases, these messages are the result of inquiry by the prophet on his own behalf or on behalf of others.

Finding a precise definition which does not immediately beg questions is difficult. One of the simplest is that of Huffmon: "an inspired speaker, under divine constraint or commission, who publicly announces an immediate revelation" (Huffmon 1976: 697). Yet even this is not without problems: What is meant by "inspired"? How is "divine constraint" defined? In what way does the revelation have to be public? His later definition is similar: "inspired speech at the initiative of a divine power, speech which is clear in itself and commonly directed to a third party" (1992: 5.477). Yet is prophetic speech always clear and not sometimes obscure? And does "speech" imply an oral message or can it be written? It seems to me that the common denominator to all the discussion above is that the prophet is a mediator who claims to receive messages direct from a divinity, by various means, and communicates these messages to recipients.

4.5 MODES OF REVELATION

4.5.1 The Terminology

Michaelsen, P. "Ecstasy and Possession in Ancient Israel: A Review of Some Recent Contributions," *SJOT* 2 (1989) 28-54.
Peterson, D. L. *The Roles of Israel's Prophets* (1981).

The terms used for the different prophetic figures and for the verbal forms about their activities imply certain things about how God revealed himself to the recipient. A number of the terms relate to sight: *ḥōzeh*, "seer," *ḥzh*, "see, have a vision," *ḥāzût*, "vision," *ḥāzôn*, "vision," *ḥizzāyôn*, "vision," *rō'eh*, "seer," *r'h*, "see," *mar'eh*, "vision." The most obvious reference is to receiving the revelation by sight. Where this is described, it is usually called a "vision," though there are also occasional references to dreams (e.g., Deut 13:2; Isa 29:7; Jer 23:28). But "vision" is also used in reference to revelations which are discussed as if they were only in the form of oral speech (2 Sam 7:17; Isa 1:1; 2:1; 21:2; Ezek 7:13; Ps 89:20). Indeed, it has been argued that visions in general lack a visual element, though this assertion is not at all convincing (on this and also the question of dreams in relation to visions, see 5.7).

The origin of *nāvî'*, "prophet," and *nb'* (nif., hitp.), "prophecy," is not agreed. Cognates elsewhere in Semitic are rare but do exist, such as *nābûm* in the Mari texts. There is no reason not to think of the root as a native Hebrew word, and any attempt to see it as a foreign borrowing has little to commend it. On the other hand, the word is not transparent and has no uses outside the prophetic context; therefore, to come up with a precise definition is difficult. The term "ecstatic behavior" has been seen as the basic connotation. This, however, is based on only a few passages, such as 1 Samuel 10:10-11, 19:20-24, and 1 Kings 18:26-29. Many other passages give no hint that a particular sort of behavior is implied beyond that associated with prophecy in general. The word seems to cover the entire variety of activity associated with prophecy including, but not limited to, ecstatic behavior (see the critical survey in Michaelsen: 40-49).

Many prophecies are presented in speech form, as if received through an audition. 1 Samuel 9:15 says explicitly that Yhwh "revealed to Samuel's ear" the matter of the choice of Saul as king. Thus, auditions were a part of the various media of revelation; nevertheless, as noted above, a prophecy such as 2 Samuel 7, which contains only speech, can still be described as a "vision" (v 17). Even if a prophecy is reported only in words, this does not necessarily mean that it was received as an audition.

4.5.2 The Question of Ecstatic Experiences and Trance States

André, G. "Ecstatic Prophesy [*sic*] in the Old Testament," *Religious Ecstasy* (1982) 187-200.

Bourguignon, E., ed. *Religion, Altered States of Consciousness, and Social Change* (1973).

Hoelscher, G. *Die Profeten* (1914).

Holm, N. G., ed. *Religious Ecstasy* (1982).

____. "Ecstasy Research in the 20th Century—An Introduction," *Religious Ecstasy* (1982) 7-26.

Michaelsen, P. "Ecstasy and Possession in Ancient Israel: A Review of Some Recent Contributions," *SJOT* 2 (1989) 28-54.
Parker, S. B. "Possession Trance and Prophecy in Pre-Exilic Israel," *VT* 28 (1978) 271-85.
Peterson, D. L. *The Roles of Israel's Prophets* (1981) 25-30.
Wilson, R. R. "Prophecy and Ecstacy: A Reexamination," *JBL* 98 (1979) 321-37.

Since the time of Hoelscher, it has been common to suppose that prophets had ecstatic experiences as the medium for their revelations; however, there has been a trend in several recent publications to deny trance states or ecstasy to the Israelite prophets. The main study has been that of Parker, though he has been followed by Petersen and, in part, by André. Yet André distinguishes "orgiastic, vigourous ecstasy" from the "calm" ecstasy of the Israelite prophets (200), which is actually quite different from Parker's views. Wilson has also contributed to the debate and is called on for support by Petersen, but Wilson more or less sidesteps the issue by concentrating on possession and stereotyped behavior and how they may be viewed in a particular society; however, he does not rule out ecstasy for Israelite prophets.

A number of issues are brought up by these studies and must be addressed if the question is to be answered; on the other hand, there are issues overlooked by them which also need consideration:

1. One of the main problems is the definition of the terms "ecstatic experience/ecstasy" and "trance." These all imply certain psychological states, though even psychologists seem to take quite divergent views about them, possibly because they are still only partially understood. Perhaps the simplest definition is, for research purposes, the "different states of consciousness that are characterised by unusual achievements, peculiar experiences and odd behaviour" (Holm: 7). The term "trance" is an almost exact synonym, this term being favored by anthropologists, whereas "ecstasy" is more often used in comparative religion (Holm: 8).

A major question is whether a distinction can be made between different sorts of trances. For example, Bourguignon distinguishes between "possession trance" and "trance" (7-8), a contrast of significance to Parker's discussion, but other specialists have not found this particular analysis useful (cf. Michaelsen: 44-45). In any case, she recognizes that possession is a particular interpretation of a situation in a particular culture. The same applies to André's distinction between "orgiastic ecstasy" and "calm ecstasy" noted above. This seems to be nothing more than a cultural manifestation of a trance rather than a different psychological state. Perhaps the only point of consensus is that trance states vary from light (in which the subject is partly aware of the surroundings and can exert some conscious will) to deep (with the subject unresponsive to the immediate environment), but beyond that is speculation and debate.

The important consideration is that the actions of the subject in a trance are heavily determined by the expectations and institutions of the society. A Siberian shaman exhibits certain behavior while in a trance which differs from that of a Haitian voodoo practitioner or a Holiness glossolalia speaker. There is no evidence that the trance state itself differs psychologically in the different individuals. Thus, the distinctions made between the types of trance among Israelite and other prophets, as asserted by André, seem nothing but willful attempts to bolster a partisan view of the "classical" Israelite prophets.

2. Even once a common view of trance from a psychological point of view is established, there still remains the difficulty of identifying an ecstatic experience in ancient and non-clinical texts. The texts of concern to us were neither written by psychologists nor even written in an idiom always comprehensible to us whose knowledge of the ancient culture is quite incomplete. Yet while granting this difficulty, one has to note that writers have often used rather arbitrary criteria when discussing the OT. No one, for example, seems to find it problematic to point to the prophets of Baal or non-Israelite prophets as experiencing a trance state. So why should one deny it for Elijah, who runs ahead of Ahab's chariot when the "hand of Yhwh" comes upon him? Similarly, the connection between music and ecstatic experiences among the sons of the prophets at the time of Saul is taken for granted (1 Sam 10:5-6, 10-13), but when a similar connection is made between Elisha's calling for a musical instrument and his giving a prophecy—a connection seemingly made by the passage itself—the association is strangely denied (e.g., Parker: 283, though he now accepts that this was arbitrary).

The experiences of shamans and others who journey in spirit to the world of spirits or to other places on earth or who see unusual sights (visions) occur in a trance state. In the OT, we have the description of Micaiah who "saw" the divine council (1 Kings 22:19-22), of Elisha who was able to see the heavenly armies (2 Kings 6:17) and who followed his servant in spirit as he went after Naaman (2 Kings 5:26). So why should we not recognize that all the prophets allegedly making such spirit journeys or seeing a vision are candidates for experiencing trances?

A prime example to demonstrate the question is Ezekiel (excluded by Parker from his study). He has visions, he makes journeys by spirit to Jerusalem, he becomes completely dumb and has other extraordinary reactions when the "hand of Yhwh" or the "spirit of Yhwh" is upon him. If Ezekiel does not have ecstatic experiences, then we have no criteria to judge that *anyone* of antiquity had such experiences. We must either accept that the language of the OT text implies such experiences for some Israelite prophets or abandon the task of trying to determine whether such experiences are at all described in any ancient text for any prophetic figures, whether the prophets at Mari, Wenamun, or the prophets of Baal.

3. A great variety of experiences of altered states of consciousness, as well as modes of receiving and passing on divine messages, is known from the cross-cultural study of prophecy. Ecstatic experiences are not just the property of prophets and may have no mediumistic function in some cases. For example, Parker has pointed out that the "possession trance" of the bands of prophets in 1 Samuel 10:5-7 and 19:20-24 is not mediumistic (271-75); however, he is wrong to conclude that this is always the case. The ecstatic experiences of shamans and others are usually mediumistic. Also, their experiences can be recalled and related to the audience after the shaman comes out of the trance. There is no reason why this could not also apply to Israelite prophets (*pace* Parker: 281).

4. Much of the time, we have no idea how the prophet received the divine message. All the text says is that "the word of Yhwh came to" so-and-so or the message is introduced by "thus says Yhwh/oracle of Yhwh" (*nĕ'um/nā'am Yhwh*). How the prophet obtained the message is not specified. It could have been by an audition or vision, or it could have been written by a scribe in his study. The message could have come through a trance state or it could have been a conscious composition. It could have come spontaneously or it could be the result of specific inquiry. In many cases, a variety of modes is possible, and we can only speculate on how it was received. Thus, it would be wrong to ascribe all prophetic oracles to ecstatic experiences; equally, we have no right to deny such experiences categorically to Israelite prophets.

Those who emphasize that a "true prophet speaks clearly and distinctly" (André: 194) ignore several facts: first, what we have is a literary report of the prophet's message, which could have been edited for readers (as the Pythian oracle's oral pronouncements were turned into hexameters by the priests); second, so-called false prophets often speak just as clearly and distinctly (e.g., Zechariah in 1 Kings 22 and Hananiah in Jer 28); third, the report of a prophet or shaman about the things seen or heard in a trance—whether given during the trance or after it—is usually intelligible; and, finally, many prophecies in the OT are obscure and even unintelligible.

The blatant double standard applied to come up with such a clear distinction between the "true" and the "false" prophets based on ecstatic experiences is demonstrated by the discussion about criticisms leveled at such prophets as Jeremiah. In some instances, they are referred to as "mad" (*mĕšuggā'*), as in Jeremiah 29:26 and Hosea 9:7. André rightly points out that we cannot use these passages to show that Jeremiah acted in a particular way, since they are given by hostile witnesses (194; also Parker: 282-83). Yet André himself then turns round and uses equally hostile passages such as Jeremiah 23:31 and Isaiah 28:7-13 to show that "false" prophets talk unintelligent nonsense (André: 194)!

In sum, we have to accept that some Israelite prophets, including some of the so-called classical prophets, seem to have had ecstatic experiences.

Equally, we have no evidence of such experiences for some of the so-called false prophets. The presence or absence of ecstatic experiences seems irrelevant to the overall question of prophecy, in Israel or outside it. The range of experience among Israelite prophets looks comparable to that known from other prophets of the ancient Near East and also modern cultures documented by anthropologists. From the point of view of modes of revelation, Israelite prophecy shows the same range and variety known all over the world, nor is there any distinction between "true" and "false" or between "classical" and other prophets.

4.6 CULTIC PROPHETS

Jeremias, J. *Kultprophetie und Gerichtsverkündigung in der späten Königszeit Israels* (1970).
Johnson, A. R. *The Cult Prophet in Israel* (1962).
Mowinckel, S. *Psalmenstudien: III. Kultprophetie und prophetische Psalmen* (1922) 4-29.
Reventlow, H. *Das Amt der Propheten bei Amos* (1962).
____. *Liturgie und prophetisches Ich bei Jeremia* (1963).
Würthwein, E. "Amos-Studien," *ZAW* 62 (1950) 10-52.

Although the OT text is not explicit about cultic prophets, Mowinckel already made a case for cultic prophecy in his *Psalmenstudien*. A. R. Johnson's work has become a standard treatment of the subject in English. Some of the arguments used in favor of postulating the existence of cult prophets are the following:

1. The story of Samuel associates him with a school or guild of prophets (1 Sam 19:18-24), yet he is also the chief cultic figure in Israel at the time.

2. Many of the attacks on "false" prophets imply that they work in groups and proclaim only peace and good for Israel. Under Ahab, not only the prophets of Baal (1 Kings 18-19) but also four hundred prophets of Yhwh are patronized by the court and seem to function as a group or guild (1 Kings 21).

3. The books of Chronicles indicate that the former cult prophets have been assimilated into the Levites and temple singers. 1 Chronicles 25:1-6 associates the sons of Asaph and others who sing and play with prophesying. 2 Kings 23:2 mentions that the priests and prophets went up with the king to the temple. That itself seems to hint at a cultic place for these particular prophets, but also the parallel passage in 2 Chronicles 34:30 has "Levites" instead of prophets. One of the sons of Asaph gives what seems to be a prophecy to Jehoshaphat (2 Chron 20:14-17).

4. The language used and the themes treated by some of the canonical prophets suggest that the writers functioned in the cult. For example, Psalms 60, 75, 82, and 110 look very much like prophetic utterances, even though a

part of the Psalter. The sons of Asaph who prophecy in 1 Chronicles 25 are evidently cult figures in that a number of psalms are ascribed to them (Ps 50, 73-83). The sons of Hanan b. Igdaliah, "the man of God," had a chamber in the temple (Jer 35:4).

Some of these arguments carry more weight than others. As discussed below (4.7), the idea of true and false prophecy begs a lot of questions. Still, the existence of cult prophets is now accepted throughout scholarship, and the real debate revolves around whether any of the written prophets arose from cult prophets. Perhaps the canonical prophets most often accepted as being cultic are Habakkuk and Nahum (cf. Jeremias, though he sees no evidence for Nahum). On the other hand, there has been a good deal of resistance to seeing some of the "classical" prophets as coming out of the cult. For example, the proposals that Amos and Jeremiah were cult prophets (Reventlow; Würthwein) have met with little sympathy. There are indeed problems with the argumentation used to prove this last point, yet one cannot help suspecting that ideology has had a heavy hand in bringing scholars to this conclusion. One cannot deny the close association that figures like Isaiah and Jeremiah had with the temple.

4.7 PROPHETIC CONFLICT: "TRUE" AND "FALSE" PROPHECY

Carroll, R. P. *From Chaos to Covenant* (1981).

____. "Night Without Vision: Micah and the Prophets," *The Scriptures and the Scrolls* (1992) 74-84.

Crenshaw, J. L. *Prophetic Conflict: Its Effect upon Israelite Religion* (1971).

DeVries, S. J. *Prophet Against Prophet* (1978).

Long, B. O. "Social Dimensions of Prophetic Conflict," *Semeia* 21 (1982) 31-43.

The idea that there were true and false prophets and prophecies is plain from the OT texts themselves. Although there is no special vocabulary for the two in Hebrew, adjectives such as "lying" prophet/prophecy may be used in the context; this process continues into the LXX, which already translates the Hebrew word *nāvî'*, "prophet," with the Greek *pseudoprophētēs*, "false prophet," in certain passages (e.g., Jer 6:13; 35[28]:1; Zech 13:2). This is an interpretation, but one which matches the intended sense of the context. The clear view in the OT text is that certain individuals were true prophets and others were false prophets, but this also represents a very tendentious point of view which has stamped its one-sided perspective on the tradition.

"Prophetic conflict" is the descriptive term used by anthropologists and others to characterize the clash between different prophetic individuals or groups. It is much better than "true" and "false" prophet. Considering the variety of prophets in the text (and in society), prophetic conflict was inevitable. This does not impugn the sincerity of individuals on one side or prove the presence of God on the other. Jeremiah accuses his opponents of not having "stood in the council of Yhwh" (23:21-22), but we have no way of knowing whether their experiences of the divine were any different from his. We do not have their side of the story; they may well have loitered around Yhwh's council as much as Jeremiah.

While standing in the council of Yhwh is one of the criteria for being a true prophet, as found here and there in the biblical text, others have also been used. According to Deuteronomy 13:2-6 and 18:15-22 a decisive criterion for distinguishing between a true and a false prophet was whether the prophet proposed going after other gods. Although there are the prophets of Baal at the time of Elijah and an occasional allegation that some prophets prophesy by Baal (e.g., Jer 2:8), they seem to have been a minority. Most of the prophets mentioned are Yahwists, including Hananiah (Jer 28) and those who opposed Micaiah (1 Kings 22:6-28).

Another "biblical" test is whether the prophecy comes to pass (Deut 13:2-6; 18:15-22). This seems of little help, however, when prophecies were seen as conditional on the response of those against whom they were directed. Jonah complained of this factor when he prophesied against Nineveh and God failed to carry out his threat against the city (Jon 3:10-4:3). Similarly, Ezekiel 33:1-20 makes the fulfillment of prophecy contingent on the response of those who hear the prophet's word. Another complicating element is the fact that there are examples of prophecies within the OT which did not take place as predicted, such as the destruction of Egypt by Nebuchadnezzar and its desolation for forty years (Ezek 29-32) or the destruction of Babylon by the Persians (Jer 50-51).

Some have suggested that personal morality was a major way of determining who was a true prophet of God. A difficulty is that we know nothing about the personal lives of most of the prophets; however, if Isaiah is anyone to go by, the activities of supposed true prophets could be such as to astound the faithful. He wandered around Jerusalem naked and barefoot for three years as a sign (something of an accomplishment in the climate, no doubt). He also had sexual intercourse with a prophetess so that they might produce children, again as a sign. The oft-repeated explanation that this was merely "Mrs. Isaiah" is contrived and apologetic—there is no suggestion of a marriage relationship.

Thus, when we examine the various means by which true prophecy might be distinguished from false, it is difficult to find any clear or consistent criteria for separating them. In many cases, the opposing prophets are very similar (e.g., Jeremiah and Hananiah [Jer 28]), and the differences between them would appear to be of little or no significance to an outsider. The text has marked out some as true and others as false, but this has been done arbitrarily according to the subjective judgment of the editors and tradents. Nehemiah followed the simplest path by condemning those prophets who opposed him (Neh 6:10-14); we have no way of knowing whether there anything else different about them.

4.8 PROPHETESSES

In traditional societies, religious specialists may be differentiated on the basis of gender. Prophecy in Israel seems mainly to have been a male affair—but not exclusively. There are several references to female prophets (*nĕvî'āh*). One of the most important is Huldah (2 Kings 22:14-20; 4.1.9). Evidently the wife of a temple official, she was consulted about the book of the law found at the time of Josiah. Her message to Josiah was that the nation would be punished for failure to follow the dictates of the book of the law; the king, however, would go to his grave in peace and not see this disaster. The prophetess Noadiah was among several prophetic figures who opposed Nehemiah, though we know nothing else about her. The other main prophetess is the woman who had sexual relations with Isaiah and bore several children by him. She is not otherwise described.

Two other women are labeled prophetesses: Miriam (Exod 15:20) and Deborah (Judges 4:4). This creates a bit of a problem, because we are given no reason for this designation, and they do not fit the role usually associated with prophets. For this reason, it is often thought that this is a late, almost honorary label, much as Moses is called a prophet. This may be the case, but perhaps matters are not so straightforward. The designation of Moses as a prophet is first found in a passage usually dated early (Hos 12:14), so the term cannot easily be dismissed for him. It has been suggested that Miriam's ability in song was the reason for her designation (Exod 15:20-21); the advantage of this argument is that it uses the very context in which Miriam is called a prophetess. Why Deborah is called a prophetess is not indicated; one might associate the title with her office of judge over Israel, but the text does not clearly make such a connection.

These reports of prophetesses are all brief, which makes it difficult to draw major conclusions. Nevertheless, from what little is known, the only difference from male prophets seems to be their sex. The behavior and messages of the prophetesses show no significant differences from those found among male prophets, recognizing that a range of behavior and message is found with both sexes. Although there may have been many more prophetesses than suggested by the few mentioned in the text, the same is also likely to be true of prophets. No special bias against female prophets is indicated in any of the passages where they are mentioned. This suggests that the proportion of male to female prophets in the text probably represents social reality.

Why there should be many more male prophets cannot easily be determined, but cross-cultural comparisons indicate that this is not an exceptional situation.

4.9 THE GESTALT OF THE PROPHET

Huffmon, H. B. "Prophecy in the Ancient Near East," *IDBSup* (1976) 697-700.
____ . "Ancient Near Eastern Prophecy," *ABD* (1992) 5.477-82

A necessary definition of a prophet is one which covers not only Israel but prophetic figures in the ancient Near East, in later Judaism, and in other pre-modern societies. In the past—and perhaps still unduly influencing the present—a variety of tendentious definitions has skewed the discussion by attempting to distance their idealized Israelite prophet from similar figures within and outside Israel. Without claiming an unproblematic definition, I have suggested that a prophet is a mediator claiming to have messages direct from a divinity, by various means, and communicating these messages to recipients.

One of the reasons this cannot be definitive is that the designation "prophet" is at least partially in the eye of the beholder, including the prophet himself. The one whom a later generation calls a prophet may have been perceived differently by his contemporaries. Or the views of a supporting faction may be quite different from those of the opponents. This is where the study of Israelite prophecy has been bedeviled by the theologically partisan views of the discussants. Such theological questions have no place in a properly sociological study. The prophet must be defined by his function and role in society, and the same applies to the prophetess. In considering the various functions and roles of prophets, the following points and characteristics need to be considered:

1. They receive messages, taken to be from God, by a variety of means: vision, audition, "angel," the "spirit" or "hand" of Yhwh, even a dream. Although one or more of these might be favored over others in a particular culture, there is no evidence that Israel or any other society rejected any of these outright. The various modes just mentioned could also involve an ecstatic (trance) state. This would not necessarily affect the general coherence of the message or the recollection of the event by the subject at a later time, but most of the time we are not given any information about the state of mind of the recipient.

2. They must also deliver the message received to the required recipient; this is often a king or ruler, but it can also be an ordinary individual. To convey the message, the prophet may use symbolic action, oral delivery, or even writing. The message may be a spontaneous revelation, but in many

cases it is the result of inquiry, either by the prophet himself or by him on behalf of others.

3. The message may be positive or negative. It may support or tear down social institutions. The type of message does not distinguish one prophet from another, since prophets may well utter one sort on one occasion and another on another.

4. Many prophets have the reputation of an ability to call on God's power to accomplish supernatural deeds: to perform signs and wonders, to benefit friends or harm enemies, to see into the spirit world and even into the future. This aura of supernatural power is not characteristic of all prophets, but the choice of an individual by a divinity itself apportions a certain sense of power to the recipient.

5. From a sociological point of view, there is no clear distinction between "pre-classical" and "classical" prophets. Such a distinction is based in part on theological judgments about the quality and nature of the prophetic message and in part on an idealized picture commensurate with what might be acceptable to a nineteenth-century Protestant. It is also shaped by the assumption that the picture of a prophet from whom a written book is allegedly preserved is somehow different from one in a prophetic legend.

6. There is no qualitative distinction between OT prophets and those known in Mesopotamia or other pre-modern cultures. A variety of functions is filled by prophetic figures in different locations. Although the OT prophets sometimes seem to be different in certain respects, this is usually based on a reading of the prophetic books, not on a careful look at the sociological context. The impression is frequently given that the OT prophets were primarily social critics and ethicists. This is based partly on a failure to consider the contents of the books as a whole and partly on a failure to recognize that the contents of prophetic books are not necessarily the product of prophets. That is, in the course of transmission and editing of the tradition, the contents of the prophetic books may well be to a significant extent the product of scribes, priests, and sages.

7. Terminology varies widely across cultures and is not the main means of identification. In the OT, various terms are used for prophetic figures. Although *nāvî'*, "prophet," is favored, followed more distantly by *hōzeh*, "seer," no clear distinction between various types can be discerned in the text as it stands. There seems to be considerable overlap in the functions of the different types as marked out by the terminology, and at most there is a concentration of function around a particular term. Also, the verbal forms (*nb'*, *ḥzh*, etc.) should not be ignored, even though their use does not always follow precisely the presence of the nouns. Although the terminology helps us initially to define what a prophet is, the identity of a prophet ultimately

depends on the context—the actions and characterization of the individual in question.

8. The concepts of true and false prophet represent theological value judgments and have no place in a sociological description. In most cases, the only thing distinguishing the true from false prophet is the identification by the text itself. That is, the text labels some prophets true and some false, but without any sort of consistent criteria. Some of the criteria mentioned (e.g., going after other gods) are irrelevant in most cases. Others are simply unhelpful (having had a divine call or having stood in the council of Yhwh) because our information is too incomplete. Whether a prophecy comes to pass is also of little use because it ignores the contingent nature of much prophecy, the fact that failed prophecies may have been quietly forgotten or re-edited to give a new interpretation, and the presence of many prophecies in the collections of "true" prophets which certainly did not happen as predicted. In short, there are no clear criteria which separate true from false, and the designation in the OT text represents the arbitrary opinion of the writers, compilers, and editors. In some cases, they do not themselves appear to be sure, as, for example, in Numbers 22-24 (5.1.3) and 1 Kings 13 (4.1.5).

5.

Diviners, Healers, and Others

This chapter looks at a group of religious specialisms which form a somewhat broad, but still definable, category. As will become clear, the practitioners in this group cannot always be easily separated from those in other chapters. Divination is an important part of daily life in many cultures. It is often at the core of healing or curing ceremonies; also, in many societies a shaman performs the duties of healing and divination. Therefore, it is useful to examine these together. Yet unlike institutions such as prophecy or priesthood, divination is generally viewed negatively, not only in the OT literature but also in modern scholarship. The importance of divination in Israelite society has generally been overlooked or ignored because of the assumption that divination is contrary to true biblical religion. Section 5.4 will address this question and attempt to allay some of the Western prejudices and misconceptions about divination. (As noted in the Preface [p. xiv], this chapter was written before the study by F. H. Cryer appeared.)

5.1 SELECTED OLD TESTAMENT TEXTS

Several of the texts important for divination have been discussed in detail elsewhere and will not be repeated here. These include Elijah (4.1.6) and Elisha (4.1.7).

5.1.1 Joseph (Gen 37, 39-50)

The story of Joseph is dominated by dreams. Already as a youth Joseph was referred to sarcastically by his brothers as a "master of dreams" (*ba'al haḥălōmôt*) because of dreams which had his parents and brothers bowing before him (37:19). He then interpreted the dreams of the chief cupbearer and the chief baker while in prison (40) and finally the dreams of Pharaoh

(41). Apart from Daniel (with whom there are a number of parallels [6.1.9]), Joseph is *the* dream interpreter. Joseph also practiced divination: "It [Joseph's cup] is the very one from which my master drinks and which he uses for divination *[nḥš]*" (44:5, 15). This may have been a form of lecanomancy (observing the pattern of oil on water), but whatever it was, there is no suggestion that Joseph's divination is to be condemned.

5.1.2 Priestly Lots: Urim/Thummim and the Ephod

Dam, C. van. *The Urim and Thummim: A Study of an Old Testament Means of Revelation* (1986).

Houtman, C. "The Urim and Thummim: A New Suggestion," *VT* 40 (1990) 229-32.

Huffmon, H. B. "Priestly Divination in Israel," *The Word of the Lord Shall Go Forth* (1983) 355-59.

Lipiński, E. "'Ūrīm and Tummīm," *VT* 20 (1970) 495-96.

Priestly modes of divination are fully approved and referred to a number of times in the text. The Urim and Thummim are mentioned in passing as devices in the hands of the priests for seeking divine decisions (Exod 28:30; Lev 8:8; Num 27:21; Deut 33:8), though they are never described in detail. It has often been argued that they were a form of lot giving binary responses—that is, only yes or no answers to questions, as indicated by 1 Samuel 14:38-42 (see below). C. van Dam has recently opposed this interpretation, however, arguing that not all such inquiries could have yielded a yes/no answer. Instead, the priest received a revelation, which was then confirmed by a special light from the Urim/Thummim, a thesis developed further by Houtman. They may well be correct, though one must keep in mind that a skilled diviner in the use of binary lots can elicit a great deal of information by the right sort of questions.

The ephod also functioned as a form of divination, though its relationship to the Urim and Thummim is not completely clear. According to the Pentateuch (Exod 28; 39), it is a part of the high priest's garments, covering the upper part of the body. Yet it is associated with the Urim and Thummim in that the breastplate attached to the ephod also housed the Urim and Thummim (Exod 28:30; Lev 8:7-8). In 1 Samuel 14, while Saul was fighting the Philistines, Ahijah the priest bore the ephod (v 3). Jonathan conducted his own personal attack. When Saul noticed Jonathan's absence, he apparently called for the ephod to consult (14:18: the MT has *'ărôn*, "ark," but the LXX has *ephoud*, "ephod"), but hearing a commotion in the Philistine camp, he interrupted the priest's inquiry by telling him to withdraw his hand (*'ěsōf yādekā*) and attacked the Philistines (vv 19-20). After an initial victory, Saul proposed to continue the fight by making a night assault. The men approved but the priest suggested that they consult God (v 36). Saul inquired (*š'l*) of God by asking a question which could be answered by yes or no, but God did not respond (v 37). Assuming from this that someone had sinned, he sought out the guilty party by means of the Thummim according to the MT (vv 38-42). However, the LXX has an interesting insight or interpretation: "If this iniquity was because of my son Jonathan or me, O Lord, God of Israel, show Urim; and if you say it was because of your people Israel, show Thummim" (v 41). This suggests two separate lots, one showing one alternative to a bipolar question and the other the other alternative. How was it possible to have no response at all (v 37), though? Here van Dam has a clear point in favor of his interpretation, which rejects the idea of binary lots. Yet it is possible that in verse 37 the ephod (or ark) is being consulted and that its means of response was more complicated. In each case, it seems to be the priest who made the official inquiry to God on behalf of the king. David also made use of the ephod (see below, 5.1.6).

5.1.3 Balaam (Num 22-24)

Balaam is given no designation in the main story, except for his father (Beor) and his town (Pethor on the Euphrates). Many of the characteristics are those of a prophet, but we also find the terminology of divination in the account. (In Joshua 13:22, he is called an "augurer" [*haqqôsēm*].) The story is well known: Balak, king of Moab, sends elders to hire Balaam to curse Israel; Balaam eventually goes with the messenger; an angel seeks to kill him and he is saved only by his ass, who sees the angel and also speaks to him; he three times blesses Israel, despite Balak's protestations.

Of interest for our problem are the various descriptions and technical terms. The god to whom Balaam prays is variously called "God" (*'ĕlōhîm*), Yhwh, El (three times in poetic sections: 23:8; 24:4, 16), and Shaddai (twice: 24:4, 16). God comes to him and speaks with him (22:19-20), manifests (or appears: nif. of *qrh*) to him (23:4-5, 15-16), and puts words into his mouth (22:38; 23:4-5, 12). Balaam asserts several times that he can speak only that which God speaks or puts into his mouth (22:38; 23:12; 24:13). God's spirit comes on him (24:2); he hears God's words, and sees the visions (*maḥăzēh yeḥĕzeh*) with unveiled eyes (*gĕlûy 'ênāyîm*) (24:4, 16). In his third attempt at cursing Israel on Balak's behalf, he does not have to seek "omens" (*nĕḥāšîm*) but instead apparently waits for God's spirit (24:1-2). He states that "augury" (*nḥš*) and "divining" (*qsm*) are unnecessary in Israel because the Israelites know immediately God's will (23:23). The messengers who come to him are said enigmatically to have divination (*qsm*) in their hands (22:7).

Balaam is presented as an ambiguous figure in the text. He is given no designation—whether diviner, prophet, or anything else. Several times the technical terminology of divination is used in the story (22:7; 23:23), but only once is such a term applied to him (24:1: *nĕḥāšîm*, "omens"). His overall image is that of a prophet—indeed, a prophet of Yhwh. The fact that he could also be called a diviner is an important datum which needs to be taken account of in any investigation (see also 5.3.1). He is indeed labeled a diviner (*haqqôsēm*) in Joshua 13:22, the only place in the Hebrew Bible where he is called anything.

On Balaam in the Deir 'Alla text, see 5.3.1.

5.1.4 Deuteronomy

Several important references occur in this book. In 13:2-6 criteria are given for knowing whether a message is from God when an individual does a "sign" (*'ôt*) or "wonder" (*môfēt*): if he suggests going after gods other than Yhwh, his message is not to be heeded, even if it comes to pass. The person with the message is referred to as either a prophet or a dreamer of dreams (*ḥōlēm [ha]ḥălôm*). No distinction is made between them, except over the matter of whether the person follows Yhwh or other gods.

In 18:9-14 is given a long list of "abominations" (*tô'ăvôt*) supposedly practiced by the other nations but to be avoided by Israel. Except for passing children through fire, most of them are types of diviners: augur (*qōsēm qĕsāmîm*), soothsayer (*mĕ'ônēn*), diviner (*mĕnaḥēš*), sorcerer (*mĕkaššēf*), caster of spells (*ḥōvēr ḥaver*), consulter of ghosts or familiar spirits (*šō'ēl 'ôv wĕyiddĕ'ōnî*), or necromancer (*dōrēš 'el-hammētîm*). (Verses 15-22 go on to discuss the "prophet like Moses" [4.1.1].) In the Blessing of Moses, the blessing given to Levi states that he (i.e., the Levites) is to have the Urim and Thummim (33:8).

5.1.5 Samuel

Texts: 1 Samuel 1-13; 15-16; 19:18-24; 25:1.

While still a youth, Samuel was in the service of Eli. At a time when there was no vision (*ḥāzôn*) in Israel, Yahweh stood by his bed and spoke to him, revealing to him the future of Eli's house (3:1-14). This experience is referred to as a "vision" (*hammar'āh*—3:15). As a result, Israel knew that Samuel was a prophet (*nāvî'*), because his predications were fulfilled (3:19-20). Because of Samuel's reputation, Saul wanted to inquire (*drš*—9:9) of him about asses which could not be found (ch. 9). Samuel is referred to as a "man of God" (9:6), with all that he says coming to pass, and is also called a "seer" (*rō'eh*). It seems that Samuel fulfilled the functions not only of priest and judge but also of prophet, seer, and diviner. Yet in 15:22-23 Samuel condemns divination, allegedly because disobedience is like the sin of divination (*qesem*) and defiance (*hafṣar*) is like iniquity and teraphim (or perhaps "the iniquity of teraphim"). Exactly what is included under *qesem* is unclear. The passage of course ignores the following story, which pictures David himself with teraphim in his house (1 Sam 19; 5.1.6).

5.1.6 David (1 Sam 19-28)

Toorn, K. van der. "The Nature of the Biblical Teraphim in the Light of the Cuneiform Evidence," *CBQ* 52 (1990) 203-22.

David is associated with a number of incidents which represent divination or could be interpreted this way. The first is in 1 Samuel 19, where he escaped being arrested by Saul's men because his wife placed teraphim in his bed to make it appear that he was still there when he had actually fled. Exactly what the teraphim were has been much discussed. A teraph often has been seen as a household god of some sort, evidently with a roughly human shape. A recent study argues that it is a figurine of the ancestor cult, an intepretation also allowed by the Mesopotamian evidence frequently invoked in the debate (Toorn).

When David was in the wilderness fleeing from Saul, Abiathar the priest came to him bringing an ephod (1 Sam 23:6). David was able to use it to avoid Saul who was pursuing him (23:8-13). The types of questions put to the ephod are those which can be answered with a yes or no. He later consulted Yhwh (*š'l baYhwh*) through the ephod when his village of Ziglag had been raided and his wives and children taken captive (30:6-8). After becoming king he also "inquired of Yhwh" (*š'l baYhwh*) about which city to settle in (2 Sam 2:1), about fighting the Philistines (2 Sam 5:19, 23), and he "inquired to Yhwh's face" (pi. *bqš 'et-pĕnê Yhwh*) about a famine (21:1). The method of inquiry and reply is not indicated in these passages, but the first could easily have been the Urim or the ephod, with yes/no answers. The response to the question about the famine is more likely to have been by vision or prophet (cf. 1 Sam 28:6), because the answer would have been harder to elicit by a bipolar form of inquiry. However, skilled diviners can learn an amazing amount even from binary answers alone, so it is possible that the Urim and Thummim or ephod were intended here.

5.1.7 Saul and the Woman of Endor (1 Sam 28)

Hoffner, H. A. "אוב" *TDOT* (1974) 1.130-34.
Lust, J. "On Wizards and Prophets," VTSup 26 (1974) 133-42.

This is the *locus classicus* on the "black arts" in the OT. Saul consults a "witch" or, in Hebrew, a *ba'ălat 'ôv*. The question is, what is an *'ôv*? One suggestion has connected it with the Sumerian word for "pit" (Hoffner). There seems to be some evidence of digging a pit as part of the ceremony to consult the dead. An example from the classical world is found in the *Odyssey* (book 11), where Odysseus wishes to consult the shade of the prophet Teiresias. He digs a pit, sacrifices sheep, and drains the blood into the pit. The shades crowd around to drink the blood, which gives them the ability to speak to the living. However, the interpretation "pit" for *'ôv* is not accepted by everyone. Johann Lust has argued that it is a form of *'av*, "father." This fits well with the idea of the ancestral spirits still having communion with the living and being available for consultation about the future and other esoteric matters, as discussed below. So does verse 13, in which the woman states that she sees *'ĕlōhîm* coming up from the earth—the shade of Samuel is a "divine being" of some sort. (Some would translate *'ereṣ* here as "underworld," but if the underworld is conceived as underneath the earth, where else could the spirit come from but out of the earth?)

A key passage is verse 6: "And Saul inquired [*š'l*] of the Lord, but the Lord did not answer him, either by dreams or by Urim or by prophets." This refers to the goal (an inquiry which results in a message from God) but makes no distinction between the modes of receiving God's message. One asks for a message, but God may respond in one of several different ways (or not at all, in this case). No qualitative distinction is made between methods commonly designated "divination" and the mode known as "prophecy."

5.1.8 Manasseh (2 Kings 21//2 Chron 33)

Manasseh is regarded by the author of 2 Kings as a most horrible king, perhaps the worst of the Israelite kings. The author does not stint in his description of Manasseh's wickedness. This includes following the practices of the Canaanites, erecting altars to Baal and an asherah, worshiping the host of heaven, and in sum doing even worse sins than the Amorites. Among these sins were passing his children through the fire, practicing soothsaying (*'ônēn*) and divination (*niḥēš*), and consulting ghosts (*'āśāh*) and familiar spirits (*yiddĕ'ōnîm*) (21:6). The account in 2 Chronicles seems based on the one in 2 Kings. 2 Kings 21:6 is very close to Deuteronomy 18:9-14, which is why passages like this usually are assigned to the Deuteronomistic History (which assumes a Deuteronomic editor). Whether Manasseh actually did all these things or whether we see in 2 Kings 21 only a stereotyped compilation of all those items that the editor regarded as evil is uncertain. One suspects that whatever original information existed, if any, has been greatly expanded to create in Manasseh the worst example the editor can imagine—the wicked king par excellence, one might say. Yet this stereotyped list is a useful source for the types of things probably fairly widely practiced in Israel at one time or another.

5.1.9 Isaiah

Ackerman, S. *Under Every Green Tree* (1992).
Lewis, T. J. *Cults of the Dead in Ancient Israel and Ugarit* (1989).

Isaiah has a number of references to divination, all of them negative and some associated with "pagan" worship or foreign practices. The people are full of Eastern ways and soothsaying (*'ōnĕnîm*) like the Philistines (2:6). Yhwh will remove the society's supports (3:1-3): warrior, judge, prophet, augur (*qōsēm*), elder, counselor, and enchanter (*nēvôn laḥaš*). A problematic passage is 8:19-22 (cf. Lewis: 128-32). The overall purpose is to prohibit the people from inquiring (*drš*) to the ghosts (*hā'ōvôt*) and familiar spirits (*hayyiddĕ'ōnîm*)—to the dead on behalf of the living. The term *'ĕlōhîm*, usually translated "God/gods," seems to be applied to the dead (v 19). The rest of the passage talks of one who has no dawn but suffers distress and darkness, who will go around wretched and hungry, and who will curse "his king and his God/gods" (vv 20-22). Who this person is, is unclear, though it has been taken as a description of the dead (Lewis: 128-32). Because the Egyptians are confounded, they will consult (*drš*) their idols, the shades (*hā'iṭṭîm*), the ghosts (*hā'ōvôt*), and the familiar spirits (*hayyiddĕ'ōnîm*) (19:3). In a passage which mentions the *rĕfā'îm* or shades of the dead and resurrection (26:13-19), there may be an allusion to divination (v 16: *ṣāqûn laḥaš*). When Ariel (Jerusalem) is besieged, its voice will come from the ground like the voice of a ghost (*'ôv*) (29:4).

In a number of passages in Second Isaiah, Yhwh emphasizes that only he knows the end from the beginning (41:21-29; 42:9; 43:9; 44:7-8; 45:20-21; 46:10; 48:3-8, 14-16). He annuls the omens of the diviners (*'ōtôt baddîm*), makes fools of the augurs (*qōsĕmîm*), and makes foolish the knowledge of the sages (44:25). As for Babylon, the daughter of the Chaldeans, her spells (*kĕšāfîm*) and enchantments (*ḥăvārîm*), her scanners of the heavens (*hōvĕrê šāmayim*) and her stargazers (*haḥōzîm bakkôkāvîm*), will not help her in her time of trouble (47:9, 12-13).

Third Isaiah has several references to what seem to be secret cults, some of which apparently have the aim of deriving esoteric knowledge from the dead (cf. Lewis; Ackerman). A passage condemning the religious practices of the people (57:3-13) is addressed to "sons of a sorceress" (v 3: *bĕnê 'ōnĕnāh*). It speaks of worshiping among the terebinths and slaughtering children in the wadis (v 5) and sacrificing on the hills (v 7). The people provoke Yhwh to anger by sacrificing in the gardens, burning incense on bricks, passing the night in tombs, and eating unclean things (65:1-7). Although the rites mentioned here are not entirely clear, the suggestion of some sort of cult of the dead is plausible. Similar is 66:3-4, which speaks of sacrificing dogs' and swine's blood, and 66:17, which talks of eating unclean animals in a ritual context.

5.1.10 Jeremiah

Jeremiah is normally thought of as a prophet, though he was also a priest (1:1). Several passages speak disparagingly of divination (14:14; 27:9-10; 29:8-9), lumping it together with false prophecy. However, one reference is quite interesting: the king sends two individuals (one of them Zephaniah the priest) to inquire (*drš*) of Yhwh (21:1-2). "To inquire" is the language of divination. He also seems to condemn those who receive messages from dreams (23:25-32; 29:8-9), but this interpretation is problematic (see 5.7 on dreams).

5.1.11 Ezekiel

Duguid, I. M. *Ezekiel and the Leaders of Israel* (1994).
Korpel, M.C.A. "Avian Spirits in Ugarit and in Ezekiel 13," *Aspects of Ugaritic Religion and Culture* (forthcoming).

The book of Ezekiel has a number of passages of relevance for the question of divination. As discussed at 4.5.2, the prophet's reception of divine messages is described in more detail in Ezekiel than in many other books. He has visions and is seized by Yhwh's spirit. In a number of passages, the elders come to "inquire" (*drš*) of Yhwh through him (14:1-4; 20:1-3). Yhwh predicts that there will no longer be false vision or "smooth divination" (*miqsam ḥālāq*) in Israel (12:21-24). Reference is made to the practice of the Babylonian king to seek advice by divination through arrows, teraphim, or liver inspection (21:26-27). Hepatoscopy is a widespread mode of divination in the ancient Near East, but the other two modes are not attested for Mesopotamia. The writer of Ezekiel apparently had no particular knowledge of Babylonian practice but was only repeating anecdotal evidence.

Chapter 13 is especially important. The first part of the chapter is a sustained attack on "false prophets" (vv 1-16). They are said not only to give false prophecies and and false visions but also to utter "lying divinations" (*qesem/miqsam kāzāv*: vv 6, 7, 9). Whether divination is being associated with prophecy as a normal thing, as visions seem to be, is a matter of debate. The references to divinations might be gratuitious slander. On the other hand, they could be recognition that some sorts of divination were a normal accompaniment of prophecy. The second part of the chapter is a condemnation of "the daughters of your people" for enigmatic practices by which they entrap souls and and hunt down lives, killing those who should live and keeping alive those who should die (vv 17-23). These women are said to prophecy (hitp. *nb'*) out of their own hearts (v 17) and to make for themselves certain bodily accouterments which apparently enable them to do this (vv 18, 20-21). Exactly what these accouterments are is difficult to say, though they seem to be some sort of headgear and something sewed to the arms or sleeves. Yhwh will deliver the innocent from their hands so that these women no longer see visions (*ḥzh*) of vanity or practice divination (*qesem qsm*) (v 23). If this passage is correctly interpreted as a reference to some sort of sorcery or casting of spells, it is probably the only passage in the OT referring to witchcraft. Otherwise, the OT is silent on witchcraft, which plays such an important part in some other societies (5.3.6).

5.1.12 Other References to Divination

Hosea has a couple of passages which may mention divination in passing. According to Hosea 3:4, Israel will go a long time without king, officials, sacrifice, ephod, and teraphim. All but the teraphim are approved institutions, in the view of most OT texts. Does this passage show a situation in which teraphim were *also* generally accepted as legitimate, perhaps even by Hosea himself? Hosea 4:12 may also refer to divination, though the exact meaning is disputed. In Zechariah 10:2, teraphim, augurs, and dreamers are all said to be false and lead the people astray. Whether all such modes of inquiry were automatically considered to be wrong by the author or only certain types is difficult to know.

2 Chronicles 16:12 refers to a foot ailment of Asa (who is completely righteous according to 2 Kings 15), for which he resorted to the physicians instead of Yhwh. Unfortunately, the reason consulting physicians was wrong is not stated. One suggestion is that "healers" (*rōfĕ'îm*) should be read as "Rephaim." If so, Asa was condemned for seeking the dead or the ancestors for healing. The suggestion is interesting but speculative. On the Rephaim and the cult of the dead, see 5.6.

On the dreams of Daniel, see 6.1.9.

5.2 THE DIVINER IN THE OLD TESTAMENT TEXT

The initial impression of the text is that all forms of divination are condemned. This especially includes seeking knowledge from familiar spirits, necromancy, and other "dark" cults. The reader's mind is imprinted with the graphic image of those who "seek unto wizards that peep, and that mutter" (Isa 8:19 AV). It seems that the text is uncompromisingly opposed to any sort of divination. As so often, though, the surface impression masks a more complicated situation.

The first exception to the sweeping condemnation is the official priestly modes of divination. The Urim and Thummim are mentioned in a variety of texts. Although never described as such, they seem to be a form of lot used to give either a yes or no answer (cf. 1 Sam 23:8-13). The other priestly means of inquiry was the ephod. This seems to have been a priestly garment. According to Exodus 28 and 39, it covered the upper torso and had attached to it a sort of breastplate which in turn housed the Urim and Thummim. Whether consulting the ephod implied using the Urim and Thummim in each case is not clear. At any rate, these objects of divination are referred to in a number of texts without any suggestion that they should not be used. The only judgment on them is that by the post-exilic period they are allegedly no longer possessed by the priesthood (Ezra 2:63; Neh 7:65).

Apart from the priestly modes (and Joseph—see below), the other forms of divination are always pictured negatively, but they are described in such a way as to suggest widespread use within the society. The exact types of divination are not always certain, though consulting the dead in some way seems to be the basis of more than one of the terms. The dominant picture of most OT texts (apart from admittedly late ones such as Daniel 12:2) is of no afterlife. Yet this does not mean that nothing survives death. Very similar to the old Greek view found in Homer, there is a certain shadowy survival of the person's life in the underworld (Sheol). The full person was not longer extant once the life (*nefeš*) had left the body—no "soul equals the person" concept here. But the dead were thought to have some sort of insight into the future, at least in the view of some circles. We also have to reckon with the possibility that there may have been views extant in Israel other than the one just outlined (5.6), and consulting the dead implied that the deceased had a more definite and active life than just a shadowy existence in Sheol.

However the dead were conceived by those who consulted them, the indications are that "dark" cults seeking esoteric knowledge were well known in Israelite society. In some way aligned with these were the teraphim. The teraphim were apparently a type of household deity, perhaps associated with an ancestor cult (5.1.6). Known as a source of inquiry for esoteric knowledge (Ezek 21:26 [Eng. 21:21]; Zech 10:2; cf. 2 Kings 23:24; Hos 3:4), they constituted a part of David's household (1 Sam 19:10-17). Whether David consulted the teraphim is not stated; on the other hand, we have no reason to deny this possibility since this seems one of their regular functions.

Perhaps the most problematic figure is that of Balaam. In the full context, he is made into a negative figure who is willing to curse Israel if God permits, and when God does not permit it, he advises on how the Moabites can subvert the Israelites by other means. However, he is a prophetic figure (though never called that as such); he also has the language of divination used with regard to him. He serves Yhwh, Elohim, and Shaddai—all legitimate names for the true God—and does nothing without receiving God's approval. Yhwh, in turn, uses him as a mouthpiece. Balaam is a good example of how the roles of prophet and diviner can be difficult to separate.

Extremely interesting in the light of all the preceding, therefore, is that the patriarch Joseph is stated explicitly to practice divination—and this without the slightest hint of criticism. Genesis 44 seems almost to be thumbing its nose at passages such as Deuteronomy 18:9-14. Apart from this, dream intepretation is also accepted as a legitimate form of determining God's mind (Joseph, Daniel). Dreamers are also equated with prophets in Deuteronomy 13:2, and dreams are one of Yhwh's modes of communication, alongside the Urim/Thummim and prophets (1 Sam 28:6). See further at 5.7.

1 Samuel 28:6 also raises an implicit question which it does not go on to address explicitly: the relationship of prophecy to divination. It does this by listing three ways in which God might respond to a query: dreams, Urim (and Thummim), prophecy. In this verse, at least, prophecy seems not to be distinguished from what are usually classified as divinatory practices. There is also the fact that divinatory terminology (especially *drš* and *š'l*) is used of inquiring of Yhwh when the answer is sought from a prophet (e.g., Jer 21:1-2; Ezek 14:1-4; 20:1-3). For a more detailed discussion of the question, see 5.5.

The one "magical" practice not widely attested is that of witchcraft or sorcery (by which is meant the malign influence spread unknowingly or deliberately by the witch/sorceror, manifested in illness, bad luck, and the like). There is one passage which suggests the existence even of this in Israel (Ezek 13:17-23), but this seems the exception. If so, the practice was either not widespread or has, for some reason or other, not been abundantly documented.

5.3 CROSS-CULTURAL PARALLELS

5.3.1 The Deir 'Alla Inscription

Delcor, M. "Le texte de Deir 'Alla et les oracles bibliques de Bala'am," VTSup 32 (1981) 52-73.
Dijkstra, M. "Is Balaam among the Prophets?" *JBL* 114 (1995) 43-64.
Hackett, J. A. *The Balaam Text from Deir 'Allā* (1980).
Hoftijzer, J., and G. van der Kooij, eds. *Aramaic Texts from Deir 'Alla* (1976).
____. *The Balaam Text from Deir 'Alla Re-evaluated* (1991).
Moore, M. S. *The Balaam Traditions* (1990).
____. "Another Look at Balaam," *RB* 97 (1990) 359-78.
Müller H.-P. "Die aramäische Inschrift von Deir 'Allā und die älteren Bileamsprüche," *ZAW* 94 (1982) 214-44.
Sasson, V. "The Book of Oracular Visions of Balaam from Deir 'Alla," *UF* 17 (1986) 283-309.
Wolters, A. "The Balaamites of Deir 'Alla as Aramean Deportees," *HUCA* 59 (1988) 101-13.

The Balaam tradition, long familiar from the account in Numbers 22-24, is now known from an inscription found at Deir 'Alla in the Jordon Valley. The inscription is difficult to read and damaged, and even its language is disputed, though everyone agrees it is a form of Northwest Semitic. The first of the two columns is the best preserved; the relationship of the first column to the second is uncertain. Balaam is called a seer of the gods (*ḥzh. 'lhn*). The gods come to him at night and he sees a vision (*wyḥz.mḥzh*). Balaam has a very negative reaction to this vision, which seems to foretell terrible things to come, including something to do with the heavens. There follows a passage referring to a number of birds, as well as activities of human beings. This passage is often taken to refer to a reversal of the normal state of things, an effect widely found in reports of the last days in apocalypses. Moore, however, takes this as a reference to ornithomancy, in which the movements of birds is a divinatory sign of what is to come.

The fragmentary state of the inscription makes interpretation very difficult, and much may never be known; nevertheless, several important points can be gleaned from it. Plainly, the Balaam story in the Pentateuch owes its origins to an earlier legend, related to the Deir 'Alla version, which was probably borrowed from outside Israel. This is hardly surprising since Israel did a good deal of borrowing. This supposition also helps to explain the ambivalent nature of the Balaam story in the OT: internally in the Numbers passage, Balaam appears as a genuine prophet-diviner of Yhwh, yet the framework and setting of the story in the Bible give him and his activities a negative connotation overall. The Balaam of Deir 'Alla is a positive character who is concerned to help the people. It has been proposed that the threat from the gods is removed by the actions and intercession of Balaam (cf. Müller: 242-43). If so, Balaam in this account has much in common with some of the later biblical prophets (cf. also the recent article by Dijkstra).

5.3.2 Egypt

Černý, J. "Egyptian Oracles," *A Saite Oracle Papyrus from Thebes in the Brooklyn Museum* (1962) 35-48.

Leclant, J. "Éléments pour une étude de la divination dans l'Égypte pharaonique," *La Divination: Études Recueillies* (1968) 1.1-23.

Lichtheim, M. *Ancient Egyptian Literature* (1973-80).

Quaegebeur, J. "On the Egyptian Equivalent of Biblical *Ḥarṭummîm*," *Pharaonic Egypt* (1985) 162-72.

Ray, J. D. *The Archive of Ḥor* (1976).

____. "Ancient Egypt," *Divination and Oracles* (1981) 174-90.

Volten, A. *Demotische Traumdeutung (Pap. Carlsberg XIII und XIV Verso)* (1942).

Williams, R. J. "The Sage in Egyptian Literature," *The Sage in Israel and the Ancient Near East* (1990) 19-30.

During the first part of the New Kingdom, kings begin to report oracles from various of the gods. These are often reported with fairly lengthy messages, with the implication that an actual voice spoke from the divine image (Leclant: 1.14-15). Also, a series of ostraca or marble chips with short written messages to the god seems to consist of queries to an oracle (Cerný: 46). How the questions were to be answered is not clear. What is clear is that the predominant mode of oracular message was by means of the statue of the god as it was carried in a bark, accompanied by priests, in a procession. Many of the reports do not say exactly how the god responded to the queries, but most of the questions were put forward in such a way that either a yes or a no answer could be given. It has been argued that the response of the god was indicated by whether the bark moved backward or advanced when a query was placed (Cerný: 44-45). This response could also have been the means of delivering many of the oracles recorded, though it seems not to have been the mode for all of them.

Stories such as those from Papyrus Westcar tell of the alleged magical exploits of sages. According to the stories preserved in it, a chief *lector*-priest of King Snefru found a lost pendant in a lake by lifting up the water; however, he is outdone by the magician Djedi who was able to rejoin a severed head to its body. He also made a prediction about the future. Many of the famous Egyptian wisemen had a comparable reputation for special powers, including the ability to see into the future. One of the Chester Beatty papyri has a treatise on "The Immortality of Writers" which mentions "those learned scribes . . . who foretold the future"; it goes on to list a number of these scribes who are sages of old, including Neferty, Imhotep, and Ptahhotep (Lichtheim: 2:176-77). Although this may in part have been allegedly based on their knowledge of *maat* and how it works in the world (Williams: 28), some of the reports seem to presuppose their mastery of the esoteric arts. The Egyptian term for "sorcerer" (Demotic *ḥry-tp*) has produced the Hebrew word *ḥarṭummîm* and Aramaic *ḥarṭōm*, often translated "magician." Yet the ultimate origin of the word is usually given as the Egyptian *ẖrw-ḥbt ḥry-tp*, "chief lector-priest" (Quaegebeur). Divination and the esoteric arts were a part of the intellectual tradition cultivated by the priests and sages.

5.3.3 Mesopotamia

Durand, J.-M. *Archives épistolaires de Mari I/1* (1988).

Finkel, I. L. "Necromancy in Ancient Mesopotamia," *AfO* 29/30 (1983/84) 1-17.

Lambert, W. G. "The <<Tamītu>> Texts," *La divination en Mésopotamie ancienne et dans les régions voisines* (1966) 119-23.

____. "The Qualifications of Babylonian Diviners," *Festschrift R. Borger* (1994).

McEwan, G.J.P. *Priest and Temple in Hellenistic Babylonia* (1981).

Nougayrol, J. "La divination babylonienne," *La Divination: Études Recueillies* (1968) 25-81.

Oppenheim, A. L. "The Interpretation of Dreams in the Ancient Near East, With a Translation of an Assyrian Dream-Book," *Transactions of the American Philosophical Society* 46 (1956) 179-354.

Renger, J. "Untersuchungen zum Priestertum in der altbabylonischen Zeit", *Zeitschrift für Assyrologie* 58 (1966) 110-88; 59 (1969) 104-230.
Sasson, J. M. "Mari Dreams," *JAOS* 103 (1983) 283-93.
Starr, I., ed. *Queries to the Sungod: Divination and Politics in Sargonid Assyria* (1990).

The importance of divination to Mesopotamian society and religion can hardly be exaggerated. Official forms of divination were invoked before any important decision by the king or government officials. Collections of texts have been published for various periods, giving eloquent testimony to the central place of divination for all political activity (e.g., Mari [Durand: 1-373]; Sargon [Starr]). Forms of divination among the masses are perhaps less abundantly attested but seem no less resorted to. The best attested mode was extispicy, looking at the innards of sacrificial animals. The main diviner was the *bārû*. Most of those documented were employees of the state, making their inquiries in the palace or temple, even accompanying the army on its campaigns, though there were those who made themselves available to the ordinary citizen, especially in connection with illness. Some *bārûs* also made prognostications based on observing the flight of birds or the movement of smoke, and divining with oil in a cup is well known, but these are less well attested than extispicy (Renger 1969: 208).

Extispicy reports and records of inquiries were compiled and used by later generations to aid in their interpretations. Some of these made on behalf of specific kings have been preserved, and the results of their inquiries can be related to definite historical events. A good example is the records from the reigns of Esarhaddon and Assurbanipal (Starr). To become a *bārû* required extensive training in order to master the accumulated data from centuries of practice. The discovery of liver models, not only in Mesopotamia but also as far away as Palestine and Etruria, indicates the type of training given. This naturally included appropriate scribal training, as well, in order to be able to read the omen compilations. According to later descriptions, the *bārû* had not only to have no physical handicap but also to be of priestly descent (Renger 1969: 213).

Records of other sorts of omens were also systematized and preserved, along with the subsequent events assumed to be their outcome. Among these was the series *Šumma izbu* on unusual or deformed births. The series *Šumma ālu* noted a variety of miscellaneous phenomena, including the behavior of animals. Although these compilations were extensively consulted, the predictions based on them usually required confirmation by extispicy (Starr: xxxii). Also recorded were celestial phenomena. These were not primarily viewed as part of an astrological system, centering on the planets and the Zodiac, which did not develop in its full form until the Hellenistic period; nor were they straightforward astronomical observation. Although various of the heavenly bodies (including Venus) were observed, such matters as eclipses and what we would call meteorological phenomena (e.g., rings around the sun or moon, thunder, clouds) and even earthquakes were also included. Toward the end of the Neo-Assyrian period, celestial observation was the dominant form of prognostication. By the Hellenistic period, the *bārû* is scarcely mentioned, though his function continued to exist (McEwan: 15).

The *šā'ilu* seems to have been concerned with dreams but evidently used other techniques as well (Oppenheim: 221-23). He might work alongside the *bārû*. We also know of women who entered this profession (*šā'iltu*), though apparently outside the temple and mainly with women as their clientele. In the Neo-Assyrian period, both sexes seem to have had low status and to have functioned mainly among the ordinary people. Necromancy was another of their activities. Necromancy itself is not very abundantly attested in the native literature, but there is evidence that it existed (Finkel).

The importance of dream interpretation is indicated by various examples in literary texts (e.g., *Epic of Gilgamesh*, Tablet 1.5 [*ANET*: 76]; Tablet 5 [*ANET*: 82-83]). The dream reports from Mari have now been published, with extensive discussion (Durand: 455-82; cf. Sasson). The interest in dream omina already attested for Old Babylonian times eventually led to the compilation of a dream-book, though the extant text probably dates from the seventh century BCE (Oppenheim: 295). Oppenheim suggested that "Mesopotamia dream-omina never reached the popularity of the other methods of divination" (238). Nevertheless, the Mari and other material show that dreams were taken seriously at both the official and popular levels.

On the the exorcist and incantation personnel (*āšipu*), see 3.3.2. On the *maḫḫû*, see 4.3.3.

5.3.4 Ugarit

Dietrich, M., and O. Loretz. *Mantik in Ugarit* (1990).
Lewis, T. J. *Cults of the Dead in Ancient Israel and Ugarit* (1989).
Loretz, O. "Nekromantie und Totenevokation in Mesopotamien, Ugarit und Israel," *Religionsgeschichtliche Beziehungen zwischen Kleinasien, Nordsyrien und dem Alten Testament* (1993) 285-315.
McLaughlin, J. L. "The *marzeaḥ* at Ugarit: A Textual and Contextual Study," *UF* 23 (1991) 265-81.
Pardee, D. J. "*Marziḫu*, *kispu*, and the Ugaritic Funerary Cult: A Minimalist View," *Aspects of Ugaritic Religion and Culture* (forthcoming).
Pitard, W. T. "A New Edition of the 'Rāpi'ūma' Texts: *KTU* 1.20-22," *BASOR* 285 (February 1992) 33-77.
Schmidt, B. B. *Israel's Beneficent Dead* (1994).

The forms of divination at Ugarit seem to have been mainly those known from Mesopotamia (Dietrich/Loretz). As a part of the international culture of the time, Ugarit would have easily imported such useful skills from the kingdoms further east. Thus, liver models and texts, birth omens, and astronominal omens are all attested. For our purposes, the main contribution of Ugarit to the discussion lies in another direction: the *marzēaḥ* institution and the question of the cult of the dead.

A great deal of discussion has centered on the *marzēaḥ* (Ugaritic *marziḫu*), well-known from the OT. This has often been seen as an institution associated with the mortuary cult, where the dead ancestors were worshiped. Another consideration here are the Rephaim (Ugaritic *rapi'uma*), who are also frequently brought into connection with the *marzēaḥ* in scholarly discussions. Who are the Rephaim? They are most often identified as the dead ancestors, especially the noble ones, who are now deified. The king list of Ugarit (*KTU* 1.113) indicates that the former kings were now seen as divine. So to remember and honor the dead heroes as now having taken their place among the gods would be a natural function of the *marzēaḥ*, and this is the *marzēaḥ*'s precise function according to many. However, there is no special connection between the *marzēaḥ* and the Rephaim, the only consistent description of the former being a place for drinking wine (McLaughlin; cf. Pitard). Pardee makes a useful distinction between the funerary cult (rites associated with burial) and the mortuary cult (later rites associated with the dead). Despite the large amount written on the subject, often with a number of misinterpretations and large measures of speculation, there is only one known text with a connection to a mortuary ritual (*KTU* 1.39).

Pardee does not deny the existence of a mortuary cult at Ugarit but only points out the little evidence we have at present. The existence of the *marzēaḥ* and the Rephaim does not by itself offer clear verification of an extensive cult of the dead. Nevertheless, it has been argued that at least one text (*KTU* 1.124) shows evidence of necromancy (Dietrich/Loretz: 205-26). If so, the argument that the evidence for necromancy is consistently late (Schmidt) runs into difficulty.

5.3.5 The Hittites

Gurney, O. R. *Some Aspects of Hittite Religion* (1977).

____ . *The Hittites* (1990).

Kammenhuber, A. *Orakelpraxis, Träume und Vorzeichenshau bei den Hettitern* (1976).

Moore, M. S. *The Balaam Traditions* (1990).

Hittite divination and oracular practice had a good deal in common with those in Mesopotamia. Indeed, some Hittite oracle compilations seem to have been borrowed from Mesopotamia. They used extispicy but also employed the observation of bird flight a great deal (Moore: 20-32). Dreams were another mode of revelation and might be evoked by incubation. Of particular interest is a passage in the "Plague Prayers of Mursilis." The passage reads as follows (*ANET*: 394):

> If, on the other hand, people are dying for some other reason, either let me see it in a dream, or let it be found out by an oracle, or let a prophet declare it, or let all the priests find out by incubation whatever I suggest to them. . . . O gods, whatever sin you behold, either let a prophet arise and declare it, or let the sibyls or the priests learn about it by incubation, or let man see it in a dream!

A similar passage is found in a prayer of Kantuzzili, a predecessor of Mursilis II, which mentions inquiring by means of dreams (*zašḫeya*), seers (^{SAL}ENSI), diviners (^{LÚ}AZU) of the Sungod by means of liver observation (Kammenhuber: 16). These passages form a remarkable parallel to 1 Samuel 28:6.

Female diviners are mentioned a number of times in the text. Referred to as "old woman" (^{SAL}ŠU.GI = Hittite *ḫašawaš*), perhaps with the connotation of "wise woman," she seems to function in some rituals of divination or incantation. These appear to be private rather than relating to the king or state. One of her main functions was to counter the evil spells of enemies of her clients.

5.3.6 Divination in Africa

Bascom, W. *Ifa Divination: Communication Between Gods and Men in West Africa* (1969).
Beattie, J., and J. Middleton, eds. *Spirit Mediumship and Society in Africa* (1969).
Evans-Pritchard, E. E. *Witchcraft, Oracles and Magic among the Azande* (1937).
Peek, P. M., ed. *African Divination Systems* (1991).

A study of divination in Africa is very useful because it shows how this art works in a living society. One of the observations which immediately presents itself is the enormous variety of aims and modes of divination. Divination functions in its own way in each society, depending on its own unique structures and needs. Divination is often resorted to in times of illness or when about to embark on some important undertaking such as a journey.

In some societies, witchcraft is central to views about illness and other misfortunes, such as among the Azande. Since witches may be unconscious of their own malign influence (unlike sorcerers, who consciously and deliberately aim to harm), divination is important to determine who is causing the problem. The Azande use the poison oracle for this and other types of inquiries. A poison derived from plants (an alkaloid with a effect similar to strychnine) is administered to a chick after the diviner puts a yes or no query.

If the chick lives, the answer is one, and if it dies, the other. The answer of the first oracle is tested by repeating the query but with the opposite sign. That is, if death meant yes in the first oracle, it would mean no in the second. The poison oracle is used not only in witchcraft accusations but also to conduct routine daily matters in the household.

Two sorts of divination might be singled out here. One is divination by spirit possession or spirit mediumship. Although this is only one mode, it is an important one. Spirit mediums usually are not, as often claimed, deviants, social misfits, or epileptics; rather, they often are well-adjusted and integrated into their community and chosen for their moral virtue. Many of them are priests of their tribal religion (Beattie/Middleton: xxiii-xxiv). The message is also often a moral one (xxvii). A second sort is *Ifa* divination (Bascom), which consists of a two-stage procedure. The first step makes use of a randomized mechanical manipulation which is used to choose a verse from a lengthy traditional list (memorized by the diviner); the verse is then used to interpret the client's situation and the response to it. The verse chosen will describe the particular sacrifice to be offered but will also contain some sort of prediction relating to the client's future, though often expressed in an ambiguous or obscure manner.

5.4 INTRODUCTION TO DIVINATION

Evans-Pritchard, E. E. *Witchcraft, Oracles and Magic among the Azande* (1937).
Frazer, J. *Belief in the Immortality of the Soul and the Worship of the Dead* (1913).
Lévy-Bruhl, L. *Primitive Mentality* (1923).
Littleton, C. S. "Lucien Lévy-Bruhl and the Concept of Cognitive Relativity," new introduction to the reprint of Lucien Lévy-Bruhl, *How Natives Think* (1985) v-lviii.
Peek, P. M., ed. *African Divination Systems* (1991).
Zuesse, Evan M. "Divination," *ER* (1987) 4.375-82.

When divination is mentioned, a certain picture impresses itself on the minds of many. This is of ignorant superstitions held by uncivilized peoples, by savages with their thinking dominated by primitive or "mythopoeic" mentality, by people without the benefit of a scientific understanding of the world. As the father of anthropology James Frazer (1.15) put it:

> I will merely say that among savages the theory of inspiration or possession is commonly invoked to explain all abnormal mental states, particularly insanity or conditions of mind bordering on it, so that persons more or less crazed in their wits, and particularly hysterical or epileptic patients, are for that very reason thought to be peculiarly favoured by the spirits and are therefore consulted as

> oracles, their wild and whirling words passing for the revelations of a higher power, whether a god or a ghost, who considerately screens his too dazzling light under a thick veil of dark sayings and mysterious ejaculations. I need hardly point out the very serious dangers which menace any society where such theories are commonly held and acted upon.

Social anthropology has moved on from Frazer's pioneering efforts. Most anthropologists who now write about magic, divination, and the like do so from a position of respect and empathy. This is in contrast with some in biblical circles where the concept of primitive mentality or mythopoeic thought still lurks. In the 1930s, E. Evans-Pritchard and others countered Lévy-Bruhl's idea of primitive mentality with the results of actual anthropological field work. Evans-Pritchard found that the day-to-day life of so-called primitive peoples was much like our own. They did not live in a world of "pan-sacralism" (cf. von Rad), nor were their lives ruled by illogical practices. Magic was a routine part of their world, but its function was very much parallel to aspects of our own lives on the social and psychological plane. The Azande and other African peoples did not assume that performing a magical rite would take the place of normal action, such as planting seeds for crops or walking faster if late getting home. They might perform magical acts in connection with these, but the magic did not replace practical activity. (It has recently been argued by Littleton that Lévy-Bruhl was widely misunderstood by his critics.)

Most people do not conduct their entire lives in a scientific manner. Indeed, outside the laboratory most scientists have just as many irrational aspects to their lives as the rest of the population—or as supposed "primitive" peoples (as Lévy-Bruhl himself noted). Modern Westerners have their social rituals, traditional customs, and non-scientific notions by which to come to terms with the world and cope with daily life. It may not be called magic, but it often has the same place in modern lives as magic in other societies. When Evans-Pritchard lived among the Azande, he recorded their use of the poison oracle (5.3.6) to confirm all their important decisions. He wrote:

> I never found great difficulty in observing oracle consultations. I found that in such matters the best way of gaining confidence was to enact the same procedure as Azande and to take oracular verdicts as seriously as they take them. I always kept a supply of poison for the use of my household and neighbours and we regulated our affairs in accordance with the oracles' decisions. I may remark that I found this as satisfactory a way of running my home and affairs as any other I know of.

When Evans-Pritchard assumed his chair in Oxford, he did not repair on a daily basis to his chicken coop with a vial of strychnine in his pocket, but he suggests that the daily lives of most Oxford dons would be no less rational and effectual if they were conducted by use of the Azande poison oracle.

So divination has an important function in many societies. Its important function has been summarized in the following way (Peek: 2, 195):

> A divination system is often the primary institutional means of articulating the epistemology of a people. . . . Divination systems do not simply reflect other aspects of a culture; they are the means . . . of knowing which underpin and validate all else. . . . It is through divination that a harmonious balance can be maintained in which a culture's most cherished values are adapted to the real world of continual flux.

The tendency to regard divination as something practiced by con artists duping ignorant people also needs correction. A good example of this view was in the second-century CE satirist Lucian. He wrote a treatise on "Alexander the False Prophet," about an individual who deceived his followers by trickery. Even when the "fake" prophet failed to escape from his own self-immolation on a giant funeral pyre, his followers interpreted his death as a divine manifestation. But the suggestion of clever tricks is even much older: it is already ascribed to the Egyptian "magicians" who opposed Moses. Yet this common apprehension is a modern misconception. Evans-Pritchard found no evidence of any attempt at trickery in the use of the poison oracle, even though that was theoretically possible and would sometimes even have been in the interests of the one conducting it.

Of course, one can go too far and explain divination and other so-called areas of magic too much in terms of Western logical terms, for these do indeed operate in societies with a world-view at times radically different from ours. To understand them properly we have to be careful of imposing our own logical categories or societal norms on the data. Divination does not have to be rationalized in Western philosophical terms to be understood and appreciated.

What is meant by divination? What sorts of activities are included under divination? Many think of divination primarily in terms of manipulation of mechanical devices such as casting lots. And many forms of divination are done at least in part by mechanical manipulation, ranging from dice and cards to shells on a tray or a basket of objects with mystical significance to mathematical grids. They would also include the priestly Urim and Thummim, and the ephod (5.1.2).

The important point is, however, that divination covers much more than mechanical manipulation. One recent discussion of divination divides the various sorts into three main categories (Zuesse): one is called "intuitive" and has to do with personal insight of the diviner; another is called "wisdom divination," including such learned skills as astrology, hepatoscopy (inspection of livers), and extispicy (inspection of intestines). But the third category has special significance: "possession divination," which is communication with spirit beings through an intermediary. This includes spirit possession, shamanism, and—perhaps surprisingly to many—prophecy. All of these forms of divination are referred to in the biblical text and will be elaborated on.

5.5 SPIRIT DIVINATION AND PROPHECY

Redford, D. B. A *Study of the Biblical Story of Joseph* (1970).

1 Samuel 28:6 is a key passage (as noted at 5.1.7). It makes no distinction between the various means of "inquiring" of God: "And Saul inquired of the Lord, but the Lord did not answer him, either by dreams or by Urim or by prophets." (This is reminiscent of a passage in the Hittite "Prayer of Mursilis"—5.3.5). Although the language of inquiry often implies a form of divination, prophecy is not set off from the divinatory modes of dream interpretation or the Urim/Thummim. It was also noted in the preceding section (5.4) that a standard classification of divination includes spirit possession or spirit divination. This immediately raises the question, How does spirit possession or spirit divination differ from prophecy? The answer implied by 1 Samuel 28:6 would seem to be that there is no difference, at least in many cases. One could seek an answer from God by various means. Two of these forms, namely Urim and dreams, fall under the heading "divination." So does prophecy, according to the context. In every case, though, even with the Urim, God is being sought as the ultimate source of the answer. God communicates, but his medium may vary.

There are a number of reasons for saying that prophecy should be classified as a form of possession divination. OT study since Wellhausen has often emphasized the uniqueness of prophecy in Israel. But this privileging of Israelite prophecy is mostly unjustified (see further at 4.4). If we look at the so-called pre-classical prophets, we find many examples of activities associated with diviners and shaman-like figures in other cultures. One example is finding lost objects. Elisha was called on to find a lost ax (2 Kings 6), and Samuel to find lost asses (1 Sam 9). It is also common for diviners in pre-modern societies to be consulted on the cause and cure of an illness and whether the person will get better. We find a similar situation with a number of the prophets: Jeroboam's wife went to the prophet Ahijah about her ill son (1 Kings 14). Elijah healed, or perhaps even brought to life, the son of the widow who gave him hospitality (1 Kings 17). A similar deed is ascribed to Elisha (2 Kings 4). Elisha also healed the leprosy of Naamah (2 Kings 5) and was consulted about the illness of Ben-Hadad, king of Damascus (2 Kings 8:7-15).

Dreams and visions are part of the diviner's art in many societies, and they have a strong place in the biblical text. Apart from the prime example of Daniel, we find Joseph as an interpreter of dreams. God made Elisha "see" (hif. *r'h*) that Hazael would become king of Damascus, suggesting a vision (2 Kings 8:13). Among the so-called classical prophets, visions are not infrequently found, especially in Ezekiel but also in Amos (7-9), Isaiah (6), Jeremiah (24-25), and Zechariah (1-8).

The question is, Are the other classical prophets different? Does not God just speak through them spontaneously without any preliminaries? Not necessarily. We know that some prophecies were the result of inquiry of the prophet or someone else (e.g., 2 Kings 8:8; Jer 21:1-2; 42:1-7; Ezek 14:1-4; 20:1-3). In other cases perhaps the prophets were not consulted as a diviner might be, but how did they receive the words ascribed to them? A frequent expression is, "The word of the Lord came to X," but we are not told *how* it came. Did the prophet perform a ritual? Was music involved, as with Elisha in 2 Kings 3:14? Was it in a dream/vision? Was it by an audition? Does an audition differ in any important way from a vision? In 2 Samuel 7:4, the "word of the Lord came to Nathan," but a little later this revelation is referred to as a "vision" (*ḥizzāyôn*: v 17).

But can one really group prophecy together with divination or even make it a subdivision of divination? After all, was not divination, as well as similar practices, forbidden to Israel? Such is stated in no uncertain terms in Deuteronomy 18:9-14 (5.1.4). Similarly, in his prophecy in Numbers 23:23 (5.1.3), Balaam states, "Lo, there is no augury (*naḥaš*) in Jacob,/No divining (*qesem*) in Israel." However, other data indicate that these passages are a Deuteronomic fiction. Deuteronomy 18 doth protest too much. How did the writer know so much about the various forms of divination if they were forbidden to Israel? Had he done anthropological fieldwork among the Canaanites? Or was he only objecting to what was common to his own society and time, perhaps in the seventh century BCE? Other passages suggest such practices continued even after Josiah's reforms (see below).

One might ask why they would have continued after the Deuteronomic dominance had been established. There are various possibilities. One of the most obvious is that the Josian reform is a literary fiction, as some suggest. But assuming there was such a reform, we cannot assume that everyone accepted Josiah's program. Perhaps the Deuteronomic view was resisted by many, as Jeremiah 44:17 indeed indicates. Another possibility is that many people may not have seen a basic conflict with their practices and such passages as Deuteronomy 18:9-14. Ask any self-designated modern witch, "Isn't witchcraft forbidden in the Bible?" The answer may well be, "Oh, only black magic is forbidden, but I practice white magic."

Various passages suggest that the practices ostensibly forbidden in Deuteronomy 18 continued long after Josiah. One of the most important is Isaiah 65:1-7, a post-exilic passage by overwhelming consensus. Despite problems of translation and interpretation, two things seem clear to most interpreters (5.1.9): (a) Private cults outside the official temple and priesthood exist and are even thriving; (b) a part of this cult concerns an attempt to gain revelations by means of necromancy—by spending the night in tombs (v 4).

Similarly, the Joseph story is dated to about the time of the Exile or even later by some (cf. Redford: 244-53), though not everyone agrees by any means. Whenever it is to be dated, Joseph is said to practice divination. Apart from the most obvious type of divination—the interpretation of dreams—there is Joseph's cup, which he has planted in Benjamin's sack of grain. It is stated that this cup is "the very one from which my master drinks and which he uses for divination" (5.1.1).

The connection between prophecy and spirit divination is further demonstrated by an examination of the various cults of the dead, considered in the next section. All this suggests that distingushing prophecy and spirit divination is difficult, if not impossible. The only possible objection—apart from those that are theologically motivated—is the question of spontaneous prophecy. In the final analysis, it really comes down to a matter of semantics and definition rather than one of a qualitative difference.

5.6 THE CULT OF THE DEAD

Ackerman, S. *Under Every Green Tree* (1992).

Barstad, H. M. *The Religious Polemics of Amos* (1984).

Berlinerblau, J. "The 'Popular Religion' Paradigm in Old Testament Research: A Sociological Critique," *JSOT* 60 (1993) 3-26.

Bloch-Smith, E. *Judahite Burial Practices and Beliefs about the Dead* (1992).

____. "The Cult of the Dead in Judah: Interpreting the Material Remains," *JBL* 111 (1992) 213-24.

Dahood, M. J. *Psalms* (1962-70).

Day, J. *Molech: A God of Human Sacrifice in the Old Testament* (1989).

Heider, G. C. *The Cult of Molek* (1985).

Lang, B. "Life after Death in the Prophetic Promise," VTSup 40 (1988) 144-56.

Lewis, T. J. *Cults of the Dead in Ancient Israel and Ugarit* (1989).

Loretz, O. "*Marziḫu* im ugaritischen und biblischen Ahnenkult: Zu Ps 23; 133; Am 6,1-7 und Jer 16,5.8," *Mesopotamica-Ugaritica-Biblica* (1993) 93-144.

Niehr, H. "Ein unerkannter Text zur Nekromantie in Israel: Bemerkungen zum religionsgeschichtlichen Hintergrund von 2 Sam 12,16a," *UF* 23 (1991) 301-6.

Pardee, D. "*Marziḫu, Kispu*, and the Ugaritic Funerary Cult: A Minimalist View," *Aspects of Ugaritic Religion and Culture* (forthcoming).

Schmidt, B. B. *Israel's Beneficent Dead* (1994).
Segal, J. B. "Popular Religion in Ancient Israel," *JJS* 27 (1976) 1-22.
Smelik, K.A.D. "Moloch, Molek or Molk-Sacrifice? A Reassessment of the Evidence Concerning the Hebrew Term Molekh," *Society of Biblical Literature Twelfth International Meeting* (Leuven: August 1994) 73 (abstract).
Smith, M. S. *The Early History of God* (1990).
____. "The Invocation of Decreased Ancestors in Psalm 49:12c," *JBL* 112 (1993) 105-7.
Smith, M. S., and E. M. Bloch-Smith. "Death and Afterlife in Ugarit and Israel," *JAOS* 108 (1988) 277-84.

A question important for the whole subject of divination is the cult of the dead. It has been axiomatic in OT studies that no afterlife is envisaged before the Exile. (True, Mitchell Dahood found many references to it in his Psalms commentary, though translations such as "Elysian Fields" and "beatific vision" did not help his case.) And it is still probably correct that the OT by and large does not think of life after death, at least in the sense of full existence of the whole person. Yet recent studies indicate that in Israel itself there was a thriving cult of the dead of some sort. This conclusion comes from a variety of considerations.

The first is the enigmatic group called the Rephaim. The Ras Shamra and Phoenician texts have led many specialists to the general conclusion that a cult of the dead was a regular part of Ugaritic religious practice. For example, the Rephaim and other texts from Ugarit suggest that the dead were periodically summoned to a banquet with the living (*KTU* 1.21 = Aqhat IVa; *KTU* 1.161 = ritual text?). Nevertheless, this interpretation has been questioned (Schmidt; cf. Pardee). Other Northwest Semitic texts may be more helpful. The living join the Rephaim when they die according to a Phoenician text (*KAI* 13.7-8 = *TSSI* 27; *KAI* 14.8 = *TSSI* 28). A Punic bilingual mentions the "divine Rephaim" (*'lnm 'r'p'm*) in the Punic text but has "sacred shades" (*dis manibus sacrum*) in the parallel Latin text (*KAI* 117). The OT picture is possibly even more complex, since the Rephaim are associated with certain primeval settlers of Palestine in some texts (e.g., Gen 14:5; 15:20; Deut 2:11, 20; 3:11, 13). However, the area in which Og of Bashan, a remnant of the Rephaim, dwells (Deut 1:4; 3:10-11; Josh 9:10; 12:4; 13:12) is the same area in which the god Rapha'u of a Ugaritic incantation seems to dwell (*KTU* 1.108): Ashtarot and Edrei. It seems that myth has been historicized, and the shades have been turned into ethnographical entities. Other passages—such as Job 26:5; Psalm 88:11-13; Isaiah 26:14, 19; Proverbs 9:18—associate the Rephaim with the dead.

Closely tied up with the Rephaim in many discussions is the institution of the *marzēaḥ*. Studies of the the *marzēaḥ* outside Israel indicate that it could sometimes be associated with a funerary cult (but see Pardee; 5.3.4). This seems to be the case in Jeremiah 16:5 in which the *marzēaḥ* is a place of mourning. It cannot be shown that the *marzēaḥ* was always a place for celebrating a cult of the dead, whether in Israel or outside it, though most references do not exclude that possibility either (cf. Barstad: 127-42; Pardee).

A related issue is that of Molek worship. Whether Molek is a deity or only a sacrifice is still debated (cf. Heider and Day with Smelik), but in any case, it seems to have been a chthonic cult associated with the underworld and with a cult of the dead. How widespread this cult was in Palestine is debatable, but it certainly existed, even in Jerusalem. Similarly, recent study of the teraphim argues that they were a common shrine to the ancestors kept in the home (5.1.6). Even the future King David had one, which his wife placed in his bed to deceive Saul's men (1 Sam 19). Confirmation of a cult of the dead in Israel comes from archeology. Elizabeth Bloch-Smith has summarized the results of studies on tombs in Palestine, especially in Judah. People were buried with a variety of personal possessions—ornaments, jewelry, favorite objects, prized possessions—but also with foodstuffs and beverages. These all suggest that the dead were being provided with things they were still in need of.

The real issue in this discussion, though, is necromancy; the term "cult of the dead" is ambiguous, and the mere existence of such cults proves little. One can have cults of the dead without assuming that the dead are available to provide aid to the living. As pointed out by several scholars (e.g., Pardee; Schmidt), a distinction should be made between a funerary cult, which relates to rites associated with burial, and a mortuary cult, which concerns later rites honoring and attending the dead. It is only the latter that comes into question with regard to seeking esoteric knowledge from the dead. Consulting the dead is mentioned in many passages apart from Deuteronomy 18 and 1 Samuel 28. One interesting passage is 2 Chronicles 16:12, where Asa is condemned for consulting the physicians (*rōfĕ'îm*). Is this a later interpretation of an original "Rephaim," as has been suggested (5.1.12)? In other words, was Asa really condemned for consulting the *dead* rather than the medics? A recent study has even seen evidence of necromancy in 2 Samuel 12:16 (Niehr).

These data show that a distinction can be made between the dominant picture of the OT and the actual beliefs and practices of the Israelite people. This does not mean that life after death was understood in the same way that it was at a later time when resurrection of the dead or the immortal soul became widely accepted. Even in pre-exilic times, something survived the person after death and could be nourished and communicated with. The shade sometimes had special insight into the future and could have this foreknowledge called forth under certain conditions or with special ceremonies. As Bernhard Lang has summarized it, "Death, for the ancient Semite, meant travel to the nether world and acquiring the status of an ancestor who was worshipped by descendants" (1988: 136).

This does not mean that a division can usefully be made along the lines of "popular" religion versus "official" religion as has sometimes been done (cf. Berlinerblau). Rather than two categories, we have to think of at least three: "popular religion," or, better, that widely practiced among the people; "official religion," the state or royal cult; "OT religious teaching," the picture arising from the OT text in its final form (though that picture is not always a unified one). "Popular religion" existed from the earliest times. "Official religion" was only a later introduction, at the time when a state or monarchy existed; thus many would put it quite late, comparatively speaking. In any case, there was no necessary conflict between state and popular religion. The state cult was primarily for the court and the capital city and perhaps an expression of loyalty to the king at other sites. The official cult did not and was not intended to oust the ages-old customs of the people; indeed, in many cases it picked up or adapted popular practices. Also, we should not think of a "popular religion" or the religion of the people as a monolithic entity. The term is really only an umbrella for all the different beliefs, cults, and forms of worship among the populace. There were no doubt many "popular religions" in Palestine, both during the monarchy and afterward.

Neither of the historical forms of worship (whether popular or official) may have found their way into the religion acceptable to the writers and editors of the OT tradition. Some minority groups might have had a great deal of influence on the biblical tradition, so that it represents the views and even practices of some groups in Israel. But the OT gives us primarily a prescriptive theological construct rather than a historical description of what was actually happening. Here and there in its criticism of the "abominations in Israel" the historical situation no doubt emerges, but such is the perspective of the writers that we cannot expect anything but a caricature much of the time.

Smith and Bloch-Smith have argued that the cult of dead was not forbidden before the middle of the eighth century. As they see it, Deuteronomy 26:14 indicates that tithes should not be used to feed the dead but does not forbid the dead to be fed. Deuteronomy 18 forbids consulting the dead through mediums but says nothing about consulting the dead directly. Some of the evidence of Smith and Bloch-Smith is subject to more than one interpretation, but the general point is well taken: the cult of the dead was a part of historical Israel and consultation of the dead was an accepted part of Israelite religion until a later time and perhaps within certain circles.

The presence of necromancy has become widely accepted. The final question is how early the practice occurred in Israelite society. Brian Schmidt has argued that there is no evidence for it before the late Judean monarchy at the earliest. If there is evidence of necromancy in Ugarit (5.3.4), however, the chances of its existence in Israel at an early time is strengthened (Schmidt himself argues against its occurrence at Ugarit). Additionally, some of the data given by Bloch-Smith suggest that a cult of the dead was known rather earlier than this; this by itself does not prove the existence of necromancy, but it would seem to allow the possibility. The question is ultimately tied up with when the text was finally edited. For a discussion of the dating of the society being described, see 7.4.

5.7 DREAMS AND DREAMERS

Carroll, R. P. *Jeremiah: A Commentary* (1986).
Durand, J.-M. *Archives épistolaires de Mari I/1* (1988).
Ehrlich, E. L. *Der Traum im Alten Testament* (1953).
Ellis, M. deJong. "The Goddess Kititum Speaks to King Ibalpiel: Oracle Texts from Ishchali," *MARI* 5 (1987) 235-66.
Gnuse, R. "A Reconsideration of the Form-Critical Structure in I Samuel 3: An Ancient Near Eastern Dream Theophany," *ZAW* 94 (1982) 379-90.
Husser, J.-M. *Le songe et la parole* (1994).
Lewis, N. *The Interpretation of Dreams and Portents* (1976).
Lindblom, J. *Prophecy in Ancient Israel* (1962).
Long, B. O. "Reports of Visions among the Prophets," *JBL* 95 (1976) 353-65.
Miller, J. E. "Dreams and Prophetic Visions," *Biblica* 71 (1990) 401-4.
Miller, P. C. *Dreams in Late Antiquity* (1994).
Niditch, S. *The Symbolic Vision in Biblical Tradition* (1980).
Oppenheim, A. L. "The Interpretation of Dreams in the Ancient Near East, With a Translation of an Assyrian Dream-Book," *Transactions of the American Philosophical Society* 46 (1956) 179-354.
Ray, J. D. *The Archive of Hor* (1976).
Sasson, J. M. "Mari Dreams," *JAOS* 103 (1983) 283-93.
Volten, A. *Demotische Traumdeutung (Pap. Carlsberg XIII und XIV Verso)* (1942).
White, R. J., ed. *The Interpretation of Dreams:* Oneirocritica *by Artemidorus (Translation and Commentary)* (1975).

Dreams and visions are important media of divine communication in most traditional societies. They were important in the ancient Near East, including Israel itself. Their popularity in comparison with other forms of divination varied with time and location, but dreams seem to have some place in almost all literature of the ancient Near East (see especially the survey in Oppenheim). Yet with regard to Israel, dreams have often been compared unfavorably with prophecy.

The terms "dream," "dreamer," and the like (Hebrew and Aramaic *ḥlm*) are not used too frequently in the Hebrew Bible: quite a few references in Genesis (though concentrated in the Joseph story); Deuteronomy 13:2-6 (Eng. 13:1-5); 1 Samuel 28:6, 15; 1 Kings 3:5-15 (Solomon's dream); a few passages in the prophets; and a number of places in Daniel. Other than these, only a few other passing references are found. Dreams seem to be treated negatively in Jeremiah (23:27-32; 29:8) and are otherwise seldom mentioned in the prophetic literature. This is has led to the conventional assertion that the OT prophets regarded dreams negatively. This sweeping generalization needs to be challenged.

First, the rarity of the root *ḥlm* in the Prophets may or may not be significant. It is found occasionally, so it is not completely avoided. As noted, Jeremiah 23:27-32 is critical, but it is in the context of an attack on "false" prophets. Dreams are only one aspect of the prophecy criticized, and other characteristics condemned (e.g., prophesying in Yhwh's name) are also typical of "true" prophets such as Jeremiah himself. Since some terms are used both positively and negatively in the prophetic literature (e.g., *nb'*), this passage by itself proves nothing about the general attitude toward dreams in Israelite society, nor does it demonstrate that dreams were a sign of false prophecy (cf. Carroll: 469-74; Husser: 162-66).

A second consideration is whether there is a clear distinction between "dream" and "vision," since the latter occurs frequently in prophetic literature. We moderns make such a distinction because we understand dreams as a normal activity of the mind during the sleep cycle, whereas visions are usually associated with an altered state of consciousness outside sleep, but we should be careful not to impose this understanding on the ancient data. There are different sorts of dreams, as was already noted by the Greek writer Artemidorus in his *Oneirocritica* (1.1-3; 4.1-2); Artemidorus distinguishes the prescient dreams (*oneiros*) from ordinary dreams. He further divides the significant dreams between "direct" and "allegorical." His insight has been taken up by modern scholars. For example, Oppenheim has made a distinction between "message" dreams, in which a direct message is conveyed, and "symbolic" dreams, which require interpretation. Although many dreams do not fall neatly into one category or the other, the two categories illustrate the important connections between dreams and other forms of divine-human communication. Dreams as direct revelations are closely related to prophecy, whereas symbolic or allegorical dreams fit very well into the wisdom tradition with its accumulation and classification of traditional knowledge. It was accepted in antiquity that not all dreams were significant or, at least, that the dreams of a king or priest may have broader significance.

Perhaps dreams are symbolic more often than visions, yet the categories of direct revelation (message) and symbolic do not necessarily separate dreams from visions. Some visions are symbolic, such as Amos 7:7-9; 8:1-3; Jeremiah 24; and the visons of Zechariah (cf. Niditch), while some dreams contain a direct message from the god(s). For example, the Mari dream in the temple of Dagan (Durand: [#233]) gives an immediate message and differs from a vision or even a prophecy only by the setting (*ANET*: 623, italics mine):

> Thus Itur-Asdu your servant . . . Malik-Dagan, a man from Shakka, ca<m>e and spoke to me as follows: "In a dream of mine I was set on going in the company of a(nother) man . . . to Mari. . . . I entered the temple of Dagan and prostrated myself. As I was prostrate, Dagan opened his mouth and spoke to me as follows: '*Did the kings of the Yaminites and their forces make peace with the forces of Zimri-Lim who moved up here?*' I said, 'They did not make peace.' Just before I went out he spoke to me as follows: '*Why are the messengers of Zimri-Lim not in constant attendance upon me, and why does he not lay his full report before me? Had this been done, I would long ago have delivered the kings of the Yaminites into the power of Zimri-Lim. Now go, I send you. Thus shall you speak to Zimri-Lim, saying: "Se[nd] me your messengers and lay your full report before me, and then I will have the kings of the Yaminites [coo]ked on a fisherman's spit, and I will lay them before you.*"'" This is what this man saw in his dream and then recounted to me.

In the OT the terminology is often seen as significant, with *ḥōlām* being normally translated as "dream," and the various forms of *ḥzh* as "vision." Husser (24-25) has distinguished them on the basis that dreams have a visual element whereas visions do not. He has recognized an important point already noted above (4.5.1); namely, that "vision" can be used of auditions and speech. Nevertheless, his attempt to dissociate "vision" from the visual is misguided, since visions often have a visual element. In some cases, the visual element is only of the deity and serves merely as the setting for an audition (cf. Gnuse: 380-81). Several passages in Job make dream(s), (*ḥălôm[ôt]*) and "vision(s) of the night," (*ḥezyôn[ôt] lailāh*), parallel (Job 7:14; 20:8). Job 4:13 associates visions of the night with sleep, and 33:15 seems to make night vision equivalent to dream. Numbers 24:4 associates seeing (*ḥzh*) and open eyes with a vision (*maḥăzeh*). Another word for vision (*mar'āh*) may have mainly words as its content (1 Sam 3:1-15; Gen 46:2); on the other hand, it may have a large visual element (Ezek 1:1; 8:3; Dan 10).

Whether there is a distinction between usage of the various terms, more important is the actual entity. The descriptions of what are called "dreams" and what are called "visions" do not necessarily differ. The vision of Micaiah, in which he eavesdrops on the divine council (1 Kings 22:13-28); Daniel's dream/vision (*ḥēlem/ḥezwā'*), in which he sees the Ancient of Days and the One Like a Son of Man (Dan 7); the Mari dream (Durand #233, quoted above); and the Mari dream or vision promising Zimri-Lim eternal sovereignty (Durand #236; Sasson: 285) have no formal distinguishing characteristics in the content of the actual message (cf. the italicized section in the quotation above). One cannot label this one a vision and that one only a dream; any distinction is merely academic.

The close relationship of dreams and prophecy is indicated by 1 Samuel 28:6, in which dreams and prophecy are evidently equal means of divine communication. Similarly, Deuteronomy 13:2-6 (Eng. 13:1-5) closely associates prophets and "dreamers of dreams." If the framework of some dream reports is taken away, the remaining divine message may be a straightforward prophecy. For example, if we compare some of the Mari dream reports (such as Durand ##227, 233, 234, 238; also Sasson 1983) with the Kititum prophecy (Ellis), we can see this easily. The Kititum prophecy may even have come through a dream, though if so, the dream framework has not been retained (cf. Ellis: 251-56). On the other hand, if we remove the dream framework from the Mari dream (Durand #233, quoted above), the remaining message (italicized in the quotation) looks just like the Kititum prophecy, or like many OT prophecies which are stated to be a word of Yhwh. Similarly, some of the oracles discussed by the Ptolemaic priest Ḥor are not clear as to their origin, whether "through dream or ecstatic or some other medium unknown to us" (Ray: 134).

A further consideration is whether the dream account describes an actual dream or whether it is only a literary creation (cf. Lindblom). We can agree from the outset that both sorts are known from ancient Near Eastern literature. Despite some apparent stylized language contributed by the recording scribe, the Mari reports almost certainly have some descriptions of genuine dreams (4.3.3). At the other extreme, the very stereotyped dreams of Daniel are unlikely to be actual experiences but careful literary creations. Yet there are many accounts which are far from clear-cut, and assessing whether they embody actual experiences, mere literary creations, or an amalgam of the two is very difficult. In the OT specifically, accounts of dreams have to be evaluated as a part of the narrative in which they occur.

5.8 SHAMANISM

Brown, J. P. "The Mediterranean Seer and Shamanism," *ZAW* 93 (1981) 374-400.

Carroll, R. P. "The Elijah-Elisha Sagas: Some Remarks on Prophetic Succession in Ancient Israel," *VT* 19 (1969) 400-15.

Diószegi, V., and M. Hoppál, eds. *Shamanism in Siberia* (1978).

Edsman, C.-M., ed. *Studies in Shamanism* (1967).

Eliade, M. *Shamanism: Archaic Techniques of Ecstasy* (1964).

Eliade, M., et al. "Shamanism," *ER* (1987) 13.201-23.

Goldammer, K. "Elemente des Schamanismus im Alten Testament," *Ex Orbe Religionum* (1972) 2.266-85.

Hultkrantz, Å. "Ecological and Phenomenological Aspects of Shamanism", *Shamanism in Siberia* (1978) 27-58.

Kapelrud, A. S. "Shamanistic Features in the Old Testament," *Studies in Shamanism* (1967) 90-96.

The word "shaman" is widely and loosely used. For that reason, it is important to be clear what is being referred to, though no definition is agreed upon even among specialists. Eliade (1964; 1987) has emphasized the technique of inducing a trance state (ecstasy) as the common features of shamanism. However, he has been criticized for focusing on the history-of-religions aspect of the problem without paying adequate attention to the sociological features of shamanism (Hultkrantz: 30-31). The shaman was first recognized as a constituent of Siberian hunting tribes, and the word "shaman" itself was borrowed from the language of one of these tribes, the Tungus. Although some would restrict the term to this specific context, this would ignore the normal anthropological procedure which recognizes that similar social phenomena may occur in various societies.

According to Hultkrantz, the "central idea of shamanism is to establish means of contacts with the supernatural world by the ecstatic experience of a professional and inspired intermediary, the shaman" (30). There are four constituent parts to shamanism (Hultkrantz: 31-51): (1) the shaman's contacts with the supernatural world; (2) the shaman as intermediary between human and supernatural; (3) inspiration from helping spirits; and (4) the shaman's ecstatic experiences. Shamanism occurs in a variety of areas over the world but is restricted to certain particular societies (Eliade, et al.; Hultkrantz: 52-54). It is found mainly in Siberia and inner Asia, North American, and South America. Although found sporadically elsewhere (Southeast Asia, Japan, Australia, Oceania), it is not a ubiquitous feature of pre-modern societies. For example, it does not exist very extensively in Africa.

If we accept Hultkrantz's strictures, shamans as such are not found in the Israelite tradition. This conclusion would seem to be widely accepted among specialists. Rather, what we discover in the OT tradition are certain features parallel to those of shamanism, and the shaman may help us to understand these particular features better (cf. Goldammer; Kapelrud; Brown).

Brown has attempted to identify a common Mediterranean mantic figure with features in common with the shaman; unfortunately, many of the features he discusses have little or no counterpart in the OT tradition and thus are helpful only in a very general way. Yet the services supplied by the shaman are sometimes the same as those for diviners and prophets in Israel: healing, finding lost objects, looking into the future. There are also a number of shamanistic characteristics to be found among the prophetic figures of the OT, such as the spiritual call and the trance state in which communication with the supernatural world takes place (4.5.2; 5.5). The stories of Elijah and Elisha are especially abundant in these (cf. Carroll), though other figures also show them, such as finding lost objects (Samuel) or curing illness (Isaiah; Ahijah).

5.9 THE GESTALT OF THE DIVINER

1. Divination was a main preoccupation in the ancient Near East. The court especially was very much concerned to guide its activities by consulting the divine world through divinatory means, but other persons seem to have used some techniques themselves or to have consulted diviners who made themselves available to commoners. The Hittite and Mesopotamian kings made a regular habit of trying to determine the will of the gods by trained diviners of various sorts.

2. Israel was no exception to the generalization that Near Eastern societies made much of divination. The evidence of the OT text and archeology shows that divination was widely used in Israelite society. The main forms of divination used by the monarchs were the priestly modes of the Urim/Thummim and the ephod. These are especially attested in texts associated with the early kings. We have no way of knowing whether the absence of attestation in texts for later monarchs is due to accident, literary design, or to an actual change in circumstances. It is possible that prophecy began to replace the priestly lots as time went on; certainly, the language of inquiry is used in regard to a number of prophets (Ahijah; Elisha; Huldah; Ezekiel).

3. The forms of divination available to the common Israelite seem to have been those associated with familiar spirits and cults of the dead. If mechanical means of divination were used, we have little evidence of them preserved. Perhaps the reason such modes as necromancy are known is due, ironically, to the fact that they are heavily censured in some of the OT texts. A number of texts describe practices which seem to fit a seance in which the dead are consulted. If these texts are correctly understood, we have several accounts which apparently refer to necromancy or related forms of divination (perhaps associated with several different periods in Israel's history). Despite the tendency of the text to condemn such practices, for the sociologist these are simply another source of information about society. The theologian might make value judgments, but sociologists want a description of what went on in society. (And the theologian would do well to take note of such inconvenient data as Joseph's divining and David's teraphim!)

4. Israel seems to have favored spirit divination. This may be one of the reasons that mechanical means are poorly attested for Israel (apart from the priestly modes). This form of divination is often overlooked in discussions, but the putting of questions to a spirit controlled by or at least available to the diviner is an important mode of divination in some societies. Yet spirit divination is not clearly distinguished from prophecy; indeed, prophecy could be considered a form of spirit divination in most instances. One might formally distinguish spontaneous prophetic revelation from spirit divination, in which the answer to a specific question is sought. But the modes of revela-

tion are often the same, and it is clear that at least some prophecies in the OT are said to be the result of divine inquiry. For example, the texts indicate that Jeremiah (37:6-10; 42) and Ezekiel (14:1-11; 20:1-3) both receive messages as a result of inquiry. It may be that many more prophecies were actively sought by the prophet but that this fact was not noted when the prophecy was written down. Thus, where other societies used extispicy by trained specialists or catalogued omens, Israel seems to have preferred consultation of spirits. This may account for the greater prominence of prophecy in Israel as compared to other Near Eastern countries.

5. The overlap between prophecy, divination, and other forms of inquiry into the divine will are well illustrated by the account of Balaam. A further passage of importance is 1 Samuel 28:6, in which Urim, dreams, and prophecy are all means by which God speaks to humans. Despite some apparent objection to dreams in some passages, there is no blanket condemnation of them. Furthermore, dreams are not necessarily distinguished from visions. The content of some dreams (and visions) is a straightforward prophetic message, once the visual framework is removed. We have no way of knowing in many cases how the divine message came, even when it is expressed in purely auditory form.

6. Some forms of divination seem to have no place in Israel. Apart from one passage in Ezekiel 13, there is no evidence that witchcraft beliefs and accusation played a role in Israelite society. Thus, we do not find accounts of people being charged with witchcraft or accused of sorcery or casting spells on opponents. If such happened in Israel, it has left no trace in the literature or archeology. Perhaps the nearest thing we have is the concept of a formalized curse pronounced against someone.

6.

The Wise

Lemaire, A. "Scribes: I. Proche-Orient ancien; II. Ancien Testament—Ancien Israël," *DBS* 12 (1992) 244-66.

The term "the wise" (wise man/men, wise woman/women, sage/s) is often used alongside social designations such as priest, prophet, and ruler, but it is rather less well defined than these. Part of our problem will be to consider what is meant by "the wise." There is also the question of whether it is a religious designation. As will be clear, the term is not used exclusively of a religious function, but religious figures are often referred to by this term. Therefore, it is important that the wise also be studied, not just the prophets, priests, and others.

6.1 SELECTED OLD TESTAMENT TEXTS

As will soon become clear, the question of the wise in the OT is not as straightforward as it is with some of the other figures. We have lengthy texts describing what prophets and priests do. We have passing references to the wise but little in the way of description or stories about the wise and their actions. One book not considered here is the Wisdom of Solomon. The reasons are its lateness (perhaps first century CE) and the clear Greek influence on it, making it problematic for discussing wisdom in ancient Israel.

6.1.1 The Wise Men of Egypt

Texts: Genesis 41; Exodus 7-8; Isaiah 19:11-15.

References to the sages of Egypt usually identify them as part of a group of court figures with special knowledge in divination and the esoteric arts; in other words, they are specialists in mantic wisdom (6.5), parallel to the wise men in the Babylonian court (Daniel; 6.1.9). In the story of Joseph the wise men and "magicians" (*ḥarṭummîm*) are called on to interpret the king's dreams (Gen 41:8). Joseph, who himself interprets the dreams, is declared wise not only because of this ability but also for his administrative skills (Gen 41:33, 39). In the account of Moses at Pharaoh's court, the wise men and magicians are used to oppose Moses and duplicate his miracles (Exod 7:11, 22; 8:3, 14). Isaiah 19:11-15 makes fun of the wise men and counselors of Pharaoh, who attempt to see into the future but do not know what Yhwh is planning.

6.1.2 Deuteronomy

Crenshaw, J. L. "Method in Determining Wisdom Influence upon 'Historical' Literature," *JBL* 88 (1969) 129-42.
McCarthy, D. J. *Treaty and Covenant* (1978).
Nicholson, E. W. *God and His People* (1986).
Weinfeld, M. *Deuteronomy and the Deuteronomic School* (1972).
____. *Deuteronomy 1-11* (1991).

Deuteronomy is not a wisdom book, unless the term "wisdom" is used in an unacceptably wide sense (cf. the criticisms of Crenshaw). The origin of the book has long been debated. The thesis of particular interest here, however, is that of Weinfeld (1972). If he is correct, the book of Deuteronomy is the product of educated scribal circles who show knowledge of international legal and literary forms. For example, he argues that the literary form of Deuteronomy has the same structure as the international treaty. This is not a new idea, though some earlier formulations of the thesis have not stood up to investigation (cf. the discussion in McCarthy; also the survey in Nicholson: 3-117). The importance of Weinfeld's proposal is that it makes a theological work—one which many theologians would make central to the OT—the product of scribes. This is supported by the extent of wisdom language in the book (Weinfeld 1991: 62-65).

It has often been noted that about 200 BCE Ben Sira (6.1.8) connected the Deuteronomic emphasis on Torah with the wisdom tradition. Yet this association is not really new, for Deuteronomy 4:6 already makes the link between wisdom and law:

> Observe them [these laws and regulations] faithfully, for that will be proof of your wisdom [*ḥokmāh*] and discernment [*bînāh*] to other peoples, who on hearing of all these laws will say, "Surely, that great nation is a wise [*ḥākām*] and discerning [*nāvôn*] people."

6.1.3 Jeremiah

Avigad, N. *Hebrew Bullae from the Time of Jeremiah* (1986).
McKane, W. *Prophets and Wisemen* (1983).
Whybray, R. N. *The Intellectual Tradition in the Old Testament* (1974).

Scribes have a prominent place in this book. Especially notable is Baruch, the scribe whose main function seems to be to act as Jeremiah's amanuensis (36). Baruch is not further designated, so we do not know whether he was a temple scribe or a friend or a disciple of Jeremiah. If he was simply someone who would hire out his scribal skills, one might wonder that he would have been willing to put his life in danger as he does here. Unfortunately, the finding of a seal of "Berekyahu b. Neriyahu the scribe" (Avigad: 28-29, 128-30) tells us little, since we have no way of knowing to what extent the picture in the book represents the historical Baruch. (There is also the fact that the names differ, even if this by itself does not preclude identity.) Most of the other references are to scribes who are part of the royal or religious administration. Baruch reads Jeremiah's words to the people in the temple from the chamber of Gemariah b. Shaphan the scribe (36:10). (It is not entirely clear, but a plausible interpretation is that Gemariah has a chamber in the temple to exercise a scribal function there.) When Gemariah's son heard Baruch's word, he went to the scribe's chamber in the royal palace to meet various officials, including Elishama the scribe (36:11-12, 20-21). (Some argue that Gemariah was probably not a scribe but that the designation "scribe" applies only to Shaphan [Avigad: 129 n. 164]; however, exactly the same argument could be used to say that Neriyahu and not Berekyahu was the scribe of the seal.)

There are also general wisdom references. The people say they are wise and have the teaching (*tôrāh*) of Yhwh, but the scribes have labored for nothing, and the wise shall be shamed (8:8-9). God asks who is wise enough to understand "this," apparently referring to the ruined land (9:11). The wise man should not glory in his wisdom but in knowledge of God (9:22-23). The plotters against Jeremiah assert that *torah* shall not fail the priest; nor counsel, the wise; nor the word, the prophet (18:18). Who the "wise" are in this verse is debated. McKane has maintained that they are the high administrative individuals (42-43), whereas Whybray has argued that this is likely a common proverb about groups of people forever talking (24-31). One of Yhwh's attributes is wisdom and understanding, and by these he established the universe (10:7, 12-13).

6.1.4 Proverbs

Bryce, G. E. *A Legacy of Wisdom* (1979).
Golka, F. W. *The Leopard's Spots* (1993).
Hermisson, H. J. *Studien zur israelitischen Spruchweisheit* (1968).

Kayatz, C. *Studien zu Proverbien 1-9* (1966).
Weeks, S. *Early Israelite Wisdom* (1994).
Whybray, R. N. *Proverbs* (1994)

The book of Proverbs has been regarded as the archetypal wisdom book. It embodies much of the terminology and also the literary formulation taken to be typical of wisdom literature. Proverbs 1-9 is composed of "instructions" (longer wisdom sayings), often by a father to a son, well-known also in Egypt and Mesopotamia. Much of the book (chs. 10-29) is composed of short proverbs without any discernable pattern of arrangement. These cover a large variety of topics. Many could arise from the experiences of people from any stratum of society. As a result, it has been suggested that the origin of these proverbs is in "clan wisdom" (*Sippenethos*). Other studies propose that even the seeming folk proverbs have a structure which is likely to be the result of learned composition (Hermisson). This view has been criticized by Golka (especially 13-14), but he accepts that the final assembly of the book was done by learned circles. There seems nothing to preclude that the book contains a mixture of folk proverbs and other sayings most likely to have arisen in a wealthy or aristocratic circle.

This suggests that large portions of the book, if not all of it, are the product of learned circles of some sort. Even if folk or clan wisdom has made its way into the book, it was probably collected and perhaps even reworked by individuals with a literary background. Chapters 1-9 are especially seen to be the product of learned and literary individuals. It was once argued that this section was quite late, post-exilic, but a good case has been made that it belongs to the period of the monarchy (Kayatz). The learned character of at least some of Proverbs is demonstrated by 22:20—24:22, which is widely believed to be dependent on the *Sayings of Amenemope* (Bryce) and thus shows acquaintance with the wisdom tradition of Egypt. Many of the proverbs discuss matters having to do with situations in a well-to-do household or even in the royal court (e.g., 14:35; 16:12-15; 25:2, 6). This does not prove that they arose in the court (Weeks), but it suggests they are not just the product of peasant wisdom; a court origin is also not excluded.

If the analogy of Mesopotamia and Egypt is anything to go by, the collection and composition of proverbs and sayings were a scribal endeavor (sayings are widespread in Egyptian literature but not proverbs, for some reason). Proverbs 25:1 refers to the proverbs of Solomon copied out by the "men of Hezekiah." Who these men were is not stated, but a reasonable inference is that they were scribes, another indication that the book as a whole is the product of scribes.

6.1.5 Job

Clines, D.J.A. *Job 1-20* (1989).

Dell, K. J. *The Book of Job as Sceptical Literature* (1991).
Hurwitz, A. "The Date of the Prose-Tale of Job Linguistically Reconsidered," *HTR* 67 (1974) 17-34.
Pope, M. *Job* (1973).
Robertson, D. A. *Linguistic Evidence in Dating Early Hebrew Poetry* (1972).
Whedbee, J. W. "The Comedy of Job," *Studies in the Book of Job* (1977) 1-39.

The book of Job is probably one of the most sophisticated books in the Hebrew Bible, indeed in the ancient world, but it is also one of the most difficult to categorize. The theme is that of theodicy: Why does God act as he does—or fail to act when elementary justice is required? This basic theological conundrum is attacked with great literary skill, though not everyone agrees on what the final answer is. One category into which the book falls is that of skeptical literature (Dell), a general category known also from Egyptian and Mesopotamian wisdom literature (e.g., the *Dispute of a Man with His Ba*; *Ludlul Bēl Nemēqi*, the *Dialogue of Pessimism*). Such literature asks questions which other literature often takes for granted and challenges conventional beliefs and religion.

When we ask who could have produced such literature, it seems unlikely that it is a folk product, whether oral or written. Chapters 1-2 and 42 are often referred to as an old folk tale to which the poem has been added. This may well be so (though some would argue that the poem is older than the *present form* of the folk tale [Hurwitz]), suggesting that the folk tale has been given its present form at a late time and by an author with considerable knowledge of literature. W. Whedbee has argued that the final form of the text shows compositional genius in which each element contributes artistically to the genre of comedy. All in all, the book as a whole shows signs of careful organization and skillful composition. It is hardly likely to be folk literature in its present form but a literary product, whatever elements have been drawn upon in its composition. The precise dating of Job is problematic. Many have put it in the post-exilic period, which is possible for the final form of the book, but there are good arguments (especially from the language) that would put the poem in pre-exilic times (Pope: xxxii-xl; Robertson).

The value of the book is the challenge it presents to conventional wisdom. The concept of action-consequence, well-known in older wisdom contexts and rooted in Deuteronomic theology, is attacked head on. That is, the idea that one's present condition is a reward for doing good or punishment for doing evil—an idea thoroughly expressed by Job's friends—is shown to be wrong, at least in Job's case. The question of theodicy, which has come to be such a major problem in any systematic theology, is the main subject of Job. The sophisticated and artistic way in which the subject is handled is a clear indication of the education and ability of the author(s)/editor(s).

6.1.6 Qohelet

Braun, R. *Koheleth und die frühhellenistische Popularphilosophie* (1973).
Crenshaw, J. A. *Ecclesiastes* (1988).
Grabbe, L. L. *Judaism from Cyrus to Hadrian* (1992).
Isaksson, B. *Studies in the Language of Qoheleth* (1987).
Loretz, O. *Qohelet und der alte Orient* (1964).
Murphy, R. *Ecclesiastes* (1993).
Schoors, A. *The Preacher Sought to Find Pleasing Words* (1992).
Whybray, R. N. *Ecclesiastes* (1989).
Young, I. *Diversity in Pre-Exilic Hebrew* (1993).

The book of Qohelet or Ecclesiastes is usually dated to the third century BCE. The main reason for this is the language. Despite a recent attempt to suggest that the language of the book could have come from a much earlier age (Young), the many characteristics shared by Qohelet with Mishnaic Hebrew makes its late date the best explanation (cf. Schoors; Isaksson [though he allows that it might be from the Persian period]). Otherwise, there is little in the book which suggests a specific age, though its content easily fits into the period of Ptolemaic rule over Palestine. The most interesting feature of the book is its skepticism. The author is willing to ask radical questions and explore the uncertainties and doubts with regard to received religious wisdom. The writer seems willing to question whether the old ideas of the rewards for religious faithfulness and obedience to God's law really stand up to human experience.

The main problem of the book is, then, similar to that of Job even though the mode of expression and approach to the problem are quite different. Beyond this agreement, there is considerable dispute regarding the exact position of Qohelet (contrast Crenshaw and Whybray). It has often been assumed that the writer was very much influenced by Greek literary and philosophical ideas (e.g., Braun). If the usual dating is correct, there is no reason why this could not be the case, but the usual evidences claimed for Greek influence are not overt and may be explained from older Near Eastern parallels in most cases (cf. Loretz). It is not necessary to resolve this problem to gain the information needed for our purposes, though some possibilities will be noted.

The writer was evidently a person of wealth and standing in society. Not only could he read and write, but he shows evidence of a good education, one incorporating traditional wisdom and perhaps even Greek literature or popular philosophy. He was also himself a teacher of young men (cf. 11:9-12:2). This all suggests an individual of aristocratic status, with wealth, position, and leisure to pursue religious and philosophical questions (cf. Whybray: 12-13). Although he shows no particular cultic interest, there is nothing to preclude his being a priest. In third-century Palestine, there was a priestly aristocracy, with the high priest's family occupying an extremely important position in the community. Other aristocratic families (e.g., the Tobiads) had also intermarried with the high priestly family, no doubt in part to advance their own family and personal ambitions. (On third-century Palestine, see Grabbe 1992: ch. 4.)

6.1.7 Ezra-Nehemiah

Grabbe, L. L. "What Was Ezra's Mission?" *Second Temple Studies: 2. Temple and Community in the Persian Period* (1994) 286-99.

In these two books, the term "scribe" is used almost entirely in reference to Ezra, along with the title "priest" (Ezra 7:6, 11, 12, 21; Neh 8:1, 4, 9, 13; 12:26, 36). The normal meaning of the term in the Persian empire of the time is only partially helpful, because Ezra is clearly not an ordinary scribe. Various suggestions have been made about a special office that Ezra may have held, but these are ultimately unconvincing (Grabbe). In the text, the main aspects of Ezra's office relate to the law of God. He is a "ready scribe in the law" (*sōfēr māhîr bĕtôrat*) of Moses, which Yhwh gave to Israel (Ezra 7:6). He had dedicated himself to studying this *torah* and to teaching it to Israel (7:10). He is a scribe in the words of Yhwh's commandments and the statutes upon Israel (v 11), a scribe in the law (*dātāʾ*) of the God of heaven (v 12). Ezra's scribalness apparently lies in his knowledge of God's law.

The only other use of the term "scribe" is in the context of gathering tithes, which Nehemiah reinstituted after they had fallen into desuetude (Neh 13:13). Placed in charge of the tithes were the (high?) priest Shelemiah, the scribe Zadok, and Pedaiah of the Levites.

6.1.8 Ben Sira

Caquot, A. "Ben Sira et le Messianisme," *Semitica* 16 (1966) 43-68.
Harrington, D. J. "The Wisdom of the Scribe According to Ben Sira," *Ideal Figures in Ancient Judaism* (1980) 181-88.
Martin, J. D. "Ben Sira's Hymn to the Fathers: A Messianic Perspective," *OTS* 24 (1986) 107-23.
Olyan, S. M. "Ben Sira's Relationship to the Priesthood," *HTR* 80 (1987) 261-86.
Skehan, P. W., and A. A. Di Lella, *The Wisdom of Ben Sira* (1987).
Stadelmann, H. *Ben Sira als Schriftgelehrter* (1980).

Written shortly after 200 BCE, Ben Sira is one of the few Jewish writings for whom the author is known and correctly named. The work itself tells us a good deal about the writer and his personal attitudes, as well as about the society in which he lived. The format of the book is similar to Proverbs 1-9 in that it is made up primarily of the genre "instruction," in which a theme is discussed in a multi-line poetic unit, often in the form of instructions to the young person or student. Many of the themes are similar to those in Proverbs, but there are others which reflect the later society of Palestine. The author may have been a priest (cf. Stadelmann; Olyan) or, if not, one who was an admirer of the priests. His hero is Simon, the high priest at the time of the Seleucid conquest (Ben Sira 50). The author also extols the scribal art, clearly speaking from the experience of the scribe. The sort of scribe he has in mind is one who is mainly occupied with God's law. Perhaps Ben Sira himself was a temple scribe; such an occupation would fit well the general outlook of his book. Of particular interest is his description of the scribe and sage, one of the few descriptions to give any detail (Ben Sira 38:24-39:11 NEB):

> A scholar's wisdom comes of ample leisure; if a man is to be wise he must be relieved of other tasks. How can a man become wise who guides the plough . . . and talks only about cattle? . . . How different it is with the man who devotes himself to studying the law of the Most High, who investigates all the wisdom of the past, and spends his time studying the prophecies! He preserves the sayings of famous men and penetrates the intricacies of parables. He investigates the hidden meaning of proverbs and knows his way among riddles. The great avail themselves of his services, and he is seen in the presence of rulers. He travels in foreign countries and learns at first hand the good or evil of man's lot. He makes a point of rising early to pray. . . . If it is the will of the great Lord, he will be filled with a spirit of intelligence; then he will pour forth wise sayings of his own and give thanks to the Lord in prayer. He will have sound advice and knowledge to offer, and his thoughts will dwell on the mysteries he has studied. He will disclose what he has learnt from his own education, and will take pride in the law of the Lord's covenant. Many will praise his intelligence; it will never sink into oblivion. The memory of him will not die but will live on from generation to generation; the nations will talk of his wisdom, and his praises will be sung in the assembly. If he lives long, he will leave a name in a thousand, and if he goes to his rest, his reputation is secure.

As with Ezra (6.1.7), the main characteristic of the scribe is handling the law of God. We also know that the term scribe was still used in its older sense of "secretary, bureaucrat" for those who functioned publicly or privately in administration or keeping records or performing secretarial duties.

Ben Sira is a good example of an exponent of "proverbial wisdom" (see 6.5 below). Although he is unlikely to have been ignorant of apocalyptic developments in some circles, he shows little or no influence from them. He seems to reject apocalyptic speculation and eschatology in general, though some have argued that 49:16 indicates a certain messianic expectation (cf. Caquot; Martin). If so, it may have been that of an earthly hero figure such as we find in such early Jewish writings as the Psalms of Solomon 17, a larger-than-life Davidic king. For Ben Sira, the main concern of wisdom is the Torah of God (24). He has brought together the Deuteronomic and the wisdom traditions (though, as noted at 6.1.2, they were never that far apart).

6.1.9 Daniel

As discussed below (6.5), Daniel is an excellent book to illustrate the connection between apocalypticism and wisdom. It holds up as examples such wise men as Daniel and his three friends. They are figures at the Babylonian court and are numbered among the ranks of the wise men and magicians who serve the king (1:17-20; 2:12-13). The wisdom possessed by Daniel is of a particular sort. "Proverbial wisdom" is not ruled out, but the emphasis is on Daniel's ability to interpret dreams and visions in order to get an insight into the future. This involves esoteric knowledge and a special sort of wisdom often referred to as "mantic." Such wisdom is certainly a gift from God (1:17) and is usually revealed either by a special revelation from God himself in a dream or vision (2:19) or by an angelic being (9:20-21). Yet it is also the product of education (1:5, 17). In addition to the wisdom content, the book of Daniel also has much in common with the prophetic books. The content is very much eschatological and, for chapters 7-12, apocalyptic. See further at 6.5.

6.1.10 Other References to Scribes

Mettinger, T. N. D. *Solomonic State Officials* (1971).

Scribes (*sôfĕrîm*) are a part of the national and religious administration according to the picture of the OT text. In a list of David's officials is Seriah the scribe (2 Sam 8:16-18) or Sheva the scribe (20:23-24) or Shavsha the scribe (1 Chron 18:15-17). The impression is that such individuals hold major government offices, perhaps supervising a number of other scribes, since they are listed alongside Zadok and Ahimelech the priests (though they were not the only priests) and Joab, who was commander in chief of the army but not the only officer. David's uncle is also said to have been a scribe (1 Chron 27:32). Among Solomon's officials are listed two scribes (1 Kings 4:2-6). The officials of Hezekiah who hear and respond to the threats of the Assyrian Rabshakeh include Shebna the scribe (2 Kings 18:18, 37; 19:2; Isa 36:3, 22; 37:2). The "royal scribe" (*sōfēr hammelek*) and the high priest together took charge of donations for the building of the temple under King Joash (2 Kings 12:11; 2 Chron 24:11). A similar function was performed by Shaphan under Josiah, even though he is just referred to as "the scribe" (2 Kings 22:3). When a scroll of the law is found in the temple, it is given to Shaphan to bring and read to the king (2 Kings 22:8-12; 2 Chron 34:15-20).

As one would expect, it seems that scribes were also to be found in other positions of administration. The scribe of the army commander was one of those executed by Nebuchadnezzar when he took Jerusalem (2 Kings 25:19; Jer 52:25). A Levitical scribe had the responsibility of registering the priests when David organized the temple personnel (1 Chron 24:6). Among the various temple offices held by Levites during the repair of the temple under Josiah was that of scribe (2 Chron 34:13). In the context of reciting Caleb's genealogy, 1 Chronicles 2:55 mentions the "families of scribes that lived at Jabez." Like much in Chronicles, this is thought by many to reflect the situation in the Persian period. Regardless, it does seem to suggest a hereditary occupation.

When we include the references in Jeremiah, it seems clear that the term "scribe" (*sôfēr*) is a general term for "secretary," ranging from those whose main job was to record in writing and all the way up to high officials in the government. In each case, though, there was still an association of the office with writing and records. Thus, the royal scribe was a government minister who had other scribes working with him. There were scribes in the temple and scribes in the army. On the other hand, we have no indication that scribes were particularly numerous or that they were accessible to the ordinary Israelite. The indications are that the scribal profession tended to run in certain families.

6.1.11 Other References to Wisdom Figures

Ahithophel the counselor of David was part of Absalom's conspiracy (2 Sam 15-17). His counsel (*'ēṣāh*) was like the word of God (2 Sam 16:23). However, when his good advice on how to defeat David was ignored, he realized he had no future and committed suicide (17:23). God's spirit will give wisdom, understanding, and counsel to the "shoot from Jesse," the idealized Davidic king (Isaiah 11:2). Fun is made of Pharaoh's counselors and sages, partly because they cannot predict the future correctly (19:11-12). The wisdom of the farmer is given by God (28:23-29). Because of insincere worship, the wisdom of the wise will fail (29:13-14). The book of Hosea ends with the statement that the wise would consider the words of the book (Hos 14:10). This is reminiscent of Daniel 12:10, which notes that the wise will understand the prophecies of the book.

There are several references to wise women. See 6.4.4.

6.2 THE WISE ACCORDING TO THE OLD TESTAMENT TEXT

Crenshaw, J. L. "Wisdom," *Old Testament Form Criticism* (1974) 225-64.
Murphy, R. E. *Wisdom Literature: Job, Proverbs, Ruth, Canticles, Ecclesiastes, Esther* (1981).

The OT text by itself does not give us a full picture of the wise, as 6.4 will discuss, but it has a number of important sets of data. First, the wisdom books (Proverbs, Job, Qohelet, Ben Sira) are designated as such because they have certain characteristics not found elsewhere or not found in such a concentrated way. Part of this is the wisdom terminology, especially the term "wise/wisdom" and the contrast between "wise/wisdom" and "foolish/folly." In some cases, these are personified as Lady Wisdom or the Foolish Woman (especially in Proverbs 1-9). (On terminology, see further at 6.4.1.)

A second characteristic of the wisdom books is their form and content. A variety of literary forms is concentrated in them, setting them off from other OT books (Crenshaw; Murphy). Apart from proverbs, the genre of instruction is frequent (Prov 1-9; Ben Sira). Of particular interest is the challenging of conventional wisdom and conventional views of God and religion as found in Job and Qohelet, sometimes designated skeptical literature. As for content, several themes are frequent. The theme of wisdom and folly is indicated by characteristic vocabulary. The interest in cosmology and how the universe works, all the way from the movements of the heavens to the activities of plants and animals is a theme of wisdom literature (Prov 6:6; 30:24-28; Job 28, 38-41). One could perhaps characterize this as an interest in all things esoteric. The wisdom literature pursues the esoteric wisdom and knowledge in a way different from much other literature, where God's hidden knowledge is recognized but the emphasis is on marveling at it and on worship rather than wanting to possess it.

Wisdom is a generic trait and not confined to one group of people. All those skilled in some trait or profession possess wisdom of a sort: the craftsman, the potter, the builder, the farmer (Isa 28:23-29). This wisdom is said to derive ultimately from God, though God might give it to some to a special degree (e.g., Bezalel in making the tabernacle: Exod 31:1-5). Others are given the label *wise* without a further specification in which area their wisdom lies (e.g., the wise woman of Tekoa: 2 Sam 14). From this point of view, anyone can be wise. Nevertheless, special emphasis is laid on the wisdom of certain individuals because of their esoteric knowledge and understanding of matters beyond the ordinary ken. This wisdom may in part be learned, but there is also an element of divine inspiration in it, which can include the gift of wise counsel possessed by some royal advisors (e.g., Ahithophel: 2 Sam 16:23). It may be individuals with mantic knowledge who can interpret dreams or perform magical acts, such as the wisemen in the Egyptian and Babylonian courts, among whom were Joseph and Daniel.

Some texts show that scribes were a part of the court and temple. No special connection is made between them and wisdom, so it may have seemed superfluous to collect such passages in the previous section. But the references to scribes become important in the light of other considerations, especially the situation elsewhere in the ancient Near East. Even some OT passages hint at the connection between the court scribes and wisdom (e.g., Isa 19:11-12; Gen 40-51; Dan 1-6). That is why the picture in the biblical text is especially incomplete for this subject as compared to prophets and some of the other religious specialists. Section 6.4 will tackle some of the problems left from the investigation of the OT text alone.

6.3 THE WISE IN THE ANCIENT NEAR EASTERN TEXTS

6.3.1 Aramaic Documents

Cowley, A. *Aramaic Papyri of the Fifth Century B.C.* (1923).
Driver, G. R. *Aramaic Documents of the Fifth Century B.C.* (1957).
Porten, B., and A. Yardeni, *Textbook of Aramaic Documents from Ancient Egypt: 1 Letters* (1986).

The Aramaic documents from the Persian period show a standard usage for the term "scribe" (*spr'*) to mean "secretary, recorder, writer, administrative official." In its consonantal form, the word "scribe" is distinguished from "document" only by context. In some letters the secretary or copyist is named at the end of the letter or elsewhere in it (e.g., Driver 4.4, 6.6, 7.10, 8.6). The term is also used of important administrative officials, such as "scribes of the treasury" (*spry 'wṣr'*: Cowley 2.12, 14) or "scribes of the provinces" (*spry mdynt'*: Cowley 17.1, 6). The association of the scribe with wisdom and the wise counselor is found in *Ahiqar*. He is referred to as "a wise and skillful scribe" (*spr ḥkym wmhyr*: *Ahiqar* 1.1), "the wise scribe, counselor of Assyria" (*[s]pr' ḥkym' y'ṭ 'twr*: *Ahiqar* 1.12), and "the wise scribe and master of good counsel" (*spr' ḥkym' wb'l 'ṭt' ṭbt'*: 2.42).

6.3.2 Egypt

Brunner, H. *Altägyptische Erziehung* (1957).
Gardiner, A. H. "The Mansion of Life and the Master of the King's Largess," *JEA* 24 (1938) 83-91.
____. "The House of Life," *JEA* 24 (1938) 157-79.
Volten, A. *Demotische Traumdeutung (Pap. Carlsberg XIII und XIV Verso)* (1942).

Williams, R. J. "Scribal Training in Ancient Egypt," *JAOS* 92 (1972) 214-21.

____. "The Sage in Egyptian Literature," *The Sage in Israel and the Ancient Near East* (1990) 19-30.

____. "The Functions of the Sage in the Egyptian Royal Court," *The Sage in Israel and the Ancient Near East* (1990) 95-98.

The sage was inseparable from the scribal tradition. Ability to read and write was confined to the relatively small elite group of trained scribes. Scribes were needed in the court and economic administration, the temple, and even the army. Because of the need for administrative staff, schools were established in the royal court. In time, the location of schools shifted to the temples. Scribes were also affiliated with the "House of Life." This was an institution with various centers, often associated with temples, devoted to the production, study, and preservation of texts, especially religious texts (Gardiner; Volten: 17-44). They were not generally for scribal training, though there is some evidence that instruction was also given (Williams: 27). The standard term for the sage was *rḫ-(3)ḫt*, "one who knows," a term which could also be generic like the Hebrew *ḥākām* (Williams: 27). In Demotic literature the term used is *rmt-rḫ*, "wise man."

The "scribes and sages" (a term found in more than one inscription) served in a variety of occupations devoted to the service of the king (Williams: 95-98). From their ranks came the advisors and counselors to the king, the officials, the diplomats, the physicians, and even the architects. The ranks were originally occupied by those of noble birth, but as time went on, the profession became open to anyone of ability, regardless of birth. Knowledge of the esoteric arts, such as the interpretation of dreams and incantations and rituals against evil spirits, was also an important part of the scribal and sapiental tradition (5.3.2).

The literature of the sages covers a wide range, much of it with parallels to the OT wisdom writings: instructions, admonitions based on traditional Egyptian concerns for order, skeptical literature, treatises in praise of the scribe, religious writings, and what might be termed magical literature. These show both the interest of the sages and the areas in which they (or at least some of them) were expected to be competent. Of considerable interest are the writings that are often designated skeptical literature. They include the *Dispute of a Man with His Ba* and the *Harper's Song* of Papyrus Anastasi. Both these question traditional beliefs and expectations about afterlife and the mortuary cult, showing that at least some sages were not afraid to go against established beliefs.

6.3.3 Mesopotamia

Denning-Bolle, S. *Wisdom in Akkadian Literature* (1992).

Harris, R. "The Female 'Sage' in Mesopotamian Literature (with an Appendix on Egypt)," *The Sage in Israel and the Ancient Near East* (1990) 3-17.
Kalugila, L. *The Wise King* (1980).
Kramer, S. N. *From the Tablets of Sumer* (1956).
____. "The Sage in Sumerian Literature: A Composite Portrait," *The Sage in Israel and the Ancient Near East* (1990) 31-44.
Lambert, W. G. *Babylonian Wisdom Literature* (1960).
____. "The Late Babylonian *Kislīmu* Ritual for Esagil," *JCS* 43-45 (1991-93) 89-106.
____. Review of S. Denning-Bolle, *Wisdom in Akkadian Literature*, *AfO* 40-41 (1993-94) 116-17.
____. "Some New Babylonian Wisdom Literature," *Emerton Festschrift* (1995) 30-42.
Sjöberg, Å. W. "The Old Babylonian Eduba," *Sumerological Studies in Honor of Thorkild Jacobsen* (1975) 159-79.
Sweet, R.F.G. "The Sage in Akkadian Literature: A Philological Study," *The Sage in Israel and the Ancient Near East* (1990) 45-65.
____. "The Sage in Mesopotamian Palaces and Royal Courts," *The Sage in Israel and the Ancient Near East* (1990) 99-107.

Discussion of the sage and the wisdom tradition is complicated in that there is no Akkadian word corresponding closely in usage to the Hebrew *ḥkm*. The wisdom literature is delineated primarily on the analogy of OT wisdom writings (Lambert 1960: 1-2). A range of "wisdom" words occurs in Akkadian literature (surveyed in Sweet: 45-65). Wisdom is preeminently associated with the gods and, as a gift from them, with the king (Sweet: 51-57; Kalugila: 38-61). This wisdom might be demonstrated in practical skills (military, technological) but also in piety. The ordinary citizens—craftsmen, soldiers, musicians—might have wisdom terms applied to them. Scribes, diviners, and counselors were also known for their wisdom, though Sweet finds no "evidence that the Akkadian wisdom terms were used with special frequency for a 'class of learned and shrewd men, including astrologers, magicians, and the like' or for persons who were 'wise, ethically and religious,' including the 'wise teacher, sage'" (65).

Sweet's study of Akkadian wisdom terminology fits well with that of Whybray's study of the Hebrew. Nevertheless, when we ask about the "intellectual tradition," there is no doubt that it was confined to a narrow circle. According to Kramer, the Sumerian sage was educator, humanist, intellectual, and spiritual guide (1990: cf. 32). The sage was also synonymous with the trained scribe, for it was from the ranks of the small numbers trained in the scribal schools (*edubba*, "tablet house") that the temple and palace officials came, as well as those who copied, preserved, and composed the literature (Sjöberg). Thus, both the temple and the court were dominated by those with their outlook and way of thinking shaped in the scribal school. (Although the king was the model of the wise man, only three Mesopotamian kings throughout their history claimed to be able to read [Sweet: 65].) Whether the *edubba* was connected with the temple is uncertain (Lambert 1960: 8). Evidence for the *edubba* as an institution after the beginning of the second millennium BCE was once unknown (Lambert 1960: 14), but it is now attested in the Late Babylonian *Kislimu* ritual (Lambert 1991-93). After that time, scribal training and learning seem to be a product of the temple, and the sages were often temple personnel.

As in Egypt, scribal training was by means of traditional literature, including collections of proverbs and instructions. These helped to incorporate the customary ethical expectations of society, but they also illustrated "the paradoxical and contradictory aspects of human destiny" (Kramer 1990: 33). This foreshadows the "skeptical tradition," which became well established in Babylonian wisdom literature (*Ludlul Bēl Nemēqi, Babylonian Theodicy, Dialogue of Pessimism*) and reached its apex in such OT books as Job and Qohelet. Passing on the literary tradition might well mean more than simply making new copies of old tablets; the writing was often updated, adapted, and recast by scribes who felt a duty to have a part in creating as well as preserving the tradition. They even compiled the traditional wisdom of some of the professions, such as the "Farmer's Almanac" from Nippur (Kramer 1956: 61-62). Although the scribal class may not have been the only ones with a claim to wisdom, there is no doubt that scribes were the carriers of the intellectual tradition. Even the "Farmer's Almanac" was not written by farmers!

6.3.4 Ugarit

Mack-Fisher, L. R. "A Survey and Reading Guide to the Didactic Literature of Ugarit: Prolegomenon to a Study on the Sage," *The Sage in Israel and the Ancient Near East* (1990) 67-80.

____. "The Scribe (and Sage) in the Royal Court at Ugarit," *The Sage in Israel and the Ancient Near East* (1990) 109-15.

Nougayrol, J. *Le Palais royal d'Ugarit: III. Textes accadiens et hourrites des Archives Est, Ouest et Centrales* (1955).

____. *Le Palais royal d'Ugarit: IV. Textes accadiens des Archives Sud (Archives Internationales)* (1956).

Rainey, A. F. "The Scribe at Ugarit—His Position and Influence," *Proceedings of the Israel Academy of Sciences and Humanities* 3 (1969) 126-47.

A great deal of didactic literature has been found at Ugarit, much of it in Akkadian or Hurrian (Mack-Fisher: 67-80). Much less is known about the training and activities of scribes at Ugarit than in the long history of Mesopotamia, but a number of scribes are known by name and even more known of a few of them (Mack-Fisher: 109-15). One seems to be referred to as the *rb spr*, "chief scribe" (*KTU* 1.75.10). By analogy, we can assume that the scribal profession worked much as it did in Mesopotamia, especially considering the strong Babylonian influence on the Ugaritic wisdom tradition (Mack-Fisher: 74).

Although how one defines "sage" is a rather subjective matter (cf. Mack-Fisher: 115), what is clear is that some of the named scribes occupied important positions as viziers and counselors of the king. The scribe Karra (Nougayrol 1955: 99, 248) seems to have been *sukkal šar Ugarit*, "vizier of the king of Ugarit" (Nougayrol 1956: 106; Rainey: 144). There was a close association between the priesthood and writing (Rainey: 128). The king apparently gave a town to one scribe as his personal estate (Mack-Fisher: 113). A large library of the scribe Rap'anu has been found in his private house. This includes not only literary and scribal works but also administrative documents, attesting to Rap'anu's importance in the court. He may even have been head of the scribal school (Mack-Fisher: 114).

6.3.5 Iran

Bailey, H. H. *Zoroastrian Problems in the Ninth-Century Books* (1943).
Boyce, M. *A History of Zoroastrianism* (1975-).
Russell, J. R. "The Sage in Ancient Iranian Literature," *The Sage in Israel and the Ancient Near East* (1990) 81-92.
____. "Sages and Scribes at the Courts of Ancient Iran," *The Sage in Israel and the Ancient Near East* (1990) 141-46.

The chief Zoroastrian deity was Ahura Mazda "Lord of Wisdom." At the heart of the cosmos lay the principle of "order" (Avestan *aša* or Old Persian *arta*, both cognates of the Sanskrit *ṛta*), very much reminiscent of Egyptian *maat*. The early (pre-Zoroastrian) Iranian priests were shaman-like figures who might give healing rituals and journey to the spirit world. Traditionally a distinction was made between innate knowledge (*āsna*) and acquired knowledge (*gaošō-sruta-*). Although much later tradition accumulated in the Zoroaster legend, the historical Zoroaster apparently embodied a variety of skills, not only being a priest but also a prophet and one who gained esoteric knowledge of the future by means of the divine spirit. The Magi or priestly class carried on the model of Zoroaster, gaining the reputation for astrological knowledge (and also giving us the word "magic" from their name). Although not all sages were priests (e.g., the hero Wīrāz was not), the intellectual tradition as a whole seems to have been carried mainly in priestly circles. This included not only scribal practice but also the large body of religious literature preserved orally (Bailey).

In Sassanian times, priests were to be found at the courts of powerful noble families as well as at the royal court (Russell: 141-46). They often seem to have had their own estates, giving them a position of prestige and power in society. Some priests served as regional judges (Russell: 143). Scribes assisted the government in administration by the keeping of all records, including those relating to taxes. Nevertheless, most scribes were from the priestly class (Russell: 145-46). The scribal and the priestly elements continued to be part of the same establishment, for the most part, and the traditional skills (such as healing) of the old Iranian priesthood were maintained from Achemenid to Sassanian times.

6.4 THE PROBLEM: WHO WERE THE WISE?

Crenshaw, J. L. "Method in Determining Wisdom Influence upon 'Historical' Literature," *JBL* 88 (1969) 129-42
McKane, W. *Prophets and Wisemen* (1983).
Whybray, R. N. *The Intellectual Tradition in the Old Testament* (1974).
____. "The Sage in the Israelite Royal Court," *The Sage in Israel and the Ancient Near East* (1990) 133-39.
Weeks, S. *Early Israelite Wisdom* (1994).

There are many references to the wise in the OT, under a variety of different terms (cf. Whybray). Unfortunately, these are mostly passing references that do not answer our major questions: Who were those known by the term "wise" (or something similar)? What significance did such designations have? Was "wise" used of a particular profession or set of professions? Who wrote the "wisdom literature" of the OT? Therefore, our study cannot just focus on the texts but must enter into one of the major debates in the study of the Israelite wisdom tradition.

6.4.1 The Terminology

The main study of terminology is that of Whybray on the intellectual tradition. The root *ḥkm* (*ḥākām*, "wise man, sage"; *ḥokmāh*, "wisdom") is especially characteristic of the books of Proverbs, Job, Qohelet, and Ben Sira; it has long been taken as the primary term for identifying wisdom writings or concerns in the OT. There are various other terms as well; however, some are more significant than others. Whybray's analysis indicates four categories: (a) those occurring only in Proverbs, Job, and Qohelet (he does not include Ben Sira in his study); (b) those occurring not only in those three books but also frequently elsewhere in the OT; (c) words characteristic of Proverbs, Job, and Qohelet but also occurring occasionally elsewhere in the OT; and (d) words exclusive to the "intellectual tradition."

Those in this last category are as important as *ḥkm* in indicating wisdom influence: *bînāh*, "understanding"; *ba'ar*, "stupid"; *kĕsîl*, "stupid"; *lêṣ*, "scoffer";

leqaḥ, "understanding, teaching"; *nāvōn*, "intelligent"; *sākāl*, "senseless, foolish"; *'ārûm*, "prudent, clever"; *tûšiyyāh*, "wisdom, success." The terms in category (c) may also be used cautiously for the same purpose: *'ĕwîl*, "fool"; *'iwwelet*, "folly"; *ḥānēf*, "godless"; *ḥēqer*, "investigation"; *'iqqēš*, "perverse, crooked"; *'ormāh*, "shrewdness, cunning"; *śkl* (hiph.), "be wise, make wise, teach"; *tĕvûnāh*, "understanding"; *tōkaḥat*, "rebuke, punishment".

After carefully working out these terminological indicators, Whybray finds a number of passages outside the wisdom books to show wisdom influence (154): Genesis 2-3; 11:1-9 (possibly); 37-50 (Joseph story); Deuteronomy 1-4; 32; 2 Samuel 9-20 and 1 Kings 1-2 (Succession Narrative); 1 Kings 3-11 (History of Solomon); Isaiah 1-39; Jeremiah; Ezekiel 28; Hosea 14:10; Micah 6:9; Psalms 1; 19:8-15; 37; 49; 51; 73; 90; 92; 94; 104; 107; 111; 119; Daniel. Whybray thus rejects some of Crenshaw's strictures about finding wisdom influence outside the wisdom literature. The interesting thing about this list is the diversity of literature within it. Those who promoted the intellectual tradition did not confine themselves to "wisdom" literature but showed an interest in a range of genres.

6.4.2 Who Wrote the Wisdom Literature?

As the study of wisdom terminology indicates, the three "canonical" wisdom books (6.1.4, 6.1.5, 6.1.6) could have been written by a number of different possible types of people in society. The choice is not unlimited, however, since most societies before modern times placed severe restrictions on an individual's choices. Most people in the ancient Near East were fully occupied in trying to get enough to eat and supply their other basic necessities. They did not have time for many other activities we take for granted today. The main requirement for intellectual activity of any kind was *leisure*. Who was able to take time away from the daily grind of working long hours for small return? Few had any such opportunity. The main sorts of figures in society who did have the necessary leisure were the upper classes, the wealthy, priests, scribes, and some others employed in government administration.

The divide between the wealthy and the vast majority of people in society was much greater in antiquity. There was really no middle class. Most wealth came from the land; there seem to have been few who made a fortune by trading or commerce. Therefore, wealth and a high position in society usually went together. Many of those with wealth would also have been involved with the court and administration in some way or the other. The king could reward those he favored with wealth and position (and position gave opportunity for wealth), and he would also have found it useful to court those powerful individuals in society who already possessed wealth and influence. Such people had the opportunity for education and the interest in pursuing or promoting intellectual activities for personal gain, for advancement of status among their peers, for entertainment, and for their own personal interest.

A good example of this is Qohelet (6.1.6). We have no clear reason to think that he was a priest or a scribe or someone involved in public life or administration. He could have been any of these, but nothing along any of these lines is indicated in his writing. What we do know is that he was someone with a good education, that he had the leisure to pursue questions about the meaning of life, and that he seems to have taught young men about his ideas (Qoh 11:9-10). The chances are that he was a member of the upper classes who had the time and interest to occupy himself with such matters.

A second group of those who had leisure for intellectual pursuits was the priests. It is often assumed that priests had no concerns beyond the cultic. On the contrary, with a secure income and plenty of spare time when not serving directly in the temple, they were the ideal group to be concerned with preserving the tradition and composing theological and other works. The temple had need of scribal skills, and it was likely to be priests or Levites who were taught these rather than laymen. The analogy from other Near Eastern peoples (6.3) is that literary activity was highest in the context of the temple and priesthood.

The third main group of people able to devote time to reading and composing literature was the scribes. They were the main group involved in administration. They had to keep records, write messages, produce inventories, create legal documents, and perhaps even keep a daybook or chronicle for the king. The term "scribe" in antiquity seemed to be used of a variety of administrative officials, from a secretary of state to a warehouse recorder. As noted above, the scribes in the temple were probably themselves priests or Levites. What they all had in common was the training to read and write. Some, if perhaps not all, had knowledge of literature and literary conventions. The scribal profession feeds on itself. It writes because it is necessary; but because it can write, it finds things to write about. Some literature may have been used as exercises in the training of novices, but it is not likely to have been written initially for that purpose.

We thus come back to Whybray's focus on an intellectual tradition in Israel (1974), except that this tradition was probably confined to a fairly narrow circle (here McKane's arguments still have considerable merit). It probably extended outward to some degree, so that Israelites visiting the temple(s) and the main urban centers would have come in contact with some of the literature by word of mouth, through public readings, or from instruction in those writings thought important for civic or religious instruction. But whatever knowledge they may have gained by such indirect means, the majority of people did not read this literature—indeed, are not likely to have read at all—and certainly were not engaged in writing it.

All these points apply to all literature of ancient Israel. Wisdom literature is of a special sort, though. The aim of theological literature is obvious. The practical writings of the everyday concourse of business, legal, commercial, and courtly affairs can be taken for granted. Wisdom literature, however, reflects a different type of writing. It comes in the category of attempts to understand the world and how it works. It can be called philosophical literature in the broadest sense. It may have theological themes and show knowledge of myths and traditions, but it is not theological literature in the narrow sense. It shows a desire to reflect on life and to ask questions, to wonder why, to seek out specialized ("hidden") knowledge. Despite the difficulties of defining "wisdom" and the justified criticism about finding wisdom influence too widely (Crenshaw), there is common consent that a wisdom tradition exists. A person in any one of the three groups just discussed could be interested in this tradition and approach and could participate by reading and even writing in it. Not all aristocrats or priests or scribes would have been concerned about "wisdom" matters, but some in each group were likely to have found wisdom attractive.

6.4.3 The Question of Schools

Crenshaw, J. L. "Education in Ancient Israel," *JBL* 104 (1985) 601-15.

Golka, F. W. "Die israelitische Weisheitsschule oder 'des Kaisers neue Kleider,'" *VT* 33 (1983) 257-70.

____. *The Leopard's Spots: Biblical and African Wisdom in Proverbs* (1993).

Haran, M. "On the Diffusion of Schools and Literacy," VTSup 40 (1988) 81-95.

Jamieson-Drake, D. W. *Scribes and Schools in Monarchic Judah* (1991).

Lemaire, A. *Les écoles et la formation de la Bible dans l'ancien Israel* (1981).

____. "The Sage in School and Temple," *The Sage in Israel and the Ancient Near East* (1990) 165-81.

____. "Education: Ancient Israel," *ABD* 2 (1992) 305-12.

Lipiński, E. "Royal and State Scribes in Ancient Jerusalem," VTSup 40 (1988) 157-64.

Millard, A. R. "An Assessment of the Evidence of Writing in Ancient Israel," *Biblical Archaeology Today* (1985) 301-12.

Puech, E. "Les écoles dans l'Israël préexilique: données épigraphiques," VTSup 40 (1988) 189-203.

Warner, S. "The Alphabet—An Innovation and Its Diffusion," *VT* 30 (1980) 82-86.

The issue of schools has long been associated with the wisdom question. Precisely what sort of schools is less often specified, but two separate types must be considered. First, the analogy of the surrounding cultures is that of scribal and priestly schools (6.3). The complicated writing systems in Mesopotamia and Egypt meant that they could be learned only after long study. Even the king habitually did not read and write (cf. 6.3.3). Therefore, schools for teaching scribes and also for training priests who may have had specialized skills (such as divining) were necessary. Second, there is the idea of universal education. Although this is a modern concept, some who argue in favor of schools seem to think that schools for teaching reading and writing to children in general existed in Israel.

The question of schools has often become entangled with that of literacy, though these are really separate issues (cf. Jamieson-Drake: 11). The following are some of the main arguments used by various scholars who argue for the concept of schools and widespread literacy (Lemaire; Millard):

1. The evidence of the OT itself. This includes the argument from the literary character of some OT texts which, it is claimed, show evidence that they were written for the use of students in schools. There are also occasional references to writing and literacy in the OT. Some passages are interpreted as hinting at the existence of schools. It is recognized, however, that this is only a minimal source of evidence.

2. Inscriptional evidence. The existence of ostraca, bullae (sealings from papyri now perished), and inscriptions are offered as proof of widespread literacy. Some of the inscriptions are abecedaries, taken to be evidence of student exercises. The use of hieratic symbols for numbers in inventories shows influence from Egypt which would have come only in a learned context.

3. The Hebrew alphabet would have been easy to learn, especially in comparison with the complex systems in Egypt and Mesopotamia.

4. The analogy of schools elsewhere in the ancient Near East.

The counter arguments include the following (Whybray 1974: 32-43; Jamieson-Drake; Golka 1983; 1994: 4-15; Haran; Puech; Lipiński; Warner):

1. Archeological information indicates that Jerusalem became an important administrative center only in the late eighth century (Jamieson-Drake). This means that the need for a large number of administrators came about only at a late date in Judah's history. These could have been supplied by means of apprenticeship or a scribal tradition passed down primarily in the family (Lipiński; Whybray 1974: 33-43).

2. The idea of universal literacy is a modern concept. It is unlikely that most Israelites were literate in the sense of being able to read literature for pleasure.

3. Those who did know how to read and write, whether well or only a bit, could have learned by private instruction rather than in formal schools.

4. There are no references to schools in Israel. Although the OT literature is primarily religious literature and does not contain writings specifically on the scribal profession, one would still expect some passing reference to schools if they existed, especially if they were found routinely in the towns and villages.

From present evidence, it seems that the idea of universal schooling for children can be dismissed. This does not mean that individuals other than the wealthy did not learn to read and write, but there is no evidence that the average Israelite learned how to write. There are few examples of writing, and those which exist can usually be put down to trained scribes, though one can argue that a few inscriptions are not the product of professionals. On the other hand, the existence of abecedaries among Palestinian inscriptions hardly demonstrates student exercises (Haran). The fact that a few nonprofessionals could write does not argue for schools. Albright has stated that the alphabetic script would have been easy to learn, though this by itself does not prove literacy for the majority. Two observations can be made: First, most languages of modern Europe—and, indeed, in the Middle East—have been written in an alphabetic script, but the widespread ability to read and write is only a recent development. Second, one does not have to go to a school to learn an alphabetic script. It could have been taught on an individual basis by literate people to other interested persons. There is simply no evidence for widespread schools for the majority of Israelite children or for widespread literacy.

Scribal schools or the like are another matter. Scribes were needed in Israel; indeed, the lack of general literacy would have made the need for professional or semi-professional scribes even more acute. The real question is not whether there were scribes or whether there was need for them but whether they were trained in what might be called a school. When we use the term "school," we tend to have in mind an institution with a set curriculum, a fixed timetable, one or more teachers, and a number of pupils. This image seems to fit the scribal and priestly schools of Egypt and Mesopotamia. There is no reason to think that scribes had to be trained in such circumstances in Israel. Scribal training to read and write could have been given on an ad hoc basis by apprenticeship. There is evidence that the scribal profession in the court ran in certain families (6.1.10). Lemaire notes that his vision of schools in Israel is not like the modern sort; rather, he points to something more like the traditional Quranic or Jewish schools, similar to the ancient Greek and Roman schools (1990: 167-68). If so, the line between such a school and a scribe who takes on apprentices or a personal tutor hired by a family is rather blurred. Perhaps the question of definition plays a larger part in the debate than has been acknowledged.

In the earlier period of the kingdoms of Israel and Judah, a large administration was unnecessary (Jamieson-Drake) and a scribal profession passed down in the family was probably sufficient. As the nations grew (e.g., Judah from the late eighth century), perhaps apprenticeship was not sufficient to produce the scribes needed, but we cannot be sure. It might have been adequate if most scribes regarded it as a duty to take on an apprentice, perhaps even to teach a son or other young relative so that the role remained within the family. From all that we can tell, young priests learned their vocation by apprenticeship. There is no reference to formal training in schools. It makes sense that a priest growing up as a boy would have learned the knowledge and skills through the family. This does not rule out formal schools, of course, but it shows that we need not postulate them to explain the situation as we know it. The same applies to scribes. In the absence of clear evidence, it seems best to keep schools in mind only as a possibility to be tested but not as an institution to be taken seriously at the moment. Judging from recent writings on the subject, the consensus of scholarship seems definitely to be moving away from the idea of schools in Israel.

6.4.4 Female Sages?

Camp, C. V. "The Female Sage in the Biblical Wisdom Literature," *The Sage in Israel and the Ancient Near East* (1990) 185-203.
Crenshaw, J. L. *Old Testament Wisdom: An Introduction* (1982).
Crook, M. B. "The Marriageable Maiden of Prov. 31:10-31," *JNES* 13 (1954) 137-40.
Harris, R. "The Female 'Sage' in Mesopotamian Literature (with an Appendix on Egypt)," *The Sage in Israel and the Ancient Near East* (1990) 3-17.
Lyons, E. L. "A Note on Proverbs 31.10-31," *The Listening Heart* (1987) 237-45.
McCreesh, T. P. "Wisdom as Wife: Proverbs 31:10-31," *RB* 92 (1985) 25-46.

We have some evidence of female scribes in Mesopotamia (Harris 1990). Does this suggest that there were female sages—"wise women"—in Israel? This proposal raises several issues. One of these is whether there was a profession of sage. This was answered in the negative, though a concentration of such individuals could be found in the ranks of the palace and temple personnel (6.4.2). A number of the references are general and show only that there were clever individuals among women as well as men. Wise women are mentioned along with men in the making of the wilderness tabernacle, but this designation is based on their craftsmanship (Exod 35:25). In Judges 5:29 Sisera's mother and her wisest ladies try to determine why he does not return. The evidence of female sages in Israel is based primarily on a few passages: the wise woman of Tekoa (2 Sam 14:2); the wise women at the siege of Abel (2 Sam 20:16); the figure of Dame Wisdom in Proverbs; the "ideal woman" (Prov 31:10-31).

It has been suggested that the wise woman of Tekoa was part of a tradition of that area. There is little evidence that there was a "wise woman tradition" associated with this town. Nevertheless, she provides an example of the sort of person who would bear the label "wise." Unfortunately, we have no specific information about her place in society. Why was she chosen to take this message to David? Was she an "ordinary" Israelite, or was she part of the aristocracy? Why was she called "wise"? Was it because of native wit and knowledge, perhaps built up by experience? Was it because of some sort of more formal education or training? It is interesting to note, as Crenshaw points out (248 n. 14), that Joab told the woman what to say.

When Joab was besieging the city of Abel, a wise woman talked to him from the wall to find out how to bring the siege to an end; her wise plan saved the city (2 Sam 20:15-22). Anyone able to save a city from sacking certainly deserves the designation "wise." Sadly, nothing further is said about her or whether she was considered wise before the event.

The figure of wisdom is problematic. First, the figure is female most likely because *ḥokmāh* is grammatically feminine. Second, it is ill-advised to attempt to draw data about the position of women in society by appeal to a personified figure, or even a goddess image, as here. The fact that Athena and Anat were warrior goddesses, for example, does not provide evidence of female warriors. Nor does the belief in the Virgin Mary as an intercessor suggest that there must be women priests in the Roman Catholic church. Without other supporting evidence, the figure of wisdom should not be used to extrapolate to Israelite society. It proves nothing by itself.

The "woman of valor" in Proverbs 31 has been variously interpreted. She has also been seen as simply Dame Wisdom in another guise (cf. McCreesh). A long-standing traditional interpretation is to see her as the ideal married woman—the model for the Israelite wife and mother (cf. Crook; Lyons). This last understanding does not exclude seeing her as the model of the wise woman; the two go together very well. But if so, it is interesting that there is nothing relating to literature in the model presented here. If these are the characteristics of the wise woman, there is no evidence that she would be part of the "intellectual tradition" described above (6.4.2).

The main difficulty is the lack of evidence. A few women are labeled "wise" in the OT, but the basis for this is not usually delineated in the context. When we ask whether these wise women—or some of them—participated in the intellectual or literary tradition, we have no way of answering the question. There is some evidence of female scribes in Mesopotamia, but these seem to have had a fairly narrow function in the system: most likely as scribes to the secluded women of the palace so that they would not have to have direct contact with male personnel (Harris). If there were female scribes or female authors of literature in Israel, this has left no clear evidence in the tradition.

6.4.5 Summary: Who Were the Wise?

Our investigation has shown that the term "wise" was a generic term, used of any intellectual ability or achievement, whether gained from learning or from native talent. It could be used of those who possessed folk wisdom as well as those with a formal education. In that sense, Whybray's "intellectual" has a good deal of merit. The wise were not a specific class or profession but encompassed all sorts of individuals from various strata of society. However, it seems that in many passages the generic term is used for a specific accomplishment, while many professions had their own types of wisdom. For example, a craftsworker had to master a number of skills which could be called "wisdom." Most references to a specific sort of "wise man" are not of this sort, though; most often they have to do with someone who is a decision-maker or counselor of some sort. Anyone can be wise, but the wise par excellence are the learned, the advisers, the counselors, the viziers—whether spiritual, political, or even private. Learned priests, advisers to the king, senior scribes all might be referred to as "wise." Even though the wise did not constitute a profession as such, the learned professions were more likely to bear the designation "wise."

It is obvious that not all those referred to as wise have a religious role, but many do. If the wise produced writings which have entered the religious canon or if the term is used of priests and teachers of God's law, then those particular wise persons must be considered along with other religious specialists.

6.5 WISDOM AND APOCALYPTICISM

Barton, J. *Oracles of God* (1986).

Collins, J. J. "Proverbial Wisdom and the Yahwist Vision," *Semeia* 17 (1980) 1-17.

____, ed. *Apocalypse: The Morphology of a Genre* (1979).

Grabbe, L. L. "The Social Setting of Early Jewish Apocalypticism," *JSP* 4 (1989) 27-47.

Hanson, P. D. "Apocalypticism," *IDBSup* (1976) 29-31.

Lambert, W. G. *The Background of Jewish Apocalyptic* (1978).

Müller, H.-P. "Magisch-mantische Weisheit und die Gestalt Daniels," *UF* 1 (1969) 79-94.

____. "Mantische Weisheit und Apokalyptik," VTSup 22 (1972) 268-93.

Rad, G. von. *Old Testament Theology II* (1965).

____. *Wisdom in Israel* (1972).

Smith, J. Z. "Wisdom and Apocalyptic," *Religious Syncretism in Antiquity* (1975) 131-56.

Stone, M. E. *Scriptures, Sects and Vision* (1980).

VanderKam, J. C. *Enoch and the Growth of an Apocalyptic Tradition* (1984).

____. "The Prophetic-Sapiential Origins of Apocalyptic Thought," *A Word in Season: Essays in Honour of William McKane* (1986) 163-76.

The relationship between wisdom and apocalypticism has been a matter of debate since von Rad's connection of the two (1965: 301-8). Although much of our evidence for apocalypticism is later than the period of primary concern here, the subject is still important for the assessment of the place of wisdom and the wise in the Israel of an earlier time—at least, it is potentially important, depending on the answer given to certain questions. Is there a connection between wisdom and apocalypticism? Von Rad's argument was that apocalypticism arose from wisdom because of its alleged ahistorical character. This point of view was sharply criticized. Many saw the very important historical thrust of apocalyptic works and thought the roots of apocalypticism lay in prophecy (cf. Hanson). More recent discussion has seen the essential truth of von Rad's claim, but from a rather different direction and for different reasons.

There is more than one type of wisdom. The type of wisdom found in works like Proverbs, the Egyptian instructions, and the traditional scribal literature of the ancient Near East is sometimes referred to as "proverbial wisdom" (cf. Collins 1980). Another sort of wisdom is that which involves esoteric knowledge relating to forces beyond the human world: "mantic wisdom" (Müller 1969; 1972). It would be a mistake to make a sharp distinction between the two since both relate to knowledge of order, the cosmos, how the world works, the essence of nature, and all those other elements which characterize wisdom. But from a modern point of view, and probably also as conceived by at least some ancients, mantic wisdom was of a different order from proverbial wisdom. Both could be taught, since the state diviners and official practitioners of mantic wisdom in the ancient Near East often learned their craft from study. Nevertheless, there was also thought to be—at least in some cases if not in all—special revelations from the divine world. Wisdom—of whatever sort—was a divine gift, but only certain special individuals received the capacity of seeing God's mind or future plans. This was the sort of wisdom to excel all other wisdom

Thus, when Daniel showed his superior wisdom it was in an act of mantic wisdom: interpreting the dream of Nebuchadnezzar (Dan 2). It is made clear that this wisdom comes from God as a special revelation, since Daniel learns the dream and its interpretation in a vision of his own. In other cases, the information is brought by an angelic being (cf. Dan 9:20-21). Nevertheless, the idea of study does not seem to be excluded, since Daniel's wisdom is first manifest in the process of his education at the Babylonian court (1:5, 17-20). The book of Daniel is a good example of mantic wisdom preserved in the Hebrew Bible, but it is a rather late book, with chapters 1-6 perhaps from the third century BCE and chapters 7-12 certainly from the mid-second. What was the earlier situation and what developments led up to the apocalyptic wisdom found in Daniel?

A number of earlier parallels to Daniel are found in ancient Near Eastern texts, especially in the Uruk and Dynastic Prophecies (Lambert; cf. 4.3.5). In these works, *ex eventu* prophecies pretend to prophesy in coded form about the reigns of various kings. They look remarkably like the long *ex eventu* prophecy of Daniel 11. Both of these look like deliberate scribal compositions for a purpose now unclear, but what emerges is that the earlier Near Eastern parallels to books like Daniel are from scribal literature. It has similarly been argued that the apocalyptic writings and related literature of the Hellenistic period are also scribal in origin (Smith). There are also clear reasons to think that Jewish apocalyptic writings could have arisen in priestly circles (Stone; Grabbe). In both instances, this could have a parallel with wisdom literature: Wisdom literature is mainly scribal in character, and some or even much wisdom literature could have come from priestly circles.

Thus, apocalyptic literature and apocalypticism as a phenomenon tell us several things. Apocalypticism has many characteristics in common with prophecy; indeed, one could argue that it is a particular form or sub-division of prophecy (Barton: 198-210; Grabbe). Some of these characteristics have developed in a new way, such as the dominance of dreams and symbolic visions in some apocalypses, but dreams and visions are a part of the prophetic tradition (5.7). Yet apocalyptic tradition also has a close relationship to mantic wisdom. Although apocalypticism as it is conventionally defined in scholarly literature (cf. Collins 1979) seems to have developed only in the Persian period or possibly later, it clearly has roots going back much earlier. Therefore, even though mantic wisdom is found explicitly only in a few late OT passages such as Daniel, the development of apocalypticism shows that mantic wisdom was an established part of the Israelite tradition. Finally, the presence of both prophetic and wisdom elements in apocalypticism (cf. VanderKam 1986) also demonstrates the related nature of these two phenomena in the same way that the activities of prophets and diviners intertwine.

6.6 THE GESTALT OF THE WISE

Bryce, G. E. "Omen-Wisdom in Ancient Israel," *JBL* 94 (1975) 19-37.

A dual problem exists in any investigation. First, there are the problems relating to the individuals referred to as "the wise." Then there is the question of the wisdom literature and tradition and what it says concerning the place of the wise in society. It is primarily, though not exclusively, through the wisdom literature that we have knowledge of the wise.

The "wise" are not easy to pin down. They definitely existed as identifiable types, not only in the OT and Jewish literature but widely in the ancient Near East. Yet when we ask what constitutes a sage, the means of answering the question are not easily available. Terminology is very important in the OT text (though, interestingly, it does not take the same weight in investigating other societies of the ancient Near East). The main term is *ḥkm* in its various forms, but there are a number of others which have special significance. In addition, some terms used in the past are actually found in such a range of contexts that their use has no special significance for determining a wisdom tradition or influence. The following points can be made about the wise and their work:

1. The wise in the broadest sense can be from any walk of life or stratum of society. The term "wise" could be used of a variety of skills, including the ability to pursue a craft or the innate wisdom of the naturally astute or practical person. Wisdom was also traditionally associated with age, gray hairs the sign of wisdom gained by experience. The craftsman, the village elder, the woman embodying traditional wisdom—all these could be called wise in their own way.

2. Despite the general usage of wisdom terminology just noted, there is a special sense in which wisdom was applied to intellectual characteristics, especially those gained or developed by formal learning, education, and study. The educated, the intellectuals, and the scribes were the wise par excellence. Although a variety of people might have been able to read and appreciate the wisdom and other literature, the number with sufficient education and leisure to compose such writings was probably quite small. Thus, we are justified in concentrating on the intellectual tradition and intellectual circles when talking of religious specialists.

3. The wise did not constitute a profession but embraced a number of professions and callings. The sage about whom we have most information, Jesus b. Sira, placed much emphasis on the priesthood and may have been a priest himself. He was also a scribe and a student of the law. He did not have the genius to challenge accepted religious dogma in the way of a Qohelet or a Job, but he is an important model of the sage and scribe. The fact that Ben Sira was centuries later than the monarchy should give us pause about assuming that sages like him existed several centuries earlier. On the other hand, there is likely to have been a significant continuum from the earlier period. That is, wisdom writings could have been authored by a priest, a scribe, a court official, or even a member of the aristocracy. Ben Sira may not show us precisely the sages of ancient Israel, but he suggests how such a person may have looked and worked.

4. The wise and wisdom concerns are not confined to the narrow range of wisdom literature. A book like Deuteronomy may be an original scribal production; it certainly seems to have many connections with the wise. It is for this reason that Ben Sira finds it so easy to unite them.

5. The OT wisdom literature shows a wide range of interests and concerns which cannot be summarized easily. These range from traditional wisdom as embodied in proverbs and instructions to interest in the workings of nature and cosmology to inquiry into the question of theodicy to question-

ing of traditional views about God and religion. While some of this could be the product of traditional folk wisdom (*Sippenethos*), much of it could only have arisen in a learned context. Even the contents and structure of the book of Proverbs appear to be the product of educated individuals, even if some of the proverbs themselves may have arisen in a traditional folk environment. A book like Qohelet is hard to imagine as being from anyone other than an educated individual with the time and leisure to reflect seriously on the meaning of life. Again, the example of Ben Sira is instructive. His own interests and characteristics could easily fit the composers of some or possibly all the OT wisdom books, yet he also shows the interests and concerns of the priests and Levites. The composers of the wisdom literature were likely to have been confined within the small circle which encompassed the priesthood, the scribal class, and the lay aristocrats.

6. Apocalyptic literature shows the importance of the mantic wisdom tradition. Although omen literature seems to have left little trace in the OT tradition directly (cf. Bryce), this does not mean that it was not around in the society. One aspect of the omen tradition, dreams and symbolic visions, is well represented in the OT text. Mantic wisdom was hardly likely to have been a late development but, rather, the underlying current only surfaces at a late stage. Mantic wisdom also overlapped considerably with prophecy. It was another means of determining the divine will, the divine plan, and the future in general.

7. The wisdom tradition unites a number of streams or institutions in Israelite society: (a) mantic wisdom, with its divinatory associations, has much in common with (b) prophecy, and the circles which carried it on seem to have included (c) priestly and (d) scribal elements. The learned tradition was not confined to one group or institution. Scribes, priests, some diviners, and some prophets will have intersected with the intellectual stratum of society. The number of those in this stratum was probably quite small relative to the population as a whole.

7.

From Text to Society

In the foregoing chapters we have looked at the various "ideal types" of religious figure: king, priest, prophet, diviner, wisdom figure. The concluding part of each chapter constructed a Gestalt of the ideal type, putting together all information available—text, archeology, anthropological studies, ancient Near Eastern texts. This chapter will take the study to its conclusions by looking at how these types interacted and functioned in society as far as it can be reconstructed. However, I shall *not* begin with the final result of the individual chapters (the Gestalt). Instead, I shall begin with the textual stage (sections 1 and 2 in each chapter). The information from the text on each ideal type is summarized as the starting point, after which the methodological principles discussed in Chapter 1 are applied in an attempt to form a coherent picture of the societal drama in which the various religious specialists performed their roles.

7.1 RELIGIOUS SPECIALISTS ACCORDING TO THE TEXTS

Although chapters 2-6 include sufficient information to be self-standing, we have to retrace our steps in part by putting aside the anthropological and other data and concentrating on the text. In other words, in this section we go back to the data and conclusions of sections 1 ("Selected Examples") and 2 ("Summary of the Text") in each chapter. At this point only the textual picture is being addressed. How that relates to the actual social situation in the light of other data and considerations will be considered later in this chapter (7.3).

7.1.1 King

Although the texts are the least informative about the monarch, he seems to have been the chief religious figure in Israel. Even the Deuteronomistic historian (Joshua-2 Kings) indicates this with the constant judging of rulers as doing righteousness in the eyes of Yhwh or doing wickedness and following the sins of Jeroboam the son of Nebat (cf. 2.2) and the consequent fate of Israel. A similar picture emerges from Chronicles, which appears to relate even the fate of the king directly to his deeds. The texts in Samuel are more forthcoming about the religious activities of the king than those in Kings or Chronicles. They show that the king (at least, from Saul to Solomon) was active in the cult, offering sacrifices and generally building and developing the temple system. Although later in the monarchy King Uzziah is said to have been smitten with leprosy for entering into the temple (2 Chron 26), no criticism is made of Saul, David, and Solomon for offering sacrifice. One brief statement even suggests that David's sons acted as priests (1 Sam 8:18; 2.1.5). David is the main innovator. He is instrumental in bringing the ark into Jerusalem and in purchasing the threshing floor on which the temple was later built. Although not allowed to build the temple himself, he made extensive preparations for it. Indeed, according to the Chronicler, David had all the material assembled and prepared, so that all Solomon had to do was assemble it like a giant prefab kit. Kings are important cultic figures, even in the present text with a good deal of anti-monarchial suspicions. Kings are cult founders; they are temple builders and sponsors of great cultic celebrations; they provide enormous numbers of sacrificial victims to the glory of Yhwh—and no doubt to their own.

7.1.2 Priests

The routine cultic activities were carried out mainly (or *solely*, according to many texts) by the priests. According to the book of Leviticus, their main function was that of butchers, cooks, and burners. Who kills the victim (the priest or the one bringing the animal is not clear: Lev 1:4-5, etc.), but the priests flay it, cut it up, burn the appropriate parts on the altar, take their allotted portions, and dispose of the rest of the animal according to the regulations for that particular sacrifice. In the view of most texts (priestly in content), there is a twofold division in the priesthood. The superior clergy are the descendants of Aaron. They have the privilege of presiding at the altar, which no Levite or lay person is allowed to do. The Levites make up the inferior priests. Their tasks are those of maintenance, cleaning, carrying, and generally assisting the priests. They are also responsible for singing, at least according to later texts such as Chronicles and Ezra-Nehemiah. This is not the full picture emerging from the text, though. Here and there are indications of different priestly groups: the sons of Aaron, the Zadokites, and even apparently those who traced their lineage to Moses (Judges 18:30). In addition, the division between priests and Levites is not made in Deuteronomy, which seems to treat all Levites as full priests. Thus, the picture that emerges from the final form of the text is a complicated—and even somewhat contradictory—one which invites further elucidation.

Priests mainly have to do with the cult, but some passages show them doing other activities. One of the chief ones is deciding and teaching the law. It makes sense that those who must pay attention to the detailed requirements of the law in their daily routine would also be the ones to preserve it, study it, interpret it, and teach it. Many of these decisions no doubt related directly to the cult (for example, the judgment of whether a leper was clean and able to enter the cult: Lev 14-15), but they are also said to be responsible for teaching the law to the people and even the king (Deut 17) and are pictured as answering questions put to them about the law (Hag 2). According to Deuteronomy and Ezekiel, they are to go even beyond this and to act as judges over civil matters, not solely but alongside other magistrates.

The text is almost uniformly negative toward other cults. Although it recognizes that such exist, it considers them contrary to God's law. Yet here and there are passages which present such worship without criticizing it. For example, Elijah builds up an altar of Yhwh which had been thrown down and sacrifices on it as proof that Yhwh is the god of Israel (1 Kings 19). The cultic personnel at other sites are seldom referred to, though Amos gives a vivid picture of the chief priest at Bethel (Amos 7). They are mostly presented as ciphers and stereotypes who carry out nefarious practices and reap their rewards by being slaughtered by true worshipers of Yhwh. Examples are the priests of Baal (1 Kings 19) and the priests of the cults removed by Josiah (2 Kings 23:20). In this, though, the text recognizes that they exist and that they have their supporters among the people. However, a full picture of society which includes these other shrines does not arise from the heavily edited text and must be reconstructed from other data and considerations.

7.1.3 Prophets

A variety of prophets is plain from the various OT texts. The uniting characteristic of prophets is their role in receiving and announcing messages from Yhwh. The messages vary greatly and are delivered to an assortment of recipients. A common theme to prophecies is a religious message, often about correct worship or activities to be encouraged or discouraged in the light of a particular religious view. A king may be criticized for allowing (or prohibiting) a particular form of worship or participating (or not participating) in the rituals of a particular cult place. Another common message is that relating to political activity: the king should (or should not) enter into a particular alliance, make peace with a superior foreign power (or not make peace but trust in Yhwh to deliver him), go to war (or not) against a particular neighbor, and so on. In some cases, prophecies relate to private individuals or more minor public ones: a message to Baruch the scribe (Jer 45) or Hananiah, the prophet who opposes Jeremiah (28).

The themes in the oracles of the written prophets are similar. The religious message predominates, often taking the form of a criticism of current religious practices and condemning the people, the nation, the king, or—generally—all of them. The political message is also frequent and may well be mixed in with the religious; the religious and the political are often not differentiated in the prophetic oracles. A significant section of the written prophets is also given over to "oracles against the nations." Although these may lie alongside similar oracles against Israel or Judah, they often form a self-contained section in a particular book. Whereas the prophecies about Israel and Judah show a mixture of the negative (usually about the current state of the nation) and the positive (often about the wonderful future, after punishment and repentance), the oracles against the nations are almost all negative: the foreign nations are in for a bad time. This coming punishment is usually seen as deserved, however, because of the evil they have committed against Israel. Some prophecies also contain what has been termed "social criticism"; however, this is a minor element in most prophetic books and usually given in very general terms.

What is plain from many prophecies is the predictive element. This is sometimes contingent on the actions of those at whom the prophecy is directed, but the prophecy explicitly foretells certain consequences or clearly implies them. Only a few give specific dates, yet a substantial number of prophecies speak fairly specifically about what will happen and even when. The tendency to see the prophets as forth-tellers and not foretellers ignores the fact that both are constituent parts of many prophecies. The prophet declares the word, vision, or so on, of Yhwh, but Yhwh knows the end from the beginning. God is able to reveal the future if God chooses. The consequences of certain actions is known to God and form a part of this future. Yhwh also knows who will be punished and who will be blessed. That many prophecies have a contingent element in them does not negate this basic consideration.

The characteristics of the individual prophets and their place in society vary considerably. A prophet like Elijah confronted religious practices with which he disagreed. He comes across as a champion of Yahwism against Baalism. However, his disciple Elisha seems to have concentrated on performing "miracles": siccing bears on insolent children, healing a poisoned pot, finding lost objects. In addition, he acted on the international scene, such as announcing a change of dynasty in Damascus, although the Damascus prophecy was a response to a query about the Aramean king's health. His interaction with the coalition of the kings of Israel, Judah, and Edom (Aram?) was another miracle: producing water for the perishing army. The information on Isaiah is not all of a piece. According to 2 Kings, he is a part of, or on good terms with, Hezekiah's court. In Isaiah, he at least has access to King Ahaz, though some of the prophecies could be taken as criticism of some of Hezekiah's policies. Many of Jeremiah's activities take place around the temple, and he has access to its chambers and the cooperation of many of the temple personnel.

7.1.4 Diviners and Shamans

The main impression of the text is that divination and similar forms of inquiry were anti-Yhwh and to be avoided and condemned. Many different passages refer to the sin of using teraphim or consulting the dead or seeking esoteric knowledge by various rites. A passage such as Deuteronomy 18:9-14 or 1 Samuel 28 seems to give the biblical view about such practices: they are wrong and to be rooted out of society. Yet other passages, sometimes overlooked, give a different picture.

Divinely sanctioned, the divinatory mechanisms of the priests played a vital role. The Urim and Thummim and the ephod were means of access to the divine will; another was dreams. These took their place alongside prophecy and do not seem to be considered less authentic or spiritual than it (1 Sam 28:6). The condemnation of the text is not against divination as such but against certain sorts. Especially important seems to be the use of divination in the context of certain cults, such as the cult of the dead. Implicit in the textual anathema of these is their place in society. Although the exact popularity of such cults cannot be determined, they seem to be well established. Whether all those who practiced the cult of the dead also looked to the dead for esoteric knowledge is not known, only that some did and in sufficient numbers to worry people such as the Deuteronomist.

Divination is a part of the shaman's craft, but the shaman is more than a diviner. Traditionally, shamans are masters of spirits and are called upon in times of illness and crisis. They may also have other functions in society, such as finding lost objects. Although the exact image of the traditional Siberian shaman is not found in the biblical text, some figures approach it in significant ways. Probably the figure most like the archetypical shaman is Elisha. He is able to harness the supernatural powers to perform miracles, to feed a large number from a small amount of food, to heal, to restore what is lost. He is able to see the supernatural world and to predict the future. These are all shamanistic traits. Other prophets also effect cures or are consulted about recovery from illness, even if they do not do all the other deeds ascribed to Elisha.

7.1.5 Sages

The term "wise," with its various forms and synonyms, is found in many different OT writings and contexts. Any specialist or professional knowledge can constitute wisdom. Wise men and women are found in different strata of society and walks of life. The farmer and the potter have their own special sort of wisdom, which ultimately derives from God. The terms can be used of anyone of intelligence. In this sense, "wisdom" is used broadly and has no particular significance for a religious specialization.

Wisdom goes beyond this general application, however, because it is especially used with regard to the intellectuals of society—the educated, the literate, and those able to appreciate literature. Again, this designation does not apply to any one single profession or social class, yet there is obviously a concentration of the wise in certain professions, such as scribes and priests, and the wealthy and aristocratic class. The intellectual tradition is primarily a learned tradition, and only those with the leisure and means can gain the required educational background and have the opportunity to pursue it.

"Sage" by itself does not specify a religious specialist. Nevertheless, the sage in ancient Israel often, if not always, fulfilled the role of religious specialist. It was not unusual for the knowledge of the sage to be considered as divinely given, even if aided by education. Their writings in many cases were religious literature; if they had other writings, these do not seem to have come down to us. Some possessed an esoteric source of knowledge which overlapped with the priest, the prophet, and the diviner. The wisdom of Daniel can only be considered as religious wisdom possessed by a religious specialist. The "sage" may have overlapped considerably with what today we might call an "intellectual," so that different types of people, with different characteristics, may have attracted this label. From the limited data available, many of these well fill the role of religious specialist.

7.2 CROSS-CULTURAL COMPARISONS

7.2.1 The Nuer

Beidelman, T. O. "Nuer Priests and Prophets," *The Translation of Culture: Essays to E. E. Evans-Pritchard* (1971) 375-415.

Evans-Pritchard, E. E. "The Nuer: Tribe and Clan," *Sudan Notes and Records* 18 (1935) 37-87.

____ . *Nuer Religion* (1956).

Johnson, D. H. *Nuer Prophets* (1994).

The prophets among the Nuer have already been discussed (4.3.6). They now need to be set in the context of other religious specialists. The most important ritual expert among the Nuer is the "earth priest" or "leopard-skin priest." This is primarily a hereditary office, residing in certain families; their major function is to purify acts of homicide and other pollutions that arise during feuds, as well as acting as mediators between the families in such situations. Of perhaps less importance are the cattle-priests, who function in regard to all aspects of cattle: fertility, health, feeding, acquiring by raiding, and the like. There are also other lesser ritual experts such as curers and diviners. The roles of prophet and priest heavily overlap. First, the most famous prophets have generally come from priestly families. For example, Ngundeng was an earth master before he was seized by a divinity. Second, there is a tendency for priests to take on prophetic functions and for prophets who are not already of the priestly lines to attempt to take on priestly roles (Beidelman: 377):

> There seems a tendency for Nuer prophets to spring from priestly lineages and sometimes for prophetic and ambitious individuals outside such lineages to try to assume priestly attributes . . . . To put it in Weber's terms, Nuer priests sometimes widen and strengthen their authority by assuming charismatic powers more often associated with prophetic figures; and Nuer prophets try to convert their charismatic powers into a more routinized authority.

Prophets must also be seen as the extreme of a continuum with other spirit-possessed individuals who may be only herbalists and healers. All prophets have some magical attributes relating to healing, warfare, and fertility. Prophets such as Ngundeng have usually attempted to regulate the place and function of magic by opposition to, and even suppression of, magical practices. Conversely, magicians would adopt the outward appearance and manner of well-known prophets (Johnson: 328). Prophets may also attempt to pass on their functions to their sons just as sons inherit the priestly office of fathers (Beidelman: 388-89, 400). On the other hand, Nuer priests often seek to augment their authority by charismatic and supernatural powers. Thus, there is a considerable overlap between the various religious specialists in Nuer society, without always a clear distinction between them (Beidelman: 404-5):

> The status of a "bull" [any person prominent because of wealth, kinship, etc.], a ghoul [one who plays and has sex with corpses], a priest, or a prophet is theoretically different but not always readily distinguishable when such labels are applied to actual data, whether case material or ideological formulations. . . . The Nuer data demonstrate similarities between priest and prophets and also, in some respects, parallels between both these and asocial or antisocial witches or ghouls.

7.2.2 The Dinka

Lienhardt, G. *Divinity and Experience: The Religion of the Dinka* (1961).

The Dinka live primarily in southern Sudan, southwest of their neighbors, the Nuer. The two seem to have influenced one another, though the exact relationship is not always clear. The priestly functions of prayer, sacrifice, and invocation of the deity for prosperity of the people and success in war are carried out by the "masters of the fishing spear." These individuals belong to certain clans with the clan-deity Flesh, who is the source of life. By the very existence and vitality of the spear masters, the life of the community is maintained (Lienhardt: 206-18).

Divination is widely practiced as well. On the simplest level this may be done by practically anyone, by manipulation of mussel shells or similar techniques. Also, the use of fetish bundles is widespread, especially to gain individual help and to curse enemies, though the possession of these is not usually admitted. But as one moves up the scale, the higher ranks of diviners are able to practice their craft because of having one of the free deities (as opposed to clan deities) in their bodies. The highest ranks of diviners are easily assimilated to the prophets, who also perform an important function. Since the really great prophets have all been from the ranks of fishing-spear masters, there is no hard-and-fast distinction between priestly, prophetic, and divinatory functions (Lienhardt: 64-80, 206-8).

7.2.3 Kiganda Religion

Rigby, P. "Prophets, Diviners, and Prophetism: The Recent History of Kiganda Religion," *Journal of Anthropological Research* 31 (1975), 116-48.

In the Kiganda religion of Uganda there is a variety of priests, prophets, diviners, and mediums who mediate between humans and the complex world of spirits. Peter Rigby (117) has noted that

> the rigid distinctions frequently made in the African context between prophets, diviners, priests, and mediums are not really applicable, and hence do not serve a useful analytical purpose; however, some differences between these roles and offices, and their incumbents, obviously do exist.

More important than the distinction between these individual specialists is that between specialists who operate on the personal level and those who function on the state level, whatever their designation.

The national shrines of the hero-gods and kings have regular priests whose service is primarily on behalf of the king. The common people will not generally go to the national shrines for their needs but to the local "spirit shrines" of the diviners, healers, and prophets. Since the national shrines are basically oriented toward the past, prophets (whose concern is with the future) usually operate on the personal level; however, there are prophets associated with the national shrines whose main function is to prophesy for the king and state officials, and some of these prophets have had considerable power over the king and his advisers. Nevertheless, some of the major national prophets began their careers as diviners. As Rigby (139) comments about one famous Kiganda prophet named Kigaanira:

> Kigaanira's case also demonstrates the close interdependence of the roles of diviner and prophet, at least for Kiganda religion. Even during the height of his powers as a politically important prophet, Kigaanira remained potentially a diviner, and when his political role was over, he returned to divination and the mediumship of Kibuuka [a Kiganda god].

The prophets at the national shrines bridge the divide between the past-oriented cult and the future-oriented function of the prophet and diviner. Finally, the fluid state of things is shown by the fact that the same individual may perform more than one role (Rigby: 132):

> It could even be argued that the very profusion and variety of terminology for Baganda priests, prophets, mediums, diviners, healers, and medicine men . . . and the constant manipulation of them, is structurally consistent with the ease with which an individual may perform several of these roles simultaneously. It is also consistent with the ability of a person to transform himself from one role to another during the course of his professional life.

7.2.4 The Shona

Bourdillon, M. *The Shona Peoples* (1982).

The Shona tribes inhabit Zimbabwe. According to their belief, the traditional diviner-healer is the *n'anga,* whose responsibility it is to communicate with the spirit world about the cause of an illness and the means of a cure (Bourdillon: 141-61). The *n'anga* is also consulted about various personal matters for which an answer is sought. While many common people have some elementary divining skills, for serious matters an individual would go only to a diviner of reputation, one who has a healing spirit. Various methods of divining are used, divining dice being especially popular. Some diviners rely entirely on their spirits, however, and receive their messages while in a possession trance. It is possible to become a *n'anga* purely by being tutored by specialists in herbal remedies and the like, but the most respected gain their abilities with the help of a healing spirit. Those who have such a spirit may gain knowledge of herbal cures by tutelage under a master, but many learn them solely by dreams and other forms of communication from their healing spirits.

The spirits possessing various individuals are ancestral spirits. A special category are the "lion spirits," who are the spirits of dead chiefs (Bourdillon: 243-49). A lion-spirit medium is mainly concerned with public affairs and thus is distinguished from the *n'anga*, but the distinction is not rigid. Sometimes a *n'anga* is consulted about public matters (especially relating to witchcraft, which is not considered in the lion spirit's domain), while some lion-spirit mediums also practice as diviners and healers. It is especially common for *makombwe* spirit mediums to be consulted on private matters. These are possessed by a particular group of lion spirits of the very early inhabitants of the country. While normal lion spirits are considered territorial, the *makombwe* spirits have more widespread influence. Thus, their mediums are not associated with a particular territory and must gain their prestige by the size of their private clientele.

Cultic functions are generally carried out by tribal elders or others within the family and relate to local and family spirits. However, the high god Mwari has an organized cult among the southern Shona (Bourdillon: 266-71). This is administered by a permanent priest and priestess, a keeper of the shrine, and a "voice." Delegations from the surrounding chiefdoms often come for oracles from Mwari, usually about public matters. The oracle may occasionally provide advice on private matters but will normally refer such requesters to lesser diviners. Because the function of this cult is similar to that of the lion spirits, lion-spirit cults are not dominant among the southern Shona as in the north.

Under the influence of Christianity, a number of native independent churches have grown up. One influential one is Johane Maranke's African Apostolic Church (Bourdillon: 287-94). Among its ecclesiastical officers are prophets and healers. The function of the prophet is primarily to diagnose the cause of illness, which the healer then proceeds to cure. While the term "prophet" is borrowed from the Bible, the function of the individual closely parallels that of the traditional diviner and is clearly an adaptation of the native religion. Healing also often takes the form of casting out evil spirits.

7.2.5 Plains Indians of North America

Lowie, R. H. *Indians of the Plains* (1954) 161-64.

In many native tribes of North America, the main religious specialist is a shaman (sometimes referred to as a medicine man or woman in older literature). These are widespread among the Plains Indians, but some tribes also have priests. For example, the Pawnee have priests whose official duty is to learn sacred songs and ritual procedure. They, rather than the chiefs, are the supreme authority of the tribe because of their care of the sacred medicine bundles, which underlie the political structure of the tribe (Lowie: 164):

> Each of the thirteen Skidi villages owned a bundle . . . . Four of the bundles were pre-eminent, and a fifth . . . took absolute precedence; the priests of these bundles rather than the titular chiefs held supreme authority. Normally, the four priests in turn assumed responsibility for the welfare of the people for the period of a year.

This office of priest is hereditary. The shamans also have features of priests in that they learn their techniques as disciples of great masters. Yet their powers of healing are supposed to derive from a particular animal who acts as the protector and source of power of the individual shaman. Treatment of illness often consists of herbal remedies and other physical means, but serious illness is treated by one who gained his technique from a visionary experience. Such shamans often specialize in one particular type of affliction. Thus, the traditional distinction made between priest and shaman is not so clear-cut in this case.

7.2.6 The Hopi

Geertz, A. W. *The Invention of Prophecy* (1994).

Knowledge of ancestral traditions (*novati*) is a source of power in the Hopi society of the American Southwest. Leadership—both secular and religious—resides largely in the possession of certain central ritual objects, but the one possessing them must also possess the tradition, songs, and ritual knowledge associated with them. One has to be a "sage" possessing esoteric knowledge to hold a position of authority in Hopi society. One element of tradition is the important ancestral myth, the "emergence myth," which describes how the Hopi and other peoples came from lower worlds into the present one. This myth is an important cultural artifact that is used as a means of understanding the world and also a basis for self-understanding for the Hopi.

A form of prophecy is attested (probably for the past several centuries at least) and well documented for the late nineteenth and twentieth centuries:

> Hopi prophecy can be formally defined as statements about the future which were reportedly pronounced by the Hopi tutelary deity, Maasaw, and by the first people who appeared at Sipaapuni, the place of the emergence of mankind (Geertz: 169-70).

Prophecies are given in several contexts: (1) in association with recitation of or reference to the emergence myth; (2) in ritual songs; and (3) in modern prose narrative such as pamphlets, newspaper interviews, and letters (often as a form of rhetoric to influence European Americans). There are no prophets, as such, because there are no revelations in the normal sense and certainly no ecstatic states. The prophecies are presented as predictions but are in fact interpretations of the core myth in the light of current events. Such events as the two world wars, the atomic bomb, space travel, and the like are alleged to have been forecast, though there is no evidence that any such predictions were ever given in advance of the event supposedly predicted; rather, these are all *ex eventu* prophecies.

Prophecy is thus a form of hermeneutic of the myth. It encourages hearers to relate primordial times and conditions to their contemporary ones:

> The present apocalyptic conditions are identified with the primordial ones, thus fusing past with present. And this fusion not only confronts past conditions with present ones, but it also provides past solutions to present problems. . . . Prophecy incorporates contemporaneous affairs into the interpretive framework of prophetic discourse and subjects those affairs and the forces behind them to evaluation in terms of conceived tradition. This evaluation, or pronouncing of judgment, derives authority from tradition and serves as a mechanism in social and political strategy (Geertz: 83, 165).

Thus, *Urzeit wird Endzeit* ("primordial time becomes endtime"). Hopi prophecy is a means of interpreting the society and its changes and crises and also a means used to change and shape the society and the attitudes within it. The prophecies often have moral or spiritual messages, as well as social and political ones. Those adumbrating the prophecies could be said to function in many ways as "sages" and interpreters of sacred texts.

Thus, Hopi prophecy has little in common with stories about the prophets in the OT, but it has many parallels to the contents of the prophetic books. As suggested at 4.4.2, some of the content of the prophetic corpus—perhaps much of it—was not uttered by prophets while under divine control but is literary prophecy. That is, many of these prophecies are religious and moral messages given in prophetic form but in fact composed by priestly, deuteronomistic, wisdom, or other writers drawing on traditional beliefs and teachings.

7.3 WHAT DID THE SOCIETY LOOK LIKE?

Carroll, R. P. "Prophecy and Society," *The World of Ancient Israel* (1989) 203-25.

Flesher, P. V. M. "Palestinian Synagogues before 70 CE: A Review of the Evidence," *Approaches to Ancient Judaism VI* (1989) 68-81.

Grabbe, L. L. "Synagogues in Pre-70 Palestine: A Re-assessment," *JTS* 39 (1988) 401-10.

____ . *Judaism from Cyrus to Hadrian* (1992).

Lewis, I. M. *Ecstatic Religion: A Study of Shamanism and Spirit Possession* (1989).

Wilson, R. R. *Prophecy and Society in Ancient Israel* (1980).

The text takes us a long way down the road toward the society, if approached carefully and critically, but there is still far to go. We can draw on other sources of information or interpretation, such as cross-cultural parallels. The picture given here is—and can be—only an intelligent guess at many points. We attempt to put the data together into a coherent whole, using analogies and deductions to make connections and patterns. In the end, though, the picture is believable only to the extent that it takes account of all the data and explains them in a cogent manner. New data could change matters drastically.

In Chapters 2-6 we looked at the various religious specialists as ideal types. I emphasize *ideal types*, because it will soon become clear, as was also noted at various points in the individual chapters, that such types seldom existed as such in society. The ideal type is an artificial construct for heuristic purposes only. It helps to clarify thinking if we focus initially on clear-cut phenomena and attempt to ask ourselves, "What was a priest (or prophet or whatever)?" and then proceed to build up various characteristics from the texts and other sources of data. But when we have to describe society as it was, things become much messier, and the ideal type which has been useful in the earlier part of the investigation must be discarded for the reality of society in all its complexity. It is also at this point that relationships between the various types of religious specialist are best explored.

Before looking at the different types as they functioned in society, the question of central versus peripheral figures should be considered. R. R. Wilson originally made the distinction between prophets, referring to central prophets and peripheral prophets (Wilson: 37-41). Wilson's particular treatment has been criticized for some weaknesses (Carroll: 216-18), the main ones being that his anthropological model (Lewis) refers to central and peripheral *cults* rather than figures and that his application does not fit some individuals, such as Jeremiah. Although these criticisms are certainly valid, the concept still seems a useful one for general purposes. With the exception of the king, the religious specialists treated in the individual chapters do tend to divide into two main groups: those who are state-sponsored or at least legitimized by the state, and those who operate in society without any official sanction and sometimes even opposed by the state. Thus, there are official state cults and then there are many other cults and cult sites, many of which may not differ from the state cult but which have no state support. There are prophets of the court and (other?) prophets in the official cult, but many other prophets as well. The king may have his diviners, and divination was practiced in a particular context by the priests, but divination was also widespread among the people. As shown below, the particular activity in question (cult operation, prophecy, divination) may have been much the same in either case, but the sphere in which it functioned and how it was received might well be affected by how it was viewed from the "official" view point of the court.

Only the official priesthood and official temple are accorded real space in the text in its final form, yet it is very clear that the monotheistic, monocultic form of worship in Israel developed very late, perhaps even in exilic or post-exilic times (3.5; 5.6). There were many cultic sites with their own priests. It has often been speculated that the Levites originated as the priests of these country cult places and were reluctantly taken into the Jerusalem cult—only as inferior clergy—after the fall of the Northern Kingdom (3.5). Although the existence of a variety of cult places seems well-enough attested, the precise relations between their clergy and Jerusalem is not spelled out in the text, because its concern is to deny the legitimacy of all cultic sites outside Jerusalem. That the Jerusalem cult personnel regarded themselves as the elite and looked on the others with disdain would not be surprising. Nevertheless, we cannot be sure that country priests were regarded as illegitimate by Jerusalem until very late in the monarchy. Thus, the old argument is perfectly believable that Deuteronomy ultimately originated in circles surrounding northern shrines and was communicated to the Jerusalem establishment only when many of these priests migrated to Jerusalem after the fall of Samaria.

Much worship in Israel centered on the cult. Although private worship cannot be excluded, it seems clear that the community very much dominated, and communal worship usually involved sacrifice and related activities. The regular worship of Elkanah and his family (1 Sam 1) seems a useful model of how Israelites worshiped. They seem to have gone up to the shrine of choice at times of public festivals. The choice of cultic site was likely to have been similar to how people choose their church or synagogue today: convenience, family tradition, personal views on worship, acceptable cult personnel, other general amenities. How the cult personnel were chosen for their jobs is likely to have varied from site to site and age to age. For instance, the cultic acts by patriarchal figures found in Genesis and Job may be fictitious with regard to the specific individuals named in the narrative; nevertheless, they probably show memory of an earlier practice when the head of the family was responsible for sacrifice, the duty being passed down to the firstborn son. The Pentateuch also seems to recognize or remember this practice when it says that the Levites are taken in place of the firstborn of Israel (Num 3:12). Even then Samuel, who was of the tribe of Ephraim, becomes a priest in the shrine at Shiloh and other cultic sites. But the usual picture of the text is of an inherited priestly function. The main qualification for priesthood in Leviticus, Numbers, and Joshua-2 Kings is physical descent. This seems to have become standard with the building of the temple in Jerusalem and is also likely to have prevailed at other cult sites. Since the priesthood carried certain privileges, the tendency would have been to pass it down through one's own family rather than allowing just anyone who chose to take the office.

Even though the text attempts to give a smooth synthetic picture, it cannot disguise the fact that there are various priestly groups and that a certain tension exists among them. The dominant picture is probably a priestly one, which divides the clergy into Aaronites, who preside at the altar, and Levites, who form the inferior clergy with more menial tasks, though Levitical duties could include positions of power in the areas of security (e.g., gatekeepers) and the fabric of the building. Deuteronomy clearly sees no such division, however, suggesting a historical development in which some viewed all priests as Levites and equal, but this view did not ultimately prevail. Stories about the sin of the Levites and about their punishment by being deprived of service at the altar were no doubt circulated to support the main priestly position (cf. Ezek 44:10-14). Yet even among the priests, there are hints at diverse groups: Ezekiel considers Zadokites alone as worthy to preside at the altar, apparently lumping the other Aaronites in with the Levites. There is also a hint at a group descended from Moses, though someone has tampered with the text at this point to disguise the fact (Judges 18:30; 3.1.3). The text thus seems to bear discrete witness to serious rivalries, which developed and were fought out in the history of the priesthood. Eventually some sort of compromise was apparently reached by the Second Temple period, since we hear nothing further of major disputes in the literature of this period. The final result of the various struggles for position was basically a twofold division of the priesthood. All "Aaronites" were priests and could carry out the duties relating to the altar. The "Zadokites" may have become a specific family of these from whom the high priests were traditionally drawn, but otherwise there is little to suggest a special position for them (but cf. Ezek 44:15). Apart from the sacrificial system, the priests had to make decisions about cultic practices, judge whether a leper could be declared clean or not (Lev 14-15), and declare on other matters of ritual purity (Hag 2). The "Levites" were responsible for the more menial functions of cleaning, carrying, provisioning, and running the temple in general. The only major change was at the time of the Maccabean revolt, when the high priesthood was taken out of the traditional ("Zadokite"?) line, an act apparently not accepted by some groups (cf. *Damascus Document* 3:21-4:4, etc.). After this, the Hasmonean, Herodean, and Roman rulers appointed priests as they saw fit, always from the line of Aaron but otherwise for political rather than religious reasons.

Whether women had a place in the temple is uncertain. The texts as finally edited make the priesthood an all-male affair. Women are not mentioned at all, except as wives or daughters. On the other hand, women are connected with various of the "pagan" (i.e., the extra-Jerusalem) cultic sites. In addition, one or two passages that allege the importation of pagan cults into the Jerusalem temple mention women. It has been widely believed and asserted that women served as cultic prostitutes in some of the "pagan" cults. Women definitely had a part to play, but their exact role is uncertain. The charge of cultic prostitution owes much to the bias of scholars who have made a theological distinction between the various cults. The actual evidence for cultic prostitution in Israel or the ancient Near East in general is very meager and subject to other interpretations (3.7). Thus, women seem to have some sort of role, probably a minor one, in some of the cults in Israel. Whether they ever had a function in the Jerusalem temple, though, is not known. Otherwise, their primary role seems to be that of lay worshiper, much as the average male Israelite. Whether the First Temple or the original Second Temple was partitioned into sections which allowed male Israelites but excluded Israelite women, as the temple of Herod did, is unknown. The few references we have suggest that women could participate as lay worshipers in the sacrificial cult (3.7).

The primary function of priestly figures was cultic, but they often had other functions as well. A form of official divination is recognized in the text. The Urim and Thummim seem to have been some sort of lot manipulated by the priests. Similar but less clear is the ephod, which was also used to ascertain God's will, evidently by a process of yes/no answers. The priests would naturally be consulted about matters of cultic procedure, but they also seem to have teaching, preserving, and decision-making functions as well. Common sense says that with the support of tithes and other dues, they had the necessary leisure to learn the religious traditions, to collect them, to study them, and to preserve them. Although writing in the Hebrew alphabet may have been more widespread than its counterpart in hieroglyphs or cuneiform, it is to be doubted that most Israelites could read or had access to books (6.4.3). The priests were the ones most likely to be able to read and write and to preserve written records of some sort. Even oral traditions would have been safer with them. They may not have been the sole guardian of the religious traditions, but they would most likely have been the main one. As long as the priesthood was diverse, the traditions preserved would have been diverse as well. There is no reason to think that some of the traditions in the OT were not preserved at shrines outside Jerusalem.

Various texts explicitly give to the priests duties other than presiding over the cult. Deuteronomy 17:8-13 regards the priests as judges, alongside lay magistrates. A similar situation is envisaged in Ezekiel (44:24), where the priests are judges. One could argue that these are "utopian" texts which do not reflect reality. Certainly, Ezekiel 40-48 is utopian in the sense that it pictures an idealized cult and state organization which did not and could not have had any reality in some if its features. Nevertheless, a comparison with the cult of the Second Temple period shows that it is partly based on reality. The general divisions and duties of priests seem to be basically accurate, and the role of the priesthood in the governance of Judah was an important one in the later period. Thus, it seems likely that local judges and magistrates would have been drawn from the priesthood, as well as the local community elders, in Second Temple times. The reality may have been different while the monarchy still existed.

Priests thus played an important role in Israelite society and were known and respected, whether at Jerusalem or at other shrines, whether priests of Yhwh or of other gods. Religious law and custom assured that revenues (tithes, offerings of various sorts, portions of most sacrifices) were made available to the priesthood so that they apparently did not normally need to have other occupations to make a living. This gave the priesthood great power. Not only were priests able to teach the will of the gods and to communicate with them and placate their anger by means of sacrifice—this itself was sufficient to make them a considerable social force—but they also had the education and leisure to conduct intellectual pursuits. They could control the national tradition and the myths of the people: the edifying tales, the moral stories, the literary exemplification of how the cosmos worked and how Israelites were to live within it.

Their control over the thought of the people could be exaggerated, since we do not know how unified the priesthood was nor how deeply into people's personal lives priests were able to delve. At a time when there were many cult places, the priesthood was probably fragmented, especially if different priests served different gods. In that situation, the teaching power and ideological control of the people were probably rather diffused, because they were not likely to have been administered by a central hierarchy; in other words, each cult place (and its priest or priests) was likely to be semi-independent. Cult centralization would have changed the situation a good deal in that the various cult personnel and cultic activities would have been concentrated in one place under one priestly hierarchy. But cult centralization in a monarchy, while increasing the power of those higher up in the hierarchy, would also take away some of the general power of the priests, because the ultimate supervisor would be the king. He would also be in a good physical position to keep an eye on the temple right next to his palace and bend its priesthood to his own ideas and concerns. Even if the result of Josiah's attempts at cult centralization are exaggerated in the tradition (2 Kings 22-23), it is clear that this was part of a move aimed at increasing his own power and authority in that part of Palestine.

Members of the court and administration would also have taken on some of the moral authority exercised by the priests. Not only did they act for the king, but they were also men of education and leisure in many cases. The priests' intellectual endeavors could also have been shared by some members of the administration, including higher officials and the lay aristocracy; at local level, even the traditional elders of the tribe or clan would have been important. The "wise" of society who were able to shape it intellectually included a range of individuals and professions: priests, scribes, aristocrats, administrators, court figures, favorites of the king. This does not mean that other members of society were not occasionally educated or concerned to pursue intellectual activities, but the concentration of such individuals must have been among those groups just listed.

Nor does it mean that there was not a substantial body of folk tradition, religious and secular. Such traditions develop in any society and are passed on from parents to children or, perhaps more often, from grandparents to grandchildren. It is the literal and figurative elders among the people who often have the position—whether by official appointment or by convention—of carrying forward the family and tribal lore. This is true not only of the tribal and village elders but also of the elderly in general, whether or not they had an official function. In a non-literate society and one in which official government communications were limited to those necessary for it to govern, the main traditions of the people would have been passed on in this way. This is why we must not exaggerate the extent to which the government may have worked on controlling the tradition. But we know from the OT literature itself that there were attempts at shaping, editing, and canalizing the tradition. We have it within the literature itself. At some indeterminate time some very specific attitudes about God, worship, and Israel's past were heavily stamped on the tradition, which was then disseminated widely throughout the community. It may well be that much of this was not done until after the end of the monarchy. But it was done, and whatever folk traditions survived were gradually altered and displaced by the official national religious story, even if some of the older traditions seem to have survived and reasserted themselves in certain movements, such as apocalypticism.

The "wise"—the intellectuals of society—were the main force who brought about this change. They were the ones who could read and write and who would have had the respect of the people. One often hears of "Deuteronomic" circles or "priestly" schools or similar literary groups to explain the preservation and editing of biblical literature. The existence of such groups is plausible, but it must be recognized that the structure of such groups was likely to have been quite different from any similar groups in a democratized and mass-educated society such as today's. The number of educated and literate people with sufficient resources to carry on such activity was extremely limited. They might exist at some larger cultic sites and perhaps in some of the larger outlying cities; however, most such people would have been concentrated in the capitals of Samaria or Jerusalem. Such circles would have normally been drawn from either the priestly or scribal classes, though there may have been the occasional lone writer or editor such as Qohelet (if he was indeed a loner). The world in which this literary and intellectual activity took place would have been a very small one in most cases. Also, there may have been the occasional productive circle outside the main centers (cf. Qumran), but much of the literary activity which led to the final set of writings making up the OT was probably carried on in Jerusalem in the very compressed world of those who possessed the intellectual ability and training to do such work.

This does not mean that all those in the intellectual circles were in agreement. It is likely—and the literature itself suggests—that there was a variety of attitudes and views, represented in some cases by different circles or "schools" of individuals. These circles/schools may have cut across the professions, so that they included priests, scribes, aristocrats, or others. That is, the tightly knit nature of the intellectual world was such that monochromatic schools of one profession or group (e.g., completely "Deuteronomistic") were not the only configuration to exist. While some ideologies may have had their focus within a particular profession such as the priesthood, others probably cut across such boundaries and divided the professions more along party lines. Thus, the hypothesized Deuteronomistic circle, for example, could have included priests, Levites, and court scribes, judging from the content of its writing and editing as reconstructed by scholars.

This emphasis on the importance of the small group of intellectuals in the shaping and transmission of the biblical tradition does not mean that folk tradition abruptly ceased. On the contrary, the displacement of traditional lore by the official religious literature and its teaching was a centuries-long affair which seems to have reached well into the Greek period and perhaps even the Roman. The mechanisms of official teaching were not likely to have been very efficient except directly around Jerusalem, but whatever their impact people do not change overnight even in a totalitarian state, and the Israelite state or states do not seem to have had the means or the will of many modern totalitarian states.

This is clear from the religious situation. Some circles were fanatical about the promotion of Yhwh and his cult as the exclusive worship for all Israelites. How early this began is not known (some would put it at the beginning of the monarchy or even earlier, but David still had his teraphim, as acknowledged even by the present heavily edited text); however, it seems to have developed a good deal of impetus toward the end of the monarchy. Assuming there is any truth in the tradition, attempts to centralize the cult already began as early as Hezekiah, but the main push came under Josiah. The plan to remove all rival cults to the temple of Yhwh in Jerusalem may not have been as successful as the text leads us to believe (cf. Jeremiah 44), but paradoxically, the destruction of Jerusalem seems to have been a major watershed in making Jerusalem the exclusive place for worship of Yhwh, who was also the only god recognized.

Thus, the Deuteronomistic ideal of one cult, one temple, and one God seems to have prevailed by the early Persian period. The "Yahweh-alone" movement had pushed out the worship of other gods, and the Jerusalem establishment had eradicated other open cults. It has been suggested that these were in some sense replaced by synagogues. Such a thesis assumes the origin of the synagogue in the exilic period or even during the period of the monarchy. This is very unlikely (Grabbe 1988; Flesher). The standard practice of worship was at a cultic site, even when Israel became monotheistic, and the synagogue concept was likely to have taken time to develop. It would have been in the Diaspora, in areas quite distant from Jerusalem, that the need for communal forms of local worship made itself felt. (Private prayer and worship are known from an early time, and could have long substituted for communal worship at the distant temple; for example, in Tobit all worship and ritual is conducted in the home or otherwise privately.) The fact is that evidence for the synagogue first appears only about the middle of the third century BCE, and evidence for synagogues in Judah comes only from the time after the Maccabean revolt. The likely development is that the synagogue arose in the Diaspora some time in the third century, spread slowly but widely, and was finally imported into Palestine, but only about the turn of the era, perhaps in the first century BCE.

Despite the official monotheistic and monocultic views, we nevertheless have evidence that underworld cults, which had once thrived openly, were still flourishing underground, as it were. As with any cult, it is difficult for outsiders to know what the appeal was to worshipers. One definite attraction, though, was that such cults seemed a source of occult knowledge—a means of finding out about the future. The idea that the dead have prescient knowledge is one widespread through the world, and the cults of the dead who seek to tap this knowledge are often close-knit clubs, open only to initiates, which conduct their activities at night in secret. This is one of the reasons that our knowledge of such cults is limited. Even if such cults were spread throughout society (as they could have been even if practiced by a minority of the population), there may have been a mixed attitude toward them. On the one hand, they were probably accepted as legitimate (except under certain rulers) and useful, but this respect was also likely to have been tinged with a certain amount of fear and aversion. Priestly circles in particular, with their authorized form of divination, would have been disdainful of such societies and perhaps even worked to discourage or even outlaw them. The negative view in the final form of the text, with its priestly overlay, strongly supports this supposition.

Divination was an important part of life in many Near Eastern cultures, as in many pre-industrial cultures studied by anthropologists. Mesopotamian temples had specialist personnel who dealt with such matters. Their activities were especially drawn on by the king and his administrators for the conduct of the affairs of state. The king would undertake no major activity without having consulted the omens, much as is the case in some societies in Africa even today. A similar state of affairs seems to have pertained in some of the other Asian peoples such as the Hittites. Although the main activity was on the plane of official government, there is evidence that ordinary people were able to avail themselves of some sorts of divination. Divination was not seen as a shady activity or a superstition but a respected profession. These practices were not frowned on but were a part of daily life.

Divination takes many different forms and varies greatly between cultures. The types of divination in Israel were not usually the same as those found in Mesopotamia (though a few cuneiform liver models suggest some use of hepatoscopy), but various modes of official and unofficial divination existed. The official method included the priestly oracles of the Urim and Thummim and the ephod, though the exact relationship between the two is still uncertain. Earlier narratives in the books of Samuel show considerable use of these, but they are not generally referred to after the reign of David. Whether this is accidental, the result of deliberate editing, or whether the use of these actually declined is impossible to say. The only statement we have is that they had vanished by the Persian period (Ezra 2:63; Neh 7:65).

There also seems to be evidence that at least some kings sought guidance by other forms of divination. The data are problematic because they are ascribed only to "wicked" kings and may, therefore, be only stereotyped slanders. But it is possible that these passages show knowledge of other non-priestly forms of divination resorted to by Israelite rulers. The most famous example is Saul's consulting of the "witch" of Endor (1 Sam 28). Solomon's stay in Gibeon may have been a deliberate attempt at the incubation of a dream (2 Kings 3). The text is not explicit on this, but Yhwh did appear to him in a dream, and the circumstances are certainly consistent with an incubation rite. The other main example is that of Manasseh (2 Kings 21//2 Chron 33). He is said to have consulted familiar spirits and practiced necromancy. Because this is a standard part of the list of "abominations" enumerated in various passages (e.g., Deut 18:9-12), it is not clear how much reliance should be placed on it. Other "wicked" kings do not have these abominations alleged for them, though, and such practices seem in any case to have been a widespread form of divination and not confined to official circles.

The main form of divination in Israel appears to have been that of spirit possession or spirit divination. How the spirits were consulted is not always stated. Other than the priestly lots, references to mechanical manipulation focus on foreign nations; however, it must be conceded that the Hebrew terminology is not always clear, and the actual means of consulting the spirits may have included lots or other forms of mechanical devices. The number of references to necromancy, esoteric cults, and associations with the cult of the dead suggest that this form of divination was well established in Israelite society. Yet even if, as noted above, the people had a mixed reaction to it, other forms of spirit divination appear to have been quite popular. The best attested mode was to consult a holy man (a "man of God") who had God's spirit and could call on it by various means to achieve second sight. This was useful in finding whether one might recover from an illness (especially if the means to do so was also revealed), to discover the location of lost objects, or to achieve deliverance from any one of the many personal disasters endemic to all people.

In contrast to cults of the dead, inquiry through holy men does not seem to have been frowned on, and they were rather more accessible to ordinary Israelites than either the official priestly form of divination or one of the dark cults. Various terms are used for these holy men: *ḥōzeh*, "seer"; *rō'eh*, "seer"; *nāvî'*, "prophet"; *'îš hā'ĕlōhîm*, "man of God." What the significance was of the different names is hard to say at this point because the text seems to use them interchangeably at times. Certainly the term "prophet" is applied to those also called "seer" or "man of God." "Man of God" seems the most generic and would probably be equivalent to "holy man" in more modern terminology. Even if the terms originally distinguished somewhat different figures at one time, usage may eventually have fused them. To add to the confusion, the verbal forms do not always agree with the nouns. Figures not labeled "prophet" in the text may still "prophesy" (nif./hitp. *nb'*), and prophets may "see visions" (*ḥzh*).

We do not read anywhere of holy women. There are a few references to prophetesses (*nĕvî'āh*). One of these is to Miriam and another to Deborah. Modern scholars have often thought that this is a much later addition to the tradition, almost an honorific to outstanding women, just as Moses and David become designated as prophets. While this analysis is plausible, one cannot help suspecting that it is simplistic (4.8). It remains true, though, that in neither case is it certain why Miriam and Deborah are so designated. Only three other women are called prophetesses. One is the woman by whom Isaiah produced several children and who is not otherwise identified (including *not* said to be his wife). A second is the prophetess Huldah, who was consulted about the book found in the temple at the time of Josiah. She may have had some sort of official capacity, either in the temple (her husband seems to have been a priest) or in the court. The last is the prophetess Noadiah, who was an enemy of Nehemiah, according to his own account (Neh 6:14).

None of these women seem to have been consulted by the people in the way that holy men were. If there were female seers and prophets to whom the people might inquire, as they did with Elisha, this has been omitted or suppressed by the text. It would not be surprising if there were none, however, since the association of certain cults with a particular sex is well-known from anthropological studies. This is partly confirmed by the fact that women are not completely absent from the text. Women were evidently associated with the esoteric arts. The woman of Endor is the main example, but Leviticus 20:27 also recognizes that women as well as men might be in command of a familiar spirit. One could argue that women are mentioned here because the reference is derogatory, but a survey of the passages does not suggest any deliberate singling out of women. For this reason, the most likely situation is that women were associated only with certain forms of divination but not others.

Most of those individuals labeled "prophet" in the text can be characterized as a subspecies of diviner. That is, they carry on their activities by means of the spirit (usually the spirit of Yhwh) and thus belong to the spirit form of divination. The type of activity does not differ in kind from that of the diviner: they receive messages from the divine which they pass on to others. Some messages come spontaneously, which some would differentiate from divination. Yet even those prophets who receive messages spontaneously or unevoked may also seek messages from Yhwh for themselves or on behalf of others. In some cases the prophet is able to declare Yhwh's will immediately. At other times he must resort to prayer, ecstasy, dreams or visions, or perhaps even the passage of time (4.9). In this he does not differ from the diviner. This brings up an important question: Can one make prophecy a subdivision of divination or is this a completely misguided endeavor?

The key—or perhaps the wild card—is the written prophets, often referred to as the "classical prophets." What do they tell us about prophecy in Israelite society? The answer is complicated, if not impossible to give. The so-called classical prophets form a body of literature with varied contents and many different themes and messages. All the prophetic books are in the name of an individual. We have almost no information on some of these "authors," such as Micah. For others (e.g., Jeremiah), there is an abundance of stories about the prophet's doings and persona. The problem is knowing whether the actual prophecies of the books were uttered by the named authors of the books. Was a particular prophecy the product of a prophet's mind, under the guidance or influence of God's spirit, uttered on a particular occasion with a specific audience in mind? If the answer is yes in each case, this may tell us a good deal about prophecy in Israel, but how often can we answer this question with a clear yes?

Even if we know that an individual prophet gave a specific prophecy to a known audience on a definite occasion—and how often can we even hope to know this?—we may still not be able to answer questions such as whether prophecy qualifies as a form of divination. The reason is that we may not know how that prophecy originated. Many of the objections to including prophecy under the rubric of divination assume information we do not have. Divination is a form of inquiry. Were the prophecies of Israelite prophets the result of inquiry? In most cases, we do not know. In some cases, the text itself states that it was. So the prophecies of the written prophets are claimed in some cases to be the responses to inquiries made of God through the prophet, or sometimes a response to the prophet's own personal inquiry. But how did the message come? Was it an audition? Did it come through a dream? Did the prophet have a vision? Did he receive the message while under the influence of drugs, alcohol, fasting, music, or other channels to an ecstatic state? Had he engaged in an incubation rite? Most of the time, we do not know; however, in some instances, the answer is definitely in the affirmative, even though these can all be the techniques or modes of the diviner.

Therefore, matters are quite complicated, even when we know what was said by whom to whom, where, and when. Generally, though, we are whistling in the dark, because we do not know how a particular prophecy arose, how it got into the book, to whom the author was speaking, what its original context was, and to what extent it has been edited. *Was the prophecy even uttered by a prophet?* In other words, the alleged prophecy could be the product of a priest in his study or a scribe in his scriptorium. This is why I have based much of my study on prophets and similar figures on stories about them rather than on the content of the alleged prophecies. The stories could be invented but probably represent real types. Whether the written prophecies coincide with what prophets actually prophesied is a much bigger question, and those who use the written prophets as their model of the only real, genuine, bona fide Israelite prophets need to consider this (4.4.2).

A major problem in modern research has been the tendency to read modern theological concerns into the message of the prophets. Failure to focus on the actual social phenomenon of the prophet has produced some potential misrepresentations of prophets in Israel. For example, prophets are often described as social critics. This seems to be not only an inadequate description but also a major distortion of the whole notion of prophet and prophecy. More accurate, judging from both the contents of the written prophets and the stories about the prophets, would be to refer to them as political and religious critics. This is because many of their messages relate to condemnation for "false" worship or failure to be as enthusiastic in the pursuit of Yahwism as the prophet thinks appropriate. Almost as important is the political element. Kings are condemned for their international relations—the negotiations, alliances, trade-links, and treaties by which the ruler attempted to secure the safety and well-being of the nation in the turbulent Near East. Yet alongside such virulent attacks on the Israelite or Judean king are found large sections of "oracles against the nations." These almost always condemn the nation in question, whether for failure to recognize the god of Israel, for

Gentile arrogance, or for its treatment of Israel. However critical the prophets seem to have been of Israel, most of them are still ultimately chauvinistic and nationalistic in their outlook.

In sum, the common element in the various characterizations of prophet is receiving and delivering messages from Yhwh. These messages may come in various forms. Some of them apparently are auditions, but many of the oracles are described as "visions," and some messages clearly come in visual form. Although dreams are less often mentioned, no clear distinction is made between them and prophecy. Sometimes the messages seem to have come unbidden and perhaps even unwelcomed. Yhwh spoke to or communicated with the prophet, who had no option but to pass that message on to the designated recipients: the people, the king, an individual, or sometimes only a book which would preserve it for a later generation. Not all prophecies were spontaneous in this way; many of them were the result of "seeking" a message from God—of inquiry by the prophet, either by himself or on behalf of someone else. The language used in such cases is not different from that relating to divination. Despite the condemnation of divination, the actual mode of revelation by Yhwh does not differ from some of the various forms classified as divination in modern study: spirit possession, dream and vision interpretation, ecstatic trance. Spontaneous prophecy may seem to be different on the surface, but the revelation and message are not essentially different from prophecy obtained by inquiry. Perhaps we are really discussing only a matter of terminology rather than different phenomena. In most cases, prophecy fits quite comfortably as a particular form of divination.

The prophets are not part of a profession as such, though there is evidence of cult prophets. Prophets seem to have come from various walks of life, all the way from priest to plowman, and their social standing was equally variable. Some were welcomed in the court and temple, whereas others were marginalized, scoffed at, or even persecuted. Such marginal figures could also be feared, though, and "peripheral prophets" might be quite influential, not only in society but also in court and government circles. A strangely garbed and perhaps mantic-spouting individual who turned up suddenly in the presence of the king in a public place and loudly delivered a word of Yhwh could command attention, however unpleasant it may have been for the royal personage. In some cases, such individuals were punished for their insolence, but it seems they were equally likely to be listened to with awe and a certain respect. Israel was said to have persecuted the prophets continually (Matt 5:12), but the prophets also evidently did their own persecuting. The priests and prophets slain or driven from their profession because of condemnation by zealot "true" prophets would know what persecution consisted of. At the very least, such zealots could make life uncomfortable for kings and high officials in a society which took prophets seriously.

7.4 WHICH SOCIETY AND WHEN?

Collins, J. J. *Daniel* (1993).

Grabbe, L. L. "Josephus and the Reconstruction of the Judean Restoration," *JBL* 106 (1987) 231-46.

____ . *Judaism from Cyrus to Hadrian* (1992).

Holladay, C. R. *Fragments from Hellenistic Jewish Authors, Volume I: Historians* (1983).

Lemche, N. P. "The Old Testament—A Hellenistic Book?" *SJOT* 7 (1993) 163-93.

Nickelsburg, G.W.E. *Jewish Literature between the Bible and the Mishnah* (1981).

Schürer, E. *The Jewish People in the Age of Jesus Christ* (1973-87).

Strange, J. "The Book of Joshua: A Hasmonaean Manifesto?" *History and Traditions of Early Israel* (1993) 136-41.

Tov, E. *Textual Criticism of the Hebrew Bible* (1992).

Up to this point, our concern has been to reconstruct as detailed a picture as possible from all the data available, keeping in mind the problematic nature of the sources. It has been recognized that the OT text provides useful and usable data, but that the appropriation of these data is problematic because of the nature of the text. Therefore, the reconstruction can only be made in broad strokes. Some may feel that more detail can be added through the use of traditio-historical criticism and that the skepticism expressed here about its usefulness is unjustified. Nevertheless, the picture here represents a "critical minimum"—the *least* that can be said with any confidence. It is a foundation on which others can build. One can only go further and give more detail with more data and refined methods. This seems far preferable to a house of cards constructed from speculation, guesswork, overinterpretation of data, and tenuous argument build upon tenuous argument.

A society has been described to some degree, but how is it to be defined in time and space? Even the critical minimum just referred to smoothes out a good deal. There is an inevitable artificiality to some degree. The data from some texts clearly relate to a somewhat different society than others. For example, the data on priests and Levites in Chronicles may well describe a later period in the society of the Second Temple period than that found in Ezra-Nehemiah. The texts used have come from a wide range of time. Because of working from the final form of the text, with its juxtaposition of data from different periods, the society reconstructed will of necessity be a composite one to some extent. With the broad brush used, the rough edges do not always appear.

It must be kept in mind, though, that the reconstruction is not just an amalgam of harmonized data from the text and anthropological and historical data from elsewhere. On the contrary, a method of "triangulation" has been used. The anthropological data are employed only to suggest how the textual data might be interpreted or whether a reconstruction is plausible or not. They have mainly a heuristic value. The data from the text have been critically scrutinized for signs of tendentious editing, alternative views, data which do not fit the editorial bias, and signs of historical development. The textual data have been used only after this critical filter has been applied.

A further point to keep in mind is that traditional societies seldom change rapidly. Institutions and customs as a whole tend to endure. Occasionally, an institution may appear or disappear very quickly as, for example, the monarchy. Any attempt to ascertain the place of the monarchy in Israelite society would have to be limited to the pre-586 period to have any relationship to the actual society. On the other hand, the cult and priesthood would have changed only gradually in most respects. Even the destruction of the temple by the Babylonians caused simply a temporary disruption. When the temple was rebuilt and the cult restored, one looks in vain for signs of major changes. Indications of some change and development are certainly in evidence (e.g., the hints at struggles between various priestly factions [3.6]), but the basic institutions persisted for long periods of time to all intents unaltered. Yet the descriptions relating to prophets, diviners, and sages are nuanced ones and would probably have applied to the society over the course of a number of centuries.

Still, much of the reconstruction is heavily dependent on data from the text, since other sources of information (e.g., archeology) tend to be quite limited. The picture we can draw is necessarily circumscribed by the deficiencies and lacks of the OT texts themselves. A major problem is the period in which the texts were created. All accept that early traditions may be found in the text, but these have been shaped by subsequent editors and tradents, and the final form of the text has been the first stage in the investigation. Some would now want to date the final form of the text even as late as the Hellenistic period; for example, Strange makes such a case for the book of Joshua. Similarly but on a broader front, N. P. Lemche argues that the "historical" material in the OT is very much parallel to that of Greek historians and is thus unlikely to be earlier than the Hellenistic period (183-84). Lemche's article is wide-ranging, and much of it is devoted to showing that the texts as we have them could not date from the early monarchy. (He begins from the first concrete datum: the physical manuscripts of the Greek text in the fourth century CE.) This means that much of what he says would still allow for the texts in the late monarchy or Persian period rather than requiring the post-Alexander age.

The growth of the text was a process which did not cease with the last major redaction. The different text-types indicate continued literary activity for many centuries, and the ancient translations and the Qumran scrolls show that no fixed text existed before 70 at the earliest. Nevertheless, it seems to me that a Hellenistic date for the final redaction/compilation for most OT writings is unlikely, with the exception of a few texts such as Qohelet, Ben Sira, and Daniel. There are several reasons for suggesting this:

1. The Qumran scrolls contain much of the OT text. The accuracy of paleographic methods is disputed, and the confidence with which many of the editors date these is hotly contested by some Qumran specialists. Nevertheless, the differences in dating are generally to be measured in decades rather than centuries. For example, many psalms were once dated to the Maccabean period. The evidence from Qumran suggests that this is unlikely.

2. A book like Daniel shows the traumas of the Maccabean persecutions. Any writing from the second century BCE, especially after 170 BCE, is likely to show some influence from the contemporary situation. Thus, any writing not showing this but dated to the Greek period would have to fall in the time of Ptolemaic rule.

3. The most conducive time for creating much of the OT would be the Persian period. The situation in the third century BCE seems less amenable to this type of editorial activity, judging from what we know of Ptolemaic rule (cf. Grabbe 1992: ch. 4).

Granted, this is not a simple question to tackle. It has been common to shove a good deal of literary activity into the Persian period, an all-too-easy solution because so much of that time in Jewish history is a blank. However, earlier efforts to put much redactional work in the so-called Exile now seem unconvincing because of the disruptions after the fall of Jerusalem. Many of the intellectuals had been killed or deported, and those left in Judah were predictably concerned with eking out a living in straitened circumstances. Those taken into captivity were not likely to have been able to carry scrolls, papyri, temple archives, or other records with them to the ruined cities and vacated country where they were taken to replace other deportees. Again, it is evident that their immediate and continuing concern was to claw out some sort of living beyond a bare existence.

It was during the Persian period that conditions seem sufficiently settled, with a functioning temple staffed by a priesthood with the necessary leisure to try to address the question of the religious tradition. The nation had suffered a great deal. Why? And what about the new situation, without king but with the high priest as the main leader of the nation? How was this all to be explained in the light of Israelite views on Yhwh and his people? These questions would have been keenly felt. The average peasant probably had other things on his mind, but even the impoverished common people may have wondered how to explain things. Priests, who were paid to be concerned with such matters, would have felt the matter even more sharply. It seems unlikely that during the entire Persian period the religious tradition would have been neglected or simply left in whatever inchoate state it found itself at this time. The Persian period seems the most likely time when much editing and writing would have taken place.

This does not preclude literary activity after the coming of Alexander. There is evidence of material that could most readily be interpreted as coming from the Greek period. However, the coming of the Greeks did not form the break in Jewish life and culture that the Babylonian captivity did (even though most Jews were clearly not taken captive by the Babylonians). The changes during the Greek period were important, but they were slow and the result of cultural influence, not the destruction of major religious institutions such as the cult and the monarchy. The next major traumatic period after the Exile was the Maccabean persecution and revolt. The post-Maccabean literature tends to reflect that crisis in some way.

4. Jewish writings indisputably dated to the Greek period do not, for the most part, closely resemble the Pentateuch, Deuteronomistic history, or the prophetic literature.

Jewish writings from the period of Ptolemaic rule do not suggest that the editing of the biblical tradition was a major activity. Perhaps one of the most certain writings is that of the chronographer Demetrius, which dates from the late-third century (Holladay: 1.51-91; Schürer: 3.513-17). It appears to presuppose the Pentateuch in much the form we have it today. This is hardly surprising in that the Pentateuch in a form very similar to the MT was evidently translated into Greek about the mid-third century. When we look at other Jewish works most likely created during the third century, we find a similar picture. Evidence indicates that parts of 1 Enoch probably belong to this period, especially 1-36 ("Book of Watchers") and 72-82 ("Astronomical Book") (Nickelsburg: 47-55; Schürer: 3.250-68). Neither of these has a counterpart in the OT. The dating of Qohelet has recently been disputed (6.1.6), but a date in the Ptolemaic period still holds the balance of the argument. Although it is part of the wisdom books, its main aim was to challenge the conventions found in Proverbs, Deuteronomy, and elsewhere. The early chapters of Daniel (Dan 1-6), also likely to have come from the third century (Collins: 35-37), resemble some other stories in the OT such as the story of Joseph (Gen 37, 39-48); however, the setting is not Israel but Babylon during the Neo-Babylonian and Persian rule, and the hero is new to the tradition. The book of Tobit is harder to date and may come from as early as the Persian period, yet it also has a figure and setting different from the main OT literature.

Ben Sira is particularly important, because the author is known and the book can be dated relatively accurately (c. 190 BCE). It has much in common with the book of Proverbs, especially Proverbs 1-9. In spite of this, the book differs in many significant ways from anything in the OT. The authorship is not accredited to an ancient figure but is clearly identified as to time and writer. The writer draws on Israelite tradition (especially chs. 44-50) and seems to know a good deal of the OT tradition in its present form (with the exception of Ezra and Daniel). This much is even clearer from the preface added by Ben Sira's grandson, who translated the book into Greek. He mentions the "law of Moses and the prophets and the other books" (Prologue), suggesting that some writings were taken as authoritative in his time (even if he unfortunately fails to list them). Thus, the Jewish literature that can be most readily dated to pre-Maccabean times looks like "post-biblical" literature, that is, literature which either presupposes much of the OT tradition or is quite distinct from it. If major literary work was being done on the OT traditions between Alexander and the Maccabees, it has left little trace.

The impression one is left with, then, is that the primary Israelite tradition was brought into order during the Persian period as a consequence of the crisis produced by the exile and restoration. The Jewish literature of the pre-Maccabean Hellenistic period often seems to presuppose the OT literature in much the same form as known to us today. Rather than attempting to put order into the earlier traditions, the Hellenistic Jewish writers appear to want to go further, either in creating new literature or in producing interpretations of the redacted tradition. They do not seem primarily concerned with developing and editing an inchoate Israelite tradition of the monarchic period (or creating one from whole cloth).

There are several things this proposal to date the main literary activity to the Persian period does *not* imply. It does not suggest that the MT was created in its entirety during this period. Although large sections of the MT may well go back to this time, it is also clear that a variety of text-types circulated for many centuries. For example, the Hebrew text of Jeremiah used by the LXX translators was probably an earlier version of that book, whereas the MT represents a later conflation and rearrangement of the text. The earlier Hebrew version continued to circulate even in Palestine, as evidenced by 4QJer^{b}. Judging from the textual variety at Qumran, there was no fixed form of the text until the first century CE or later.

Another point is that this does not imply a fixed canon. The growth of the canon is a complex question, and it probably proceeded over a lengthy period of time, with some parts (e.g., the Pentateuch) becoming accepted as authoritative scripture before other parts. But, again, the fixing of the canon in the present form cannot be demonstrated before the first century CE, if even then. It is clear that some books were accepted as scripture in some circles even though they did not eventually become a part of the standard Jewish canon.

Thus, we can only presume that the editing of the Israelite tradition took place over a period of time, and it continued to develop to some extent well into the Greek period when we know that some books were most likely written. Nevertheless, there is little evidence of the Greek period in the bulk of the OT text. The prophecies against foreign nations seldom include the Greeks. They are mainly against nations encountered by Israel in the monarchic period, such as Assyria, Babylon, and those immediately around Palestine. The Persians are also not usually included, though this could be because the tradition viewed Persian rule favorably (note the occasional prophecy against Elam, however, which could be a reference to Persia: Jer 49:34-37). Even the genealogy in an admittedly late book like Nehemiah (Neh 12:22, 26) seems not to reach the end of Persian rule (cf. Grabbe 1987).

8.

Concluding Essay

This has been a socio-historical study. Religious specialists are known in all societies and have roles and functions befitting the particular societal institutions and expectations. The psychological and social needs of people seem to be very similar across the world throughout history. Until modern times these needs were usually met in whole or in part by religious institutions and beliefs. People want to know about the basic questions of life. Where did the world come from? What sustains it? What happens after death? Are there supernatural or unseen forces which might help or hinder one's activities? How can they be appeased or enlisted in aid? Is there a divine world to be understood and catered to and also called on for assistance? What does the future hold? What is the answer to those questions which cannot be answered by human ability and knowledge?

In the simplest societal organizations, the religious needs may be overseen by designated family members. For example, the head of the family or the eldest son might traditionally act as priest or cultic functionary. The role or office is performed on a part-time basis, as one of the duties carried on by this particular member of the family. Yet even at a simple level of societal complexity, some individuals take on the full-time role of religious specialist, especially of particular sorts (e.g., shaman) because a special training or calling is needed. And as societies grow larger and more complex, it is likely that some individuals will become professionals to meet part of the religious needs of the community or state.

Although religious needs seem remarkably similar from society to society, the religious institutions and religious specializations which develop to meet them vary considerably. Yet even here there seems to be a limited range of institutions and specialists, with the variety due primarily to the particular emphasis, distribution, and permutations within the limited selection of modes available. A cult with priests and other cult personnel is one institution found ubiquitously. Other widespread specialists are diviners, prophets, spirit masters, witch-finders, healers, shamans, counselors, and preachers. These may be associated with a state or local cult, or they may practice privately without any institutional base. But some selection from these occurs within almost all societies known.

Religion often operates in more than one register in society. There may be, for example, a differentiation between the state or national or royal cult which is supported centrally and the religion of the masses. Societies organized as states generally have such a national cult, though it does not usually function as an established church in the way that Christianity has in modern European history. That is to say, while the state cult may support the monarchy or central government and require some sort of nominal allegiance from all citizens, it does not exclude local cults and other forms of worship. And these local cults may be the primary outlet for religious devotion. In the polytheistic context of most ancient Near Eastern countries, a multiplicity of cults serving a variety of deities was the norm. The idea that one cult should aggressively proselytize or seek to oust the others was little known outside Israel (and perhaps even only in certain circles within Israel) before the rise of Christianity. What is often referred to as "popular religion" flourished alongside state-sanctioned forms of worship.

Thus, the question is not whether ancient Israel had religious specialists but what sort and to what extent these can be determined from the sources available to us. To many readers it may seem strange that one should even suggest that there might be a problem with determining the structure of Israelite society. However, a crisis is developing among historians of ancient Israel. A growing number now question whether the OT text can at all be used in trying to reconstruct Israel's history. The problematic nature of the OT traditions as historical sources has long been recognized to a lesser or greater extent. It is universally accepted that the contents of the Hebrew Bible have a long history and reached their final form only quite late during the Second Temple period. The problems of long growth, repeated editing, and community authorship are nothing new.

Yet until recently, most historians accepted that important earlier traditions could be teased out of the mass of late tradition, and that the broad outlines of Israel's history could be accepted with confidence. A significant minority of biblical scholars is now challenging this view. Some of them argue that we should reject the OT tradition altogether, while others are extremely skeptical about the use of the biblical text, even if they do not reject it entirely. Whether one wholly agrees with this view, its proponents still have a point. Even some well-known practitioners of traditio-historical criticism have called into question the possibility of using the methods of form and source criticism to sort out early traditions.

In the long run, it may be that the traditio-historical methods will survive in their present or revised form and that they or new methods will restore confidence in using the OT as a historical source. However, at this point it seems to me that it would be an error to assume that the source analyses found in the major commentaries and monographs can be used with confidence in such a study as I am doing. The problem of using the OT text has to be faced and dealt with. There is a severe gap between text and society, and we must consider explicitly the methodological problems in trying to bridge it.

In theory we could use other sources, such as archeology and inscriptions. Unfortunately, neither of these tell us very much about religion in Palestinian society in the mid-first-millennium BCE. For the question of religious specialists, we either use the text or we abandon the subject. So my approach has been to begin with the position of the skeptics. The one thing we have is the text—in its Masoretic form or, in some cases, in a slightly different form as attested by the LXX, Qumran scrolls, or other textual sources. When the text reached the form available to us is not certain, but the Persian period is a reasonable compromise for much of it. We know that some portions of it probably belong to the Greek period (Daniel, probably Qohelet). Some critics are now postulating that the main OT tradition is even the product of Hellenistic times. For a number of reasons, I find that rather unlikely (see 7.4). Despite problems, the Persian period seems the best candidate; in any case, it can serve for present purposes.

But there is a further problem. The biblical text is a theological construct. It has been preserved and edited by idealogues whose main concern has been to promote a particular view of religion and history. Can we hope to extract historical information about society from such an artificial creation? It is not just the lateness of the text but its very nature which creates the gap between text and society. How can we use a late theological text to reconstruct society?

Despite the problems, I believe the gap can be bridged—to some extent, at least—because of the nature of sociological history. The questions we must answer are different from those of political or other historians who need to write about specific events. If we want to know whether a particular event took place or in what form or when, we must have historiographical sources to provide this information. When we ask about a society, the time frame is usually much broader and the sources of potential value are of a different order. A work of fiction may not tell us about a historical event, but most works of fiction have the society of the author as the background. In the societies of the ancient Near East—as in most traditional societies—things seem to have changed only slowly.

Unless the writers have completely invented the social institutions in the text, even unhistorical texts tell us something about the society. Is it possible that the writers have invented the society in their writings? For example, have the writers attempted to create an ideal of the "true prophet" rather than describing the way prophets actually were? We cannot rule that out, at least in the details. Nevertheless, there are two reasons to discount the extent of invention with regard to religious specialists. The first is that the expected stereotypes are not there. When we look at the various prophetic stories and traditions, we see a variety of prophetic figures with different styles and techniques. Of particular interest is the fact that such "false prophets" as Hananiah look remarkably similar to "true prophets" like Isaiah. If the writers wished to create clear stereotypes, they missed a wonderful opportunity. The second reason is the application of cross-cultural parallels. What these show is that the images of religious specialists in the OT text are plausible for the most part. Plausibility is not by itself sufficient to prove historicity, but it is a first hurdle which must be passed.

It is important to be clear what cannot be demonstrated by the methodological approach I have just outlined. It will not establish the validity of the individual events or personages in the text. For example, the stories about Jeremiah and Hananiah cannot be assumed to tell us about real persons who did particular things during the reign of the last king of Judah. The persons and events may have been real, but we have not demonstrated them so. On the other hand, we do not need such demonstration. What we can say is that the text is highly likely to be presenting us with information on prophetic figures who had features in common with Jeremiah and Hananiah, as well as suggesting the existence of prophetic conflict and the likelihood that prophets took different positions on the events of the day.

The limits of the text thus have to be faced. There will be much we cannot do and cannot know. It benefits no one to overinterpret the texts in a gross manner, as is sometimes done. What we can do is reconstruct the ancient society in its broad outlines. The fine details and the historical development of the institutions would require more reliable sources. Some scholars feel they can go much further through the use of traditio-historical methods. Perhaps they are right, but we cannot assume that in the present climate. The method I propose is aimed at providing a critical minimum. It will create a backbone, a framework to which additional detail can be added. It is a picture which can only be improved, one hopes, rather than needing complete revision.

What kind of society emerges from this investigation and what is the place of the various religious specialists in it? The society of Palestine in the mid-first-millennium BCE was a part of the broader society of the ancient Near East. Whether there had been a united kingdom of Israel under a David or Solomon is currently debated, but the only indubitable situation is that a Northern Kingdom, called Israel, and a Southern Kingdom, called Judah, existed by the ninth-eighth century. The Assyrian inscriptions attest this.

These were small kingdoms under the rule of the Assyrians from the mid-eighth century. The Northern Kingdom was incorporated into the Assyrian empire as a province about 722 BCE, losing its king and upper class, along with some portion of its population. Other peoples were evidently brought in as settlers, but how many and what portion of the population they made up is unknown. The Southern Kingdom continued on for another 135 years, first as an Assyrian vassal and then as a Babylonian one. In spite of the impression of the text, these were simply two more small kingdoms of the west, most of the time caught in the web of the large empires.

We would thus expect to find influences from the great civilizations of Mesopotamia and Egypt, but because of the difference in size and circumstances, we would also expect to find dissimilarities. There is no reason to think that Israel had unrelated spiritual needs, though its way of expressing and fulfilling them may have been different. Like many other Near Eastern peoples, Israel had its temple and cult sites. Eventually, the cult sites outside Jerusalem were eliminated, but this was not until quite late, either shortly before or perhaps even after the fall of Jerusalem in 587/6 BCE. Similarly, the main means of determining the divine will in Mesopotamia was by use of divination, especially extispicy, but also by prophets. Israel matched this but with a different emphasis.

The primary structure of government all over the ancient Near East was monarchy. It is difficult to find any attested deviation from this administrative format. Israel was no exception. Granted, there is a strong anti-monarchic tradition in the OT text, but to what extent it matched real life is a question. Was this perhaps mainly a post-exilic development, even if it had pre-exilic roots? In any case, the predominant message of the text is pro-monarchic, although individual kings may be criticized. From the earliest external attestation of the kingdoms of Israel and Judah, they are monarchies and remained so until turned into provinces of the Mesopotamian empires.

The king was responsible only to the gods, but there was a universal tradition that he had serious responsibilities toward his people and would be called to account if he neglected his duties. He was obligated to uphold justice throughout the land and to see that his people were able to live in peace and free from want. For "every man to sit under his own vine and fig tree" was not just an Israelite ideal. Nor was the burden of protecting the widow and the orphan confined to the Hebrew tradition. This was expected of all kings, and for many of them we have inscriptions making claims that they fulfilled their duties. Hammurabi assures us that he was chosen as king "to promote the welfare of the people, . . . to cause justice to prevail in the land, to destroy the wicked and the evil, that the strong might not oppress the weak" (*Codex Hammurabi*, Prologue 1; *ANET*: 164).

A significant role of the king in establishing peace and prosperity was the proper maintenance of the divine cult. There could be serious consequences for neglect of this, not just for the king personally but for all the people. When the king sinned, the whole country suffered. The king was head of the cult, and the many priests serving at cult sites around the country were merely his surrogates. The concept of separation of the divine and the mundane, or the civil and the religious, was not one which would have been readily understood. And the notion that the priesthood could oppose the king and carry on independently of the monarchy also had little place in their thinking.

Israel was no different. The king was responsible to Yhwh, the national God from all that can be determined, though by no means the only divinity to be worshiped until the late monarchy at the earliest. The state cult was also under royal jurisdiction and control. Beginning with David and extending to Josiah, a variety of texts shows the king as the chief actor in establishing, overseeing, and modifying (sometimes drastically) the cult. Texts dealing with early kings also show the king fulfilling a role in the cult. No OT text shows the king as the chief cultic figure, with the priests only filling in for him as it were, though this has been postulated on the analogy of the kings elsewhere in the ancient Near East. Some OT texts seem to wish to counter any idea that the king could preside at the altar, especially the example of Uzziah in 2 Chronicles 26:16-21 or of the "prince" (*nāśî'*) in Ezekiel 44-48. But it is interesting that these are universally accepted as late texts. Therefore, the view that the king should not preside at the altar may not have been dominant when there actually was a king.

The existence of the state cult, with the king at its head, does not usually preclude other cults and cult sites. According to the OT tradition, the kingdom of Israel had royal cult sites at Dan and Bethel. In Judah the royal cult site seems to have been confined to Jerusalem, though possibly other sites such as Arad were also royal shrines. Besides the state shrines or temples, worship places seem to have been found around the country. This is normal. By the Second Temple period, Israelite religion became dominated by the monotheistic and monocultic view, but this appears to have come about only gradually. The worship of gods besides Yhwh is sporadically attested; however, the Israelite onomasticon indicates that Yhwh was the main deity (that is, the divine element in most names preserved both in the biblical tradition and in inscriptions and ostraca is a form of Yhwh).

Near Eastern temples usually have a diversity of personnel. Besides officials who preside over the cult itself, temples need administrators, workmen, maintainers, and suppliers. Important in Mesopotamia were diviners. Distinctions between different personnel are indicated by individual terminology, but generic terms such as "priest" do not always exist and the clear-cut distinction assumed between priestly and other functions is not always found.

Within the OT text several different views of the Israelite priesthood are found. Some speak of the "Levitical priests," some of "priests and Levites" or Aaronites and Levites, and some of Zadokites and Levites. The concept of the priesthood that prevailed in the Second Temple period was one of priests who officiated at the altar and of lower clergy (Levites) with other duties. The diversity within the OT text is often thought to reflect struggles within the priesthood before the final outcome was achieved. This may well be true. For example, among those who migrated to Judah after the fall of the Northern Kingdom seem to have been cult personnel from its temples and shrines. These are widely thought to have been the origin of the Levites.

The cult was only one means of communicating and serving the gods. Especially important in Mesopotamian royal cults were diviners and others who had responsibility for trying to determine the will of the gods and what the future held. The king performed no major act of state without inquiring of the deity. The OT text does not have extensive data on the question, but there are references to similar consultations of Yhwh. One mode was the priestly "lots," the Urim and Thummim and the ephod. Another is less clear from the text but has been inferred from several hints: cultic prophets. Court prophets are known from the four hundred prophets of Ahab (1 Kings 22:6), and figures like Isaiah and Hananiah (Jer 26) probably also filled this role. But just as the temple and cult were ultimately under the jurisdiction of the king, so the court prophets and cult prophets may not have been clearly distinguished. Remember that the main function of the *bārûs* (diviner-priests) in Mesopotamia was to serve the king, even if they were connected with a temple.

As well as official prophecy and divination, prophets and diviners also arose and functioned among the people. The needs that impelled the king to seek divine guidance had their counterpart among the general populace. Would the crops succeed? Would a sick relative recover? Would the merchant return safely from this journey, or should it be postponed to a more auspicious time? The ones to answer these questions were those with special powers or insight, the prophets and diviners. One might refer to such individuals as professionals, but this must be understood in a particular way. The "professional prophet" has a negative connotation in OT study because it has usually been assumed that no "true prophet" ever plied his trade for pay. This is a simplistic assessment. So-called true prophets such as Elijah and Elisha accepted gifts of various sorts; some of the "classical prophets" seem to have been cult prophets, with support from the temple and state; and we have no way of knowing how most of the prophets earned their living. Also, anthropological study attests that many professional figures take up their task as a result of a divine call, sometimes even against their will.

Diviners function mainly as inquirers. They receive their messages from the world beyond as a response to questions put to it. Because of the prejudice in the text against many forms of divination, we have only hints about modes other than the official priestly ones. We do not know whether diviners among the people regularly inquired of Yhwh, for example. What does seem clear is that some forms of divination were closely associated with cults of the dead. It is evidently a worldwide belief that the dead can have special insight into the future or into the mind of the gods. Although the edited OT tradition is opposed to cults of the dead, hints in the text, as well as archeology, attest their extensive presence in Israelite society.

Divination takes many forms, especially mechanical manipulation, but other forms also tend to give binary responses limited to yes/no answers. But divination is not limited to mechanical or similar types. What is often overlooked is the extent of spirit divination in many societies. In this area, it is difficult if not impossible to distinguish between prophecy and spirit divination. The prophet may differ from the diviner in receiving spontaneous messages from the deity without any instigation. This fact might be the one distinctive characteristic of prophecy. Yet we have many examples in the OT text where the prophet receives a divine message as a result of inquiry, either on his own behalf or on behalf of someone else. So in this area at least, prophecy is only a form of divination, and various OT texts do not suggest that one mode was preferable to another. A question might be put to God, but the response might come by a variety of conduits, whether lots, dreams, oracles, or prophecies.

The wise occupy an interesting place in any discussion of religious specialists. Wisdom terminology can be used of many different people and situations within society. The farmer carries on his trade by wisdom; the spinner is wise in her craft; the potter, the weaver, the jeweller, and many others have special skills for which they can be called wise. The elders of the community may be wise because of experience and also may be the repositories of the community traditions and folk wisdom. Men and women wise by reputation may be sought out at the local level for advice and counsel. The nature of wisdom is such that wisdom at all levels is recognized and appreciated.

For our purposes, however, the main interest is in the intellectual tradition, the sphere of wisdom due to instruction and learning. It is primarily in this sphere that reference is also made to divine wisdom and its gift to some humans. Wisdom as measured by knowledge of God's *torah*, and personal piety is often referred to in the wisdom literature, but the context is usually a learned one. One may fear God without formal education, but knowledge of God's law and divine insight are usually the products of wise teacher and apt pupil. The wisdom sections of the OT, while appreciating wisdom in all its forms, from ant to craftsworker, focus on the intellectual form of wisdom. This is the wisdom of the scribe, the counselor, the priest, the intellectual.

Thus, it becomes rapidly clear why the sages are an important part of the sphere of religious specialists, for they are the ones who produced much or even all of Israel's religious literature. One does not need a formal education to receive a call to be Yhwh's prophet. On the other hand, much of the content of the prophetic books probably arose from the hand of sages, whether themselves prophets or only producing oracle-like compositions as a vehicle for their message. It can be taken for granted that the wise did not form a monolithic group. To be called wise did not identify one as part of a profession; rather the wise encompassed a number of professions. Under this rubric might be priests, Levites, professional scribes, court counselors and other officials, prophets and masters of the diviners' arts.

Not all prophets and diviners were participants in the intellectual circles, and perhaps not all priests or Levites or even scribes. But those with the necessary education and leisure to participate in intellectual endeavors were probably always few and concentrated in the capital. And they had different interests, concerns, and points of view—nor were these likely to have been all the same for one professional group. In other words, not all priests took the same stance; priests could criticize priests, and priests could pursue non-priestly interests, such as cosmology. Similarly, lay aristocrats may have had definite views about the cult or about the divine. Not all who wrote about worship or the cult or God were necessarily priests or prophets; nor were those who expressed opinions about "secular" matters, such as proper conduct in the presence of the king or how to succeed in life, always non-priests. The priestly, the Deuteronomic, the wisdom, and much of the prophetic literature were all likely products of wisdom circles of one sort or another. In those days long before universal state education or even literacy, no others had the necessary training and opportunity to read, appreciate, and write literature.

As has already been often hinted at, the neat divisions of religious specialists is illusory. This was true in the ancient Near East, is known from anthropological study, and is evident for ancient Israel as well. Some specialisms were strictly proscribed to all but a select few. Only the males of a particular section of Israel could serve at the altar, for example, and only a few men would be king. Most specialisms were not so restricted in membership, however, and people from all walks of life practiced in many of them. Despite the use of Weberian ideal types, it has not been easy to separate some of the religious specialists because they do not fall into neat categories. All specialists are to some extent intermediaries, whether the priest at the sacrifice, the diviner casting lots, or the prophet in a trance. They are the channels between the human world and the divine. One might ask God's will, but the answer might come by priestly lot, by dream, by vision, or even by an event which requires interpretation. Only a select few could be priests at the altar, but prophets could be found in chapel, court, and countryside. Priests could divine and so could many others. With the right education and mental ability, any of these could take a place among the intellectuals.

Not only were the functions of the various religious specialists not clearly differentiated, but the same individual might fulfill more than one role. The priest casting the Urim and Thummim was acting as a diviner. A number of the prophets were also priests. Scribes could be found among the priests and Levites; being a scribe was also a hereditary profession in certain families. The neat, watertight categories we so often work with exist only in our own minds, not in society.

All societies are messy affairs. They are amorphous and constantly changing in small ways, if not in larger. When we think we have pinned some aspect down, it has a way of slipping away in the welter of ambiguous or contrary examples. This fact well applies to modern living societies which can be observed and computerized by professional social scientists. The social historian trying to delve into a long-dead society, known only from late, heavily edited, and blatantly tendentious texts, can hardly hope to do more than present a plausible reconstruction which does not attempt a precision beyond the limits of our sources. Speculation is easy and can be very interesting, but it is not history and it is not sociology. Our desire to know must not lead us into claiming more than the nature of the data allows.

Some may find the bare outline presented here far too sketchy for their tastes. I contend that it is a start, a foundation on which to build. The superstructure can be added when reliable data are available. All the various disciplines of OT study have their part to play in trying to find these trustworthy data which can serve as stable building blocks in constructing a model of ancient Israelite society.

Bibliography

Abba, R. "Priests and Levites in Deuteronomy," *VT* 27 (1977) 257-67.

Ackermman, Susan. *Under Every Green Tree: Popular Religion in Sixth-Century Judah.* HSM 46. (Atlanta: Scholars Press, 1992).

Ahn, Gregor. *Religiöse Herrscherlegitimation im achämenidischen Iran: Die Voraussetzungen und die Struktur ihrer Argumentation.* Acta Iranica 31; Textes et Mémoires 17 (Leuven: Peeters, 1992).

Albertz, Rainer. *A History of Israelite Religion in the Old Testament Period: Volume 1: From the Beginnings to the End of the Monarchy; Volume 2: From the Exile to the Maccabees* (London: SCM, 1994).

Amerding, Carl Edwin. "Were David's Sons Really Priests?" *Current Issues in Biblical and Patristic Interpretation.* Ed. G. F. Hawthorne (Grand Rapids, Mich.: Eerdmans, 1975) 75-86.

André, Gunnel. "Ecstatic Prophesy [*sic*] in the Old Testament." In *Religious Ecstasy: Based on Papers Read at the Symposium on Religious Ecstasy Held at Åbo, Finland, on the 26th-28th of August 1981.* Ed. N. G. Holm (Stockholm: Almqvist and Wiksell, 1982) 187-200.

Auld, A. Graeme. "Prophets through the Looking Glass: Between Writings and Moses," *JSOT* 27 (1983) 3-23.

_____ . "Prophets through the Looking Glass: A Response to Robert Carroll and Hugh Williamson," *JSOT* 27 (1983) 41-44.

_____ . "Prophets and Prophecy in Jeremiah and Kings," *ZAW* 96 (1984) 66-82.

_____ . "Prophecy in Books: A Rejoinder," *JSOT* 48 (1990) 31-32.

Aune, David E. *Prophecy in Early Christianity and the Ancient Mediterranean World* (Grand Rapids, Mich.: Eerdmans, 1983).

Avigad, Nahman. *Hebrew Bullae from the Time of Jeremiah: Remnants of a Burnt Archive* (Jerusalem: Israel Exploration Society, 1986).

Bailey, Harold H. *Zoroastrian Problems in the Ninth-Century Books: Ratanbai Katrak Lectures* (Oxford: Clarendon, 1943).

Barstad, Hans M. *The Religious Polemics of Amos: Studies in the Preaching of Am 2,7B-8; 4,1-13; 5,1-27; 6,4-7; 8,14.* VTSup 34 (Leiden: Brill, 1984).

_____ . "No Prophets? Recent Developments in Biblical Prophetic Research and Ancient Near Eastern Prophecy," *JSOT* 57 (1993) 39-60.

_____ . "Lachish Ostracon III and Ancient Israelite Prophecy," *EI* 24 (1993) 8*-12*.

_____ . "Akkadian 'Loanwords' in Isaiah 40-55—And the Question of Babylonian Origin of Deutero-Isaiah." In *Text and Theology: Studies in Honour of Professor dr. theol. Magne Sæbø Presented on the Occasion of His 65th Birthday.* Ed. A. Tångberg (Oslo: Verbum, 1994) 36-48.

Bartlett, John R. "Zadok and his Successors at Jerusalem," *JTS* 19 (1968) 1-18.

Barton, John. *Oracles of God: Perceptions of Ancient Prophecy in Israel after the Exile* (London: Darton, Longman and Todd, 1986).

Bascom, William. *Ifa Divination: Communication Between Gods and Men in West Africa* (Bloomington and Indianapolis: Indiana University, 1969).

Beard, Mary. "Priesthood in the Roman Republic." In *Pagan Priests: Religion and Power in the Ancient World*. Ed. M. Beard and J. North (London: Duckworth, 1990) 17-48.

Beard, Mary, and John North, eds. *Pagan Priests: Religion and Power in the Ancient World* (London: Duckworth, 1990).

Beattie, John, and John Middleton, eds. *Spirit Mediumship and Society in Africa* (London: Routledge, 1969).

Beaulieu, Paul-Alain. "The Historical Background of the Uruk Prophecy." In *The Tablet and the Scroll: Near Eastern Studies in Honor of William W. Hallo*. Ed. M. E. Cohen, et al. (Bethesda, MD: CDL Press, 1993) 41-52.

Beidelman, T. O. "Nuer Priests and Prophets." In *The Translation of Culture: Essays to E. E. Evans-Pritchard*. Ed. T. O. Beidelman (London: Tavistock, 1971) 375-415.

Berlinerblau, J. "The 'Popular Religion' Paradigm in Old Testament Research: A Sociological Critique," *JSOT* 60 (1993) 3-26.

Biggs, Robert D. "More Babylonian 'Prophecies,'" *Iraq* 29 (1967) 117-32.

_____ . "The Babylonian Prophecies and the Astrological Texts," *JCS* (1985) 86-90.

_____ . "Babylonian Prophecies, Astrology, and a New Source for 'Prophecy Text B,'" *Language, Literature, and History: Philological and Historical Studies Presented to Erica Reiner*. Ed. F. Rochberg-Halton. AOS 67. (New Haven, Conn.: American Oriental Society, 1987) 1-14.

Bleeker, C. J. "The Position of the Queen in Ancient Egypt." In *The Sacral Kingship: Contributions to the Central Theme of the VIIIth International Congress for the History of Religions (Rome, April 1955)* NumSup 4. (Leiden: Brill, 1959) 261-68.

Blenkinsopp, Joseph. *A History of Prophecy in Israel* (London: SPCK, 1984).

Bloch-Smith, Elizabeth. *Judahite Burial Practices and Beliefs about the Dead*. JSOTSup 123; JSOT/ASOR Monograph Series 7 (Sheffield: JSOT, 1992).

_____ . "The Cult of the Dead in Judah: Interpreting the Material Remains," *JBL* 111 (1992) 213-24.

Borger, Rykle. "Gott Marduk und Gott-König Šulgi als Propheten: Zwei prophetische Texte," *BO* 28 (1971) 3-24.

Bourdillon, M. *The Shona Peoples*. Rev. ed. (Gweru, Zimbabwe: Mambo, 1982).

Bourguet, Marie-Noëlle, et al., eds. *Between Memory and History* (Chur, Switzerland: Harwood, 1990) (= *History and Anthropology* 2/2).

Bourguignon, Erica, ed. *Religion, Altered States of Consciousness, and Social Change* (Columbus: Ohio State University, 1973).

Bowman, R. A. *Aramaic Ritual Texts from Persepolis*. University of Chicago Oriental Institute Publication 91 (Chicago: University of Chicago Press, 1970).

Boyce, M. *A History of Zoroastrianism*. Vols. 1- HdO I.8.1 (Leiden: Brill, 1975-).

_____ . *Zoroastrians: Their Religious Beliefs and Practices*. Library of Religious Beliefs and Practices (London: Routledge & Kegan Paul, 1979).

_____ , ed. *Textual Sources for the Study of Zoroastrianism*. Textual Sources for the Study of Religion (Manchester: Manchester University, 1984).

_____ . "On the Antiquity of Zoroastrian Apocalyptic," *BSOAS* 47 (1984) 57-75.

_____ . *Zoroastrianism: A Shadowy but Powerful Presence in the Judaeo-Christian World.* Friends of Dr. Williams's Library Lecture (London: Dr Williams's Trust, 1987).

Braun, R. *Koheleth und die frühhellenistische Popularphilosophie*. BZAW 130 (Berlin/ New York: de Gruyter, 1973).

Brett, M. G. "Literacy and Domination: G. A. Herion's Sociology of History Writing," *JSOT* 37 (1987) 15-40.

Brown, John Pairman. "The Mediterranean Seer and Shamanism," *ZAW* 93 (1981) 374-400.

Brunner, Hellmut. *Altägyptische Erziehung* (Wiesbaden: Harrassowitz, 1957).

Bryce, Glendon E. "Omen-Wisdom in Ancient Israel," *JBL* 94 (1975) 19-37.

_____ . Review of R. N. Whybray, *The Intellectual Tradition in the Old Testament*, *JBL* 94 (1975) 596-98.

_____ . *A Legacy of Wisdom: The Egyptian Contributions to the Wisdom of Israel* (Lewisburg: Bucknell University, 1979).

Burke, Peter. "Overture: the New History, its Past and its Future." In *New Perspectives on Historical Writing*. Ed. P. Burke (Cambridge: Polity Press, 1991) 1-23.

Burstein, S. M. *The Babyloniaca of Berossus*. SANE 1/5 (Malibu: Undena, 1978).

Buss, M. J. "An Anthropological Perspective upon Prophetic Call Narratives," *Semeia* 21 (1982) 9-30.

Camp, Claudia V. "The Female Sage in the Biblical Wisdom Literature." In *The Sage in Israel and the Ancient Near East*. Ed. J. G. Gammie and L. G. Perdue (Winona Lake, Ind.: Eisenbrauns, 1990) 185-203.

Caquot, André. "Ben Sira et le Messianisme," *Semitica* 16 (1966) 43-68.

Carroll, Robert P. "The Elijah-Elisha Sagas: Some Remarks on Prophetic Succession in Ancient Israel," *VT* 19 (1969) 400-15.

_____ . "Twilight of Prophecy or Dawn of Apocalyptic?" *JSOT* 14 (1979) 3-35.

_____ . *From Chaos to Covenant: Uses of Prophecy in the Book of Jeremiah* (London: SCM, 1981).

_____ . *Jeremiah: A Commentary*. OTL (London: SCM, 1986).

_____ . "Poets Not Prophets: A Response to 'Prophets Through the Looking-Glass,'" *JSOT* 27 (1983) 25-31.

_____ . "Prophecy and Society." In *The World of Ancient Israel: Sociological, Anthropological and Political Perspectives, Essays by Members of the Society for Old Testament Study*. Ed. R. E. Clements (Cambridge University Press, 1989) 203-25.

_____ . "Whose Prophet? Whose History? Whose Social Reality? Troubling the Interpretative Community Again: Notes Towards a Response to T. W. Overholt's Critique," *JSOT* 48 (1990) 33-49.

_____ . "Night Without Vision: Micah and the Prophets." In *The Scriptures and the Scrolls: Studies in Honour of A. S. van der Woude on the Occasion of his 65th Birthday*. Ed. F. García Martínez, et al. VTSup 49 (Leiden: Brill, 1992) 74-84.

_____ . "On Representation in the Bible: An *ideologiekritik* Approach," *JNSL* 20 (1994) 1-15.

Černý, Jaroslav. "Egyptian Oracles." In *A Saite Oracle Papyrus from Thebes in the Brooklyn Museum* (Papyrus Brooklyn 47.218.3). Ed. R. A. Parker (Providence: Brown University, 1962) 35-48.

Charpin, Dominique. "L'Andurârum à Mari," *MARI* 6 (1990) 253-70.

Childs, Brevard S. *Isaiah and the Assyrian Crisis*. Studies in Biblical Theology, Second Series 3 (London: SCM, 1967).

Clements, Ronald E. *Isaiah and the Deliverance of Jerusalem: A Study of the Interpretation of Prophecy in the Old Testament*. JSOTSup 13 (Sheffield: JSOT, 1980).

_____ . *Isaiah 1-39*. NCB (London: Marshall, Morgan & Scott; Grand Rapids: Eerdmans, 1980).

_____ , ed. *The World of Ancient Israel: Sociological, Anthropological and Political Perspectives: Essays by Members of the Society for Old Testament Study* (Cambridge: Cambridge University Press, 1989).

Clines, David J. A. "The Evidence for an Autumnal New Year in Pre-exilic Israel Reconsidered," *JBL* 93 (1974) 22-40.

_____ . "New Year," *IDBSup* (1976) 625-29.

_____ . *Ezra, Nehemiah, Esther*. CBC (London: Marshall, Morgan & Scott; Grand Rapids: Eerdmans, 1984).

_____ . *Job 1-20*. WBC 17 (Dallas: Word, 1989).

_____ . "The Nehemiah Memoir: The Perils of Autobiography," *What Does Eve Do to Help? and Other Readerly Questions to the Old Testament*. JSOTSup 94 (Sheffield: Sheffield Academic, 1990) 124-64.

Cody, Aelfred. *A History of Old Testament Priesthood*. AnBib 35 (Rome: Pontifical Biblical Institute, 1969).

_____ . "The Phoenician Ecstatic in Wenamūn: A Professional Oracular Medium," *JEA* 65 (1979) 99-106.

Coggins, R. J. *Haggai, Zechariah, Malachi*. Old Testament Guides (Sheffield: JSOT, 1987).

Collins, John J. *The Apocalyptic Vision of the Book of Daniel*. HSM 16 (Atlanta: Scholars, 1977).

_____ . "Proverbial Wisdom and the Yahwist Vision." In *Gnomic Wisdom*. Semeia 17. Ed. J. D. Crossan (Atlanta: Scholars Press, 1980) 1-17.

_____ . *Daniel*. Hermeneia (Minneapolis: Fortress, 1993)

_____ , ed. *Apocalypse: The Morphology of a Genre*. Semeia 14 (Atlanta: Scholars, 1979).

Cook, J. M. *The Persian Empire* (London: J. M. Dent, 1983).

Coote, Robert B., and Keith W. Whitelam. *The Emergence of Early Israel in Historical Perspective*. The Social World of Ancient Israel 5 (Sheffield: JSOT, 1987).

Corney, R. W. "Zadok the Priest," *IDB* 4 (1962) 928-29.

Cowley, A. *Aramaic Papyri of the Fifth Century B.C.* (1923; reprinted Osnabruck: Otto Zeller, 1967).

Crenshaw, James L. "Method in Determining Wisdom Influence upon 'Historical' Literature," *JBL* 88 (1969) 129-42 (reprinted in J. L. Crenshaw, ed., *Studies in Ancient Israelite Wisdom* [Library of Biblical Studies; New York: Ktav, 1976] 481-94).

_____ . *Prophetic Conflict: Its Effect upon Israelite Religion*. BZAW 124 (Berlin/New York: de Gruyter, 1971).

_____ . "Wisdom." In *Old Testament Form Criticism*. Ed. J. H. Hayes (San Antonio: Trinity, 1974) 225-64.

_____ . "The Birth of Skepticism in Ancient Israel." In *The Divine Helmsman: Studies on God's Control of Human Events, Presented to Lou H. Silberman*. Ed. J. L. Crenshaw and S. Sandmel (New York: Ktav, 1980) 1-19.

_____ . *Old Testament Wisdom: An Introduction* (Louisville: John Knox; London: SCM, 1982).

_____ . "Education in Ancient Israel," *JBL* 104 (1985) 601-15.

_____ . *Ecclesiastes*. OTL (London: SCM, 1988).

Crook, Margaret B. "The Marriageable Maiden of Prov. 31:10-31," *JNES* 13 (1954) 137-40.

Cross, Frank M. *Canaanite Myth and Hebrew Epic* (Cambridge: Harvard, 1973).

Cryer, Frederick H. *Divination in Ancient Israel and Its Near Eastern Environment: A Socio-Historical Investigation*. JSOTSup 142 (Sheffield: Sheffield Academic Press, 1994).

Culley, Robert C., and Thomas W. Overholt, eds. *Anthropological Perspectives on Old Testament Prophecy*. Semeia 21. (Chico: Scholars, 1982).

Dahood, Mitchell J. *Psalms*. 3 vols. AB (Garden City, N.Y.: Doubleday, 1962-70).

Dam, Cornelius van. *The Urim and Thummim: A Study of an Old Testament Means of Revelation*. 2 vols. Theologische Hogeschool van de Gereformeerde Kerken in Nederland te Kampen. (Kampen: van den Berg, 1986).

David, A. Rosalie. *The Ancient Egyptians: Religious Beliefs and Practices* (London-Boston: Routledge and Kegan Paul, 1982).

Davies, Philip R. *Daniel*. Old Testament Guides. (Sheffield: JSOT, 1985).

_____ . *In Search of "Ancient Israel."* JSOTSup 148. (Sheffield: JSOT, 1992).

_____ . "God of Cyrus, God of Israel: Some Religio-Historical Reflections on Isaiah 40-55." In *Words Remembered, Texts Renewed: Essays in Honour of John F.A. Sawyer*. Ed. Jon Davies, Graham Harvey, and Wilfred G.E. Watson. JSOTSup 195 (Sheffield Academic Press, 1995) 207-225 .

Day, John. *Molech: A God of Human Sacrifice in the Old Testament*. University of Cambidge Oriental Publications 41 (Cambridge University Press, 1989).

_____ . *Psalms*. Old Testament Guides (Sheffield: JSOT, 1990).

Dearman, John Andrew. *Property Rights in the Eighth-Century Prophets: The Conflict and its Background*. SBLDS 106 (Atlanta: Scholars, 1988).

Delcor, M. "Le texte de Deir 'Alla et les oracles bibliques de Bala'am," *Congress Volume: Vienna 1980*. VTSup 32 (Leiden: Brill, 1981) 52-73.

Dell, Katharine J. *The Book of Job as Sceptical Literature*. BZAW 197. (Berlin: de Gruyter, 1991).

Denning-Bolle, Sara. *Wisdom in Akkadian Literature: Expression, Instruction, Dialogue*. Mededelingen en Verhandelingen van het Vooraziatisch-Egyptisch Genootschap "Ex Oriente Lux" 28 (Leiden: Ex Oriente Lux, 1992).

Deselaers, P. *Das Buch Tobit: Studien zu seiner Entstehung, Komposition und Theologie*. Orbis biblicus et orientalis 43 (Freiburg: Universitätsverlag, 1982).

DeVries, Simon J. *Prophet Against Prophet. The Role of the Micaiah Narrative (I Kings 22) in the Development of Early Prophetic Tradition* (Grand Rapids, Mich.: Eerdmans, 1978).

_____ . *1 Kings*. WBC 12 (Waco, Tex.: Word, 1985).

Dietrich, Manfred, and Oswald Loretz (with contributions by others). *Mantik in Ugarit: Keilalphabetische Texte der Opferschau—Omensammlungen—Nekromantie*

(Abhandlungen zur Literatur Alt-Syrien-Palästinas 3; Münster: UGARIT-Verlag, 1990).

Dijkstra, Meindert. "Is Balaam Among the Prophets?" *JBL* 114 (1995) 43-64.

Diószegi, V., and M. Hoppál, eds. *Shamanism in Siberia*. Bibliotheca Uralica 1 (Budapest: Akadémiai Kiadó, 1978).

Donner, H., and W. Röllig. *Kanaanäische und aramäische Inscriften, Mit einem Beitrag von O. Rössler*. Vols. 1-3 (Wiesbaden: Harrassowitz, 1962-64).

Driver, G. R. *Aramaic Documents of the Fifth Century B.C.* Rev. ed. (Oxford: Clarendon, 1957).

Duguid, Iain M. *Ezekiel and the Leaders of Israel*. VTSup 56 (Leiden: Brill, 1994).

Durand, Jena-Marie. *Archives épistolaires de Mari I/1* (Archives royales de Mari 26; Paris: Editions Recherche sur les Civilisations, 1988).

Eaton, John H. "The Psalms and Israelite Worship." In *Tradition and Interpretation: Essays by Members of the Society for Old Testament Study*. Ed. G. W. Anderson (Oxford: Clarendon, 1979) 238-73.

Edsman, Carl-Martin, ed. *Studies in Shamanism*. Scripta Instituti Donneriani Aboensis 1 (Stockholm: Almqvist and Wiksell, 1967).

Ehrlich, Ernst Ludwig. *Der Traum im Alten Testament*. BZAW 73 (Berlin: Töpelmann, 1953).

Eliade, Mircea. *Shamanism: Archaic Techniques of Ecstasy*. Bollingen Series 76 (Princeton, N.J.: Princeton University, 1964).

Eliade, M., et al. "Shamanism," *ER* (1987) 13.201-23.

Ellenson, David H. "A Note on Peter Berger's 'Charisma and Religious Innovation: The Social Location of Israelite Prophecy,'" *Bits of Honey: Essays for Samson H. Levey*. Ed. S. F. Chyet and D. H. Ellenson. SFSHJ 74 (Atlanta: Scholars, 1993) 229-32.

Ellis, Maria deJong. "The Goddess Kititum Speaks to King Ibalpiel: Oracle Texts from Ishchali," *MARI* 5 (1987) 235-66.

_____ . "Observations on Mesopotamian Oracles and Prophetic Texts: Literary and Historiographic Considerations," *JCS* 41 (1989) 127-86.

Emerton, J. A. "Priests and Levites in Deuteronomy," *VT* (1962) 129-38.

Emmerson, Grace I. *Isaiah 56-66*. Old Testament Guides (Sheffield: JSOT, 1992).

Engnell, Ivan. *Studies in Divine Kingship in the Ancient Near East* (Oxford: Blackwell, 1943; reprint 1967).

Evans-Pritchard, E. E. "The Nuer: Tribe and Clan," *Sudan Notes and Records* 18 (1935) 37-87.

_____ . *Witchcraft, Oracles and Magic among the Azande* (Oxford: Clarendon, 1937).

_____ . *Nuer Religion* (Oxford/New York: Oxford University Press, 1956).

Fahey, Tony. "Max Weber's *Ancient Judaism*," *American Journal of Sociology* 88 (1982) 62-87.

Fiensy, David. "Using the Nuer Culture of Africa in Understanding the Old Testament: An Evaluation," *JSOT* 38 (1987) 73-83.

Finkel, Irving L. "Necromancy in Ancient Mesopotamia," *AfO* 29/30 (1983/84) 1-17.

Finkelstein, J. J. "Amiṣaduqa's Edict and the Babylonian 'Law Codes,'" *JCS* 15 (1961) 91-104.

Flesher, P. V. M. "Palestinian Synagogues before 70 CE: A Review of the Evidence," *Approaches to Ancient Judaism VI: Studies in the Ethnography and Literature of Judaism*. BJS 192 (Atlanta: Scholars, 1989) 68-81.

Fohrer, G. *History of Israelite Religion* (Nashville: Abingdon, 1972).

Fowler, Jeaneane D. *Theophoric Personal Names in Ancient Hebrew: A Comparative Study*. JSOTSup 49 (Sheffield: JSOT Press, 1988).

Frankfort, Henri. *Kingship and the Gods: A Study of Ancient Near Eastern Religion as the Integration of Society and Nature* (with a new Preface by Samuel Noah Kramer; Chicago/London: University of Chicago, 1948; reprint 1978).

Frankfurter, David. *Elijah in Upper Egypt: The Apocalypse of Elijah and Early Egyptian Christianity*. Studies in Antiquity and Christianity (Minneapolis: Fortress, 1993).

Frazer, James G. *Belief in the Immortality of the Soul and the Worship of the Dead*. 3 vols. The Gifford Lectures, 1911-12 (London: Macmillan, 1913).

Frye, Richard N. *History of Ancient Iran*. Handbuch der Altertumswissenschaft, 3.7 (Berlin/New York: de Gruyter, 1984).

Gammie, J. G., and L. G. Perdue, eds. *The Sage in Israel and the Ancient Near East* (Winona Lake, Ind.: Eisenbrauns, 1990).

Gardiner, Alan H. *The Admonitions of an Egyptian Sage from a Hieratic Papyrus in Leiden (Pap. Leiden 344 recto)* (Leipzig: Hinrichs, 1909).

_____ . "The Mansion of Life and the Master of the King's Largess," *JEA* 24 (1938) 83-91.

_____ . "The House of Life," *JEA* 24 (1938) 157-79.

Garelli, Paul, ed. *Le palais et la royauté (archéologie et civilisation)*. XIXe Recontre Assyriologique Internationale (Paris: Librairie Orientaliste Paul Geuthner, 1974).

Geertz, Armin W. *The Invention of Prophecy: Continuity and Meaning in Hopi Indian Religion* (Berkeley/Los Angeles/London: University of California, 1994).

Gibson, John C. L. *Textbook of Syrian Semitic Inscriptions*. Vols. 1-3 (Oxford: Clarendon, 1975-).

Glazier-McDonald, B. *Malachi: The Divine Messenger*. SBLDS 98 (Atlanta: Scholars, 1987).

Gnuse, Robert. "A Reconsideration of the Form-Critical Structure in I Samuel 3: An Ancient Near Eastern Dream Theophany," *ZAW* 94 (1982) 379-90.

Goedicke, Hans. *The Report of Wenamun* (Baltimore: Johns Hopkins, 1975).

Goldammer, K. "Elemente des Schamanismus im Alten Testament," *Ex Orbe Religionum: Studia Geo Widengren*. NumenSup 22 (Leiden: Brill, 1972) 2.266-85.

Goldstein, Jonathan A. "The Historical Setting of the Uruk Prophecy," *JNES* 47 (1988) 43-46.

Golka, Friedemann W. "Die israelitische Weisheitsschule oder 'des Kaisers neue Kleider,'" *VT* 33 (1983) 257-70.

_____ . *The Leopard's Spots: Biblical and African Wisdom in Proverbs* (Edinburgh: T & T Clark, 1993).

Goodfriend, Elaine Adler, and Karel van der Toorn. "Prostitution," *ABD* (1992) 5.505-13.

Gordon, Robert P. "From Mari to Moses: Prophecy at Mari and in Ancient Israel." In *Of Prophets' Visions and the Wisdom of Sages: Essays in Honour of R. Norman Whybray on his Seventieth Birthday*. Ed. H. A. McKay and D.J.A. Clines. JSOTSup 162 (Sheffield: JSOT, 1993) 63-79.

Grabbe, Lester L. "Josephus and the Reconstruction of the Judean Restoration," *JBL* 106 (1987) 231-46.

_____ . "Synagogues in Pre-70 Palestine: A Re-assessment," *JTS* 39 (1988) 401-10.

_____ . "The Social Setting of Early Jewish Apocalypticism," *JSP* 4 (1989) 27-47.

_____ . "Reconstructing History from the Book of Ezra." In *Studies in the Second Temple: The Persian Period.* Ed. P. R. Davies. JSOTSup 117 (Sheffield: JSOT, 1991) 98-107.

_____ . *Judaism from Cyrus to Hadrian: Vol. 1: Persian and Greek Periods; Vol. 2: Roman Period* (Minneapolis: Fortress Press, 1992; reprinted London: SCM, 1994).

_____ . *Leviticus.* Old Testament Guides (Sheffield: JSOT, 1993).

_____ . "Prophets, Priests, Diviners and Sages in Ancient Israel." In *Of Prophets' Visions and the Wisdom of Sages: Essays in Honour of R. Norman Whybray on his Seventieth Birthday.* Ed. H.A. McKay and D.J.A. Clines. JSOTSup 162 (Sheffield: JSOT, 1993) 43-62.

_____ . "What Was Ezra's Mission?" *Second Temple Studies: 2. Temple and Community in the Persian Period.* Ed. T. C. Eskenazi and K. H. Richards. JSOTSup 175 (Sheffield: JSOT, 1994) 286-99.

Gray, John. "Sacral Kingship in Ugarit." In *Ugaritica VI.* Ed. F. A. Schaeffer. Mission de Ras Shamra 17 (Paris: Mission Archéologique de Ras Shamra, 1969) 289-302.

Gray, Rebecca. *Prophetic Figures in Late Second Temple Jewish Palestine: The Evidence from Josephus* (Oxford: Clarendon, 1993).

Grayson, A. K. *Babylonian Historical-Literary Texts.* Toronto Semitic Texts and Studies (Toronto/Buffalo: University of Toronto, 1975).

Grayson, A. K., and W. G. Lambert, "Akkadian Prophecies," *JCS* 18 (1964) 7-30.

Guillaume, Alfred. *Prophecy and Divination among the Hebrews and Other Semites.* The Bampton Lectures 1938 (London: Hodder and Stoughton, 1938).

Gunneweg, A. H. J. *Leviten und Priester: Hauptlinien der Traditionsbildung und Geschichte des israelitisch-jüdischen Kultpersonals.* FRLANT 89 (Göttingen: Vandenhoeck & Ruprecht, 1965).

Gurney, O. R. "Hittite Kingship." In *Myth, Ritual, and Kingship: Essays on the Theory and Practice of Kingship in the Ancient Near East and in Israel.* Ed. S. H. Hooke (Oxford: Clarendon, 1958) 105-21.

_____ . *Some Aspects of Hittite Religion.* Schweich Lectures 1976 (London: British Academy [Oxford University Press], 1977).

_____ . *The Hittites* (London: Penguin, 1990).

Güterbock, Hans G. "The Hittite Temple According to Written Sources." In *Le temple et le culte.* XXe Recontre Assyriologique Internationale. Uitgaven van het Nederlands Historisch-Archeologische Instituut te Istambul 37 (Istanbul: Nederlands Historisch-Archeologische Instituut, 1975) 125-32.

Hackett, Jo Ann. *The Balaam Text from Deir 'Allā.* HSM 31 (Atlanta: Scholars Press, 1980).

Hallo, W. W. "Akkadian Apocalypses," *IEJ* 16 (1966) 231-42.

Halpern, Baruch. *The First Historians: The Hebrew Bible and History* (San Francisco: Harper and Row, 1988).

Hanson, P. D. *The Dawn of Apocalyptic* (Philadelphia: Westminster, 1973).

_____ . "Apocalypticism," *IDBSup* (1976) 29-31.
_____ . "From Prophecy to Apocalyptic: Unresolved Issues," *JSOT* 15 (1980) 3-6.
Haran, M. "On the Diffusion of Schools and Literacy." In *Congress Volume: Jerusalem 1986*. Ed. J. A. Emerton. VTSup 40 (Leiden: Brill, 1988) 81-95.
Harrington, D. J. "The Wisdom of the Scribe According to Ben Sira." In *Ideal Figures in Ancient Judaism: Profiles and Paradigms*. Ed. J. J. Collins and G. W. E. Nickelsburg. SBLSCS 12 (Atlanta: Scholars, 1980) 181-88.
Harris, Rivkah. "The Nadītu Woman," *Studies Presented to A. Leo Oppenheim, July 7, 1964* (Chicago: Oriental Institute, 1964) 106-35.
_____ . "The Female 'Sage' in Mesopotamian Literature (with an Appendix on Egypt)." In *The Sage in Israel and the Ancient Near East*. Ed. J. G. Gammie and L. G. Perdue (Winona Lake, Ind.: Eisenbrauns, 1990) 3-17.
Hartman, L. F., and A. A. Di Lella. *The Book of Daniel*. AB 23 (Garden City: Doubleday, 1978).
Hauer, C. E. "Who Was Zadok?" *JBL* 82 (1963) 89-94.
Heider, George C. *The Cult of Molek: A Reassessment*. JSOTSup 43 (Sheffield: JSOT, 1985).
Helck, Wolfgang. "Priester, Priesterorganisation, Priestertitel," *LdÄ* 4 (1982) 1084-97.
Henshaw, Richard A. *Female and Male: The Cultic Personnel: The Bible and the Rest of the Ancient Near East*. Princeton Theological Monograph Series 31 (Allison Park, Penn.: Pickwick, 1994).
Herion, Gary A. "The Impact of Modern and Social Science Assumptions on the Reconstruction of Israelite History," *JSOT* 34 (1986) 3-33.
Hermann, Siegfried. "Prophetie in Israel und Ägypten: Recht und Grenze eines Vergleiches," *Congress Volume: Bonn 1962*. VTSup 9 (Leiden: Brill, 1963) 47-65.
Hermisson, H. J. *Studien zur israelitischen Spruchweisheit*. WMANT 28 (Neukirchen-Vluyn: Neukirchen Verlag, 1968).
Hoelscher, Gustaf. *Die Profeten* (Leipzig: Hinrichs, 1914).
Hoffner, Harry A. "Second Millennium Antecedents to the Hebrew *'ōḇ*," *JBL* 86 (1967) 385-401.
_____ . "אוב" *TDOT* (1974) 1.130-34.
Hoftijzer, J., and G. van der Kooij, eds. *Aramaic Texts from Deir 'Alla*. Documenta et Monumenta Orientis Antiqui 19 (Leiden: Brill, 1976).
_____ . *The Balaam Text from Deir 'Alla Re-evaluated: Proceedings of the International Symposium Held at Leiden 21-24 August 1989* (Leiden: Brill, 1991).
Holladay, C. R. *Fragments from Hellenistic Jewish Authors, Volume I: Historians*. TT 20, Pseudepigrapha Series 10 (Atlanta: Scholars, 1983); *Volume II: Poets: The Epic Poets Theodotus and Philo and Ezekiel the Tragedian*. TT 30, Pseudepigrapha Series 12 (Atlanta: Scholars, 1989).
Holm, Nils G., ed. *Religious Ecstasy: Based on Papers Read at the Symposium on Religious Ecstasy Held at Åbo, Finland, on the 26th-28th of August 1981* (Stockholm: Almqvist and Wiksell, 1982).
_____ . "Ecstasy Research in the 20th Century—An Introduction." In *Religious Ecstasy: Based on Papers Read at the Symposium on Religious Ecstasy Held at Åbo,*

Finland, on the 26th-28th of August 1981. Ed. N. G. Holm (Stockholm: Almqvist and Wiksell, 1982) 7-26.

Houtman, C. "The Urim and Thummim: A New Suggestion," *VT* 40 (1990) 229-32.

Huffmon, Herbert B. "Prophecy in the Mari Letters." In *Biblical Archaeologist Reader* (1970) 3.199-224 (reprinted from *BA* 31 [1968] 101-24).

_____ . "Prophecy in the Ancient Near East," *IDBSup* (1976) 697-700.

_____ . "Priestly Divination in Israel." In *The Word of the Lord Shall Go Forth: Essays in Honor of David Noel Freedman in Celebration of His Sixtieth Birthday*. Ed. C. L. Meyers and M. O'Connor. ASOR Special Volume Series 1 (Winona Lake, Ind.: Eisenbrauns, 1983) 355-59.

_____ . "Ancient Near Eastern Prophecy," *ABD* (1992) 5.477-82

Hultkrantz, Å. "Ecological and Phenomenological Aspects of Shamanism." In *Shamanism in Siberia*. Ed. V. Diószegi and M. Hoppál (Budapest: Akadémiai Kiadó, 1978) 27-58.

Hunger, H., and Stephen A. Kaufman. "A New Akkadian Prophecy Text," *JAOS* 95 (1975) 371-75.

Hurwitz, A. "The Date of the Prose-Tale of Job Linguistically Reconsidered," *HTR* 67 (1974) 17-34.

Husser, Jean-Marie. *Le songe et la parole: Etude sur le réve et sa fonction dans l'ancien Israël*. BZAW 210 (Berlin-New York: de Gruyter, 1994).

Isaksson, Bo. *Studies in the Language of Qoheleth, With Special Emphasis on the Verbal System*. Acta Universitatis Upsaliensis: Studia Semitica Upsaliensia 10 (Stockholm: Almqvist & Wiksell, 1987).

Jacobsen, T. "Early Political Development in Mesopotamia," *ZA* 52 (1957) 91-140.

Jamieson-Drake, David W. *Scribes and Schools in Monarchic Judah: A Socio-Archeological Approach*. JSOTSup 109. Social World of Biblical Antiquity 9 (Sheffield: Almond Press, 1991).

Japhet, Sara. *I & II Chronicles: A Commentary*. OTL (London: SCM, 1993).

Jenkins, Keith. *Re-Thinking History* (London—New York: Routledge, 1991).

Jepsen, Alfred. *Nabi: Soziologische Studien zur alttestamentlichen Literatur und Religionsgeschichte* (Munich: Beck, 1934).

Jeremias, Jörg. *Kultprophetie und Gerichtsverkündigung in der späten Königszeit Israels*. WMANT 35 (Neukirchen: Neukirchener Verlag, 1970).

Jeyes, Ulla. "The Nadītu Women of Sippar." In *Images of Women in Antiquity*. 2d ed. Ed. A. Cameron and A. Kuhrt (London: Routledge, 1993) 260-72.

Johnson, Aubrey R. *The Cult Prophet in Israel*. 2d ed. (Cardiff: University of Wales, 1962).

_____ . *Sacral Kingship in Ancient Israel*. 2d ed. (Cardiff: University of Wales, 1967).

Johnson, Douglas H. *Nuer Prophets: A History of Prophecy from the Upper Nile in the Nineteenth and Twentieth Centuries*. Oxford Studies in Social and Cultural Anthropology (Oxford: Clarendon Press, 1994).

Johnson, Marshall D. *The Purpose of the Biblical Geneaologies*. 2d ed. (Cambridge University Press, 1988).

Kákosy, Lászlo. "Orakel," *LdÄ* 4 (1982) 600-6.

Kalugila, Leonidas. *The Wise King: Studies in Royal Wisdom as Divine Revelation in the Old Testament and Its Environment*. CBOTS 15 (Lund: Gleerup, 1980).

Kammenhuber, Annelies. *Orakelpraxis, Träume und Vorzeichenshau bei den Hettitern.* Texte der Hethiter 7 (Heidelberg: Carl Winter, 1976).

Kapelrud, Arvid S. "Shamanistic Features in the Old Testament." In *Studies in Shamanism.* Ed. C.-M. Edsman. Scripta Instituti Donneriani Aboensis 1 (Stockholm: Almqvist and Wiksell, 1967) 90-96.

Kayatz, Christa. *Studien zu Proverbien 1-9: Eine form- und motivgeschichtliche Untersuchung unter Einbeziehung ägyptischen Vergleichsmaterials.* WMANT 22 (Neukirchen-Vluyn: Neukirchen Verlag, 1966).

Kees, Hermann. *Das Priestertum im ägyptischen Staat vom Neuen Reich bis zur Spätzeit.* 2 vols.. Probleme der Ägyptologie 1 (Leiden: Brill, 1953-58).

Kent, R. G. *Old Persian.* 2d ed. AOS 33 (New Haven: American Oriental Society, 1953).

Knight, Douglas A., ed. *Julius Wellhausen and His* Prolegomena to the History of Israel. Semeia 25 (Chico: Scholars, 1983).

Korpel, Marjo C. A. "Avian Spirits in Ugarit and in Ezekiel 13," *Aspects of Ugaritic Religion and Culture.* Proceedings of the Ugaritic Conference, Edinburgh July 1994. Ed. N. Wyatt and W. Watson. (Münster: UGARIT-Verlag, forthcoming).

Kramer, Samuel Noah. *From the Tablets of Sumer* (Indian Hills, CO: Falcon's Wing Press, 1956).

_____ . *The Sacred Marriage Rite: Aspects of Faith, Myth, and Ritual in Ancient Sumer* (Bloomington: University of Indiana, 1969).

_____ . "The Sage in Sumerian Literature: A Composite Portrait." In *The Sage in Israel and the Ancient Near East.* Ed. J. G. Gammie and L. G. Perdue (Winona Lake, Ind.: Eisenbrauns, 1990) 31-44.

Kraus, Hans-Joachim. *Worship in Israel: A Cultic History of the Old Testament* (Oxford: Blackwell, 1966).

_____ . *Theology of the Psalms* (Minneapolis: Augsburg; London: SPCK, 1986).

_____ . *Psalms 1-59: A Commentary* (Minneapolis: Augsburg, 1988).

_____ . *Psalms 60-150: A Commentary* (Minneapolis: Augsburg, 1989).

Kuhrt, Amélie. "Usurpation, Conquest and Ceremonial: from Babylon to Persia." In *Rituals of Royalty: Power and Ceremonial in Traditional Societies.* Ed. D. Cannadine and S. Price (Past and Present Publications; Cambridge: Cambridge University, 1987) 20-55.

Lambert, W. G. *Babylonian Wisdom Literature* (Oxford: Clarendon, 1960).

_____ . "The <<Tamītu>> Texts." In *La divination en Mésopotamie ancienne et dans les régions voisines.* Bibliotheque des Centres d'Études Supérieures Spécialisés (Paris: Presses Universitaires de France, 1966) 119-23.

_____ . "The Seed of Kingship." In Le palais et la royauté. Ed. G. Garelli. XIXe Recontre Assyriologique Internationale (Paris: Librairie Orientaliste Paul Geuthner, 1974) 427-40.

_____ . *The Background of Jewish Apocalyptic.* Ethel M. Wood Lecture, University of London, 22 Feb. 1977 (London: Athlone, 1978).

_____ . "The Late Babylonian *Kislīmu* Ritual for Esagil," JCS 43-45 (1991-93) 89-106.

_____ . "Prostitution." In *Außenseiter und Randgruppen: Beiträge zu einer Sozialgeschichte des Alten Orients* (Xenia: Konstanzer Althistorische Vorträge und Forschungen 32; ed. V. Haas; Konstanz: Universitätsverlag Konstanz, 1992) 127-57.

_____ . Review of S. Denning-Bolle, *Wisdom in Akkadian Literature*, *AfO* 40-41 (1993-94) 116-17.

_____ . "The Qualifications of Babylonian Diviners," *Festschrift R. Borger* (1994).

_____ . "Some New Babylonian Wisdom Literature," *Emerton Festschrift* (Cambridge University Press, 1995) 30-42.

Lanczkowski, Günter. "Das Königtum im Mittleren Reich." In *The Sacral Kingship: Contributions to the Central Theme of the VIIIth International Congress for the History of Religions (Rome, April 1955)*. NumSup 4 (Leiden: Brill, 1959) 269-80.

_____ . "Ägyptischer Prophetismus im Lichte des alttestamentlichen," *ZAW* 70 (1958) 31-38.

_____ . *Altägyptischer Prophetismus*. Ägyptologische Abhandlungen 4 (Wiesbaden: Harrassowitz, 1960).

Lang, Bernhard. *Monotheism and the Prophetic Minority: An Essay in Biblical History and Sociology*. The Social World of Biblical Antiquity 1 (Sheffield: Almond Press, 1983).

_____ , ed. *Anthropological Approaches to the Old Testament*. Issues in Religion and Theology 8 (Philadelphia: Fortress; London: SPCK, 1985).

_____ . "Life after Death in the Prophetic Promise." In *Congress Volume Jerusalem 1986*. Ed. J. A. Emerton. VTSup 40 (Leiden: Brill, 1988) 144-56.

Langhe, R. de. "Myth, Ritual, and Kingship in the Ras Shamra Tablets." In *Myth, Ritual, and Kingship: Essays on the Theory and Practice of Kingship in the Ancient Near East and in Israel*. Ed. S. H. Hooke (Oxford: Clarendon, 1958) 122-48.

Larsen, Mogens Trolle. "The City and Its King: On teh Old Assyrian Notion of Kingship." In Le palais et la royauté. Ed. G. Garelli. XIXe Recontre Assyriologique Internationale (Paris: Librairie Orientaliste Paul Geuthner, 1974) 285-300.

Leclant, Jean. "Éléments pour une étude de la divination dans l'Égypte pharaonique." In *La Divination: Études Recueillies*. Ed. A. Caquot and M. Leibovici. 2 vols. (Paris: Presses Universitaires de France, 1968) 1.1-23.

Lemaire, André. *Les écoles et la formation de la Bible dans l'ancien Israël*. OBO 39. (Freiburg [Schweiz]: Universitätsverlag; Göttingen: Vandenhoeck & Ruprecht, 1981).

_____ . "The Sage in School and Temple." In *The Sage in Israel and the Ancient Near East*. Ed. J. G. Gammie and L. G. Perdue (Winona Lake, Ind.: Eisenbrauns, 1990) 165-81.

_____ . "Education: Ancient Israel," *ABD* 2 (1992) 305-12.

_____ . "Scribes: I. Proche-Orient ancien; II. Ancien Testament—Ancien Israël," *DBS* 12 (1992) 244-66.

Lemche, Niels Peter. *Early Israel: Anthropological and Historical Studies on the Israelite Society before the Monarchy*. VTSup 37 (Leiden: Brill, 1985).

_____ . "The Old Testament—A Hellenistic Book?" *SJOT* 7 (1993) 163-93.

Levenson, Jon D. *Theology of the Program of Restoration of Ezekiel 40-48*. HSM 10 (Missoula: Scholars, 1976).

Lévy-Bruhl, Lucien. *Primitive Mentality* (New York: Macmillan, 1923).

Lewis, I. M. *Ecstatic Religion: A Study of Shamanism and Spirit Possession*. 2d ed. (London/New York: Routledge, 1989).

Lewis, Naphtali. *The Interpretation of Dreams and Portents.* Aspects of Antiquity (Toronto/Sarasota, Fla.: Samuel, Stevens, Hakkert, 1976).

Lewis, Theodore J. *Cults of the Dead in Ancient Israel and Ugarit.* HSM 39 (Atlanta: Scholars Press, 1989).

Lichtheim, Miriam. *Ancient Egyptian Literature.* 3 vols. (Berkeley and Los Angeles: Univerity of California, 1973-80).

Lienhardt, G. *Divinity and Experience: The Religion of the Dinka* (Oxford: Clarendon, 1961).

Lindblom, J. *Prophecy in Ancient Israel* (Oxford: Blackwell, 1962).

Lipiński, E. "Ūrīm and Tummīm," *VT* 20 (1970) 495-96.

_____ . "Royal and State Scribes in Ancient Jerusalem." In *Congress Volume: Jerusalem 1986.* Ed. J. A. Emerton. VTSup 40 (Leiden: Brill, 1988) 157-64.

Littleton, C. Scott. "Lucien Lévy-Bruhl and the Concept of Cognitive Relativity," new introduction to the reprint of Lucien Lévy-Bruhl, *How Natives Think* (Princeton, N.J.: Princeton University, 1985) v-lviii.

Livingstone, Alasdair. *Court Poetry and Literary Miscellanea.* State Archives of Assyria 3 (Helsinki: Helsinki University, 1989).

Loewe, Michael, and Carmen Blacker, eds. *Divination and Oracles* (London: George Allen & Unwin, 1981).

Long, Burke O. "The Effect of Divination upon Israelite Literature," *JBL* 92 (1973) 489-97.

_____ . "Reports of Visions among the Prophets," *JBL* 95 (1976) 353-65.

_____ . "Prophetic Authority as Social Reality." In *Canon and Authority: Essays in Old Testament Religion and Theology.* Ed. G. W. Coats and B. O. Long (Philadelphia: Fortress, 1977) 3-20.

_____ . "Social Dimensions of Prophetic Conflict," *Semeia* 21 (1982) 31-43.

Loretz, Oswald. *Qohelet und der alte Orient* (Freiburg: Herder, 1964).

_____ . "Nekromantie und Totenevokation in Mesopotamien, Ugarit und Israel." In *Religionsgeschichtliche Beziehungen zwischen Kleinasien, Nordsyrien und dem Alten Testament: Internationales Symposion Hamburg 17.-21. März 1990.* Ed. B. Janowski, et al. OBO 129 (Göttingen: Vandenhoeck & Ruprecht, 1993) 285-315.

_____ . "*Marziḥu* im ugaritischen und biblischen Ahnenkult: Zu Ps 23; 133; Am 6,1-7 und Jer 16,5.8." In *Mesopotamica-Ugaritica-Biblica: Festschrift für Kurt Bergerhof zur Vollendung seines 70. Lebensjahres am 7. Mai 1992.* AOAT 232. Ed. M. Dietrich and O. Loretz (Neukirchen-Vluyn: Neukirchener Verlag, 1993) 93-144.

Lowenthal, David. *The Past Is a Foreign Country* (Cambridge: Cambridge University, 1985).

Lowery, R. H. *The Reforming Kings: Cult and Society in First Temple Judah.* JSOTSup 120 (Sheffield: JSOT Press, 1991).

Lowie, R. H. *Indians of the Plains.* American Museum of Natural History (New York: McGraw-Hill, 1954); 161-64 are reprinted in W. A. Lessa and E. Z. Vogt, *Reader in Comparative Religion: An Anthropological Approach.* 2d ed. (New York/ London: Harper and Row, 1965), 452-54.

Lust, J. "On Wizards and Prophets," *Studies on Prophecy: A Collection of Twelve Papers.* VTSup 26 (Leiden: Brill, 1974) 133-42.

Lyons, E. L. "A Note on Proverbs 31.10-31." In *The Listening Heart: Essays in Wisdom and the Psalms in Honor of Roland E. Murphy, O. Carm.* Ed. K. G. Hoglund, et al.. JSOTSup 58 (Sheffield: JSOT, 1987) 237-45.

McCarthy, Dennis J. *Treaty and Covenant.* 2d ed. (Rome: Pontifical Biblical Institute, 1978).

McCreesh, T. P. "Wisdom as Wife: Proverbs 31:10-31," *RB* 92 (1985) 25-46.

McEwan, Gilbert J. P. *Priest and Temple in Hellenistic Babylonia.* Freiburger altorientalische Studien 4 (Wiesbaden: Steiner, 1981).

Mack-Fisher, Loren R. "A Survey and Reading Guide to the Didactic Literature of Ugarit: Prolegomenon to a Study on the Sage." In *The Sage in Israel and the Ancient Near East.* Ed. J. G. Gammie and L. G. Perdue (Winona Lake, Ind.: Eisenbrauns, 1990) 67-80.

_____ . "The Scribe (and Sage) in the Royal Court at Ugarit." In *The Sage in Israel and the Ancient Near East.* Ed. J. G. Gammie and L. G. Perdue (Winona Lake, Ind.: Eisenbrauns, 1990) 109-15.

McKane, William. *Prophets and Wisemen* (1965). Reprinted with new introduction (London: SCM, 1983).

McLaughlin, John L. "The *marzeaḥ* at Ugarit: A Textual and Contextual Study," *UF* 23 (1991) 265-81.

Malamat, Abraham. *Mari and the Early Israelite Experience.* Schweich Lectures 1984 (Oxford University Press for the British Academy, 1989).

_____ . "A New Prophetic Message from Aleppo and its Biblical Counterparts." In *Understanding Poets and Prophets: Essays in Honour of George Wishart Anderson.* Ed. A. G. Auld. JSOTSup 152 (Sheffield: JSOT, 1993) 236-41.

Manor, Dale W., and Gary A. Herion. "Arad," *ABD* (1992) 331-36.

Martin, James D. "Ben Sira's Hymn to the Fathers: A Messianic Perspective," *OTS* 24 (1986) 107-23.

Matthews, Victor H., and Don C. Benjamin. *Social World of Ancient Israel, 1250-587* BCE (Peabody, Mass.: Hendrickson, 1993).

Mayes, A. D. H. *Israel in the Period of the Judges.* Studies in Biblical Theology, second series 29 (London: SCM, 1974).

_____ . *The Old Testament in Sociological Perspective* (London: Marshall Pickering, 1989).

Meeks, W. A. *The Prophet-King: Moses Traditions and the Johannine Christology.* NovTSup 14 (Leiden: Brill, 1967).

Mettinger, Tryggve N. D. *Solomonic State Officials: A Study of the Civil Government Officials of the Israelite Monarchy.* CBOTS 5 (Lund: Gleerup, 1971).

_____ . *King and Messiah: The Civil and Sacral Legitimation of the Israelite Kings.* CBOTS 8 (Lund: Gleerup, 1976).

Michaelsen, Peter. "Ecstasy and Possession in Ancient Israel: A Review of Some Recent Contributions," *SJOT* 2 (1989) 28-54.

Millard, A. R. "An Assessment of the Evidence of Writing in Ancient Israel," *Biblical Archaeology Today: Proceedings of the International Congress of Biblical Archaeology, Jerusalem 1984* (Jerusalem: Israel Exploration Society, 1985) 301-12.

Miller, James E. "Dreams and Prophetic Visions," *Biblica* 71 (1990) 401-4.

Miller, J. Maxwell. *The Old Testament and the Historian.* Guides to Biblical Scholarship, Old Testament (Minneapolis: Fortress, 1976).

Miller, J. Maxwell, and John H. Hayes. *A History of Ancient Israel and Judah* (Minneapolis: Fortress; London: SCM, 1986).

Miller, Patricia Cox. *Dreams in Late Antiquity: Studies in the Imagination of a Culture* (Princeton, N.J.: Princeton University, 1994).

Mooney, James. *The Ghost-Dance Religion and the Sioux Outbreak of 1890*. Fourteenth Annual Report of the Bureau of Ethnology, 1892-93 Part 2 (Washington, DC: Government Printing Office, 1896; reprinted Lincoln: University of Nebraska, 1991).

Moore, Michael S. *The Balaam Traditions: Their Character and Development*. SBLDS 113 (Atlanta: Scholars Press, 1990).

_____ . "Another Look at Balaam," *RB* 97 (1990) 359-78.

Moran, William L. "New Evidence from Mari on the History of Prophecy," *Biblica* 50 (1969) 15-56.

Mowinckel, Sigmund. *Psalmenstudien*. Parts 1-6 (Skrifter utgit av Videnskapsselskapets i Kristiania II: Hist.-Filos. Klasse; Oslo: Dybwad, 1921-24).

_____ . *The Psalms in Israel's Worship*. 2 vols. Oxford: Blackwell, 1962). Reprinted with a foreword by R. K. Gnuse and D. A. Knight. The Biblical Seminar 14 (Sheffield: JSOT, 1991).

Müller, H.-P. "Magisch-mantische Weisheit und die Gestalt Daniels," *UF* 1 (1969) 79-94.

_____ . "Mantische Weisheit und Apokalyptik," *Congress Volume, Uppsala 1971*. VTSup 22 (Leiden: Brill, 1972) 268-93.

_____ . "Die aramäische Inschrift von Deir 'Allā und die älteren Bileamsprüche," *ZAW* 94 (1982) 214-44.

Murphy, Roland E. *Wisdom Literature: Job, Proverbs, Ruth, Canticles, Ecclesiastes, Esther*. Forms of Old Testament Literature (Grand Rapids, Mich.: Eerdmans, 1981).

_____ . *Ecclesiastes*. WBC 23A (Dallas: Word Books, 1993).

Nicholson, Ernest W. *God and His People: Covenant and Theology in the Old Testament* (Oxford: Clarendon, 1986).

Nickelsburg, G. W. E. *Jewish Literature between the Bible and the Mishnah* (Philadelphia: Fortress, 1981).

Niditch, Susan. *The Symbolic Vision in Biblical Tradition*. HSM 30 (Atlanta: Scholars, 1980).

Niehr, Herbert. "Ein unerkannter Text zur Nekromantie in Israel: Bemerkungen zum religionsgeschichtlichen Hintergrund von 2Sam 12,16a," *UF* 23 (1991) 301-6.

Nissinen, Marti. "Die Relevanz der neuassyrischen Prophetie für die alttestamentliche Forschung." In *Mesopotamica-Ugaritica-Biblica: Festschrift für Kurt Bergerhof zur Vollendung seines 70. Lebensjahres am 7. Mai 1992*. AOAT 232. Ed. M. Dietrich and O. Loretz (Neukirchen-Vluyn: Neukirchener Verlag, 1993) 217-58.

Noort, E. *Untersuchungen zum Gottesbescheid in Mari*. AOAT 202 (Neukirchen-Vluyn: Neukirchener Verlag, 1977).

North, John. "Diviners and Divination at Rome." In *Pagan Priests: Religion and Power in the Ancient World*. Ed. M. Beard and J. North (London: Duckworth, 1990) 51-71.

Nougayrol, Jean. *Le Palais royal d'Ugarit: III. Textes accadiens et hourrites des Archives Est, Ouest et Centrales*. Mission de Ras Shamra 6 (Paris: Imprimerie Nationale, 1955).

_____ . *Le Palais royal d'Ugarit: IV. Textes accadiens des Archives Sud (Archives Internationales)*. Mission de Ras Shamra 9 (Paris: Imprimerie Nationale, 1956).

_____ . "La divination babylonienne." In *La Divination: Études Recueillies*. Ed. A. Caquot and M. Leibovici. 2 vols. (Paris: Presses Universitaires de France, 1968) 1.25-81.

O'Connor, David, and David P. Silverman, eds. *Ancient Egyptian Kingship*. Probleme der Ägyptologie 9 (Leiden: Brill, 1995).

Olyan, Saul M. "Ben Sira's Relationship to the Priesthood," *HTR* 80 (1987) 261-86.

_____ . *Asherah and the Cult of Yahweh in Israel*. SBLMS 34 (Atlanta: Scholars, 1988).

Oppenheim, A. Leo. "The Interpretation of Dreams in the Ancient Near East, With a Translation of an Assyrian Dream-Book," *Transactions of the American Philosophical Society* 46 (1956) 179-354.

_____ . *Ancient Mesopotamia: Portrait of a Dead Civilization* (Chicago/London: University of Chicago, 1964).

Orlinsky, Harry M. "The Seer in Ancient Israel," *Oriens Antiquus* 4 (1965) 153-74.

_____ . "The Seer-Priest and the Prophet in Ancient Israel," *Essays in Biblical Culture and Bible Translation* (New York: Ktav, 1974) 39-65 (= *The World History of Jewish People*: Vol. 3. *Judges* [ed. B. Mazar; New Brunswick, N.J.: Rutgers University Press, 1971]).

Otto, Walter. *Priester und Tempel im hellenistischen Ägypten: Ein Beitrag zur Kulturgeschichte des Hellenismus*. 2 vols. (Leipzig-Berlin: Teubner, 1905-8).

Overholt, Thomas W. "Prophecy: The Problem of Cross-Cultural Comparison," *Semeia* 21 (1982) 55-78 (= B. Lang, ed. *Anthropological Approaches to the Old Testament* [1985] 60-82).

_____ . *Prophecy in Cross-Cultural Perspective: A Sourcebook for Biblical Researchers*. SBLSBS 17 (Atlanta: Scholars, 1986).

_____ . *Channels of Prophecy: The Social Dynamics of Prophetic Activity* (Minneapolis: Fortress, 1989).

_____ . "Prophecy in History: The Social Reality of Intermediation," *JSOT* 48 (1990) 3-29.

_____ . "'It Is Difficult to Read,'" *JSOT* 48 (1990) 51-54.

Pardee, Dennis J., updated and revised by Jonathan T. Glass. "Literary Sources for the History of Palestine and Syria: The Mari Archives," *BA* 47 (1984) 88-99.

_____ . "*Marziḫu*, *kispu*, and the Ugaritic Funerary Cult: A Minimalist View," *Aspects of Ugaritic Religion and Culture*. Proceedings of the Ugaritic Conference, Edinburgh July 1994. Ed. N. Wyatt and W. Watson (Münster: UGARIT-Verlag, forthcoming).

Parker, A. C. *The Code of Handsome Lake, the Seneca Prophet*. New York State Museum, Bulletin 163 (Albany: State Museum, 1913).

Parker, Richard A., ed. *A Saite Oracle Papyrus from Thebes in the Brooklyn Museum* (Papyrus Brooklyn *47.218.3*) (Providence, R.I.: Brown University, 1962).

Parker, Simon B. "Possession Trance and Prophecy in Pre-Exilic Israel," *VT* 28 (1978) 271-85.

_____ . "Official Attitudes toward Prophecy at Mari and in Israel," *VT* 43 (1993) 50-68.

Parpola, Simo, and Kazuko Watanabe. *Neo-Assyrian Treaties and Loyalty Oaths*. State Archives of Assyria 2 (Helsinki: Helsinki University, 1988).

Paul, Shalom. *Amos*. Hermeneia (Minneapolis: Fortress, 1991).

Peek, Philip M., ed. *African Divination Systems: Ways of Knowing*. African Systems of Thought (Bloomington and Indianapolis: Indiana University, 1991).

Petersen, David L. *The Roles of Israel's Prophets*. JSOTSup 17 (Sheffield: JSOT, 1981).

_____ , ed. *Prophecy in Israel: Search for an Identity*. Issues in Religion and Theology 10 (Philadelphia: Fortress; London: SPCK, 1987).

Pitard, Wayne T. "A New Edition of the 'Rāpi'ūma' Texts: *KTU* 1.20-22," *BASOR* 285 (February 1992) 33-77.

Pope, Marvin. *Job*. AB 15. 3d ed. (Garden City, N.Y.: Doubleday, 1973).

Porten, B., and A. Yardeni. *Textbook of Aramaic Documents from Ancient Egypt: 1 Letters*. Hebrew University, Department of the History of the Jewish People, Texts and Studies for Students (Jerusalem: Hebrew University, 1986).

_____ . *Textbook of Aramaic Documents from Ancient Egypt: 3 Literature, Accounts, Lists*. Hebrew University, Department of the History of the Jewish People, Texts and Studies for Students (Jerusalem: Hebrew University, 1993).

Pritchard, James B., ed. *Ancient Near Eastern Texts Relating to the Old Testament* 3d ed. with supplement (Princeton: Princeton University, 1969).

Puech, E. "Les écoles dans l'Israël préexilique: données épigraphiques," *Congress Volume: Jerusalem 1986*. Ed. J. A. Emerton. VTSup 40 (Leiden: Brill, 1988) 189-203.

Quaegebeur, Jan. "On the Egyptian Equivalent of Biblical *Ḥarṭummîm*," *Pharaonic Egypt: The Bible and Christianity*. Ed. Sarah Israelit-Groll (Jerusalem: Magnes, 1985) 162-72.

Rad, Gerhard von. *Old Testament Theology: II The Theology of Israel's Prophetic Traditions* (San Francisco: Harper & Row, 1965).

_____ . *Wisdom in Israel* (Nashville: Abingdon, 1972).

Rainey, Anson F. "The Scribe at Ugarit—His Position and Influence." In *Proceedings of the Israel Academy of Sciences and Humanities* 3 (1969) 126-47.

Ramsey, George W. "Zadok," *ABD* 6 (1992) 1034-36.

Ray, J. D. *The Archive of Ḥor*. Texts from Excavations, Second Memoir (London: Egypt Exploration Society, 1976).

_____ . "Ancient Egypt." In *Divination and Oracles*. Ed. M. Loewe and C. Blacker (London: George Allen & Unwin, 1981) 174-90.

Redford, Donald B. *A Study of the Biblical Story of Joseph (Genesis 37-50)*. VTSup 20 (Leiden: Brill, 1970).

Reiner, Erica, in collaboation with David Pingree. *Babylonian Planetary Omens, Part Two: Enūma Anu Enlil, Tablets 50-51*. Bibliotheca Mesopotamica 2/2 (Malibu: Undena, 1981).

Rendtorff, Rolf. *The Problem of the Process of Transmission in the Pentateuch*. JSOTSup 89 (Sheffield: JSOT Press, 1990).

Renger, J. "Untersuchungen zum Priestertum in der altbabylonischen Zeit," *Zeitschrift für Assyrologie* 58 (1966) 110-88; 59 (1969) 104-230.

Reventlow, H. *Das Amt des Propheten bei Amos*. FRLANT 80 (Göttingen: Vandenhoeck & Ruprecht, 1962).

_____ . *Liturgie und prophetisches Ich bei Jeremia* (Gütersloh: Mohn, 1963).

Rigby, P. "Prophets, Diviners, and Prophetism: The Recent History of Kiganda Religion," *Journal of Anthropological Research* 31 (1975), pp. 116-48.

Riley, William. *King and Cultus in Chronicles: Worship and the Reinterpretation of History*. JSOTSup 160 (Sheffield: JSOT Press, 1993).

Ringgren, Helmer. "Akkadian Apocalypses." In *Apocalypticism in the Mediterranean World and the Near East: Proceedings of the International Colloquium on Apocalypticism, Uppsala, August 12-17, 1979*. Ed. D. Hellholm (Tübingen: Mohr[Siebeck], 1983) 279-86.

Robertson, David A. *Linguistic Evidence in Dating Early Hebrew Poetry*. SBLDS 3 (Atlanta: Scholars Press, 1972).

Rogerson, J. W. *Anthropology and the Old Testament*. Growing Points in Theology (Oxford: Blackwell, 1978).

Ross, J. F. "Prophecy in Hamath, Israel, and Mari," *HTR* 63 (1970) 1-28.

Ruppert, L. *qāsam*, *TWAT* 7 (1990) 78-84.

Russell, James R. "The Sage in Ancient Iranian Literature." In *The Sage in Israel and the Ancient Near East*. Ed. J. G. Gammie and L. G. Perdue (Winona Lake, Ind.: Eisenbrauns, 1990) 81-92.

_____ . "Sages and Scribes at the Courts of Ancient Iran." In *The Sage in Israel and the Ancient Near East*. Ed. J. G. Gammie and L. G. Perdue (Winona Lake, Ind.: Eisenbrauns, 1990) 141-46.

Sacral Kingship, The: Contributions to the Central Theme of the VIIIth International Congress for the History of Religions (Rome, April 1955). NumSup 4 (Leiden: Brill, 1959).

Saggs, H.W.F. *The Greatness that Was Babylon*. Great Civilization Series (London: Sidgwick and Jackson, 1962).

_____ . *The Greatness that Was Assyria*. Great Civilization Series (London: Sidgwick and Jackson, 1984).

Sasson, Jack M. "An Apocalyptic Vision from Mari?: Speculations on *ARM* X:9," *MARI* 1 (1982) 151-67.

_____ . "Mari Dreams," *JAOS* 103 (1983) 283-93.

Sasson, Victor. "The Book of Oracular Visions of Balaam from Deir 'Alla," *UF* 17 (1986) 283-309.

Schaeffer, Claude F.-A., ed. *Le Palais Royal d'Ugarit, 3: Texts accadiens et hourrites des Archives Est, Ouest et Centrales*. Mission de Ras Shamra 6 (Paris: Imprimerie Nationale, 1955).

_____ . *Le Palais royal d'Ugarit, 4: Texts accadiens des Archives Sud (Archives internationales)*. Mission de Ras Shamra 9 (Paris: Imprimerie Nationale, 1956).

Schlichting, Robert. "Prophetie," *LdÄ* 4 (1982) 1122-25.

Schmidt, Brian B. *Israel's Beneficent Dead: Ancestor Cult and Necromancy in Ancient Israelite Religion and Tradition*. Forschungen zum Alten Testament (Tübingen: Mohr[Siebeck], 1994).

Schoors, A. *The Preacher Sought to Find Pleasing Words: A Study of the Language of Qoheleth*. Orientalia Lovaniensia Analecta 41 (Leuven: Peeters/Departement Orientalistiek, 1992).

Schürer, E. *The Jewish People in the Age of Jesus Christ*. Rev. G. Vermes, et al. 3 vols. in 4 (Edinburgh: T & T Clarke, 1973-87).

Segal, J. B. "Popular Religion in Ancient Israel," *JJS* 27 (1976) 1-22.

Seux, M. J. *Épithétes Royales akkadiennes et sumériennes* (Paris: Letouzey et Ané, 1967).

_____ . "Königtum. B. II. und I. Jahrtausend," *RLA* 6 (1980-83) 140-73.

Shupak, Nili. *Where Can Wisdom Be Found? The Sage's Language in the Bible and Ancient Egyptian Literature*. OBO 130 (Fribourg: Universitätsverlag; Göttingen: Vandenhoeck & Ruprecht, 1993).

Sjöberg, Å. W. "The Old Babylonian Eduba." In *Sumerological Studies in Honor of Thorkild Jacobsen on His Seventieth Birthday, June 7, 1974* (Oriental Institute of the University of Chicago, Assyriological Studies 20; Chicago-London: University of Chicago, 1975) 159-79.

Skehan, P. W., and A. A. Di Lella, *The Wisdom of Ben Sira*. AB 39 (Garden City: Doubleday, 1987).

Smelik, Klaas A. D. "Moloch, Molek or Molk-Sacrifice? A Reassessment of the Evidence Concerning the Hebrew Term Molekh," *Society of Biblical Literature Twelfth International Meeting* (Leuven: August 1994) 73 (abstract).

Smith, Jonathan Z. "Native Cults in the Hellenistic Period," *HR* 11 (1971-72) 236-49.

_____ . "Wisdom and Apocalyptic." In *Religious Syncretism in Antiquity*. Ed. B. A. Pearson (Atlanta: Scholars, 1975) 131-56.

_____ . "European Religions, Ancient: Hellenistic Religions," *Encyclopaedia Britannica*. 15th ed. (Chicago: Encyclopaedia Britannica, 1985), *Macropaedia* 18.925-27.

Smith, Mark S. *The Early History of God: Yahweh and the Other Deities in Ancient Israel* (San Francisco: Harper, 1990).

_____ . "The Invocation of Decreased Ancestors in Psalm 49:12c," *JBL* 112 (1993) 105-7.

Smith, Mark S., and Elizabeth M. Bloch-Smith. "Death and Afterlife in Ugarit and Israel," *JAOS* 108 (1988) 277-84.

Smith, Morton. *Palestinian Parties and Politics That Shaped the Old Testament* (New York: Columbia, 1971).

Soden, Wolfram von. "Zur Stellung des 'Geweihten' (*qdš*) in Ugarit," *UF* 2 (1970) 329-30.

_____ . *The Ancient Orient: An Introduction to the Study of the Ancient Near East* (Grand Rapids, Mich.: Eerdmans, 1994).

Stadelmann, H. *Ben Sira als Schriftgelehrter: einer Untersuchung zum Berufsbild des vormakkabäischen Sofer unter Berücksichtigung seines Verhältnisses zu Priester-, Propheten- und Weisheitslehrertum*. WUNT 2. Reihe, Nr. 6 (Tübingen: Mohr[Siebeck], 1980).

Stanford, Michael. *The Nature of Historical Knowledge* (Oxford: Blackwell, 1986).

Starr, Ivan, ed. *Queries to the Sungod: Divination and Politics in Sargonid Assyria*. State Archives of Assyria 4 (Helsinki: Helsinki University Press, 1990).

Stoebe, Hans Joachim. *Das zweite Buch Samuelis*. KAT 8/2 (Gütersloh: Gütersloher Verlagshaus, 1994).

Stolper, Matthew W. "The *šaknu* of Nippur," *JCS* 40 (1988) 127-55.

Stone, Michael E. *Scriptures, Sects and Vision: A Profile of Judaism from Ezra to the Jewish Revolts* (Oxford: Blackwell, 1980).

Strange, John. "The Book of Joshua: A Hasmonaean Manifesto?" *History and Traditions of Early Israel: Studies Presented to Eduard Nielsen, May 8th 1993*. Ed. A. Lemaire and B. Otzen. VTSup 50 (Leiden: Brill, 1993) 136-41.

Sweet, Ronald F.G. "The Sage in Akkadian Literature: A Philological Study." In *The Sage in Israel and the Ancient Near East*. Ed. J. G. Gammie and L. G. Perdue (Winona Lake, Ind.: Eisenbrauns, 1990) 45-65.

_____ . "The Sage in Mesopotamian Palaces and Royal Courts." In *The Sage in Israel and the Ancient Near East*. Ed. J. G. Gammie and L. G. Perdue (Winona Lake, Ind.: Eisenbrauns, 1990) 99-107.

Talshir, Zipora. *The Alternative Story: 3 Kingdoms 12:24 A-Z*. Jerusalem Biblical Studies 6 (Jerusalem: Simor, 1993).

Tarragon, Jean-Michel de. *Le culte à Ugarit d'aprés les textes de la pratique en cunéiformes alphabétiques*. Cahiers de la Revue Biblique 19 (Paris: Gabalda, 1980).

Taylor, J. Glen. *Yahweh and the Sun: Biblical and Archaeological Evidence for Sun Worship in Ancient Israel*. JSOTSup 111 (Sheffield: JSOT, 1993).

Thompson, Thomas L. *Early History of the Israelite People From the Written and Archaeological Sources*. Studies in the History of the Ancient Near East 4 (Leiden: Brill, 1992).

Tigay, Jeffrey H. *You Shall Have No Other Gods: Israelite Religion in the Light of Hebrew Inscriptions*. HSS (Atlanta: Scholars, 1986).

Tooker, Elisabeth. "On the New Religion of Handsome Lake," *Anthropological Quarterly* 41 (1968) 187-200.

Toorn, Karel van der. "The Nature of the Biblical Teraphim in the Light of the Cuneiform Evidence," *CBQ* 52 (1990) 203-22.

_____ . "The Babylonian New Year Festival: New Insights from the Cuneiform Texts and their Bearing on Old Testament Study," *Congress Volume Leuven 1989*. VTSup 43 (Leiden: Brill, 1991) 331-44.

Tov, Emmanuel. *Textual Criticism of the Hebrew Bible* (Assen/Maastricht: Van Gorcum; Minneapolis: Fortress, 1992).

Trafzer, C. E., and M. A. Beach, "Smohalla, the Washani, and Religion as a Factor in Northwestern Indian History," *American Indian Quarterly* 9 (1985) 309-24.

Trigger, B. G., et al. *Ancient Egypt: A Social History* (Cambridge University Press, 1983).

Tuell, Steven Shawn. *The Law of the Temple in Ezekiel 40-48*. HSM 49 (Atlanta: Scholars, 1992).

Ussishkin, D. "The Date of the Judaean Shrine at Arad," *IEJ* 38 (1988) 142-57.

VanderKam, James C. *Enoch and the Growth of an Apocalyptic Tradition*. CBQMS 16 (Washington, DC: Catholic Biblical Association, 1984).

_____ . "The Prophetic-Sapiential Origins of Apocalyptic Thought." In *A Word in Season: Essays in Honour of William McKane*. Ed. J. D. Martin and P. R. Davies. JSOTSup 42 (Sheffield: University Press, 1986) 163-76.

Volten, Aksel. *Demotische Traumdeutung (Pap. Carlsberg XIII und XIV Verso)*. Analecta Aegyptica 3 (Copenhagen: Einar Munksgaard, 1942).

Wallace, A.F.C. "Halliday Jackson's Journal to the Seneca Indians, 1798-1800," *Pennsylvania History* 19 (1952) 117-47, 325-49.

_____ . *The Death and Rebirth of the Seneca* (New York: Random House, 1969).

Walsh, Jerome T. "The Contexts of 1 Kings XIII," *VT* 39 (1989) 355-70.

Warner, S. "The Alphabet—An Innovation and its Diffusion," *VT* 30 (1980) 82-86.

Weber, Max. *Ancient Judaism*. Trans. and ed. H. H. Gerth and D. Martindale (Gencoe, Ill.: The Free Press, 1952).

_____ . *The Sociology of Religion*, in G. Roth and C. Wittich, eds., *Economy and Society*. 2 vols. (Berkeley/Los Angeles: University of California, 1978)

Weeks, Stuart. *Early Israelite Wisdom*. Oxford Theological Monographs (Oxford: Clarendon, 1994).

Weinfeld, Moshe. *Deuteronomy and the Deuteronomic School* (Oxford: Clarendon, 1972).

_____ . "Ancient Near Eastern Patterns in Prophetic Literature," *VT* 27 (1977) 178-95.

_____ . *Deuteronomy 1-11*. AB 5 (New York: Doubleday, 1991).

Weippert, Manfred. "Assyrische Prophetien der Zeit Asarhaddons und Assurbanipals." In *Assyrian Royal Inscriptions: New Horizons in Literary, Ideological, and Historical Analysis (Papers of a Symposium Held in Centona [Siena] June 26-28, 1980)*. Ed. F. M. Fales (Rome: Istituto per l'Oriente, 1981) 71-115.

Weiser, Arthur. *The Psalms: A Commentary* (London: SCM, 1962).

Wellhausen, Julius. *Der Text der Bücher Samuelis* (Göttingen: Vandenhoeck und Ruprecht, 1871).

_____ . *Prolegomena to the History of Israel* (Edinburgh: A. and C. Black, 1885). Reprinted with a Foreword by D. A. Knight. Scholars Press Reprints and Translations Series (Atlanta: Scholars, 1994).

Wenham, G. J. "Were David's Sons Priests?" *ZAW* 87 (1975) 79-82.

Whedbee, William J. "The Comedy of Job." In *Studies in the Book of Job*. Ed. R. Polzin and D. Robertson. Semeia 7 (Atlanta: Scholars Press, 1977) 1-39.

White, Robert J., ed. *The Interpretation of Dreams:* Oneirocritica *by Artemidorus (Translation and Commentary)*. Noyes Classical Studies (Park Ridge, N.J.: Noyes, 1975).

Whitelam, Keith W. *The Just King: Monarchical Judicial Authority in Ancient Israel*. JSOTSup 12 (Sheffield: JSOT, 1979).

Whitley, C. F. *Koheleth: His Language and Thought*. BZAW 148 (Berlin/New York: de Gruyter, 1979).

Whybray, R. N. *The Intellectual Tradition in the Old Testament*. BZAW 135 (Berlin/New York: de Gruyter, 1974)

_____ . *Isaiah 40-66*. NCB (London: Marshall, Morgan & Scott; Grand Rapids: Eerdmans, 1975).

_____ . *The Second Isaiah*. Old Testament Guides (Sheffield: JSOT, 1983).

_____ . *The Making of the Pentateuch: A Methodological Study*. JSOTSup 53 (Sheffield: JSOT, 1987).

_____ . *Ecclesiastes*. NCB (London: Marshall Morgan and Scott; Grand Rapids, Mich.: Eerdmans, 1989).

_____ . "The Sage in the Israelite Royal Court." In *The Sage in Israel and the Ancient Near East*. Ed. J. G. Gammie and L. G. Perdue (Winona Lake, Ind.: Eisenbrauns, 1990) 133-39.

_____ . *Proverbs*. NCB (London: Marshall Morgan and Scott; Grand Rapids, Mich.: Eerdmans, 1994).

Widengren, Geo. "The Sacral Kingship of Iran," *The Sacral Kingship: Contributions to the Central Theme of the VIIIth International Congress for the History of Religions, Rome, April 1955*. NumSup 4 (Leiden: Brill, 1959) 242-57.

Wilcke, Claus. "Zum Königtum in der Ur III-Zeit." In Le palais et la royauté. Ed. G. Garelli. XIXe Recontre Assyriologique Internationale (Paris: Librairie Orientaliste Paul Geuthner, 1974) 177-232.

Wilhelm, Gernot. "Marginalien zu Herodot: Klio 199." In *Lingering over Words: Studies in Ancient Near Eastern Literature in Honor of William L. Moran*. Ed. T. Abusch, et al. HSS 37 (Atlanta: Scholars, 1990) 505-24.

Williams, Ronald J. "Scribal Training in Ancient Egypt," *JAOS* 92 (1972) 214-21.

_____ . "The Sage in Egyptian Literature." In *The Sage in Israel and the Ancient Near East*. Ed. J. G. Gammie and L. G. Perdue (Winona Lake, Ind.: Eisenbrauns, 1990) 19-30.

_____ . "The Functions of the Sage in the Egyptian Royal Court." In *The Sage in Israel and the Ancient Near East*. Ed. J. G. Gammie and L. G. Perdue (Winona Lake, Ind.: Eisenbrauns, 1990) 95-98.

Williamson, H.G.M. "The Origins of the Twenty-Four Priestly Courses: A Study of 1 Chronicles xxiii-xxvii," *Studies in the Historical Books of the Old Testament*. VTSup 30 (Leiden: Brill, 1979) 251-68.

_____ . "A Response to A. G. Auld," *JSOT* 27 (1983) 33-39.

Wilson, Bryan R. *Magic and Millennium: A Sociological Study of Religious Movements of Protest among Tribal and Third-World Peoples* (London: Heinemann, 1973).

Wilson, Robert R. *Genealogy and History in the Biblical World*. Yale Near Eastern Researches 7 (New Haven, Conn.: Yale, 1977).

_____ . "Prophecy and Ecstacy: A Reexamination," *JBL* 98 (1979) 321-37.

_____ . *Prophecy and Society in Ancient Israel* (Minneapolis: Fortress, 1980).

_____ . *Sociological Approaches to the Old Testament* (Philadelphia: Fortress, 1984).

Winkle, D. W. van. "1 Kings XIII: True and False Prophecy," *VT* 39 (1989) 31-43.

Wolff, Hans Walter. *Joel and Amos* (Hermeneia; Philadelphia: Fortress, 1977).

Wolters, Al. "The Balaamites of Deir 'Alla as Aramean Deportees," *HUCA* 59 (1988) 101-13.

Woude, A. S. van der. "Micah in Dispute with the Pseudo-Prophets," *VT* 19 (1969) 244-60.

Wurthwein, E. "Amos-Studien," *ZAW* 62 (1950) 10-52.

Yamauchi, Edwin M. "Cultic Prostitution: A Case Study in Cultural Diffusion." In *Orient and Occident: Essays Presented to Cyrus H. Gordon on the Occasion of his Sixty-fifth Birthday*. Ed. H. A. Hoffner. AOAT 22 (Neukirchen-Vluyn: Neukirchener Verlag, 1973) 213-22.

Young, Ian. *Diversity in Pre-Exilic Hebrew*. Forschungen zum Alten Testament 5 (Tübingen: Mohr, 1993).

Yoyotte, Jean. "L'inscriptions hiéroglyphiques de la statue de Darius à Suse," *Cahiers de la délégation archéologique française en Iran* 4 (1974) 181-83.

Zimmerli, W. *Ezekiel*. Hermeneia (Philadelphia: Fortress, 1979-83).

Zuesse, Evan M. "Divination," *ER* (1987) 4.375-82.

Index of Modern Authors

Citation Index